單手拍掌
One Hand Clapping

單手拍掌
One Hand Clapping

翁笑雨 Xiaoyu Weng
侯瀚如 Hou Hanru

GUGGENHEIM

目錄
Contents

The Solomon R. Guggenheim Foundation

贊助方致辭
Sponsor's Statement

何鴻毅家族基金與古根海姆美術館聯袂推動跨年度的中國當代藝術項目，集策展研究、藝術委任創作與拓建館藏為主要元素，「單手拍掌」是此項目的第三回合暨閉幕展。對我們雙方來說，其過程就是在一個創新且充滿發展前景的領域裏且行且思。

我們的初衷是支持一個能結合古根海姆國際視野的中國當代藝術項目，但它實際上已超越地域藩籬和文化分野。這個項目中的展覽、出版和公眾活動不單呈現出華人藝術家在不同文化語境下的創作，更展示了當代藝術作為一種全球性現象是何其複雜。古根海姆借助其專業優勢，把各地華人藝術家融入當前的多重論述。

本項目所啟發出來的問題，或許超越了它所賦予的答案。對於團隊為激發興趣和深化理解所作的大膽嘗試，本人由衷敬佩。我更期望這些值得研究和思考的問題，能推動大家繼續為當代藝術作出貢獻。

這次閉幕展的參展藝術家曹斐、段建宇、林一林、黃炳和楊嘉輝，皆以不落窠臼、獨樹一幟的藝術實踐而膺選。對於這五位藝術家，以及促成本次展覽的古根海姆領導層和策展人員，本人謹此致以最誠摯的祝賀。

何猷忠
何鴻毅家族基金主席

One Hand Clapping is the third and final exhibition of The Robert H. N. Ho Family Foundation Chinese Art Initiative, a multiyear curatorial research, art-commissioning, and collection-building project with the Solomon R. Guggenheim Museum. The initiative has been an experimental foray into new and promising territory for both our foundation and the museum.

Conceived as a Chinese art initiative in support of the Guggenheim's international vision, this project in fact reaches beyond the confines of geographical and cultural categorization. Even as the exhibitions, publications, and progams engage with Chinese artists and their creativity in diverse contexts, they also recognize the complexity of contemporary art practice as a global phenomenon. The Guggenheim has built upon its expertise to integrate Chinese artists into multiple discourses.

The project may have opened up more questions than it answered. I applaud the bold steps it has taken to drive interest in and catalyze deeper understanding of the subject. And I hope these questions or areas of inquiry will continue to motivate investigation and new experimentation, and contribute to the field of contemporary art.

For this final exhibition, artists Cao Fei, Duan Jianyu, Lin Yilin, Wong Ping, and Samson Young have been selected for their innovative and individualistic practices. I offer my congratulations to them, as well as to the Guggenheim's leadership and the curatorial staff who have realized the exhibition.

Robert Yau Chung Ho
Chairman, The Robert H. N. Ho Family Foundation

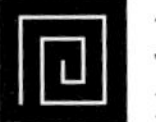

何鴻毅家族基金
THE ROBERT H. N. HO FAMILY FOUNDATION

館長致辭
Director's Foreword

自2013年伊始，所羅門·R·古根海姆美術館「何鴻毅家族基金中國藝術計劃」一直致力於加深美術館與現今中國藝術家的合作，並在美術館所關心的全球藝術項目中展現他們的視野和令人振奮的作品。這個計劃的展覽、公教活動和新的委任作品以及隨後形成的古根海姆館藏集中體現了今天大中華地區的鮮活藝術能量。在計劃的最新也是最終回中，我們邀請了五位藝術家：曹斐、段建宇、林一林、黃炳和楊嘉輝為題為「單手拍掌」的展覽來創作新的作品。展覽的一大亮點在於這些藝術家對我們當下技術化的「介導現實」之干預和互動。對於其中一些參展藝術家來説，這也是首次在紐約美術館展出他們重要的作品。

「單手拍掌」由何鴻毅家族基金中國藝術副策展人翁笑雨、何鴻毅家族基金中國藝術策展顧問侯瀚如再次聯手——這兩位策展人在該計劃第二次展覽「故事新編」(2016–17)中的合作獲得了各方佳評。另外，在翁笑雨的帶領下，該計劃見證了古根海姆通過創新的出版物、數字內容和公共項目使得本土和國際的觀眾更加積極參與和了解來自大中華地區的新藝術。始於第一次展覽「汪建偉：時間寺」，「何鴻毅家族基金中國藝術計劃」逐漸建立起自己的影響，該計劃不僅將今天中國的藝術實踐突顯為全球語境中不可或缺的一部分，而且力求展示這些實踐如何洞見我們當下最為迫切的現實。美術館最終收藏了十三位藝術家、藝術團體的26件作品，這些不同媒介的作品共同組成「何鴻毅家族基金藏品」。來自世界其他地方的藝術作品將在美術館落地生根，此舉打破古根海姆美術館以歐美藝術為衡量標準的傳統。這些充滿活力的新作品為這個時代的藝術和更深的跨文化交流打下了堅實的基礎並提供更廣闊的視角。我們只有如此拓展館藏和項目，才能回應美術館作為任重道遠的文化大使之挑戰。

為了進一步促進與參展藝術家和同行的合作，該計劃也構建了一個全球美術館網絡以接受部分委任作品的其他版本的捐贈。在由古根海姆三星亞洲藝術高級策展人兼全球藝術高級顧問孟璐(Alexandra Munroe)帶領的古根海姆亞洲藝術計劃的支持下，這個知識、學術和共同信守的網絡確保了這些藝術作品在國際平台上的流通和傳播，並保證其持久的生產力和影響力。

「單手拍掌」標誌著「何鴻毅家族基金中國藝術計劃」告一段落，這也是一個我們與何鴻毅家族基金長期合作的重要里程碑。我們深深地感謝何鴻毅家族基金的創始人何鴻毅先生，以及基金會的主席何猷忠先生，感謝他們為這次充滿雄心的探索所提供的遠見，也感謝他們一路以來持續的支持。我們的合作夥伴們對於進一步發展中國藝術文化的學術研究、創新和受眾之熱忱與投入非同凡響，我們很期待和他們展開下一個新的合作篇章。基金行政總裁黎義恩(Ted Lipman)先生和營運總監鍾妙芬女士的睿智建議讓該計劃獲益良多，他們的貢獻不勝枚舉，對我們的成功至關重要。

我們同樣要對所羅門·R·古根海姆基金會董事會表示感謝。我們尤其要感謝董事長William L. Mack和主席Wendy Fisher對我們在亞洲及其他地區工作不遺餘力的支持。感謝基金會董事蔡思賢(Cindy Chua-Tay)、基金會名譽董事John S. Wadsworth, Jr.以及他的妻子Susy的領導，他們對於古根海姆拓寬在亞洲的藝術使命提供了激勵和變革性的支持。

最後，我們要對參與此次展覽的五位藝術家致以最誠摯的謝意，他們的思考和實踐持續啟發著我們。我們珍惜與他們以及其他八位藝術家和藝術團體共同建立的關係，他們為「何鴻毅家族基金中國藝術計劃」的成功作出無比貢獻，也為古根海姆持續呈現和詮釋來自世界各地的藝術實踐的努力添磚加瓦。

Richard Armstrong
所羅門·R·古根海姆美術館
館長與基金會主席

Since its inception in 2013, The Robert H. N. Ho Family Foundation Chinese Art Initiative at the Solomon R. Guggenheim Museum has deepened the museum's commitment to collaborating with living Chinese artists to present visionary and stimulating work within the context of the Guggenheim's dedicated global arts programs. The initiative's exhibitions, programs, and new commissions — and the subsequent entry of the works into the Guggenheim's collection — epitomize the fresh artistic energy coming out of Greater China today. For the initiative's latest and last iteration, we have invited five artists — Cao Fei, Duan Jianyu, Lin Yilin, Wong Ping, and Samson Young — to create new works responding to our current technologically mediated reality. These new commissions culminate in the presentation of the group exhibition *One Hand Clapping*. For some of the artists, this is the first substantial presentation of their work in a New York museum.

Organized by Xiaoyu Weng, The Robert H. N. Ho Family Foundation Associate Curator of Chinese Art, and Hou Hanru, Consulting Curator, The Robert H. N. Ho Family Foundation Chinese Art Initiative, *One Hand Clapping* builds on the success of the curators' previous collaboration on the second commission and exhibition of the initiative, *Tales of Our Time* (2016–17), which was enthusiastically received by diverse audiences. Moreover, the initiative has seen the Guggenheim, under the guidance of Weng, facilitate the engagement of both local and international communities with new art from Greater China through innovative publications, digital content, and public programming. Starting with its first presentation, *Wang Jianwei: Time Temple* (2014), The Robert H. N. Ho Family Foundation Chinese Art Initiative has built its legacy not only by foregrounding art practices from China today as integral elements in global discourse, but also by communicating how these practices provide insight into urgent contemporary realities. The museum has been able to acquire a total of twenty-six works by thirteen artists and groups across a range of media to form The Robert H. N. Ho Family Foundation Collection. Alongside the artworks from other parts of the world that stake positions beyond the Guggenheim's traditional Euro-American parameters, these new works lay an essential foundation for fostering wider perspectives on the art of our time and deeper cross-cultural interactions. It is only by expanding our collection and programming in this way that we can respond to the challenge of adapting the role of museums as meaningful cultural agents.

In addition to enabling collaborations with participating artists and colleagues, the initiative has also established a network of museums around the world that receive donations of select editioned artworks produced through the commissions. Under the auspices of the Guggenheim's Asian Art Initiative, led by Alexandra Munroe, Samsung Senior Curator, Asian Art, and Senior Advisor, Global Arts, such a network of knowledge, scholarship, and commitment ensures the circulation and dissemination of these artworks at the international level and, consequently, their generative and enduring influence.

One Hand Clapping marks the completion and fulfillment of The Robert H. N. Ho Family Foundation Chinese Art Initiative, and an important milestone in our long-term relationship with The Robert H. N. Ho Family Foundation. We are deeply grateful to Robert H. N. Ho, Founder, and Robert Y. C. Ho, Chairman, for sharing their vision for this ambitious venture and their lasting support along the way. We recognize partners whose enthusiasm and dedication to furthering the scholarship, innovation, and accessibility of Chinese art and culture are remarkable, and we look forward to opening a new chapter in our collaboration. The initiative has also benefited from the wise counsel of Ted Lipman, Chief Executive Officer, and Anita Chung, Chief Operating Officer; their contributions have been as myriad as they have been significant to our success.

The Solomon R. Guggenheim Foundation Board of Trustees also deserves thanks. We are particularly grateful to William L. Mack, Chairman, and Wendy Fisher, President, for their unwavering support of our work in Asia and beyond. The leadership of Trustee Cindy Chua-Tay and Trustee Emeritus John S. Wadsworth, Jr., and his wife, Susy, in their commitment to expanding the Guggenheim's mission to include art from Asia has also been encouraging and transformative.

In conclusion, the Guggenheim extends its deepest gratitude to the five artists whose work is featured here and whose thinking and practices inspire us. We cherish the relationships we have fostered with them and with the other eight artists and groups who have contributed to the success of The Robert H. N. Ho Family Foundation Chinese Art Initiative and the Guggenheim's ongoing endeavor to present and interpret art practices from around the world.

Richard Armstrong
Director, Solomon R. Guggenheim
Museum and Foundation

致謝 Acknowledgments

「單手拍掌」是「何鴻毅家族基金中國藝術計劃」在所羅門·R·古根海姆美術館第三回也是最終回的委任作品展覽。在過去的五年中，該計劃不僅拓展了美術館致力於全球視野的目標，也進一步加深了其與本土和全球之間複雜話語的緊密聯繫。我們向所羅門·R·古根海姆美術館館長與基金會主席Richard Armstrong致以最誠摯的謝意，他的遠見使得這一系列以研究和委任創作為基礎的展覽和活動得以實現。我們也將最真誠的感謝獻給三星亞洲藝術高級策展人兼全球藝術高級顧問孟璐(Alexandra Munroe)，她在此計劃的實施過程中給予了關鍵性的支持和指導。藝術總監、詹妮弗與大衛·斯多克曼首席策展人Nancy Spector則在計劃過程中提供了富有洞見的評論和評估。我們也對亞洲藝術助理策展人安輝景(Kyung An)不可或缺的工作表示感謝，她一絲不苟且敬業地協調了整個展覽。

在計劃發展的過程中，我們試圖挑戰、解構並重新定義充滿爭議的「中國當代藝術」之概念，並呈現近十年來最具思想性和啟發性的藝術作品。承蒙在何猷忠先生領導下的何鴻毅家族基金對我們工作的信任和視野啟迪，在這裏，我們尤其要感謝基金行政總裁黎義恩(Ted Lipman)先生，他的熱情和支持促進了我們真誠的合作；營運總監鍾妙芬(Anita Chung)女士以她的美術館專業經驗為我們的研究和策展提供了重要的參考；公共關係及宣傳經理湯惠德(Janet Tong)女士和行政及項目經理黃翠玲(Scarlet Wong)女士也在協調計劃的各個方面發揮了重要作用。我們將繼續發展、研究、呈現和傳播古根海姆何鴻毅家族基金收藏的藝術作品和它們所帶來的知識。

沒有什麼能比與藝術家合作並實現他們富有野心的遠見和作品來得更有意義了。我們對參與最終回展覽的藝術家：曹斐、段建宇、林一林、黃炳和楊嘉輝致以最深厚的感謝。在無數的會議、郵件、Skype電話和微信溝通裏，他們大膽的想像、敏銳的社會批判和頑皮的幽默塑造了這個展覽和新的委任作品。和他們的作品一樣，這些藝術家朝著未來之藝術，激發、鼓勵和創造著可能性。

這本畫冊絕不因循守舊，它不僅作為展覽的記錄，也是藝術計劃實現過程的一個積極組成部分，和我們委任作品的精神一樣，畫冊通過組合多樣、複雜的作者聲音和視覺材料去創造意義。我們非常感謝編輯Andrew Maerkle的出色貢獻，他的投入、開放和經驗使我們的策展理念得到最大程度的實現。除了我們的兩篇策展論述，我們邀請了哲學家許煜撰寫有關科技未來的分支及其對人類影響的論述短文；另外，他的《論中國的技術問題》一書對我們展覽最初的設想有著指導意義。我們感謝他慷慨地分享其具有原創性和批判性的研究。另外，詩人黃裕邦、烏青和張羞的詩歌進一步拓展了我們想像力和美學的視界。打工詩人許立志的哥哥許宏志、文集《新的一天》(作家出版社，2015)的編輯秦曉宇和藍獅子出版社，對我們重新出版許立志的部分詩歌提供了莫大的支持。

這本出版物的雙語和跨學科特性不僅需要熟練的溝通技巧也需要變通的思維方式，我們的中文編輯吳建儒和Maerkle共同工作，致力於此，與以下譯者緊密合作以確保準確和及時地交付本書的內容：杜可柯、費正華(Jennifer Feeley)、顧愛玲(Eleanor Goodman)、賈世怡(Breanna Chia)、柯夏智(Lucas Klein)、李佳桓、莫修、徐晞文、徐丹羽、余小蕙、張思銳和朱又佳。

繼上一個展覽畫冊《故事新編》的成功合作之後，我們再次與屢獲殊榮的設計工作室Wkshps(前稱為Project Projects)合作設計本次展覽畫冊。Wkshps的合夥人吳承桓(Chris Wu)及其同事陳穎(Janet Chan)對本書的獨特內容做出了富有創造力的回應。他們充滿活力的概念和創新的設計體現在本書的各個方面，尤其在視覺溝通層面加強了藝術家創作的概念手稿、參考材料和作品方案部分，讓讀者可以更深入地參與到我們與這些藝術家討論、發展委任作品的策展過程之中。

出版和多媒體部門的菁英同事們是這本畫冊得以出版的支柱，他們成功地協作跨越不同時區的諸多作者們。我們要特別感謝出版和多媒體創意總監Lisa Naftolin，她敏銳地評價道，制作一本如此複雜的書，本身就是一個生產具有持久影響力新知的過程。我們也要感謝出版人Diana Murphy，編輯經理Elizabeth Zechella，製作副總監Melissa Secondino，高級制作經理Jonathan Bowen和制作經理助理Shiori Kawasaki的貢獻。此外，在Naftolin的領導和平面設計總監、首席平面設計師Marcia Fardella的指揮下，出版和

One Hand Clapping is the third and final commission and exhibition of The Robert H. N. Ho Family Foundation Chinese Art Initiative at the Solomon R. Guggenheim Museum. In the past five years, the initiative has not only expanded the museum's commitment to global perspectives, but also deepened its engagement with discourses on the ever more complex relations between the local and global. Profound thanks are due to Richard Armstrong, Director, Solomon R. Guggenheim Museum and Foundation, whose foresight has enabled the undertaking of this series of research- and commission-based exhibitions and programs. Our deepest appreciation also goes to Alexandra Munroe, Samsung Senior Curator, Asian Art, and Senior Advisor, Global Arts, for her crucial and steadfast leadership and support of the project's development. Nancy Spector, Artistic Director and Jennifer and David Stockman Chief Curator, has provided insightful critique and important commentary throughout. We are grateful as well for the indispensable support of Kyung An, Assistant Curator, Asian Art, who coordinated all aspects of the exhibition with great meticulousness and dedication.

Through the initiative, we have sought to challenge, deconstruct, and redefine contested notions of "contemporary Chinese art," and to present some of the most thoughtful and provocative artworks of the past decade. We are deeply indebted to The Robert H. N. Ho Family Foundation, under the direction of Chairman Robert Y. C. Ho, for inspiring and trusting our vision. In particular, we thank Ted Lipman, Chief Executive Officer, whose passion and insight have nourished a true collaboration. Anita Chung, Chief Operating Officer, lent her museum expertise to our partnership, pointing out important directions in our research and implementation. Janet Tong, Public Relations and Communications Manager, and Scarlet Wong have also been instrumental in coordinating different fronts of the initiative. We look forward to continuing to develop, research, present, and disseminate the knowledge of the artworks forming The Robert H. N. Ho Family Foundation Collection at the Guggenheim.

Nothing is more rewarding than collaborating with artists to realize their ambitious proposals. We offer our most profound thanks to the artists Cao Fei, Duan Jianyu, Lin Yilin, Wong Ping, and Samson Young, who are featured in this final exhibition. Their bold imagination, sharp social critique, and quirky humor informed our ideas and shaped the new commissions through hundreds of meetings, emails, Skype calls, and WeChat messages. These artists, like the works they made, inspire, encourage, and innovate possibilities for a future art to come.

This catalogue is by no means conventional. It is intended to serve not merely as a document of the exhibition, but also as an active component in the realization of the project — in the spirit of commissioning — by assembling and making meaning through a diverse range of complex voices and visual materials. We are immensely grateful for the exceptional job done by our editor Andrew Maerkle, whose commitment, openness, and experience have enabled the realization of the curatorial vision to its full extent. Alongside our two curatorial essays, we have invited the philosopher Yuk Hui to contribute an essay on the bifurcation of technological futures and its implications for humanity. Yuk's book *The Question Concerning Technology in China: An Essay in Cosmotechnics* (Urbanomic, 2016) was instrumental in our initial thinking about the framing around this exhibition. We thank him for his generosity in sharing his original and critical research. In addition, the poetry of Nicholas Wong, Wu Qing, and Zhang Xiu has further expanded our imaginative and aesthetic horizons. Xu Hongzhi, brother of the worker-poet Xu Lizhi (1990–2014); Qin Xiaoyu, editor of the anthology *A New Day* (Xin de yi tian, The Writers Publishing House, 2015); and Blue Lion Cultural Creativity Company, Hangzhou, have provided great support in our effort to reprint a selection of Xu's poems.

The bilingual and interdisciplinary nature of this publication not only requires skillful coordination but also fluid thinking. Together with Maerkle, our dedicated Chinese editor Jianru Wu has worked closely with the following translators to ensure accurate and timely delivery of the content of the book: Breanna Chia, Du Keke, Jennifer Feeley, Eleanor Goodman, Lucas Klein, Alvin Li, Aurora Tsui, Xu Danyu, Yu Hsiao-hwei, Sirui Zhang, Wayne Zhou, and Yvette Zhu.

This is our second collaboration with the award-winning design studio Wkshps (formerly Project Projects) in designing a catalogue. Building upon the success of the previous exhibition catalogue, *Tales of Our Time*, studio partner Chris Wu and his associate Janet Chan responded to the unconventional materials of this book with brilliant creativity. Their conceptual rigor and innovative approach are evident in every aspect of the book; in particular, their design enhances the visual communication of the section where we present concept drawings, reference materials, and plans by each of the artists in order to engage readers in the curatorial process of developing the commissions with the artists.

The talents of the Publishing and Digital Media Department were the backbone of the production of this catalogue, which entailed managing a large team of contributors across multiple time zones. Our appreciation especially goes to Lisa Naftolin, Creative Director, Publishing and Digital Media, who incisively commented that the making of a book of such complexity is itself a process of generating new knowledge that has lasting influence. We also thank Publisher Diana Murphy; Managing Editor Elizabeth Zechella; Associate Director, Production, Melissa Secondino; Senior Production Manager Jonathan Bowen; and Assistant Production Manager Shiori Kawasaki for their astute contributions. Furthermore, under Naftolin's leadership and the guidance of Marcia Fardella, Director, Graphic Design, and Chief Graphic Designer, the team conceived an innovative holistic approach for the exhibition's identity and for the initiative as a whole. Naomi Leibowitz, Associate Director, Creative Strategy and Operations, and Stephan Knuesel, Digital Media Producer, organized the video and digital materials on our website and in the Guggenheim App; Caitlin Dover, Senior Editor, Interactive, produced a dedicated blog series.

Occupying two tower galleries at the museum with five entirely new projects executed in diverse mediums, an exhibition of this creative and logistical magnitude depends on the diligent staff of every department at the Guggenheim. Each member of the Project Team has contributed to this exhibition's realization. Special recognition is due to Rob McGarry, Senior Project Manager, who ably managed the budget and liaised with the artists, the museum's departments, and outside vendors, and Jade Ong, Associate Project Manager, who offered crucial support and excellent interpretation for the communication and production of the show. Michael Sarff, Associate Director, Exhibition Management, solved every puzzle that came up in the exhibition's production process with extraordinary professionalism. Jaime Krone, Director,

多媒體部門為展覽和整個計劃的視覺概念和媒體形象構想了創新的方案。創意戰略及運營副總監Naomi Leibowitz和數字媒體制作人Stephan Knuesel為展覽整合了古根海姆網站以及app中的錄像和數碼資料;Caitlin Dover,高級互動媒體編輯為此展覽製作了一個博客系列。

五件跨媒介的全新藝術作品,占據了美術館的兩個塔樓展廳,如此具有創意和實施規模的展覽依賴於古根海姆每個部門的勤奮員工。這個項目團隊的所有成員為展覽的實現做出了貢獻。特別要感謝高級項目經理Rob McGarry,他負責在藝術家、美術館部門和外部供應商之間的聯絡,有效地安排了項目預算;還有項目副經理王祖玉(Jade Ong)也為展覽的溝通和制作提供了關鍵的支持和出色的同聲傳譯。展覽管理副總監Michael Sarff用卓越的專業精神解決了展覽制作過程中的所有難題。展覽設計總監Jaime Krone提供了出色的設計方案以實現藝術家的意圖。媒體藝術技術總監Piotr Chizinski在安裝多媒體作品過程中解決了所有的新技術難題。設備部門資深經理Richard Avery和展覽服務總監Eric Lindveit協助我們在展廳中實現了頗具挑戰的作品。我們也感謝展覽管理總監Clare Bell和她領導的展覽管理部門。

將全新的藝術作品和觀念傳遞給更廣闊的觀眾群體,無論遠近,都絕非易事。媒體公共關係部門總監Sarah Eaton和高級公關Kristina Parker的工作使展覽得到了廣泛的媒體關注;基金會和合作部門宣傳總監Renee Dumouchel和全球宣傳經理Alisha Levin制定了有效的宣傳策略。在策展人們創意的指導下,公共項目總監Christina Yang、公共項目副經理Anthea Song和前任副經理Evelyn Peng 組織了展覽的公共項目,將藝術家探討的問題擴展到各領域和公眾中去。委任項目的特殊性在于克服過程中諸多不確定因素,對此團隊表現出靈活的、勇於擔當的精神。我們對藝術品修復保存部門的工作表示感謝,在副館長和首席藝術品修復師Lena Stringari的領導下,資深基時媒體藝術品修復師Joanna Phillips、紙本藝術與攝影修復師Jeffrey Warda、資深繪畫修復師兼修復保存事務副總監Julie Barten、物件藝術修復師Esther Chao以及計算機藝術修復研究員Jonathan Farbowitz確保了展品的順利安裝和妥善收藏。我們的登記部門總監、登記員Mary Louise Napier和登記部門副總監Michele Heinrici,登記員Lisa Blanchard,保證了藝術品順利自海外運入。我們感謝發展部門總監、副館長Catherine Carver Dunn和機構發展副總監Katie Lisa,她們與基金會進行了重要的溝通協調工作。我們同樣感謝收藏總監、資深策展人Tracey Bashkoff,收藏部副策展人Lauren Hinkson,收藏部策展助理Lidia Ferrara,感謝他們在作品收藏過程中考慮周全的建議。最后,策展部門的優秀實習生孔主裕(Grace Hong)和劉笑容(Sharon Liu)協助了翻譯、研究和行政工作。

如果沒有藝術家畫廊的鼎力協助,「單手拍掌」在時間如此有限的情況下恐怕無法得以實現。我們感謝馬凌畫廊(香港、上海)的馬淩(Edouard Malingue)和江馨玲(Lorraine Malingue);維他命藝術空間(廣州、北京)的胡昉和張巍;科隆Gisela Capitain畫廊的Gisela Capitain;Team畫廊(紐約、洛杉磯)的José Freire以及博而勵畫廊(北京、紐約)的包文麟(Waling Boers)。

「何鴻毅家族基金會中國藝術計劃」附屬委員會在這第三回展覽伊始便對藝術家遴選、展覽策展方向和收藏策略提供建議。奎松市菲律賓大學藝術研究教授,Jorge B. Vargas美術館及菲律賓研究中心策展人Patrick Flores自本計劃第一次展覽便參與此工作。此次還有三位頗具聲望的同僚加入他的行列:香港M+博物館副館長、首席策展人鄭道煉;紐約巴德學院策展研究中心策展研究生項目總監、赫塞爾美術館首席策展人Lauren Cornell以及上海當代藝術博物館館長龔彥。感謝他們充滿啟發的洞見。

除了參展藝術家之外,還有許多尊敬的同事與我們分享了知識和觀點。我們想特別感謝e-flux期刊的創刊編輯穆柏安(Brian Kuan Wood)和自由撰稿人、編輯Jesi Khadivi對書中一些文本提出的反饋。亞洲藝術文獻庫(香港、紐約)董事會主席杜柏貞(Jane DeBevoise)一如既往地提供慷慨的咨詢和支持。愛丁堡大學Talbot Rice 畫廊總監Tessa Giblin參與了楊嘉輝項目的研究。我們也感謝哲學家和理論家Marc Auge、Franco“Bifo” Berardi和許煜,他們近年來的學術研究在此次策展思考和研究中激發了許多頗具靈感的討論。我們還要感謝安靜(Lee Ambrozy)、白慧怡(Stephanie Bailey)、Jeanne Gerrity、Prem Krishnamurthy、Scott Norton、歐寧、Barbara Pollack、Laurel Ptak、王旭和鄢醒。

最後,我們感謝家人的支持和關愛。翁笑雨感謝她的父親翁紀軍和母親張慧靜,即便離家千里之外,他們一致鼓勵她追逐夢想。侯瀚如感謝他的妻子艾華蓮(Evelyne Jouanno)和女兒侯仲儀(Kim Hou)以及他的父親侯保源、母親王小薇和兄長侯海如。

如最初構想,「單手拍掌」為所羅門·R·古根海姆美術館的「何鴻毅家族基金中國藝術計劃」畫上了句號。我們感謝一路走來攜手同行的所有人,你們的參與讓我們的工作更有意義,也為此計劃產生的影響力以及我們在古根海姆開展全球藝術項目的下一階段作出貢獻。

翁笑雨
何鴻毅家族基金
中國藝術副策展人

侯瀚如
何鴻毅家族基金
中國藝術計劃策展顧問

Exhibition Design, provided ingenious design solutions to realize the artists' proposals. Piotr Chizinski, Head of Media Arts, took on all challenges in expertly installing multimedia works incorporating exciting new technologies. Richard Avery, Senior Manager, Facilities, and Eric Lindveit, Director, Exhibition Services, allowed us to realize some of these challenging works in the galleries. We thank Clare Bell, Director of Exhibitions, for managing the output of all these outstanding team members.

It is never easy to translate radical new artworks and ideas for wider audiences near and far. Sarah Eaton, Director, Media and Public Relations, and Kristina Parker, Senior Publicist, worked hard to generate media interest; Renee Dumouchel, Director, Communications, Foundation and Collaborations, and Alisha Levin, Manager, Global Communications, created effective communications strategies. Under the curators' creative guidance, Christina Yang, Director of Public Programs; Anthea Song, Associate Manager, Public Programs; and Evelyn Peng, former Associate Manager, implemented the exhibition's public program, opening up the issues explored by the artists to various fields and publics. The commissioning aspect of the project demanded a flexible, can-do spirit in the face of many uncertainties in the process. We are thankful for the efforts of the Conservation Department. Led by Lena Stringari, Deputy Director and Chief Conservator, together with Joanna Philips, Senior Conservator, Time-based Media; Jeffrey Warda, Senior Conservator, Paper and Photographs; Julie Barten, Senior Painting Conservator and Associate Director, Conservation Affairs; Esther Chao, Conservator, Objects; and Jonathan Farbowitz, Fellow, Conservation of Computer-based Art, the department staff ensured that all objects were installed and entered the collection with utmost care. Our registrars MaryLouise Napier, Director of Registration; Michele Heinrici, Associate Director, Registrar; and Lisa Blanchard, Registrar, safeguarded the artworks' arrival from overseas. We thank Catherine Carver Dunn, Deputy Director, Advancement, and Katie Lisa, Associate Director, Institutional Development, who performed important work with the foundation. We are also grateful to Tracey Bashkoff, Director, Collections, and Senior Curator; Lauren Hinkson, Associate Curator, Collections; and Lidia Ferrara, Curatorial Assistant, Collections, for their thoughtful advice throughout the acquisition process. Finally, the excellent Curatorial Interns Grace Hong and Sharon Liu assisted with translation, research, and administrative tasks.

The production of *One Hand Clapping* would not have been possible in such a short amount of time without the tremendous support of the artists' galleries. We thank Lorraine Malingue and Edouard Malingue of Edouard Malingue Gallery, Hong Kong and Shanghai; Hu Fang and Zhang Wei of Vitamin Creative Space, Guangzhou and Beijing; Gisela Capitain of Galerie Gisela Capitain, Cologne; José Freire of Team Gallery, New York and Los Angeles; and Waling Boers of Boers-Li Gallery, Beijing and New York.

The Robert H. N. Ho Family Foundation Chinese Art Initiative Subcommittee was formed at the outset of this third cycle to advise on the selection of artists, the curatorial direction of the exhibition, and collection strategy. Patrick Flores, Professor of Art Studies, University of the Philippines, and Curator, Jorge B. Vargas Museum and Filipiniana Research Center, University of the Philippines, Quezon City, has served in this capacity since the first commission of the initiative. This time, he was joined by three other prestigious colleagues: Doryun Chong, Deputy Director and Chief Curator, M+, Hong Kong; Lauren Cornell, Director of the Graduate Program and Chief Curator of the Hessel Museum of Art, CCS Bard, New York; and Gong Yan, Director, Power Station of Art, Shanghai. Their insights were indispensable.

In addition to the participating artists, many esteemed colleagues have shared their knowledge and ideas with us. We would especially like to thank Brian Kuan Wood, Founding Editor, *e-flux Journal*, and Jesi Khadivi, writer and editor, for their thoughtful feedback on some of the texts in this volume. Jane DeBevoise, Chair of the Board of Directors, Asia Art Archive, Hong Kong and New York, always provides generous counsel and support. Tessa Giblin, Director, Talbot Rice Gallery, the University of Edinburgh, contributed to Samson Young's research. We also acknowledge philosophers and theorists Marc Auge, Franco "Bifo" Berardi, and Yuk Hui, whose recent intellectual works sparked many inspirational discussions during the curatorial thinking and research of this exhibition. We also thank Lee Ambrozy, Stephanie Bailey, Jeanne Gerrity, Prem Krishnamurthy, Scott Norton, Ou Ning, Barbara Pollack, Laurel Ptak, Wang Xu, and Yan Xing.

Finally, we thank our family members for their loving support. Xiaoyu Weng thanks her father, Weng Jijun, and mother, Zhang Huijing, who have always encouraged her to pursue her dreams, even somewhere thousands of miles from home. Hou Hanru thanks his wife, Evelyne Jouanno, and daughter, Kim Hou; his parents, Hou Baoyuan and Wang Xiaowei; and his brother, Hou Hairu.

One Hand Clapping concludes The Robert H. N. Ho Family Foundation Chinese Art Initiative at the Solomon R. Guggenheim Museum as it was initially conceived. We are grateful to everyone who has accompanied us along the way. Your participation has made our work all the more meaningful, and has contributed to the initiative's impact and legacy as we forge the next phase of global arts programming at the Guggenheim.

Xiaoyu Weng
The Robert H. N. Ho Family Foundation Associate Curator of Chinese Art

Hou Hanru
Consulting Curator, The Robert H. N. Ho Family Foundation Chinese Art Initiative

Project Team

Art Services and Preparation
David Bufano, Director, Art Services and Preparation
Elisabeth Jaff, Senior Preparator
Jeffrey Clemens, Senior Preparator

Conservation
Lena Stringari, Deputy Director and Chief Conservator
Julie Barten, Senior Painting Conservator and Associate Director, Conservation Affairs
Joanna Phillips, Senior Conservator, Time-based Media
Esther Chao, Conservator, Objects
Jeffrey Warda, Senior Conservator, Paper and Photographs
Hillary Torrence, Manager, Conservation
Jonathan Farbowitz, Fellow, Conservation of Computer-based Art

Curatorial
Nancy Spector, Artistic Director and Jennifer and David Stockman Chief Curator
Alexandra Munroe, Samsung Senior Curator, Asian Art, and Senior Advisor, Global Arts
Xiaoyu Weng, The Robert H. N. Ho Family Foundation Associate Curator of Chinese Art
Hou Hanru, Consulting Curator, The Robert H. N. Ho Family Foundation Chinese Art Initiative
Kyung An, Assistant Curator, Asian Art
Grace Hong, Sharon Liu, and others, Interns, Asian Art

Development
Catherine Carver Dunn, Deputy Director, Advancement
Mary Anne Talotta, Director, Individual Development
Pamela Taite, Director, Special Events
Katie Lisa, Associate Director, Institutional Development

Director's Office
Richard Armstrong, Director, Solomon R. Guggenheim Museum and Foundation
Lindsey Cash, Senior Assistant to the Director and Director's Office Coordinator
Linnea Wilson, Director's Office Assistant

Education
Kim Kanatani, Deputy Director and Gail Engelberg Director of Education
Sharon Vatsky, Director of School and Family Programs
Christina Yang, Director of Public Programs
Anthea Song, Associate Manager, Public Programs
Evelyn Peng, Associate Manager, Public Programs

Exhibition Design
Jaime Krone, Director, Exhibition Design
Lucie Rebeyrol, Junior Exhibition Designer

Exhibition Management
Clare Bell, Director of Exhibitions
Michael Sarff, Associate Director, Exhibition Management
Rob McGarry, Senior Project Manager
Jade Ong, Associate Project Manager

Exhibition Services
Eric Lindveit, Director, Exhibition Services
Paul Bridge, Senior Manager, Exhibition Installations
Barry Hylton, Senior Manager, Exhibition Installations
Derek Deluco, Senior Technician
Piotr Chizinski, Head of Media Arts
Mark Argue, Manager, Exhibition Construction
Mary Ann Hoag, Head of Exhibition Lighting
And team

Fabrication
Christopher George, Director, Fabrication
Peter Mallo, Chief Framemaker
Peter Brayshaw, Chief Cabinetmaker
Steven Ott, Cabinetmaker
Ross Caudill, Fabricator
Marcel Walker, Cabinetmaker

Facilities
Peter Read, Director of Facilities, Fabrication and Office Services
Michael Zall, Associate Director, Facilities Operations
Richard Avery, Senior Manager, Facilities
Ian Felmine, Chief Engineer
And team

Global Communications
Tina Vaz, Deputy Director, Global Communications
Renee Dumouchel, Director, Communications, Foundation and Collaborations
Sarah Eaton, Director, Media and Public Relations
Kristina Parker, Senior Publicist
Alisha Levin, Manager, Global Communications

Graphic Design
Marcia Fardella, Director, Graphic Design and Chief Graphic Designer
Janice I-Chiao Lee, Associate Director, Graphic Design
Peter Raphael Castro, Graphic Designer and Production Manager

Interactive
Laura Kleger, Director, Interactive
Maria Slusarev, Associate Director, Website and Interactive Experience
Robert Duffy, Associate Director, Interactive Technology and App
Caitlin Dover, Senior Editor, Interactive
Daniel Yang, Web Developer
Joey Pfeifer, Designer, Interactive
Josie Rubio, Interactive Producer
Grace Tung, Manager, Interactive
Emelia Meckstroth, Associate Manager, Interactive

Legal
Sarah Austrian, Deputy Director, General Counsel, and Assistant Secretary
Marianna Horton Mermin, Senior Associate Counsel
Lee White Galvis, Associate General Counsel

Library and Archives
Jillian Suarez, Associate Librarian

Marketing
Holly Campbell, Associate Director, Marketing
Essie Lash, Senior Manager, Marketing
Alexandra Barber, Senior Digital Marketing Manager
Harineta Rigatos, Digital Marketing Manager
Alexa Revans, Marketing Associate
Elizabeth Cosgrove, E-mail Marketing Coordinator

Photography
David Heald, Director of Photographic Services and Chief Photographer
Monique Romney, Image Archive Assistant
Susan Wamsley, Digital Asset Manager

Publishing and Digital Media
Lisa Naftolin, Creative Director, Publishing and Digital Media
Diana Murphy, Publisher
Naomi Leibowitz, Associate Director, Creative Strategy and Operations
Melissa Secondino, Associate Director, Production
Elizabeth Zechella, Managing Editor
Jonathan Bowen, Senior Production Manager
Rebecca Sears, Senior Editor, Digital Media
Stephan Knuesel, Digital Media Producer
Shiori Kawasaki, Assistant Production Manager
Kayla Elam, Publishing Assistant

Registrar
MaryLouise Napier, Director of Registration
Michele Heinrici, Associate Director, Registrar
Lisa Blanchard, Registrar

Retail
Gigi Loizzo, Director, Retail Strategy and Operations
Katherine Lock, Senior Manager, Merchandise and Product Development
Ed Fuqua, Manager, Retail Analysis and Merchandise

Security
Emily Schluter, Associate Director, Security
And team

Theater Operations
Brenda Gray, Director of Theater Operations
Julia Hahn-Gallego, Manager of Theater Operations
And team

Visitor Experience
Trevor Tyrrell, Director, Visitor Experience
Emily Johnson, Senior Manager, Group Sales and Box Office
Nicole Fernandez, Visitor Experience Manager, Analysis and Planning
Brian Wilson, Manager, Visitor Experience
And team

翁笑雨
Xiaoyu Weng

詩和遠方
Poetry and Place Afar

電影《十年》(2015)以2025年的香港為背景，編織了一齣黑色政治諷刺劇，預想了這座城市在中國大陸政權統治下可能的命運。盡管是想像未來，但影片裏既沒有出現地外生命形式和外星世界，也沒有出現太空飛船、機器人、賽博格或人工智能等帶有科幻意味的技術。相反，片中的城市景觀看上去跟當今的香港基本無異，但是人們的日常生活卻時不時地被政治暗殺、自焚抗議等極端戲劇化的事件打斷，兒童也開始做起秘密警察的工作(讓人回想到文化大革命期間的紅衛兵)。《十年》通過探索政治獨立、社會矛盾和人性價值等議題，描繪了一幅與中國政府所宣揚的、建立於經濟騰飛和軍事實力基礎之上的全民幸福神話大相徑庭的未來圖景。

其實無論是在中國國內還是海外，有關中國之未來的主流政治想像裏都彌漫著這一神話的論調。如果把「中國」和「未來」作為兩個關鍵詞放到谷歌上一搜，出來的結果大都與經濟、技術相關，比如中國GDP預計將於2030年之前超過美國[1]；中國公司，特別是國防技術創新領域的公司，正在重點開發人工智能[2]，等等。一方面，中國政府樂於得到此類關注，並將其轉化為鞏固國內政權的宣傳材料。雖然因為「大躍進」等政治運動造成的人道主義災難而飽受詬病[3]，毛澤東於1957年提出的極度理想主義的口號「超英趕美」在某種程度上已經變成現實。另一方面，在全球媒體和政客的鼓吹下，這些預測延續了冷戰思維模式，即將「未來」博弈於為爭奪全球霸權而進行的軍事和

Set in Hong Kong in 2025, the film *Ten Years* (2015) is a dark political satire speculating about the city's fate under mainland China's rule. Although it imagines the near future, the film is devoid of extraterrestrial life-forms, alien worlds, or sci-fi-infused technology such as spacecraft, robots, cyborgs, and artificial intelligence. Rather, the Hong Kong it depicts resembles that of the present, but day-to-day life is interrupted by dramatic events such as political assassinations and acts of self-immolation, while children work as secret police (recalling the Red Guards of the Cultural Revolution). Raising questions about political autonomy, social tensions, and human values, *Ten Years* projects a vision of the future that counters the myth of happiness for all promoted by the Chinese government on the basis of economic success and military prowess.

This myth pervades the political imagination of China's future, both within the country and beyond. Consider that a Google search combining the keywords "China" and "future" returns predominantly economy- and technology-related results: China's GDP is predicted to overtake that of the United States before 2030,[1] and Chinese companies — especially those working in national

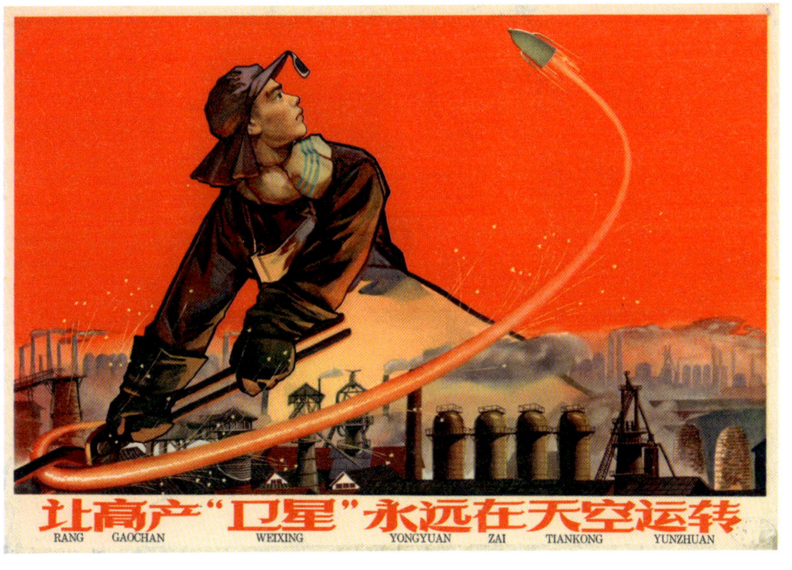

鍾在本，《讓高產「衛星」永遠在天空運轉》，1958，海報，反映了大躍進時期(1958–62)中國政府不切實際的經濟和科技增長目標

Zhong Zaiben, *Let the "Sputnik" of high production circle around the sky forever*, 1958. Poster demonstrating the unrealistic targets for economic and technological growth set by the Chinese government during the Great Leap Forward era (1958–62)

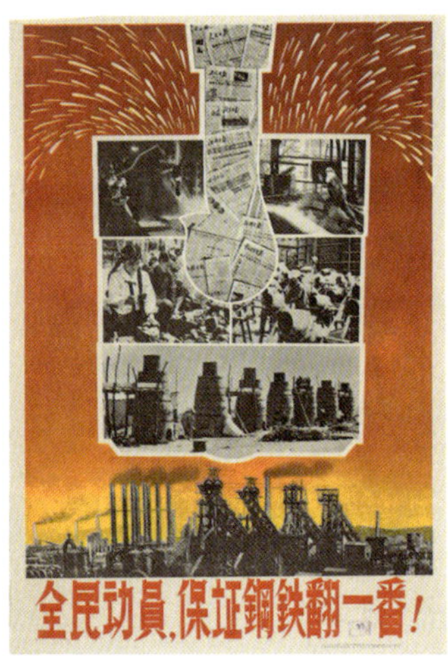

匿名創作者，《全民動員，保證鋼鐵翻一番！》，1985，海報。大躍進期間的各種荒謬举措，其中一項是政府動員全民在家裏後院煉鋼，与此同时饑荒奪取數百萬人的生命。
Unknown artist, *Mobilize the whole population, to make sure that steel is doubled!*, 1958. Poster. The campaign to mobilize the populace to mass-produce steel in "backyard furnaces" is remembered as one of the follies of the Great Leap Forward era, when government policy resulted in a famine that took millions of lives.

經濟競賽。[4]但冷戰已經證明，競爭的結果並不那麼明了，各方都被困在一種互相依賴，彼此分化的複雜動態關係中，在資源、貿易、移民、債務的全球網絡已成形的今天就更是如此。「以競爭為基礎的未來概想」持續至今，它與不僅席捲中國，也遍及世界各地的加速技術發展之間有什麼樣的聯繫？全球與本土之間越發錯綜複雜的關係對於我們共同的技術未來將產生何種影響，這些影響又將如何啟發我們重新審視本土-全球二元關係？

要回答上述具有挑戰性的問題，重新思考本土-全球關係這一隱喻可以為我們提供一個出發點。哲學家許煜認為，本土的文化、政治身份已經無法作為全球的對立面孤立存在，全球狀態不僅僅只是一個空間概念，同時也是一種時間體驗。許煜引用法國人類學家安德烈·勒魯瓦-古蘭（André Leroi-Gourhan）的說法，指出技術體系的同步效果將個體限定在一種去人性化的、「近乎於完全機械化的律動」當中。[5]全球化的同化和均質化進程借助諸如電訊、物流、金融等不斷擴張的技術系統已經「跨越了所有疆域」。在這個意義上（同時也鑒於上文所提出的，大家對「中國的未來」將如何塑造世界的極度好奇），「中國」便已不僅僅是一片地理疆域，更是一個時間的概念。因此，重新思考哲學、藝術意義上的「未來」，也許可以給我們提供中國文化想像與世界之關係的新的可能性。

defense innovation — are prioritizing AI.[2] On the one hand, the Chinese government welcomes this attention and turns it into propaganda for securing internal power. Although discredited by the humanitarian disasters resulting from political campaigns such as the Great Leap Forward,[3] Mao Zedong's recklessly idealistic 1957 slogan "Surpass Britain, Catch America" (*chao Ying gan Mei*) has to an extent become a reality. On the other hand, sensationalized by politicians and media outlets around the world, these forecasts perpetuate the Cold War mentality that equates the future with military and economic competition for global supremacy.[4] But as the Cold War showed, the endgame is not so obvious, as all the players are locked into an intricate dynamic of interdependency and differentiation — all the more so now, with the establishment of global networks of resources, trade, migration, and debt. How does the perpetuation of "a future based on competition" connect with technological developments not only in China, but across the world as well? What implications do the increasingly complex relations between the global and local have for our collective technological future, and how do they inspire us to reconsider the local-global binary?

A reconsideration of the metaphor of the local-global relationship can provide a starting point for answering these challenging questions. Arguing that the cultural and political identity of the local can no longer be isolated in opposition to the global, the philosopher Yuk Hui proposes that the global condition is not simply a spatial concept but is now also a temporal experience. Yuk cites French anthropologist André Leroi-Gourhan's observation that the synchronization effect of technological systems conditions individuals in a dehumanizing "rhythmicity that has reached a stage of almost total mechanicity."[5] Globalization's processes of synchronization and homogenization "traverse every territory" via an ever-expanding array of technological systems, from telecommunications to logistics and finance. In this sense, given the intense interest in how its future will shape the world, "China" is not just a geographical territory but also a temporal concept. Thus rethinking the *future* — as a philosophical and artistic idea — might lead us to new possibilities for the cultural imagination of China in relation to the world.

One Hand Clapping

It is against this backdrop that we began to conceive the ideas around the third and final commission of The Robert H. N. Ho Family Foundation Chinese Art Initiative at the Solomon R. Guggenheim Museum. Conclusions always prompt imagination of what comes after. Formerly a vision of a future that would provide happiness for all, dreamed of by many artists, the promise of technological utopia has been gradually corrupted by the exploitation of financial capitalism, so that global techno-capitalist development is now the dominant mode of everyday life. How can art continue to be relevant under these conditions? If the imperative of art is to reimagine life, in the belief that doing so can free us from the general drift of the world, and perhaps ultimately redirect it, then this imperative is all the more urgent today.

When art engages with issues concerning the future, how does it inform our understanding of the present? We have invited five artists — Cao Fei, Duan Jianyu, Lin Yilin, Wong Ping, and Samson Young — to reflect on this question with us. In doing so, we provided them with fifteen keywords as a foothold for approaching their new commissions: future; technology; system; myth; ghost; groundlessness; disaster; chaos; absurdity; uncanny; medium; togetherness; existence; humanity; and utopia. By no means are the resulting artworks illustrations or literal interpretations of these words; on the contrary, through the dialogue between artist and curator, the process of creating new works actively addresses the tension between the thinking of the making and the act of the making, while allowing the concepts and materials that constitute the work to reciprocally influence the making in mind.

This intriguing process mirrors the always uncertain ontological status of art, which escapes fixed definition. It brings to mind the seemingly absurd image of "one hand clapping," derived from the Zen koan that asks, "We know the sound of two hands clapping. But what is the sound of one hand clapping?"[6] The idea is initially baffling, but the mere proposal of the question brings its possibility into existence, and once we accept the possibility, we are invited down a path of multiple horizons. Similarly, the commitment to art involves continuous contemplation of life's unanswerable questions, especially those concerning the future. It is through this untenability, which actively engages our critical agencies, that we find connections between the framework of this exhibition and the implications of its title, *One Hand Clapping*.

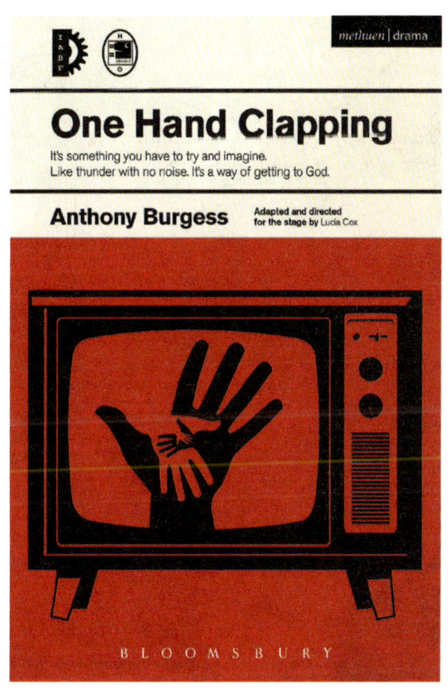

露西亞・考克斯改編自安東尼・伯吉斯小說《孤掌難鳴》〈英文原題為*One Hand Clapping*〉的同名舞台劇劇本封面，第一版〈倫敦，Methuen Drama出版社，1961〉
Cover of Lucia Cox's stage adaptation of Anthony Burgess's eponymous novel, *One Hand Clapping* (London: Methuen Drama, 1961)

First, "one hand clapping" evokes ideas of "solitude" and "working alone." Whereas there is a tendency in current liberal art discourses to equate "socially engaged art practice" with open political resistance, "one hand clapping" suggests the possibility of "disengagement" as an alternate form of resistance. This was already manifested in the Chinese tradition of the literati recluse, and is also recognizable in Theodor W. Adorno's idea of art as the social antithesis of society. No matter what forms it takes, art is neither directly reflective of society, nor is it obviously useful to society. All the more so in dark times, the freedom of art finds its greatest potential in its reimagination of life through a rich and productive *un*reasonableness that puts the rhetoric of truth into doubt.

Second, the title itself indexes issues of cultural origins and appropriation. Now a global cultural

單手拍掌

正是在上述背景下，我們開始構思「何鴻毅家族基金中國藝術計劃」在古根海姆美術館的第三也是最後一個展覽。「尾聲」總會讓人對「將來」浮想聯翩。在歷史的進程中，很多藝術家曾在技術烏托邦的允諾中看到了幸福大同的未來圖景，如今這幅圖景卻被金融資本主義的剝削漸漸侵蝕，全球技術–資本主義發展已成為日常生活的主導模式。在這種環境下，藝術如何保持相關性？如果藝術的使命在於重新想像生活，並相信她能借此把我們從時代的洪流中解放出來，甚至最終重新引導這股洪流，那麼這個使命在今天就顯得更加緊迫。

當藝術介入有關未來的問題時，她能為我們對當下的理解帶來何種影響？我們邀請了五位藝術家：曹斐、段建宇、林一林、黃炳和楊嘉輝來共同思考這個問題。我們為藝術家提供了十五個關鍵詞，作為他們此次委任創作的基礎線索：未來、技術、系統、神話、幽靈、失重、災難、混沌、荒誕、詭異、媒介、團結、存在、人性、以及烏托邦。展覽最終呈現的作品絕不是上述關鍵詞的圖示解析或直接闡釋，恰恰相反，通過藝術家與策展人之間的持續對話，此次新作品的創作過程積極回應了「創作的思考」與「創作的行為」之間的張力，同時，允許構成作品的材料和觀念與「思維中的創作」形成相互影響的關係。

這一豐富的過程呼應了藝術拒絕固化定義、總是不確定的本體狀態。這個過程也讓人聯想到禪宗公案裏的一個看似荒誕的意象：「單手拍掌」——「吾人知悉二掌相擊之聲，然則獨手拍之音又何若？」[6]看到這個問題，一開始誰都會覺得困惑，但是問題的提出本身就預示了其答案存在的可能，一旦我們接受了這一可能性，就能跟著踏上一條通向多重視野的道路。同樣，對藝術的專注意味著去不斷思考生命中那些沒有答案的問題，尤其是關於未來的叩問。這一無解的探詢調動著我們的批判能動性，正是通過它，此次展覽的框架與展覽題目《單手拍掌》的涵義之間建立起了聯繫。

首先，「單手拍掌」讓人聯想到「獨處」和「獨自工作」。盡管今天的人文話語系統傾向於把「社會參與性藝術實踐」等同於公開的政治抵抗，「單手拍掌」暗示了另一種可能性，即「抽身而出」作為一種另類抵抗形式。這一點在中國文人隱世的傳統中已有體現，德國哲學家阿多諾（Theodor W. Adorno）討論的「藝術作為社會的反命題」說的也是類似的議題。實際上，不管藝術採取何種表現形式，她既不是社會的直接反映，也對社會也沒有明顯的利用價值。時代越是險惡便越是如此：只有借助其豐富且具有生產性的「不合理」來對真理的修辭提出質疑，藝術的自由才能在對生活的重新想像中發揮最大的潛力。

其次，這個題目本身就索引了文化出處和挪用的問題。如今「獨手拍之音」的意象可能已經成為了全球文化的一種陳詞濫調，在各種語境中被反覆引用，從J.D.賽林格（J. D. Salinger）《九故事》（1953）的卷首引語，到安東尼·伯吉斯（Anthony Burgess）1961年的同名小說，以及1974年的一部關於羽翼樂隊（Wings）的電影。[7]此外，它也為粵語流行歌手林子祥1994年的同名單曲和專輯《單手拍掌》提供了靈感，然而，林子祥的「單手拍掌」一詞並不是來自中文語境，也沒有直譯自日文，卻是借道了戰後美國垮掉一代的文化轉譯。此外，禪宗公案的起源本來就非常複雜：日文裏的kōan一詞以中文的「公案」（gong'an）為原型，而誕生於唐朝（618–907）的這一佛教禪修方式實際是「公府之案牘」的簡寫，指「官府辦公的案件文卷」。[8]從中國到日本，再經由西方挪用回到中國，「單手拍掌」在文化傳播過程中不斷變形變異。

此次展覽我們再次借用它做題目，希望通過上述幽靈般的迴路，檢驗在這個不斷擴張卻日趨扁平的全球傳播系統下，意義是如何被生產、省略以及重述的。這一「再挪用」的行為也表達了本次中國藝術計劃不易調和的矛盾狀態：一方面參展藝術家被框定在「中國性」的集體形象中，但另一方面，作為創作個體，他們都在積極消解這種定義；他們的實踐被放到一個外國語境（古根海姆美術館）呈現和解讀，但同時又被寄予投射回他們自己所屬文化的期待。於是，當藝術作為一種抵抗時，她反覆切換於對社會認同的介入和介出中。這一辯證的過程促使藝術獲得某種激進的獨一性，模糊所謂起源問題，同時迴避本質主義，使其超越僅僅是對世界的簡單反饋。正是在這種意義上，藝術實踐可以成為一種「單手拍掌」式的實踐。

除此以外，「單手拍掌」的謎題也指向未來。它是一個尚未到來的聲音，一個我們無法辨識直到它不再曾是的聲音。在中文的詞源學裏，「未來」是一個複合詞，由「尚未、未嘗」的「未」字和「即將到來」的「來」字組成。和公案的隱喻一樣，這一有關未來的謎題擁有自己的生命，並會繼續不斷地借用、解構和轉換其自身。委任創作總是具有挑戰和冒險精神，因為我們，作為策展人和藝術家，永遠無法確信什麼時候完成了創作，又是什麼完整了作品。但這種對於「尚未到來」之物的不確定總是與期待和希望息息相關，也正是這曖昧的躊躇滿志定義著人性與未來的關係。

檮杌的冷記憶

在古代中國，歷史意識與未來想像之間的關係化身為神話裏的怪獸——檮杌。這種兇殘成性又富有洞察能力的怪獸「在認知層面獲得了與歷史的同一性」，而且可以「預見未來」。[9]通過喚起歷史事件的暴力和野蠻，檮杌警醒世人勿讓悲劇在未來重演。它同時也體現著一種原始的、卻不再被當代社會珍視的動物性精神。在描寫後現代文化語境中技術當道的今天與未來時，讓·鮑德里亞（Jean Baudrillard）指出，我們在現代化進程中毀掉的不是人性，而是非人性和獸性，一種人與生俱來的獸性。[10]

banality, referenced everywhere from the epigraph of J. D. Salinger's *Nine Stories* (1953) to the titles of Anthony Burgess's 1961 novel and a 1974 film about the band Wings,[7] "one hand clapping" also inspired the 1994 song and album by Cantopop singer George Lam; however, the title, "Danshou paizhang," was not translated directly from Japanese, but arrived via the detour of postwar American Beat culture. Moreover, the practice of koan already has complex origins: the Japanese term *kōan* derives from the Chinese *gong'an*, the Chan Buddhist practice that emerged in the Tang dynasty (618–907), which in turn is an abbreviation of *gongfu zhi andu*, referring to "case documents of the public law court."[8] From China to Japan and back again via Western appropriation, "one hand clapping" has metamorphosed continuously in the process of cultural transmission.

In borrowing it again as the exhibition title, we hope to test—through such a phantom circuit—how meaning is fabricated, omitted, and restated in our ever expanding but flattening global communication systems. This act of reappropriation expresses this initiative's irreconcilable condition: the participating artists are framed by the collective image of "Chineseness," while as individuals they actively dissolve such framing; and their practices are presented and interpreted in a foreign context (the Guggenheim) but are expected to project back to their culture of origin. Art as a form of resistance is intertwined in a process of constant engagement and disengagement with social identification. This dialectical process drives art to become radically singular, to blur questions of origin, bypass essentialism, and be more than a reflection of the world. It is in this sense that artistic practice can be a practice of "one hand clapping."

Further, the conundrum of "one hand clapping" also points to the future. It is a sound yet to come, a sound we do not recognize until it is no longer what it was. In Chinese etymology, *future* is a compound word combining the characters for "not yet" (*wei*) and "to come or arrive" (*lai*). Like the metaphor of the koan, the conundrum inevitably has a life of its own and continues to appropriate, deconstruct, and transform itself. Commissioning is a risky business, since we, as curators and artists, are never sure when to complete the work and what completes it. But the uncertainties of this something "yet to arrive" are always entangled with the expectations and hopes that characterize humanity's relation to the future.

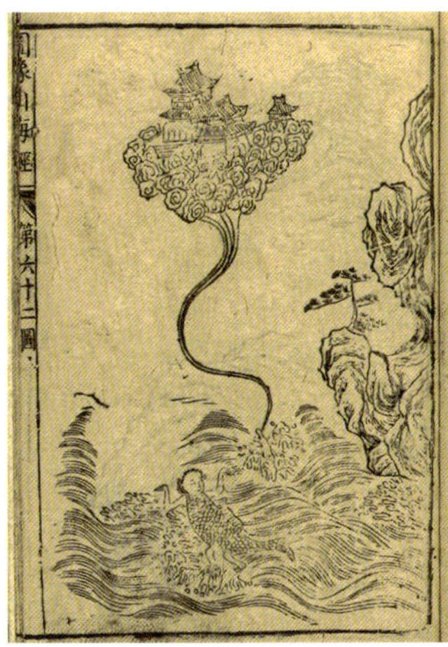

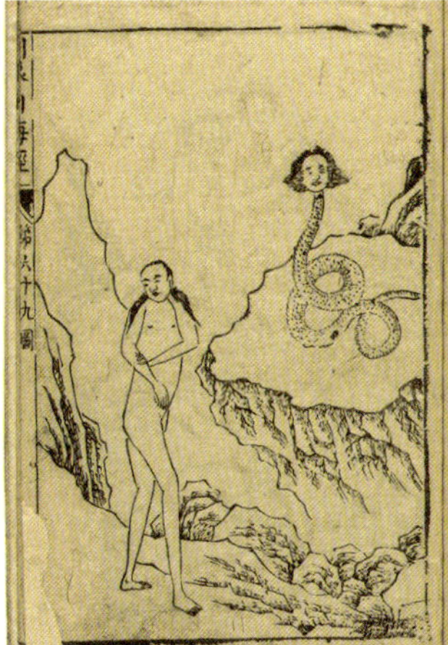
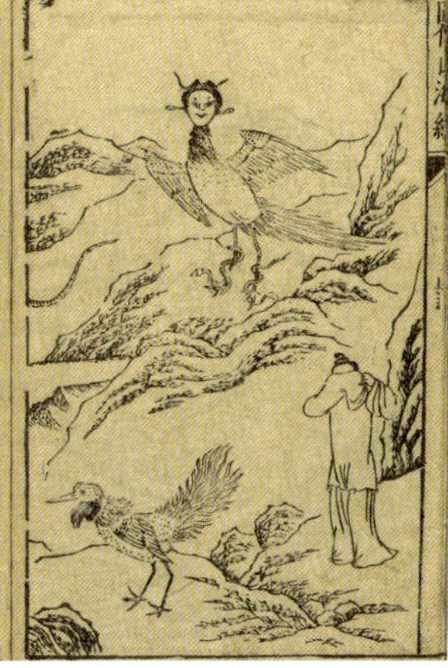

選自明代《有圖山海經》，1597–1620
Illustrations from a Ming-dynasty edition of *Classic of Mountains and Seas*, 1597–1620

Cool Memories of Taowu

In ancient China, the relationship between historical consciousness and the imagination of the future was embodied in the mythical monster Taowu. With its ferocious nature and visionary magic, Taowu "acquired cognitive identity with history" and could "foresee the future."[9] Evoking the violence and brutality of historical events, Taowu cautions against repeating similar mishaps in the future. It also speaks to a primordial and animalistic

受到鮑德里亞的啟發，段建宇嘗試挖掘她在日常生活的邊緣人物身上發現的動物性和原始狀態。在她為本次展覽創作的全新系列繪畫《春江花月夜》(2017-18)裏，這種獸性體現在繪畫的中心人物中：比如流浪於嘈雜城市的乞丐和街頭藝人；趴在自制輪板上滑行的殘疾人；吹笛女人的長髮拖地，卷起來形成巨蛇般的庇護所；還有穿梭於陰影之間的狼人。段建宇造型的靈感來源多元，包括唐朝的文學作品(該系列的題目就援引自張若虛[約660-720年]的一首詩)，周臣(1460-1535)、蔣兆和(1904-1986)的經典水墨作品，以及社會主義現實主義的宣傳畫等等。她的異質想像不僅跨越了歷史的時空，也超越了區別動物與人類、自然與神性之間的現代性分割。

鮑德里亞筆下獸性的毀滅實際上指向了現代技術統治論社會的野心，其目標就是要利用機械管理清除一切無秩序和非理性的跡象。盡管我們當前的社會大有走向「人神」(Homo deus)的趨勢，即一種經過技術強化、基因改造，不受原始恐懼和需求困擾的物種[11]，段建宇對這種「完美」的存在並不感興趣。她畫中的人物瘋癲滑稽，不受控制，如同一則影射未來返祖現象的寓言。通過關注那些總是被人忽略，但又各有特色的生命，她的繪畫也揭示出那些所謂「對社會無貢獻」群體受到的擠壓和排除。段建宇那些原本「不值一提」的畫中人，實際上質疑了藝術表現機制在塑造文化想像從而維護社會秩序中扮演的共犯角色。這些毫不妥協的詭異形象是全球化均質進程中逸出常規的不協調音。最終展現在我們眼前的，是一片包含著美學與政治雙重維度的奇異風景。

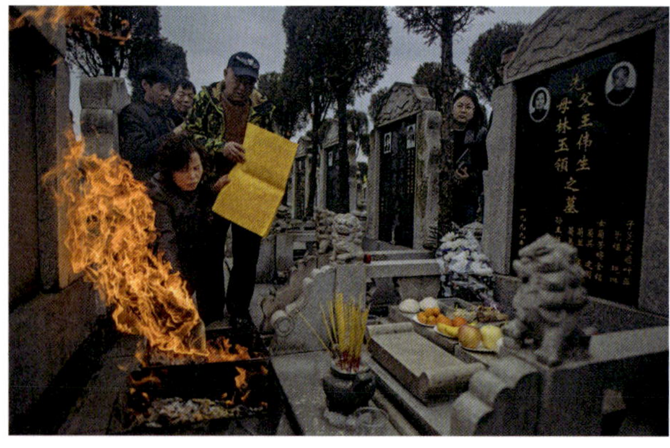

清明節期間，一位女士在先人墓碑前燒冥幣，上海公墓，2017年4月4日。
A woman burns ghost money before a gravestone as an offering to her ancestors during the annual Qingming Festival, or Tomb Sweeping Day, at a public cemetery in Shanghai, April 4, 2017.

spirit that is no longer celebrated in contemporary society. Writing about the techno-present and future against the postmodern backdrop, Jean Baudrillard speculates that what we have destroyed in the process of modernization is not humanity, but inhumanity and bestiality: the bestiality inherent to humans.[10]

Inspired by Baudrillard's insight, Duan Jianyu seeks to excavate the animality and primordiality she sees manifested in marginalized figures in everyday life. In her new painting series produced for this exhibition, *Spring River in the Flower Moon Night* (2017–18), this is apparent in the central figures she has created: the beggars and street jugglers wandering amid the urban chaos; the "cripples" rolling around on their DIY wheeled boards; the lute players whose long hair touches the ground and coils into big, snakelike shelters; the werewolves scuttling through the shadows. Informed by Tang-dynasty literary motifs (the series title, *Chun jiang hua yue ye* in Chinese, is taken from the famous poem by Zhang Ruoxu [ca. 660–720]), classic ink works by Zhou Cheng (1460–1535) and Jiang Zhaohe (1904–1986), and Socialist Realist propaganda, Duan enunciates an idiosyncratic vision that transcends modern divisions of animal, human, nature, and the divine, as well as historical epochs and places.

The destruction of bestiality Baudrillard identifies is in fact the ambition of a modern technocratic society that seeks to purge from itself all hints of disorder and irrationality by machine management. Whereas our current societies presage a coming *Homo deus* — a species of technologically augmented, genetically engineered humans who are free from primal fears and necessities[11] — Duan is not interested in such "perfect" beings. Her characters are unruly allegories of an atavism for the future. By focusing on overlooked but unique lives, her paintings expose the exclusionary practices targeting those who are deemed socially unproductive. Her otherwise disregarded characters prompt questions about the complicity of mechanisms of representation in shaping the cultural imagination and maintaining social order. Through their uncanny and uncompromising imagery, they are eccentric, out-of-sync notes in the homogenized composition of globalization. The result is a fantastic landscape that has both aesthetic and political dimensions.

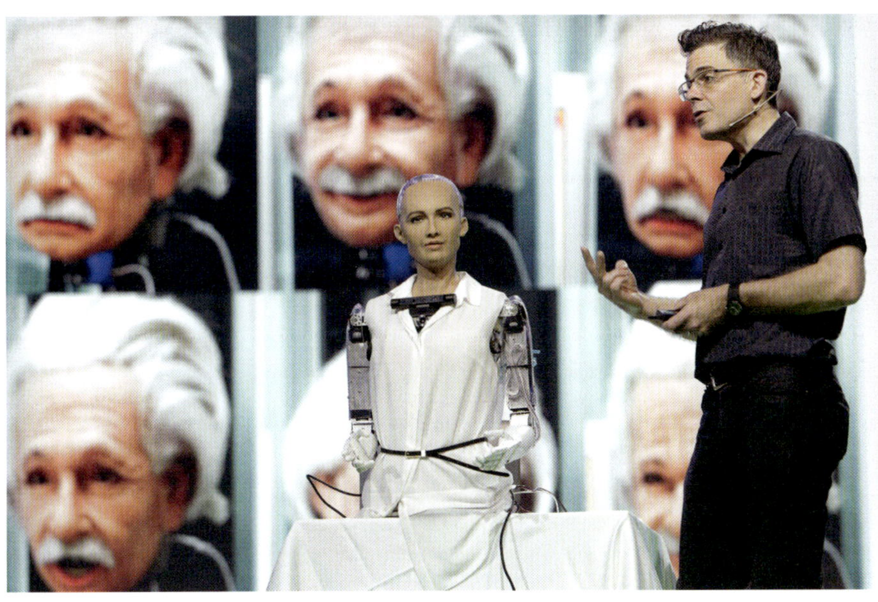

漢森機器人技術公司創始人兼CEO大衛・漢森正在解釋創造機器人Sophia的過程，Sophia是一個超仿真、臉部有女性特徵的機器人。全球移動互聯網大會，北京，2016年4月29日。
David Hanson, founder and CEO of Hanson Robotics, describes the process of creating Sophia, an ultrarealistic female humanoid robot, at the Global Mobile Internet Conference in Beijing, April 29, 2016.

The Afterlife of Obsolescence

A keen observer of the everyday, Wong Ping scavenges for mundane events to alchemize into fable-like animations. In *Dear, can I give you a hand?* (2018), he focuses on a seeming paradox: how are we to reconcile the contradiction of eagerly anticipating the future while simultaneously approaching death? In Wong's native Hong Kong, the issues surrounding the aging population often hide out of sight. Because of the insanely high real estate prices, the deceased must bid on plots for their cinerary caskets, and services encouraging burial at sea advertise the gimmick of virtual tomb sweeping. Replacing ancient tradition, the latter involves creating an online account for the deceased with profiles and passwords; users log on to pay their respects through digital renderings of the offerings customarily burned or presented at real graves.[12]

An actual encounter inspired the narrative of *Dear, can I give you a hand?* One afternoon, Wong stumbled across an old man who had discarded a bag of VHS tapes in a public recycling bin. His curiosity piqued, Wong opened the lid to discover a collection of carefully packed pornographic films. Building on this event, Wong draws a parallel between the obsolete media format and the marginalized aging population, who are dismissed as economically and biologically barren. In Wong's dystopian future, longevity is sinful and virtual tomb sweeping the norm, but when families gather before the computer to observe the annual memorial rites, they forget the log-in information! In another scene, caretakers switch on the virtual reality headsets of their wheelchair-bound charges, who are calmed by views of the sunset across the passing seasons, while they themselves, addicted to their smartphones, keep on swiping and refreshing their social media feeds.

Wong's nonsensical and risqué humor upsets our social norms. Exemplified by the elderly protagonist who lusts after his daughter-in-law, Wong's invented characters have profane desires and struggle with human nature. The voice of the animation's narrator—performed by the artist himself—relates everything in an expressionless tone that belies the narrative's provocativeness. Such moral equivocation challenges contemporary sensibilities modeled on codes of political correctness. After all, the deadpan delivery cannot

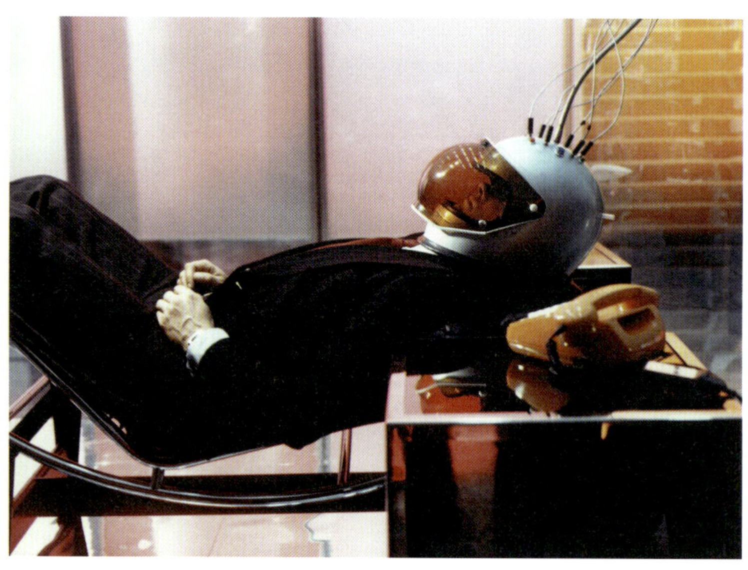

法斯賓德，《世界旦夕之間》，1973年，16毫米電影。研究員正在運行由「身份單元」組成的模擬世界程序。這些「身份單元」相信自己是真實的人類。與此同時，運行程序的研究員也開始懷疑他們的世界其實也是一個模擬現實。
Rainer Werner Fassbinder, *World on a Wire*, 1973. 16 mm film. In this film produced for German television, researchers running a simulation program populated by "identity units" who believe they are actual human beings begin to suspect that their own world is also a simulation.

荒廢之物的來世

黃炳對日常生活有敏銳的觀察力，煉金術般地將平凡事件轉化成寓言式的動畫作品。在《親，需要服務嗎？》(2018)中，他將焦點對準了一個看似矛盾的、有關存在的問題：一邊是對未來的急切期盼，一邊是不斷接近死亡的事實，我們如何協調兩者？

在藝術家居住的香港，人們對人口老齡化的相關問題常常避而不談。由於房地產價格高昂，骨灰龕位年年短缺，很多鼓勵海葬的服務機構開始推銷網上掃墓。取代古老殯葬傳統的這項服務需要用戶首先在網上為去世的親人創建一個帳戶，填寫個人信息，並設置密碼，用戶登錄後可以向死者奉獻數字祭品，而這些祭品過去都是在實體的墓前焚化或供奉的。[12]

《親，需要服務嗎？》的故事靈感來源於藝術家在真實生活裏的一次遭遇。一天下午，黃炳看到一位老人將一袋VHS錄像帶扔進了一個公共垃圾回收箱。心生好奇的他打開垃圾桶的蓋子，發現裏面是一套打包得整整齊齊的黃色錄像帶。從這件小事出發，黃炳在過時的媒體形式與邊緣化的老年人之間找到了某種聯繫：如同因為過時而被扔掉的錄像帶，老年人常常被社會視為於經濟和生物層面都沒有生產力的群體。在黃炳的敵托邦未來裏，長壽變成一種罪過，網上掃墓也已習以為常，但當一家人聚到電腦前參加一年一度的紀念儀式時，他們發現自己居然忘了登錄信息！在另一個場景中，坐在輪椅上的老人頭戴VR眼鏡，只要看護人員打開眼鏡的開關，老人便可以從虛擬的四季變幻落日景象裏獲得平靜，而看護人員自己則埋首於智能手機，不停滑動手指刷屏幕，更新社交媒體上的信息。

黃炳無厘頭、甚至有些猥褻的幽默顛覆了我們的社會準則。正如那個對自己兒媳想入非非的老年主人公所示，黃炳創造的人物都懷揣齷蹉的欲望，掙扎在人性邊緣。動畫片的旁白由藝術家親自配音，他不帶任何感情色彩的聲音叛離了敘事本身的挑釁意味。這種道德上的撩撥挑戰了我們建立於政治正確原則基礎上的當代感知力。畢竟，冷面幽默的敘述風格也掩蓋不了人們隱藏在謹慎、尊重和規範行為之下的困惑、憤怒與焦慮。

在《親，需要服務嗎？》中，黃炳利用他特有的視覺語言，通過華麗、復古波普式的色彩強化了敘事的荒誕性。動畫片在一面電視牆上循環播放，顯示器背面以透明殼蓋處理使其內部「器官」暴露在外，不禁讓人想起外殼半透明的老式任天堂掌上遊戲機。錄像牆周圍是一大片蹦蹦跳跳的玩具假牙——宛如某個高燒夢魘裏的香港鬼故事場景。這件裝置作品華麗艷俗、惡作劇般的氛圍營造了一個張力十足的空間，時間在其中懸置於一個已經過時的未來。

誰是0-1-0：單子與二進制碼

也許我們可以把作為控制論和數字電腦基石的二進制碼及其1-0-1-0的數字序列視為「單手拍掌」的又一類化身。1701年，法國耶穌會傳教士白晉(Joachim Bouvet)從中國寄了一本《易經》給德國通才G. W. 萊布尼茨(G. W. Leibniz)，後者就是根據對這本《易經》的翻譯和誤讀發明了二進制。[13] 萊布尼茨後來有關「單子論」(1714)的論述預測了一個技術統治的未來。他認為世界是由無數「單子」構成，「單子」是「沒有組成部分」但性質不同的

conceal the confusion, rage, and anxiety repressed beneath outward displays of prudence, respect, and good behavior.

Dear, can I give you a hand? employs Wong's unique visual language of gaudy, retro-pop colors to intensify the narrative's absurdity. The animation is looped on a wall of video monitors, the backs of which are designed to expose their internal "organs," reminiscent of the old, translucent-covered Nintendo Game Boy console. Behind the video wall spreads a constellation of tacky jumping denture toys — like something from a Hong Kong ghost story in a fever dream. The installation's flashy, mischievous atmosphere creates a contested space where time is suspended in an already outdated future.

Who Is 0–1–0: The Monad and the Binary Code

We could consider the binary code and its 1-0-1-0 sequences — the foundation of cybernetics and all digital computers[13] — another embodiment of "one hand clapping." Its inventor, G. W. Leibniz, drew inspiration from his translation and misreading of the *I Ching*, a copy of which was sent to him from China by the French Jesuit Joachim Bouvet in 1701. Leibniz's subsequent treatise, the "Monadology" (1714), predicts a technocratic future. Leibniz believed that the world is composed of an infinite number of "monads" — simple substances with "no parts," although varying in quality — that form compounds. Convinced that the universe is ruled according to a perfect order, which he attributed to God, he claimed that these monads are generated by divinity and expressed in accordance with God's infinite will.[14]

The monad has in turn become the namesake for small function units in the contemporary practice of functional programming, with programmers chaining "monads" together to create complex compositions. But who creates the "perfect order" here? Are computer programmers "playing God" by writing the systems that control contemporary society? Or, are they literally creating "God" through the development of AI and optimized machine-humans? Perhaps, since the laws of the universe can be reduced to binary code on a subatomic level, we are living in a planetary computer, and our reality is a programmed simulation, as visualized in Rainer Werner Fassbinder's 1973 TV serial, *World on a Wire*.[15]

Lin Yilin offers a humorous take on these fantasies in the multimedia installation he created for *One Hand Clapping, Monad* (2018). Lin uses VR technology to simulate a few simple basketball movements, but rather than having users share the experience of the basketball player — modeled on the Chinese American NBA star Jeremy Lin, whose athleticism has become an inspiration for Asian Americans struggling with negative stereotypes about their masculinity — he puts them in the position of the ball itself. The moment Lin Yilin's VR headset and chair are activated, the visual and physical simulation disorients the user and external reality drops away as the perspective shifts from that of the player to that of the basketball. Parts of the brain signal the body to create the sensation of being bounced around, while the conscious mind struggles to process the strange view of the surroundings. Yet the realness of the experience elicits an ontological dissonance. It may be absurd to imagine how a basketball feels, but this is precisely the work's point. Whereas Hollywood films seek to build empathic connections between the story's heroes and viewers, in the VR world, the participants do not merely watch other people in an invented reality; they themselves inhabit that reality. This interchange of subjectivity and objectivity opens the possibility of an affective evolution in our relations with the "other." We can *be* the other, rather than simply express commiseration *for* the other. Lin suggests that if we can achieve this with a basketball, then it could be applied to other categories of subjectivity, and possibly even extended to conflicts over political and racial differences.

Ballads of Automation

Imagine a near future in which China is an automated utopia: product delivery drones fly over the three-century-old Fenghuang Ancient Town in Hunan Province; liberated Foxconn workers play mahjong or read poetry to each other in the now defunct workers' lounge; and although the air pollution remains, a citywide air-purifying respirator covering Beijing refreshes around the clock.

A few decades ago, the utopic vision of an automated communist future already found inspiration in the lyrics of revolutionary workers' ballads: "Listen to the party, committed to automation, our prospects beautiful as a

簡單實體。它們互相結合，形成複合物。萊布尼茨堅信宇宙運行遵循一種完美的秩序，他將這秩序歸結為上帝，宣稱單子由神創造，並呈現上帝無限的意志。[14]

「單子」這個名稱隨後被當代電腦編程實踐的函數式編程借用，來命名最小函數單位，而程序員的工作就是把大量「單子」串聯到一起，創造出複雜的結構。但在此時此處到底是誰在創造「完美的秩序」？電腦程序員是在「扮演上帝」嗎？因為他們編寫的系統仿佛控制了當代社會。抑或，他們正在通過開發人工智能以及優化「人—機」合體，貨真價實地創造著「上帝」？也許因為整個宇宙的規律在亞原子層面都可以被還原為二進制碼，我們生活的地球其實就是一台巨大的行星計算機，而我們身處的現實則是一個被編碼的擬像，就像導演賴納·維爾納·法斯賓德（Rainer Werner Fassbinder）1973年的電視劇《世界旦夕之間》裏所想像的那樣。[15]

林一林在他為《單手拍掌》創作的多媒體裝置《單子》（2018）中，以幽默的手法詮釋了上述奇思妙想。他用VR技術模擬了幾個簡單的籃球動作，但觀眾參與的角色卻不是籃球手，而是籃球本身。球手的原型是美籍華裔NBA明星林書豪，他充滿陽剛氣質的運動員形象與許多有關亞洲男性形象的偏見形成對比，因此也成為了亞裔美國人追隨的偶像。裝置的VR頭盔和座椅一啟動，視覺和身體的模擬環境讓使用者突然失去方向感，隨著視角從球手轉換到籃球，外部現實也跟著慢慢瓦解。大腦的一部分示意身體去制造被碰來撞去的感覺，而理性意識卻在奮力處理周圍環境奇怪的視野。經驗的真實性最終激起一種自我本體的失調。試圖體驗一顆「籃球」的感覺和經歷聽起來可能很荒唐，但這正是作品的意圖所在。好萊塢電影總是試圖在故事主角與觀眾之間建立起共情關係，而在VR的世界裏，參與者不只是觀看虛構現實中其他人的一舉一動，他們自己就是那個現實的一部分。這一主體

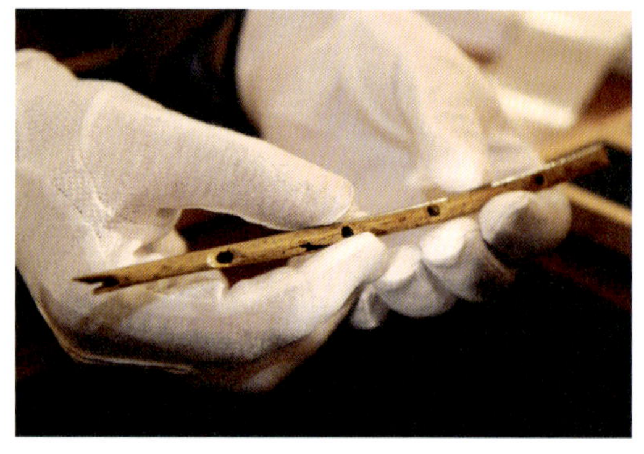

一名德國杜賓根大學的考古學家手上拿著舊石器時代的鳥骨長笛。
An archaeologist at the University of Tübingen, Germany, handles a Paleolithic bird-bone flute.

painting!"[16] And in the most popular line from the revolutionary opera *On the Docks* (1964): "The big crane, so impressive! Everything lifted in its effortless grasp!"[17] Produced during the Cultural Revolution, *On the Docks* portrays Communist Party members and dockworkers who collaborate with the new machinery to ensure the successful shipment of wheat to Africa before a typhoon arrives. Aiding anti-imperialist struggles in Asia, Africa, and Latin America, the courageous performance on the docks exemplifies the lofty ideals of international communism. This vision of an automated future is no Chinese novelty. History is littered with blueprints for unrealized techno-utopias and work-free leisure societies. For example, in his BBC series *All Watched Over by Machines of Loving Grace*, Adam Curtis describes how last century's "cyberdelic" counterculture movement gave birth to the Californian Ideology, which believed that cybernetic systems would liberate humankind from tedious labor.[18] More recently, theories such as Fully Automated Luxury Communism (FALC) aim to "embrace automation to its fullest extent."[19] Referencing Marxist theories of technological development, FALC counts on AI, robotics, and synthetic biology to bring about a postcapitalist leisure society—without unequal wealth distribution—that resonates with traditions of both futurist optimism and social democracy.

Centering on a speculative fiction film, Cao Fei's multimedia installation *Asia One* (2018) visits some of China's most advanced industrial facilities, including the world's first fully automated, unmanned sorting center in Kunshan, Jiangsu Province. Cao is no stranger to telling stories about factories in China. Her acclaimed project *Whose Utopia* (2006) documents a lighting factory in the Pearl River Delta and its workers, who are mostly migrants from rural areas. While *Whose Utopia* highlights the migrant workers' personal stories against the dominant state narrative of economic growth, *Asia One* investigates the tension between human labor and automation, testing the possibilities for an ultimate utopia and shifting the focus from individual dreams to the collective future.

The film shows the sleek infrastructure, speedy robots, and effortless flow of products in the industrial facilities, but something unsettling simmers beneath the surface. Where does the human body reside? Have we finally

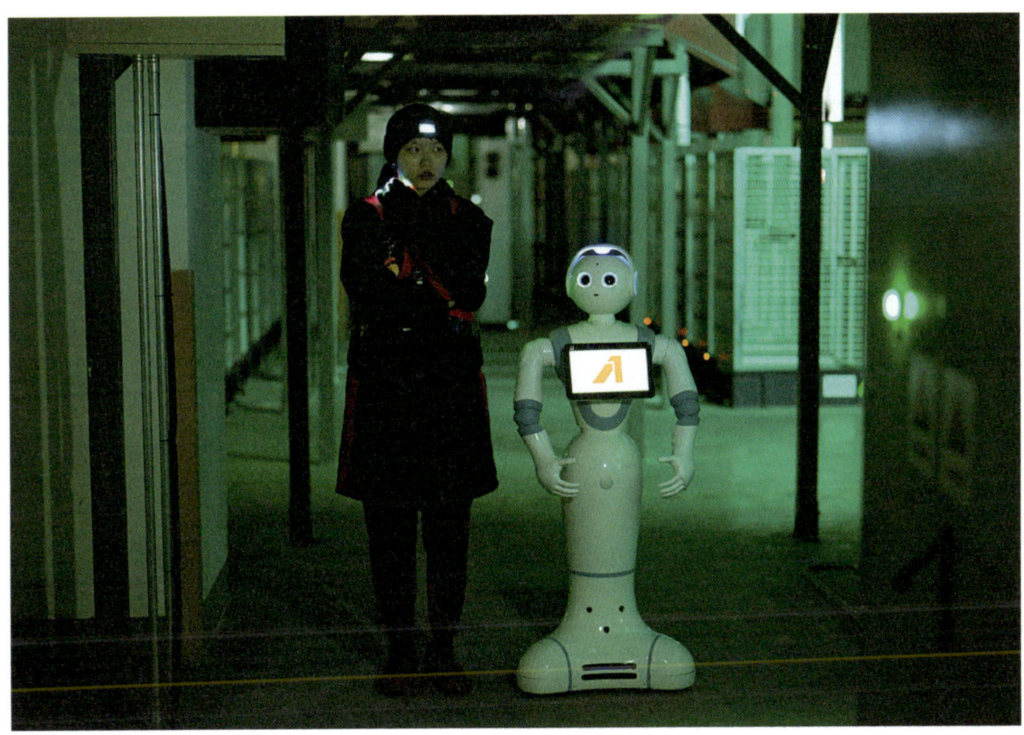

曹斐，《Asia One》，2018（局部），多頻彩色錄像，尺寸可變，所羅門・R・古根海姆美術館，紐約，何鴻毅家族基金藏品，2018.12
Cao Fei, *Asia One*, 2018 (detail). Multichannel color video installation, with sound, dimensions variable overall. Solomon R. Guggenheim Museum, New York, The Robert H. N. Ho Family Foundation Collection 2018.12

been emancipated by machines, or are we ensnared in a new confinement—trapped into "buying the world while staying at home"?[20] In pursuit of ever greater efficiency, we increasingly remove physical interactions from everyday life. But in minimizing messy human interactions, we run the risk of eliminating human nature altogether. Without capricious, erratic, irrational behavior, what might remain?

Impossible Instruments?

Musical instruments tell intimate stories about humanity. Consider the forty-thousand-year-old bird-bone flute found in the Hohle Fels cave in southwest Germany. Not only does it look familiar, it also sounds familiar, as demonstrated by the replica made by archaeologist Wulf Hein.[21] Hearing this little flute and imagining how prehistoric musicians would have blown through its V-shaped notch collapses the millennia separating us from them.

Scientists have spent centuries investigating how musical instruments produce sound, and experimenting with how to reverse engineer their properties. Such inquiries anticipate the emergence of music synthesizers, which are not only novel instruments for producing electronic timbres, but also an attempt to imitate traditional instruments. Although such imitation was sought by the music industry as a means to economize production, the desire to "perfect" the imitation continues growing. From Moog's first commercially manufactured synthesizer in the mid-1960s to the current use of algorithms to digitally simulate instruments, there has been a relentless obsession with claiming "authenticity" through technical refinement. But what kind of authenticity?

In *Possible Music #1 (feat. NESS & Shane Aspegren)* (2018), Samson Young problematizes notions of authenticity and explores their broader cultural implications. In his project, an array of "impossible musical instruments" anchors a sonic and sculptural environment scattered with objects, drawings, and videos. Ranging from a twenty-foot-long trumpet to a tuba so massive no human lung can play it, these whimsical instruments do not really exist, but by implementing a set of physical models derived from the University of Edinburgh's NESS (Next Generation Sound Synthesis) project, Young was able to imagine the sounds

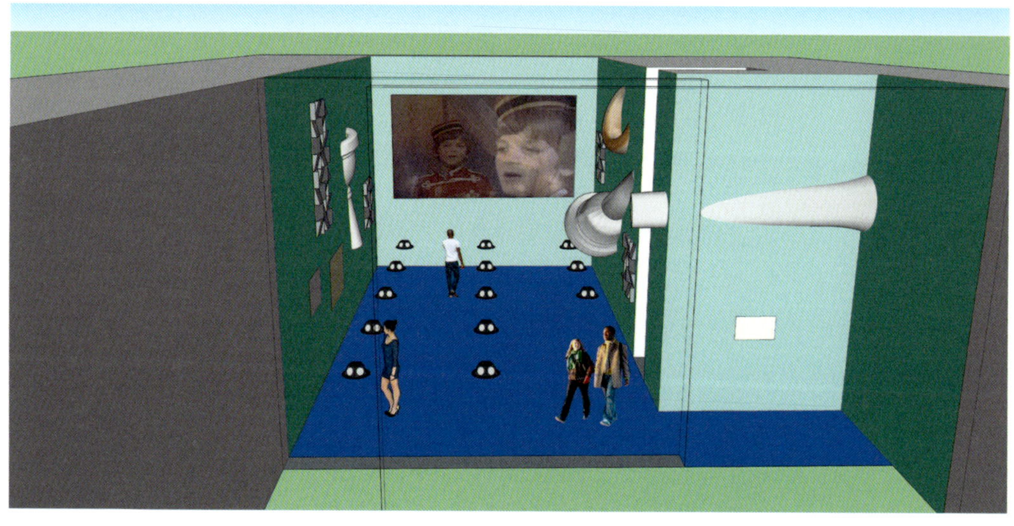

楊嘉輝，《Possible Music #1（feat. NESS & Shane Aspegren）》，2018（數碼效果圖）。所羅門·R·古根海姆美術館，紐約，何鴻毅家族基金藏品，2018.17
Samson Young, *Possible Music #1 (feat. NESS & Shane Aspegren)*, 2018 (digital rendering). Solomon R. Guggenheim Museum, New York, The Robert H. N. Ho Family Foundation Collection 2018.17

與客體的互換為我們與「他者」的關係開啟了一條情感進化的可能性路徑。我們可以「成為」他者，而不只是表達對他者的同情憐憫。林一林的作品幽默地提議，如果我們能與一顆籃球產生共情，那麼這可能也適用於其他類型上的主體，甚至可以延伸到政治與種族差異引發的衝突。

自動化歌謠

想像在不久的將來，中國變成了一個自動化的烏托邦：送貨的無人機盤旋在有著三百多年歷史的鳳凰古城上空；從工廠解放出來的富士康工人在已經廢棄的工人休息室裏打麻將或朗誦詩歌；雖然空氣污染問題還在，但一個覆蓋北京的空氣淨化器二十四小時運轉，為全城提供清潔空氣。

早在幾十年前，革命工人歌謠便在自動化的共產主義未來這一烏托邦願景裏尋找靈感：「聽黨的話，搞自動化，咱們的前景，美如畫！」[16]當然還有革命樣板戲《海港》(1964)裏那句最流行的唱詞：「大吊車，真厲害，成噸的鋼鐵，它輕輕地一抓就起來！」[17]編排於文化大革命期間的《海港》刻畫了共產黨黨員和碼頭工人如何配合新機器，搶在颱風來襲之前將運往非洲的援助稻種搬運上船。為支援亞非拉地區的反帝鬥爭，人們在碼頭上英勇奮鬥，充分體現了國際共產主義的崇高理想。其實，這一自動化的未來願景並非中國獨創。歷史上，有太多未能實現的技術烏托邦和沒有成型的無工作休閑社會暢想。比如，在BBC電視紀錄片系列《在慈愛的機器監視下》中，導演亞當·柯蒂斯(Adam Curtis)就描述了上世紀六十年代網絡迷幻的反文化運動如何催生出加州意識形態，後者相信控制論可以把全人類從單調的勞動中解放出來。[18]近年來，包括「全自動豪華共產主義」(FALC)在內的一些的理論則以「在最大程度上全面擁抱自動化」為目標。[19] FALC援引馬克思主義理論裏有關技術發展的部分，認為依靠人工智能、機器人，以及合成生物學可以建設一個消除財富不公平分配的後資本主義休閑社會，其論述與未來主義的樂觀精神以及社會民主主義理想的傳統遙相呼應。

曹斐的多媒體裝置《Asia One》(2018)以一部科幻思辨式影片為核心，呈現了中國一些最先進的自動化工業設施，包括位於江蘇省昆山市的世界首個全自動無人配送中心。這並不是曹斐第一次講述中國工廠的故事。她廣為人知的作品《誰的烏托邦》(2006)記錄的就是珠三角地區的一家照明設備廠以及其工人(大部分是農民工)的生活狀態。《誰的烏托邦》凸顯了在國家經濟發展的主流敘事下農民工的個人故事，而新片《Asia One》則考察了人類勞動力與自動化之間的張力關係，通過檢驗一個終極烏托邦的可能性，將關注焦點從個體夢想轉向集體未來。

我們在影片裏看到光鮮高級的設備設施、行動高效迅速的機器人，以及流暢無阻的產品傳輸，但這一切的背後似乎總有某種令人不安的東西若隱若現。人的身體到哪去了？機器究竟是解放了我們，還是將我們推入了一個新的陷阱，受困於「坐在家裏買遍世界」？[20]為了追求更高的效率，我們不斷削減日常生活裏人與人的身體互動，因為在這過程中常常充斥著混亂的情緒和行為。可是為了避免這些看似無用的互動，我們很有可能連人性本身都丟掉了。當我們沒有了心血來潮，沒有了不合常規的非理性行為，剩下的還能有什麼呢？

they would make and to compose for them. Each instrument generates a specific composition and is activated at precise intervals through a computer program. Yet none are actualized in complete material form; their fragmentary parts — a mouthpiece, a reed, a body — beg for phantom instrumentalists. The blaring, martial orchestration of Young's environment signifies an invisible conductor whose body either never existed or has yet to be materialized.

Between recitals, the beating of drums reverberates among the unusual objects, which evoke the ruins of a civilization from another time. The objects' differing visual and material qualities — from smooth and hard-edged to rough and bulky, bodily and concrete to virtual and digital — suggest the potential for metamorphosis. Despite its disembodiment of musicians and instruments, computer modeling of the sounds and properties of instruments claims to be scientific. Young's fictional approach, however, ridicules the very idea of an "authentic" object and, by extension, the subject and cultural authenticity it claims. If the birth of music is a critical moment in the birth of humanity, then what will be our last musical instrument, and what might survive after our civilization ends? What might a new world give birth to, and what would it sound like?

After the Future

The Robert H. N. Ho Family Foundation Chinese Art Initiative concludes with *One Hand Clapping*. The initiative has engaged with ongoing intellectual and political discourses on reimagining local and global relations by singling out Greater China as a site for artistic production. As such, it can perhaps be compared to the titular koan. While much is left for reflection, the problem is no longer one of simply developing new narratives or looking at the world from the viewpoint of China. Itself a product of globalization, the notion of the "local" must resist its own framing as an isolated locality; instead, like "one hand clapping," the future of locality could actively appropriate and transform the global.

Romanticizing escape from the local scene, the phrase "poetry and place afar" (*shi he yuanfang*) is a popular meme circulating among young Chinese people on the internet.[22] It speaks to the generation who grew up in economically competitive social environments and feel imprisoned by the tedium of nine-to-five jobs, yet are afraid to quit because of the high mortgage payments on their condo apartments. "Poetry and place afar" expresses their longing for hope, imagination, and freedom. This longing was also deeply felt by the poet Xu Lizhi (1990–2014). In his three years working on the assembly line at Foxconn, Xu wrote hundreds of poems before killing himself at age twenty-four by jumping from the workers' dormitory. Far from envisioning the happiness of the FALC society, Xu saw himself as a misplaced screw, dropping "straight down, with a faint sound," lost to the factory floor.[23] But as long as there is poetry, there is imagination, curiosity, and freedom. In the concluding passages of his book *After the Future*, autonomist philosopher and media activist Franco "Bifo" Berardi advocates that the political task of the future is to foster a "cognitarian self-consciousness" and "sensibility of social solidarity, of human empathy, of gratuitous activity — of freedom, equality, and fraternity" for all.[24] It is at the intersection of poetry, therapy, and paradigmatic creation where the new space of activism emerges.

In this catalogue, we reprint selected poems by Xu Lizhi alongside those by the young poets Wu Qing and Zhang Xiu, whose "nonsense style" poetry employs direct language to address trivial activities and subjects. Radically negating conventions of signifier and signified, poetics and symbolism, they unravel the hypocrisy of grand

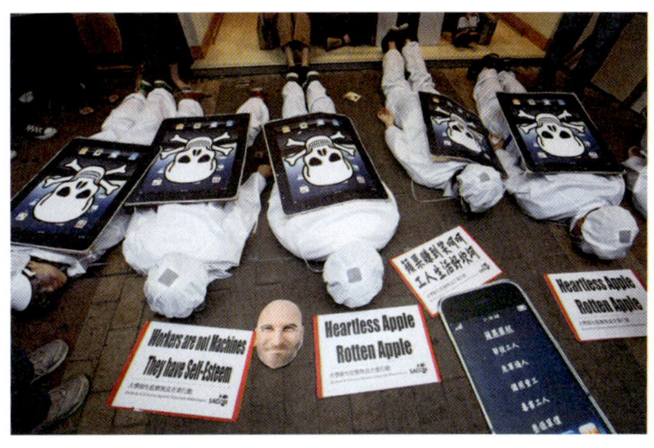

大學生穿著成富士康工人，背後掛著印有骷髏頭和交叉骨圖案的模擬iPad，堵在香港蘋果高級經銷商的門口，2011年5月7日。
University students dressed as Foxconn workers and carrying mock iPads featuring skull-and-crossbones motifs block the entry to an Apple Premium Reseller shop in Hong Kong, May 7, 2011.

不可能樂器？

樂器總是述說有關人類文明的親密故事。比如在德國西南部Hohle Fels洞穴出土的那支骨笛，考古學家沃弗·海恩（Wulf Hein）制作了一個它的複製品來嘗試演奏，盡管骨笛有著四萬年的歷史，但它卻讓我們感到無比親切，不僅外形上看起來熟悉，就連發出的聲音也不讓人陌生。[21] 聽著笛音，想像著史前的演奏家們如何把嘴唇貼在V形切口上吹出聲響，橫亙於我們之間的數萬年光陰就這樣瞬間崩塌了。

幾個世紀以來，科學家一直孜孜不倦地研究各類樂器的發聲原理，試圖根據其特性來反向設計制造其物理結構，這些實驗也催生了音樂合成器。合成器不光是制作電音的新型樂器，同時也試圖模擬傳統樂器。盡管音樂產業開發模擬技術在某種層面上是為了降低制作成本，但追求「完美」模擬音色的欲望也在不斷增長。從1960年代中期第一台投入商業生產的穆格合成器問世，到今天利用計算機算法做數字擬音，人們對通過改進技術提高「眞實」程度的執著始終不變。但這究竟是一種什麼樣的「眞實」？

在作品《Possible Music #1（feat. NESS & Shane Aspegren）》（2018）中，楊嘉輝質疑了眞實性的概念，並探討了它們更廣泛的文化意義。在他構建的聲音環境裏，錯落有致地散放著各種物品、草圖和數字動畫，其中的一系列「不可能樂器」是裝置的重點。這些稀奇古怪的樂器在現實中並不存在，比如6米長的小號，或者巨大到人類肺活量根本不可能吹奏的大號等等。但借助蘇格蘭愛丁堡大學NESS（Next Generation Sound Synthesis，次代聲音合成）實驗室研發的一套物理模型，楊嘉輝得以能夠想像它們的音色，並為之譜曲。每一件樂器有一段相應的曲目，在電腦程序的控制下被精確且週期性地激活。但這些樂器沒有一件完整成型，它們散落的零件部位，

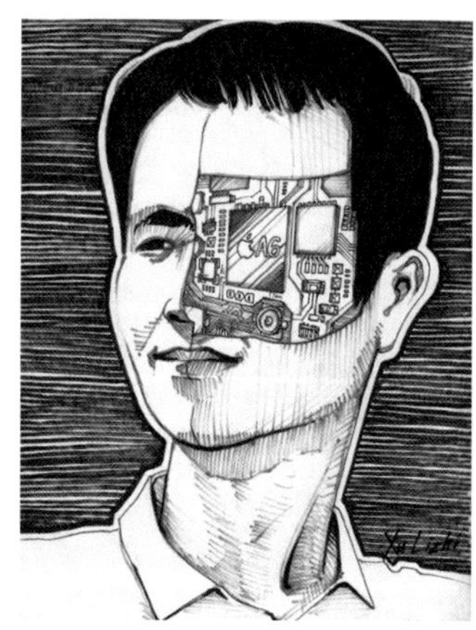

亨利·盧克，《許立志肖像》，2014，紙上馬克筆，30.5×22.9 cm
Henry Luke, *Portrait of Xu Lizhi*, 2014. Ink on paper, 30.5×22.9 cm

一個吹口、一個簧片、或者一個管身，彷彿在召喚著幽靈般的樂器演奏者。楊嘉輝製作的軍事管弦樂環境，聲音宏亮，暗示著一位看不見的樂隊指揮。只不過這位指揮的肉身卻無處可尋，它要麼從未存在過，要麼尚在成形之中。

演奏間隙軍鼓擊打的聲響繚繞在這些奇特物品之間，彷佛一個來自另一時代的文明所留下的廢墟。這些樂器部件有的光滑銳利，有的粗糙大塊，有的具有實體，有的則是虛擬和數字的，它們彼此迥異的視覺和物質特性暗示著「變異」的可能性。盡管沒有音樂家和樂器的實體存在，電腦的聲音建模以及模擬樂器物理構成，往往仍稱其本身是一種科學的過程。楊嘉輝虛構的創作手法反過來嘲諷了所謂「眞實客體」的概念，從而進一步質疑了其主張的主體與文化眞實性。如果音樂的誕生是人類文明史上的關鍵時刻，那麼人類的最後一件樂器會是什麼？我們的文明終結之後，什麼又可以倖存？新世界將催生出何種事物，它又會發出什麼樣的聲響？

未來之後

「單手拍掌」是「何鴻毅家族基金中國藝術計劃」的最終展覽項目。該計劃致力於調動當下的知識與文化話語，通過聚焦大中華地區的藝術生產現場，重新想像本土與全球之間的關係。盡管留待反思的東西還很多，我們所面對的問題已不再僅僅是如何以中國的視角觀察世界或書寫新的敘事。「本土」這一概念，本身作為全球化的產物，決不能將其自身局限於孤立的本土性框架中；相反，本土性的未來，正如「單手拍掌」一樣，應該能夠積極侵入、挪用並最終改變全球化的格局。就此，我們也許可以將這些思考與作為本次展覽題目的同名公案作比。

近年來，有一個網絡詞彙「詩和遠方」在中國的年輕人中流行。這個詞因為表達了某種對逃離本土環境的浪漫化想像，讓在講求經濟競爭的社會中成長起來的新一代人感到心有戚戚。[22] 這代人一方面對朝九晚五的生活深感厭倦，一方面又因背負高額房貸而沒有勇氣放棄工作。「詩和遠方」表達了他們對希望、想像和自由的向往。也許，詩人許立志（1990–2014）也曾深刻感受到這種渴念。他在富士康流水線上工作的三年期間，寫下了數百首詩，之後卻從工人宿舍樓上縱身一躍，結束了自己二十四歲的年輕生命。許立志從來不曾夢想過「全自動豪華共產主義」社會下的幸福生活，他將自己視為一顆被放錯位置的「螺絲」，「垂直降落，輕輕一響」，消失於工廠地面上。[23] 但哪裏有詩，哪裏就有希望、想像和自由。哲學家及激進主義者弗蘭克·比弗·貝拉迪（Franco "Bifo" Berardi）在其《未來之後》一書的結論部分提出，未來的政治任務是培養認同全人類「自由、平等和博愛」的「認知上的自我意識」以及「對社會團結、人類共情、無償活動的感知力」。正是在詩歌、治愈與創造的交界處，萌發出行動主義的新空間。[24]

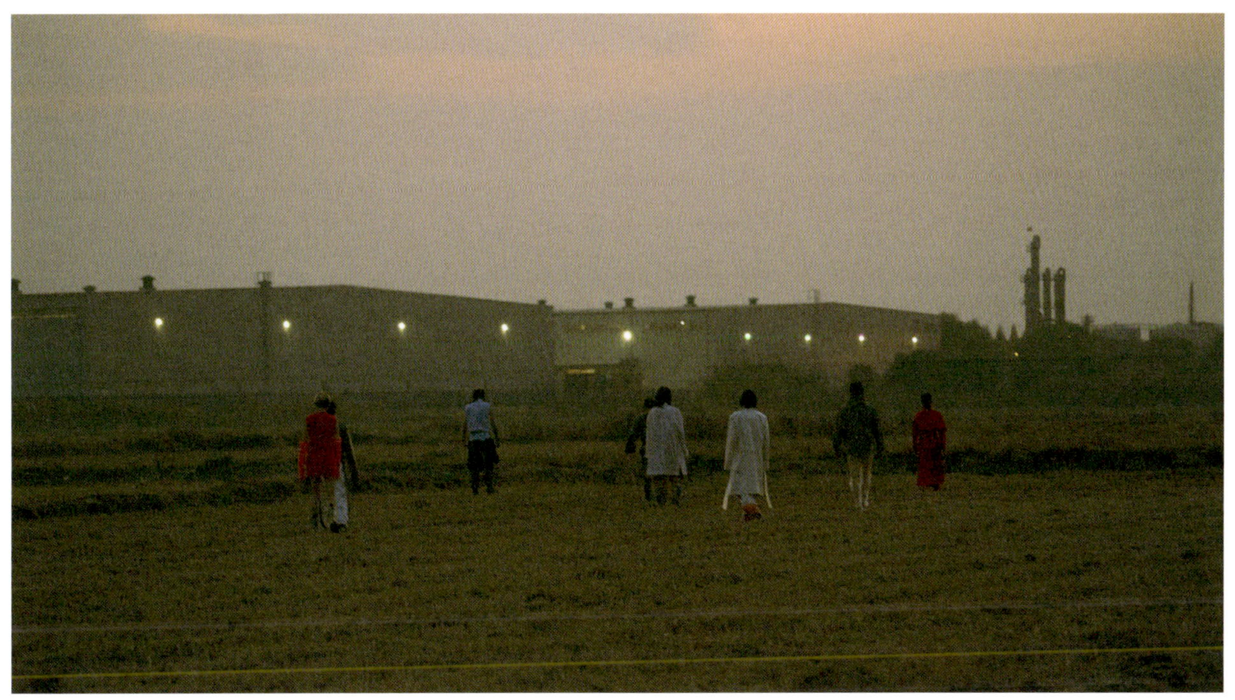

曹斐，《Asia One》，2018（局部）
Cao Fei, *Asia One*, 2018 (detail)

在本次展覽的畫冊中，我們重印了部分許立志的詩歌，同時摘選了年輕詩人烏青和張羞的作品，烏與張的「廢話體」詩歌用簡單甚至有些粗俗的語言描述了看似無關緊要的日常和主題。通過徹底否定能指與所指、詩學與象徵的傳統結構，他們的作品讓宏大敘事和主流話語的虛僞性暴露無遺。我們還委任了香港年輕詩人黃裕邦創作新的詩歌系列《黑暗改編》。黃裕邦在作品中想像了2052年的香港，粵語被禁，但雙語詩人們利用人工智能，經過多重翻譯，對粵語進行編碼，將其寫進詩歌，以此抵制當局對粵語的清洗。這是份有關一場詩性革命的提案，也是對「單手拍掌」又一次未來主義式的挪用。

narratives and mainstream discourses. We have also commissioned a new cycle of poems by Hong Kong-based poet Nicholas Wong, "Dark Adaptation." Wong imagines a Hong Kong of 2052 where Cantonese is banned but bilingual poets collaborate to resist the language's erasure by coding it into poetry through multiple layers of AI-facilitated translation. This is a proposal for a poetic revolution, and another instance of the futuristic appropriation of "one hand clapping."

1 傑奧夫・科爾文(Geoff Colvin),《研究:2030年中國將超越美國成為全球最大經濟體》(「Study: China Will Overtake the U.S. as World's Largest Economy Before 2030」),《財富》雜誌,2017年2月9日,http://fortune.com/2017/02/09/study-china-will-overtake-the-u-s-as-worlds-largest-economy-before-2030/。
2 約翰・李(John Lee),《中國技術領域的崛起:一個互聯網帝國的誕生》(「The rise of China's tech sector: The making of an internet empire」),《*the interpreter*》,2017年5月4日,https://www.lowyinstitute.org/the-interpreter/rise-china-s-tech-sector-making-internet-empire。
3 1958到1962年的「大躍進」是一場試圖通過快速工業化和集體化將中國從農業經濟體改造成社會主義社會的全國性經濟、社會運動。香港大學教授、歷史學家馮客(Frank Dikötter)在他的著作《毛澤東的大饑荒:1958–1962年的中國浩劫史》(美國紐約,Bloomsbury出版社,2010年)中,通過中共公開的檔案,全面考察了大躍進展開的原因、經過和關鍵轉折點,講述了大躍進從農業、工業、貿易、住宅、到自然環境的破壞,宏偉的集體主義計劃如何演變成百姓求生存的鬥爭和變形,最後導致四千五百萬人死亡的悲劇。
4 關於當前中美關係如何反映了歷史上老牌大國與新興勢力之間的矛盾,以及兩個超級大國如何避免未來戰爭的可能性,參見格雷厄姆・艾利森(Graham Allison),《注定一戰:美國和中國能否逃脫修昔底德陷阱?》(*Destined for War: Can America and China Escape Thucydides's Trap?*),美國波士頓,Houghton Mifflin Harcourt出版社,2017年。
5 許煜,《論中國的技術問題》(*The Question Concerning Technology in China: An Essay in Cosmotechnics*),美國法爾茅斯,Urbanomic出版社,2016年12月,第281頁。更多請參閱許煜為本畫冊撰寫的文章《走向技術未來的分支》。本畫冊第106–113頁。
6 從中國的禪宗傳統發展而來,「公案」在日本的禪宗佛教包含了沈思和離散的修行方式,用思考謎題一般的案件作為工具來打破理性意識的限制,從而獲得「空」的本質領悟。公案「單手拍掌」公認源於日本禪師白隱慧鶴(Hakuin Ekaku,1686–1769),這位改革者的貢獻在於將現代「公案」練習系統化,在臨濟禪學院首次被典型地展示於學徒。再者,從避開經典絕對主義的傳統中發展而來,白隱慧鶴不遵循西方對作者權的預設。這個公安存在著大量不同的英文譯本。此處引述的版本由於被J.D.塞林格引作《九故事》(美國波士頓Little,Brown出版社,1953)一書的序言而流行。此外,參考鈴木大拙(D. T. Suzuki)《公案練習》,選自《禪宗佛教文選(第二卷)》(英國倫敦Luzac出版社,1933),第1至165頁,該著作被認為是最早關於公案練習的英文著作。
7 這些只是其他很多跟「禪宗智慧」有關的樂隊名和書名裏最膾炙人口的例子。《九故事》引用了此公案的全文。小說和電影標題都為《One Hand Clapping》。
8 羅伯特・沙夫(Robert H. Sharf),《如何用禪宗公案去思考》(「How to Think with Chan *Gong'an*」),章節選自《通過案例去思考:中國文化史的專業知識》(*Thinking with Cases: Specialist Knowledge in Chinese Cultural History*),費俠莉(Charlotte Furth)等編輯,美國火奴魯魯,夏威夷大學出版社,2007年,第207–10頁。更多信息參見魯思・福勒・佐佐木(Ruth Fuller Sasaki)和三浦一舟(Miura Isshū),《禪塵:公案的歷史與臨濟宗的公案研究》(*Zen Dust: The History of the Koan and Koan Study in Rinzai [Linji] Zen*),美國紐約,Harcourt,Brace & World出版社,1967年,以及斯蒂芬・海爾(Steven Heine)和戴爾・S・賴特(Dale S. Wright)編輯,《公案:佛教禪宗的文本和語境》(*The Koan: Texts and Contexts in Zen Buddhism*),英國牛津,牛津大學出版社,2000年。
9 王德威,《歷史與怪獸:二十世紀中國的歷史,暴力與虛構寫作》(*The Monster That Is History: History, Violence, and Fictional Writing in Twentieth-Century China*)美國伯克利,加利福尼亞大學出版社,2004年,第6–7頁,中文譯本由台灣麥田出版社於2011年出版。
10 讓・鮑德裏亞(Jean Baudrillard),《斷片集:冷記憶III,1991–95》(*Fragments: Cool Memories III*,1991–95),美國紐約,Verso出版社,1997年,第10頁。中文譯本由南京大學出版社於2009年3月出版。
11 參見尤瓦爾・諾亞・赫拉利(Yuval Noah Harari),《未來簡史:從智人到智神》(*Homo Deus: A Brief History of Tomorrow*),美國紐約,Harper出版社,2017年(中文譯本由中信出版社於2017年2月出版),以及本畫冊許煜的文章《走向技術未來的分支》。
12 網上掃墓的例子參見Wangshangsaomu.com。
13 諾伯特・維納(Norbert Wiener),《控制論:或動物與機器中的控制與通信》(*Cybernetics: Or Control and Communication in the Animal and the Machine*),第二版,美國劍橋,麻省理工大學出版社,1965年,第12–13頁。
14 G.W.萊布尼茨(G. W. Leibniz),《哲學原理,或單子論》(「The Principles of Philosophy, or, the Monadology」),收錄於《哲學文集》(Philosophical Essays),Roger Ariew和Daniel Garber翻譯,印第安納波斯利,Hackett出版社,1989年,第213–25頁。中文譯本參考《單子論》,選自《西方哲學名篇選讀》(上),翰水法、翰林合、張祥龍編,中國北京大學出版社,2014年,第229–49頁。
15 這一觀點在大眾媒體上也越來越受歡迎:參見菲利普・鮑爾(Philip Ball),《我們也許生活在一個電腦程序裏,但可能也沒什麼關係》(「We might live in a computer program, but it may not matter」),BBC.com,2016年9月5日,http://www.bbc.com/earth/story/20160901-we-might-live-in-a-computer-program-but-it-may-not-matter。
16「聽黨的話,搞自動化,咱們的前景,美如畫!」出自《工人歌謠選》,中華全國總工會宣傳部編,中國北京工人出版社,1961年。
17「大吊車,真厲害,成噸的鋼鐵,它輕輕地一抓就起來!」出自《革命現代京劇海港主旋律樂譜》,上海京劇團海港劇組集體改編,中國北京,人民文學出版社,1972年。
18《在慈愛的機器監視下》(*All Watched Over by Machines of Loving Grace*),180分鐘,三集,由亞當・柯蒂斯(Adam Curtis)編劇並導演,於2011年5月23日至6月6日期間在英國BBC頻道2上播放。
19 布賴恩・麥錢特(Brian Merchant),《全自動豪華共產主義》(「Fully automated luxury communism」),《衛報》,2015年3月18日,https://www.theguardian.com/sustainable-business/2015/mar/18/fully-automated-luxury-communism-robots-employment。
20 選自曹斐的短篇小說《淘寶》(2010),重新收錄於本畫冊,第147頁。
21 海恩(Wulf Hein)在赫爾佐格(Werner Herzog)2010年的電影《忘夢洞》(*Cave of Forgotten Dreams*)中吹奏過骨笛復制品。他的評論道:「這支笛子有五聲音階,簡直令人驚訝。它跟我們今天聽到的音樂是一個調性。」
22 這個短語的出處是中國音樂人、公眾人物高曉松在網上發表的一篇文章,後來被他寫進自己2016年發布的一首歌裏,歌名叫《生活不止眼前的苟且》。
23 選自《一顆螺絲掉在地上》,2014年,參見本畫冊,第133頁。
24 弗蘭克・比弗・貝拉迪(Franco "Bifo" Berardi),《未來之後》(After the Future),美國奇科,AK Press出版社,2011年,第163頁。

1 Geoff Colvin, "Study: China Will Overtake the US as the World's Largest Economy Before 2030," *Fortune*, February 9, 2017, http://fortune.com/2017/02/09/study-china-will-overtake-the-u-s-as-worlds-largest-economy before-2030/.

2 John Lee, "The Rise of China's Tech Sector: The Making of an Internet Empire," *the interpreter*, May 4, 2017, https://www.lowyinstitute.org/the-interpreter/rise-china-s-tech-sector-making-internet-empire.

3 Lasting from 1958 to 1962, the Great Leap Forward was an economic and social campaign that aimed to transform China from an agrarian economy into a socialist society through rapid industrialization and collectivization. See Frank Dikötter, *Mao's Great Famine: The History of China's Most Devastating Catastrophe 1958–1962* (New York: Bloomsbury, 2010), for a comprehensive account of this period.

4 See Graham Allison's *Destined for War: Can America and China Escape Thucydides's Trap?* (Boston: Houghton Mifflin Harcourt, 2017) for an of-the-moment analysis of how current relations between the United States and China reflect historical patterns of conflict between established and rising powers, and how the two superpowers might avoid war in the future.

5 Yuk Hui, *The Question Concerning Technology in China: An Essay in Cosmotechnics* (Falmouth, UK: Urbanomic, 2016), p. 281. For more, see also Yuk's contribution to this catalogue, "For the Bifurcation of Technological Futures," on pp. 106–113.

6 Drawn from the Chinese Chan tradition, the koan in Japanese Zen Buddhism encompasses a meditative and discursive discipline that uses the contemplation of riddle-like "cases" as a vehicle for breaking through rational consciousness to gain insight into the nature of the void. The "one hand clapping" koan is distinct in that it was originated by the Japanese monk Hakuin Ekaku (1686–1769), the reformer credited with systematizing modern koan practice, and is typically the first presented to novices in the Rinzai school of Zen. Moreover, emerging from a tradition that eschews the literalism of scripture, Hakuin's koan does not conform to Western assumptions of authorship. Numerous variations of it exist in English translation. The version cited above was popularized by its use as the epigraph to J. D. Salinger's *Nine Stories* (Boston: Little, Brown, 1953). See also D. T. Suzuki, "The Koan Exercise," in *Essays in Zen Buddhism (Second Series)* (London: Luzac, 1933), pp. 1–165, for one of the earliest treatises on koan practice in English.

7 These are only the most prominent examples among others including band names and books on "Zen wisdom." The koan is quoted in full in *Nine Stories*; the novel and film titles are both *One Hand Clapping.*

8 Robert H. Sharf, "How to Think with Chan *Gong'an*," in *Thinking with Cases: Specialist Knowledge in Chinese Cultural History*, ed. Charlotte Furth et al. (Honolulu: University of Hawai'i Press, 2007), pp. 207–10. For more, see Ruth Fuller Sasaki and Isshū Miura, *Zen Dust: The History of the Koan and Koan Study in Rinzai (Linji) Zen* (New York: Harcourt, Brace & World, 1967), and Steven Heine and Dale S. Wright, eds., *The Koan: Texts and Contexts in Zen Buddhism* (Oxford: Oxford University Press, 2000).

9 David Der-Wei Wang, *The Monster That Is History: History, Violence, and Fictional Writing in Twentieth-Century China* (Berkeley: University of California Press, 2004), pp. 6–7.

10 Jean Baudrillard, *Fragments: Cool Memories III, 1991–95*, trans. Emily Agar (New York: Verso, 1997), p. 10.

11 For more, see Yuval Noah Harari, *Homo Deus: A Brief History of Tomorrow* (New York: Harper, 2017), as well as Yuk, "Bifurcation of Technological Futures."

12 For an example of a virtual tomb sweeping website, see Wangshangsaomu.com, accessed November 13, 2017, http://www.wangshangsaomu.com/.

13 Norbert Wiener, *Cybernetics: Or Control and Communication in the Animal and the Machine*, 2nd ed. (Cambridge: MIT Press, 1965), pp. 12–13.

14 G. W. Leibniz, "The Principles of Philosophy, or, the Monadology," in *Philosophical Essays*, trans. Roger Ariew and Daniel Garber (Indianapolis: Hackett, 1989), pp. 213–25.

15 This idea is also gaining traction in the mass media. See Philip Ball, "We Might Live in a Computer Program, but It May Not Matter," BBC.com, September 5, 2016, http://www.bbc.com/earth/story/20160901-we-might-live-in-a-computer-program-but-it-may-not-matter.

16 From the song "Mei ru hua" [Beautiful as a painting], in Zhonghua quanguo zonggonghui xuanchuan bu, ed., *Gongren geyao xuan* [An anthology of workers' ballads] (Beijing: Beijing gongren chubanshe, 1961). Author's translation.

17 Shanghai jingjutuan "Haigang" juzu, ed., *Geming xiandai jingju zhuxuanlü yuepu* Haigang [Score of the main themes in the modern revolutionary Peking opera *On the Docks*] (Beijing: Renmin wenxue chubanshe, 1972). Author's translation.

18 *All Watched Over by Machines of Loving Grace*, written and directed by Adam Curtis, aired May 23 to June 6, 2011, on BBC Two, United Kingdom, 180 min. in three parts.

19 Brian Merchant, "Fully Automated Luxury Communism," *The Guardian*, March 18, 2015, https://www.theguardian.com/sustainable-business/2015/mar/18/fully-automated-luxury-communism-robots-employment.

20 From Cao's short story "Taobao" (2010), reprinted on p. 147 of this volume.

21 Hein plays the flute in Werner Herzog's 2010 film *Cave of Forgotten Dreams*. Hein comments, "[It is] astonishing that this flute is pentatonic. This is the same tonality that we are used to hearing today."

22 The phrase originated with Gao Xiaosong, a famous musician and public figure in China, who first expressed the idea in an essay he published online and then in the lyrics of a song he wrote and released in 2016, "Life Is More Than Drifting Along" (*Shenghuo buzhi yanqian de gouqie*).

23 From "A Screw Falls to the Ground" (2014), trans. Eleanor Goodman, reprinted on p. 133 of this volume.

24 Franco "Bifo" Berardi, *After the Future*, ed. Gary Genesko and Nicholas Thoburn (Chico, CA: AK Press, 2011), p. 163.

侯瀚如
Hou Hanru

單手拍掌？散論可能的現實

Clapping with One Hand? Fragmentary Notes on Possible Realities

誰人沒愛過一場，歡呼與愛傷
想哭便讓淚流，付你那些要付的帳
你快再別叫嚷，不需她都歡暢
上帝也不可以，單手拍掌
——林子祥《單手拍掌》[1]

1

「砰！！！」一個籃球被一架無人機自古根海姆美術館圓形大廳中庭上方的天花板拋下，從六層樓高墜落地面，發出的巨響迴盪在空蕩的建築裏；同時，籃球向著頭戴虛擬實境裝備的觀眾奔去。緊跟著，觀眾看到華裔（或者更準確地說，是台裔）NBA球星林書豪的虛擬影像；他剛一出現，觀眾旋即化身為投向籃網的那個球。一旁，藝術家正躺在籃球落地處，並開始順著圓形大廳的坡道翻滾而上，頑強地對抗著地心引力，直到抵達美術館最高處。這一切同時發生。一開始看似毫無關聯的籃球、藝術家和觀眾，像產生連鎖反應的不同元素，慢慢聚攏，形成一股不可阻擋的動力。這，是林一林為「何鴻毅家族基金中國藝術計劃」委任新作所想像的場景。

林一林的作品情節讓人想起伽利略從比薩斜塔同時扔下兩個不同重量的球體來證明自由落體定律的故事——一個孤膽戰士為追求真理，挑戰彼時宗教、意識形態和政治權威的英雄傳奇。林一林自言他的行為受萊布尼茨（G. W. Leibniz）《單子論》所啟發，此書認為，構成宇宙的每一個「單純實體」（simple substance）或「單子」（monad），都有其自身的完滿性或自足性，同時也反映出宇宙的某個部份。[2]作為在美國努力求生存和發展藝術生涯的中國移民藝術家，林一林把自己視為「單子」：一個擁有自身宇宙、獨立自足的生命體。他把NBA有史以來首位華裔美籍球員及目前活躍於聯盟的少數亞裔球員之一的林書豪，看成殊途同歸的另一個「單子」。在萊布尼茨的觀點裏，上帝是統治宇宙的外部力量，而林一林和林書豪則必須向多少帶有文化或種族偏見的當權者——不論是藝術機構或籃球教練——證明自己的價值。他們兩人雖然素未謀面，在各自領域努力奮鬥的孤獨經驗，卻如出一轍。林一林表示，「我一直有看NBA的比賽，一個有趣的現象是，華裔或中國球員總是一個傷退或離場以後，另一個才進入。如果把他們看作一個個同類的『單子』，林書豪的身體條件是最普通的一個，但他身上的各種元素組合和遭受的種族問題，經歷成功和同樣的失敗。我感興趣的是這種戲劇性，可能部分原因是同樣姓林。」[3]

林一林是都會人群中一位特立獨行的行為藝術家，他把自己的身體當作表演工具，用來測試在急速發展的城市化和全球化世界中，個體與環境之間的張力。他走遍世界各地，從中國到美國，以及其他地方，實行這種看似安靜、毫不引人注意卻極其尖銳的行為介入。某次，他甚至帶著和自己真人等大的肖像照片從家鄉

Who has never been in love before, cheers
and pain
You want to cry then let it flow, pay what you
have to pay
No use shouting now, no need to keep
her happy
'Cause not even God can clap with one hand
— George Lam, "Clapping with One Hand"[1]

1

"Bang!!!" A basketball is dropped by a drone from the dome of the Guggenheim's rotunda atrium and falls six stories to the ground, sending a resounding echo through the empty building. The next moment, a viewer wearing virtual reality headgear encounters a virtual image of Jeremy Lin, the NBA basketball star of Chinese or in fact Taiwanese origin. Lin's image has only just appeared when the viewer is transformed into the ball itself and shot at the basket. Off to the side, the artist, lying exactly where the ball hit the ground, starts rolling up the ramp of the rotunda, straining against gravity to reach the highest point of the building. Seemingly happening all at once, everything is swept up in a swirl of confusion. Although initially disconnected, the ball, artist, and viewer are gradually pulled together, like the elements in a chain reaction, into an inexorable dynamic. This is the scene Lin Yilin envisions in his proposal for *One Hand Clapping*, the final exhibition of new commissions for The Robert H. N. Ho Family Foundation Chinese Art Initiative at the Solomon R. Guggenheim Museum.

Lin's scenario recalls the story about Galileo Galilei dropping two spheres of differing masses from the Leaning Tower of Pisa to demonstrate the law of free fall — a heroic legend of a lonely warrior challenging the religious, ideological, and political authorities of the time in pursuit of truth. Lin himself says his action is inspired by G. W. Leibniz's "Monadology," which proposes that the "simple substances," or "monads," that constitute the universe each have their own perfection or self-sufficiency while also reflecting an aspect of the universe.[2] A Chinese immigrant artist struggling to survive and build his career in the United States, Lin sees himself as a monad: a self-contained being that represents its own cosmos. He sees Jeremy Lin, the first Chinese American in NBA history, and one of

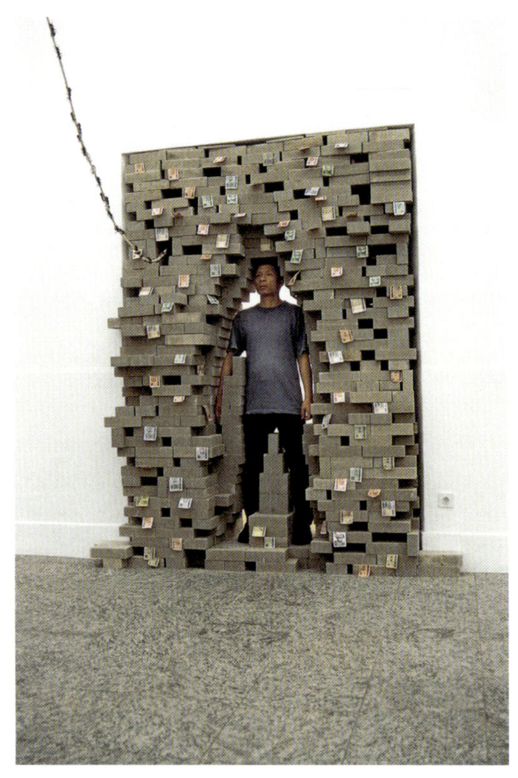

林一林，《XX億零一個》，1998，行為表演現場
Lin Yilin, *X Billion and First Person*, 1998. Performance view

廣州一路到瑞士伯爾尼，藉以觀察不同的社會如何看待自我。其實，他將這一等身肖像視為模糊眞實的我和再現的我界線的「另一個我」，或一個樣貌一樣的旅途同伴。對林一林而言，孤獨的遊牧者(nomad)，或者說「單子」，正代表了藝術家(傑出的籃球員也是一種藝術家)奇特而孤獨的特有身份，他所體現的是一個獨一無二的宇宙。這樣一個像「單子」的個體，注定永遠是個異鄉人，只能用自己發明但沒有誰能眞正理解的語言來表達自我，在這次的新作中，林一林藉由觀眾參與分享的方式，強化了這個感覺，他通過虛擬現實來表達眞實的我和想像的我之間的張力，並揭示出今天身份生產的新規範。但他的人生目標，或命運，乃在追逐那不可企及的眞相之音，那是單手拍掌的聲音，如禪宗公案所示：雙手互拍會發出聲音，而單手又能拍出什麼聲音？[4]

然而，今天不再是浪漫主義藝術家的太平盛世。藝術家作為人類「單子」，揭示了一個迫切的議題：在一個對特立獨行和靈魂自由的個人仍然充滿偏見和壓迫的世界，藝術家，尤其是那些具有移民背景的藝術家，將何去何從？這個問題在馬克·費舍(Mark Fisher)所稱「資本主義現實主義」的意識形態佔主導地位的時代，尤顯重要。「資本主義現實主義」用自己製造的現實來取代「眞實」，形成了

only a few Asian players currently active in the league, as another monad who has gone through similar experiences. Whereas God is the external power governing the cosmos in Leibniz's vision, the two Lins have had to prove themselves to authorities — whether art institutions or basketball coaches — that are not without cultural and racial prejudices. Although the two have never met, they share the solitary experience of striving for achievement in their respective fields. Lin Yilin states, "I've always followed NBA basketball, and an interesting phenomenon I noticed is that when one Chinese or Chinese American player gets injured or retires, another comes in to take his place. If we see each of these players as the same type of 'monad,' then Jeremy Lin's physical attributes are the most ordinary of them all, but the elements he embodies in combination with the racism that he encounters mean that he experiences equal amounts of success and failure. This theatricality is what interests me — maybe in part because we share the same last name. As such, he and I also constitute our own type of 'monad.'"[3]

A lonely performer amid urban crowds, Lin Yilin deploys his body as a performative instrument for testing the tensions between individuals and their environments in a rapidly transforming world of urbanization and globalization. He has carried out his quiet and unspectacular but penetrating interventions across the world, from China to the United States and beyond. Once, he even carried his own life-size photographic portrait — which he saw as an alter ego or company-like proxy that blurred the lines between his real and represented self — all the way from his native Guangzhou to Bern, Switzerland, in an experiment with how the self is perceived in different societies. For Lin, the lonely nomad, or monad, represents exactly what an artist (and an outstanding basketball player is an artist of a sort, too) should be: singular and solitary, incarnating a unique universe. Such a monad-like entity is condemned to being an eternal stranger who expresses himself only in a language of his own invention, which no one else really understands. This feeling is underscored by his use of virtual reality in his new work to represent the tension between actual and imagined selves in a way that is shared by the audience, revealing the new norms of identity production today. But his life's goal, or destiny, is to chase the unreachable sound of the truth. This is the sound of one hand clapping, as suggested by the Zen koan: "Two hands clap and there is a sound. What is the sound of one hand clapping?"[4]

But these are no longer the halcyon days of romantic artistic heroes. The status of the artist as human monad reveals an urgent issue: what is to become of artists, especially those of immigrant backgrounds, in a world still marked by prejudices and oppression against those who are different, independent, and free-souled? This is particularly critical at a time dominated by the ideology Mark Fisher has identified as Capitalist Realism, which substitutes "the real" with the reality of its own making, engendering a pervasive atmosphere wherein even imagining an alternative to capitalism becomes impossible.[5] It is in the very heart of this "real world" — in which museums are the apparatus for imposing the conditions of the real world onto the idealized freedom of the "art world" — where every "radical" gesture counts as an attempt to achieve an "impossible victory" over the absolute power of the "system."

Carried out in the empty museum, Lin's ball dropping also recalls Daniel Buren's (in)famous intervention into the Guggenheim architecture at the *Guggenheim International Exhibition* of 1971.

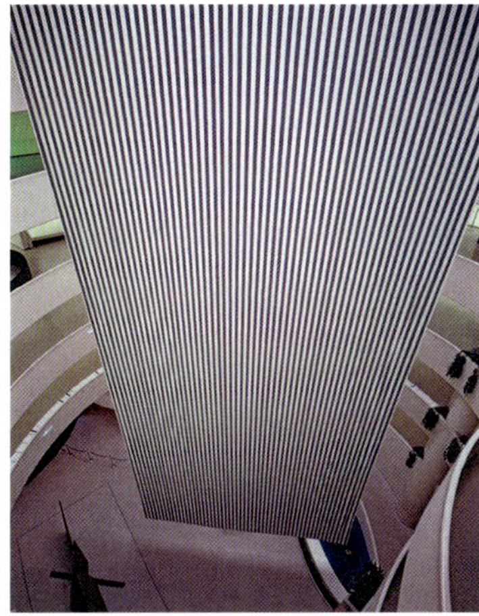

丹尼爾・布罕，《繪畫-雕塑》，1971，裝置現場
Daniel Buren, *Peinture-Sculpture* (*Painting-Sculpture*), 1971. Installation view

Buren suspended a huge banner painted with his signature vertical stripes in the void of the rotunda, obstructing sight lines across the space and prompting complaints from other exhibiting artists. He had to withdraw the "work" before the opening, but took a photo before doing so — the photo is now an icon of institutional critique. Implicitly dealing with issues regarding the social role of the immigrant, Lin's project extends that institutional critique into a direct confrontation with political reality. Lin's gesture can be seen as an heir to Buren's and, in fact, an even more rebellious provocation. It brings us back to the fundamental questions of existence today: How can we survive Capitalist Realism? How can we preserve the right to be a monad — a free soul that can still live with the beautiful imagination of clapping with one hand?

Lin Yilin is by no means an isolated and lonely genius. Following Gerald Raunig's concept of the "dividuum,"[6] or sharing the destiny of the different, Lin is singular and exceptional, but also "haunted" by many "ghosts" of diverse cultures, or "a multiplicity of me." This is a new image of the author — one that reinvents the modern individual intellectual hero as "a transversal intellect." As Raunig states:

> New challenges emerge when the position of the General Intellect, of a mass, multiple and militant intellectuality, is negotiated today. The intellect that does not close itself off in the single author-individual, the intellect that does not sublate the flows of social knowledge in a communitarian, general, universal unity, invents itself in machinic capitalism as a transversal intellect. This intellect is transversal, because it emerges in traversing the singularities of thinking, speaking, writing, fabricating knowledge: a machinic-dividual stream of thinking that moves across the dichotomy of individual and community, permeates individuals and collectives, inhabits the spaces, things, landscapes between them and allows new forms of disobedience to emerge, new forms of noncompliance, new dissemblages.[7]

一種總體氛圍，讓連想像資本主義之外的其他方案都變得不可能。[5]在這個「現實世界」的核心之中——博物館在其中扮演了將現實世界的條件強加諸於「藝術界」理想化之上的機制——每一個「激進的」姿態，都是為從「制度」的絕對權力那兒贏得一場「不可能的勝利」所作的努力。

林一林讓籃球從空蕩的美術館上空落下，讓人想起1971年「古根海姆國際展」上，丹尼爾·布罕（Daniel Buren）對古根海姆美術館建築（惡名）昭著的介入。布罕將一面畫有其個人標誌性的豎條紋大旗，從上到下懸掛在圓形大廳當中，阻擋了整座美術館的視線，引起了其他參展藝術家的抱怨。他在被迫於開幕前撤下這件「作品」所拍的那張照片如今成了機構批判的象徵。林一林的作品含蓄地觸及移民所扮演的社會角色的問題，並且將機構批判延伸為與政治現實的直接對抗。他的姿態和布罕異曲同工，甚至更加叛逆和挑釁。它讓我們反思今天關於存在的根本命題：如何在資本主義現實主義中，繼續活下去？如何保有作為「單子」的權利？保有一顆仍能生活在單手拍掌的美麗想像之中的自由靈魂！

林一林絕非一位孤立存在的孤獨天才。按傑拉德·勞尼格（Gerald Raunig）的「分人」（dividuum）[6]或與異者共命運的概念，林一林儘管與眾不同，但也受許多不同文化的「鬼魂」、或著說「許許多多的我」所糾纏。這是一個新的作者形象——將現代個別的智力英雄重塑為「橫截的智力」。如勞尼格所寫道：

> 此刻，一旦「普遍智能」的位置被重新檢討，新的挑戰勢必隨即出現。「普遍智能」意指一種群體式的、多元的、帶有戰鬥動能的智識。這樣的智能不閉鎖於單一的作者個人中，這樣的智能也不會將流動的社會知識先吸納後否決，固定為社群、共通、普世的體系。也因之，這樣的智能以橫截的智能形式，在機器資本主義的條件下發明自己。這樣的智能具有橫截走勢，它橫越各個獨特的思維、論說、書寫，由此構築知識：一種機器－分人的思想流，它截斷了個人和共同體二分法，滲入個人和集體之中，進駐到它們之間的空間、事物和景觀內部，並且允許新的不服從形式的出現；新的違規形式；新的解體。[7]

2

現於林一林家鄉廣州生活和工作的畫家段建宇，探索著中國的「城鄉結合部」的狀況——多數人至今仍住在此過渡地帶。這些長期備受忽視和邊緣化、仍然一貧如洗的居民，也在尋找自己能在「現代化」當中存活下來的方式，他們頑強地尋找著自己生命的意義。這兒遠離都會媒體的聚光燈，為草根智慧、創意、活力、詩性、性衝動和思想自由提供了一塊沃土。這兒常被新興的都會人視為一個令人難以置信的不真實的世界、或超現實的世界。民工的流動以及跟蹤他們的藝術家、導演和知識份子，如賈樟柯、劉小東和歐寧，串起了城市和城鄉結合部這個中間地帶的特殊聯繫。

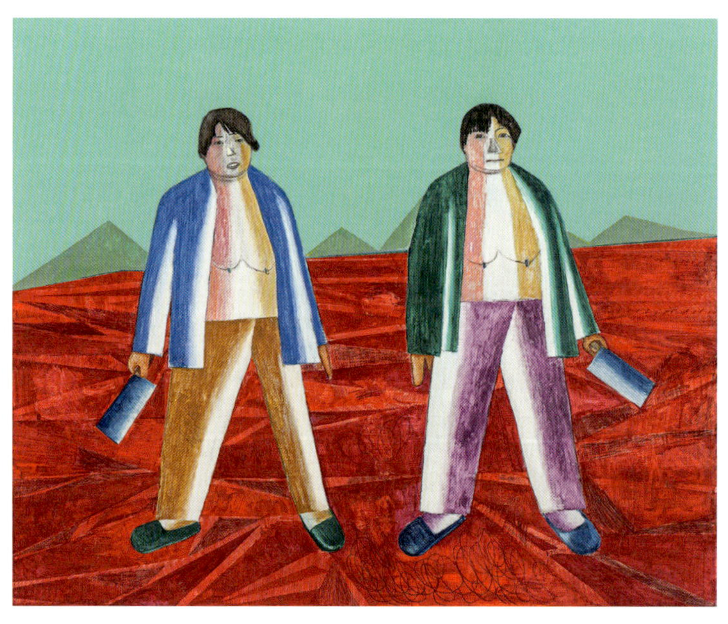

段建宇，《殺，殺，殺馬特No.1》，2014，布面油畫，181×217 cm
Duan Jianyu, *Sharp, Sharp, Smart No. 1*, 2014. Oil on canvas, 181×217 cm

2

Based in Lin Yilin's hometown, Guangzhou, the painter Duan Jianyu investigates the world in transition between rurality and urbanity in China. This transient territory is where the majority of the population still live. Largely overlooked and marginalized, its inhabitants remain poor, but are also searching for their own way to survive "modernization," stubbornly seeking their own meaning in life. Far from the spotlight of the metropolitan media, this is a land fertile in folk wisdom, ingenuity, vivacity, poetry, sexual impulse, and mental freedom. It is a world often viewed by the burgeoning urban population as unbelievably unreal, or surreal. The special links between the urban world and this in-between rural-urban realm are woven mainly by the flows of migrant workers and the artists, filmmakers, and intellectuals who follow them, such as Jia Zhangke, Liu Xiaodong, and Ou Ning. Through her painting practice, Duan Jianyu herself acts as an insightful and empathic witness to this situation. She presents in her paintings the realities, dreams, fantasies, and values of the inhabitants of this "floating world," from country men and women to the teenagers who celebrate *shamate* (the term is a phonetic play on the English "smart") — a subculture that jumps across online and real world communities, blending strains of global youth culture ranging from English punk to Japanese glam rock and anime — and claim their right to recognition, beauty, and the fulfillment of "primitive" needs like sex and food. She insists, however, that "painting is an alternate reality that parallels the real world, but it is not real in the moral sense. In my paintings I like to build relational structures for exploring and studying the abstract relations among different things. They originate from the known reality, but they also differ completely from that reality."[8]

While witnessing the fate of the rural population who have failed to "integrate" into globalizing urban society, Duan revisits a wide

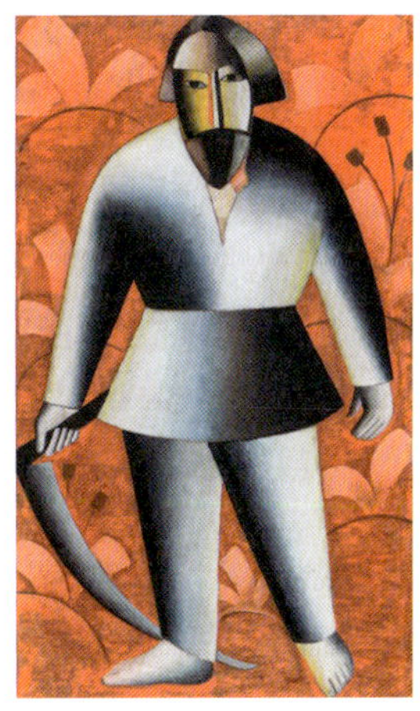

卡茲米爾・馬列維奇，《割草機》，1911–12，
布面油畫，114.3 × 67.2 cm
Kazimir Malevich, *The Mower*, 1911–12.
Oil on canvas, 114.3 × 67.2 cm

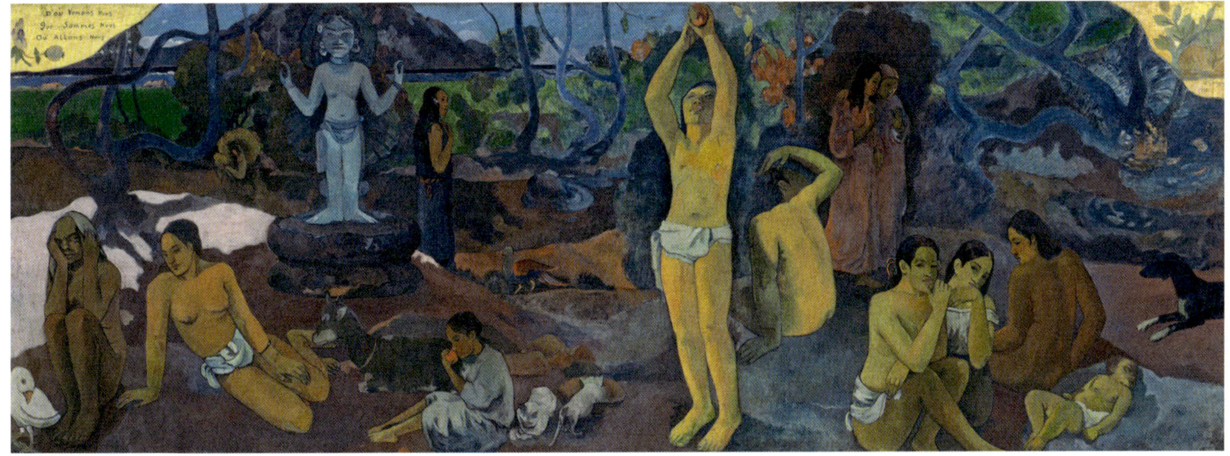

保羅・高更，《我們從何處來？我們是誰？我們向何處去？》，
1897–98，布面油畫，139.1 × 374.6 cm
Paul Gauguin, *Where Do We Come From? What Are We? Where Are We Going?*, 1897–98. Oil on canvas, 139.1 × 374.6 cm

段建宇通過其繪畫實踐，以敏銳的洞察力和同情心見證了這個獨特的狀態。從鄉村男女到追捧「殺馬特」的青少年（殺馬特是英文smart的音譯，興起於互聯網和現實生活中的亞文化，結合從英國朋克到日本華麗搖滾和動漫等全球年輕人的文化。殺馬特主張擁有被認可、美和滿足如性和食物等「原始」需求的權利），段建宇在畫中呈現這個「浮世」的居民，他們的現實生活、夢想、奇思幻想和價值觀。儘管如此，段建宇堅稱：「繪畫是平行於現實世界的另一個真實的世界，這種真不是道德意義的真。我喜歡在繪畫中搭建這些關係結構，探索和研究各種事物的抽象關係。它們的來源是已知的現實，但它們又不完全等同於現實。」[8]

段建宇見證了那些未能「融入」全球化城市的農村人口的命運，同時重新探索多位不同藝術家前輩，從馬列維奇（Kazimir Malevich，1878–1935）到蔣兆和（1904–1986）和周臣（1460–1535），以及古代鬼魅故事如十八世紀作者蒲松齡的《聊齋誌異》和旨趣相同的其他民間文學。段建宇本身也是位優異的小說家，這讓她能想像和建構一個超現實的平行世界，在其中，美醜、生死、天堂地獄，都變得沒有什麼差別了。正如「單手拍掌」讓我們看到抓住真相的「其他方式」或「超越之境」，段建宇筆下勾勒出的人物既是有血有肉的真實人物，同時也是鬼魅幻影。然而，對藝術家，可能也對任何仔細觀察它的人來說，這個世界比現實世界更加真實，當我們花時間去遊弋這個非凡之地時，會感到彷彿被帶到了另一個世界，但同時又被社會現實放大的引力強行拉回。段建宇的世界雖在美學上受馬列維奇後期農民肖像畫的啟發，但和保羅·高更繪畫世界的聯繫卻更為密切。兩位藝術家都提出同樣的問題：我們從何處來？我們是誰？我們向何處去？

3

離林一林生長、段建宇居住之地相隔不遠，在中國內地和前英國殖民地邊界的另一頭，有一位叫黃炳的香港年輕人。他和他的「同胞們」在面對生存環境變動的現實下，不斷質疑著「一國兩制」的實際意涵，及其在快速變遷的世界、在中國正崛起成為一個新的全球勢力的條件中，如何得以持續。黃炳通過創造一個超現實的平行世界，揭露香港的現實，同時也對之進行抵抗——香港已成為測試當前全球權力重新分配下，中國和國際社會之間交涉談判的新秩序的實驗室。然而，黃炳使用的語言不是繪畫，而是低解析度、扁平形式的動畫片。黃炳大學讀的是多媒體設計，但未能掌握精密的電腦編程技術。他幾乎是迫不得已下選擇聚焦極其簡單的格式，甚至類似上個世紀八十年代八位元電玩的幼稚動畫，這最終成了他的個人美學風格。諷刺的是，他說道，「有趣的是，人們把它看成是我的『風格』，因為這基本上是我力所能及做的一切。」[9] 儘管藝術家為人謙遜，他實際上創造了一種獨一無二的感知力。他發現了一種直率簡潔，

range of artistic precedents, from Kazimir Malevich (1878–1935) to Jiang Zhaohe (1904–1986) and Zhou Chen (1460–1535), as well as ancient ghost tales like eighteenth-century author Pu Songling's *Strange Stories from a Chinese Studio* (*Liao zhai zhi yi*), and other examples of popular literature in the same vein. This allows Duan, who is a remarkable fiction writer in her own right, to envision and construct a surreal, parallel world where the differences between beauty and ugliness, life and death, or heaven and hell become *in*different. Just as "clapping with one hand" shows us "another way" or "realm beyond" for grasping the truth, the figures that emerge from Duan's brush are at once real bodies with flesh and blood and also phantoms. However, this world — for the artist, and probably for anyone who observes it closely — is more real than the real one. Spending time in this extraordinary place, one has the sensation of being transported to the beyond while at the same time being forcefully pulled back by the amplified gravity of the social reality. Although aesthetically inspired by Malevich's peasant portraits, Duan's world turns out to be even more intimately linked to that of Paul Gauguin. Both artists raise the same question: *Where Do We Come From? What Are We? Where Are We Going?*

3

Not far from where Lin Yilin was raised and Duan Jianyu lives, on the other side of the border between the Chinese mainland and the former British colony, there is a young man in Hong Kong named Wong Ping. Questioning what "one country, two systems" actually means, and how it can be sustained in a rapidly changing world where China is emerging as a new global power, Wong and his "compatriots" must confront the reality of their living conditions. Wong does so by imagining a lurid alternate reality that at once exposes and resists the everyday reality of Hong Kong, which has become a laboratory for testing the new order being negotiated between China and the international community amid the current global redistribution of power. However, Wong's language is not painting, but the low-resolution, flat form of animated video.

Wong studied multimedia design at university but was unable to master sophisticated computer coding. Almost by default, he opted to focus on the format of extremely simple and even naïve animations reminiscent of 1980s-era 8-bit video games, and this eventually became his personal aesthetic. Ironically, he says, "I think it's funny people see it as my 'style,' because it's basically all I can do."[9] Despite such modesty, the artist has in fact created a thoroughly unique sensibility. He has discovered a straightforward, succinct, but innately ironic and amusing visual language for expressing his vision of the world. Having grown up in an environment informed by video games, digital image making, underground music, and introverted, obsessive *otaku* subculture,[10] Wong is part of a generation who are trying to reinvent their own life values — their identities and joys — during a frustrating and painful moment in Hong Kong's transition back to Chinese rule, as hope for the democratic and autonomous society promised by China has been replaced only by disappointment. Wong is of course involved in the grassroots protest and resistance movement, but his commitment to the cause turns out to be radically personal and singular. He produces videos clips for his underground musician friends like the band My Little Airport, whose "campus songs" (*xiaoyuan gequ*) criticize the erosion of social values by neoliberal capitalism and political oppression, and give voice to the deep pain of the young people. But after taking to the streets to protest, he returns home to plunge into his own reality — an endless darkness "decorated" by occasional sexual and cerebral thrills — expressed through animated narratives relating his own fantasies and sense of helplessness in the face of the impasse gripping Hong Kong. Whereas many people use money making, material consumption, and sex as palliatives for their frustration, Wong's videos reference emblems of the economic miracles and cultural ascendancy of the "good old days" before the handover, but turn them into overexcited yet quasi-impotent phallic symbols. At the same time, they recount dark stories of prostitution, poverty, and corruption in a playful but ultimately desperate manner that contrasts with their graphically extravagant images and settings.

Now, after all the oscillation between hope and disappointment in Hong Kong politics, Wong has shifted his imagination into a totally new field, or fear, for his latest project: examining how, on top of all the other desperations, society

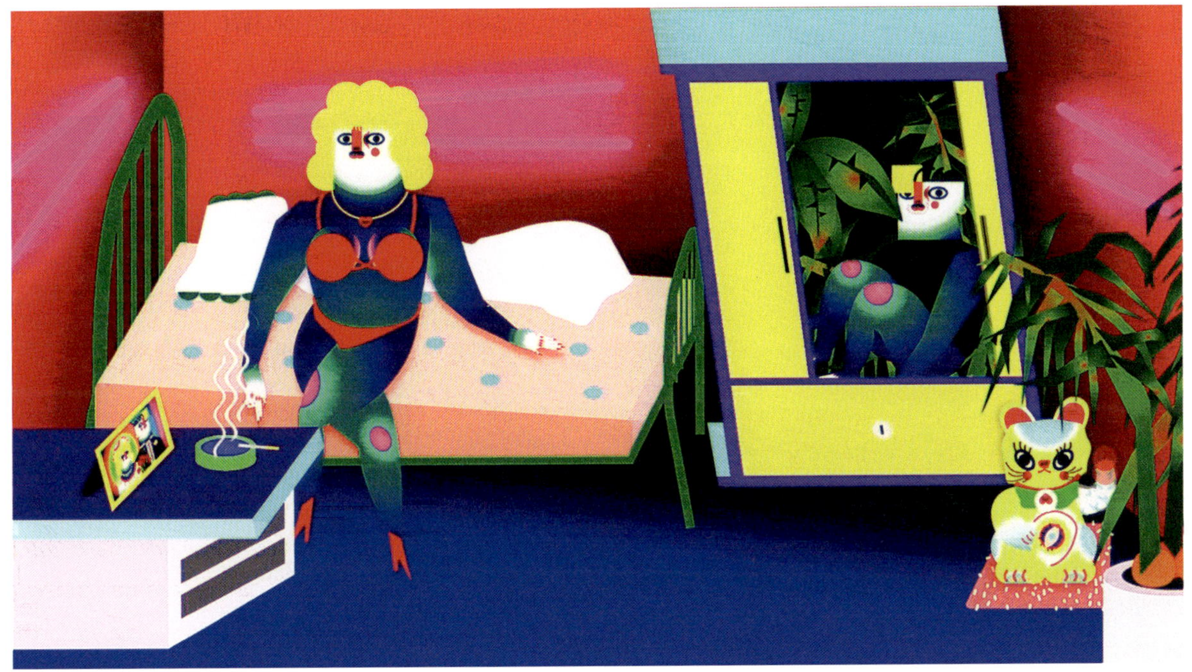

黃炳，《慾望Jungle》，2015，彩色動畫錄像
Wong Ping, *Jungle of Desire*, 2015. Animated video

但先天上充滿諷刺和趣味性的視覺語言，來表達他的世界觀。

黃炳成長在一個受電玩、數字影像製作、地下音樂以及內向、癡迷的「宅男」亞文化所形塑的環境。在香港回歸中國統治這個令人沮喪和痛苦時刻，在中國承諾一個民主自治社會的希望被失望所取代之際，他所屬的這個世代正試圖重塑自己的人生價值以及身份認同和歡樂。黃炳當然參與了民間基層發起的抗議和抵制運動，但做出非常個人化而獨特的奉獻，例如，他為朋友、地下樂隊「My Little Airport」製作短視頻——該樂隊的「校園歌曲」批判新自由資本主義和政治壓迫對社會價值的侵蝕，為年輕人的失落和痛苦發聲。然而，結束街頭抗議後回到家中，他所面對的是另一個現實——永無止盡的黑暗，偶爾靠性和大腦刺激來「點綴」。他用動畫故事來講述面對香港所陷入的僵局時，自己的幻想和無力感。當很多人把賺錢、物質消費和性，作為舒緩挫折感的緩衝器時，黃炳的錄像指涉了香港移交前那段「美好往昔」的經濟奇蹟和文化優勢的象徵——例如因粵語流行曲《獅子山下》而家喻戶曉的「獅子山精神」——但將之轉化為過度興奮卻又幾乎性無能的陽具符號。同時，他的錄像用一種風趣但最終是絕望的方式——這又恰恰和視覺上極其奢華的圖像和場景成反照——講述著嫖妓、貧窮和腐敗的黑暗故事。

在經歷了香港的政治不斷在希望和絕望之間游移擺盪之後，黃炳的最新創作將想像力轉移到另一個全新的領域，審視社會如何處理老齡化的問題，以及其背後普遍的恐懼感。這是一個經常被忽視但愈來愈迫切的挑戰，尤其在這個數字經濟和人工智能威脅並剝奪著許多人工作權利的時代，就連年輕人都必須為他們遙遠的未來擔心。在他訴諸此題材的新動畫片裏，藝術家對我們提出警告：未來將一改往昔，長壽是一種犯罪。此時，一個家庭故事就成了這樣：

> 兒子對妻子說：「我怎樣都不忍心把父親送到外面老人院去。」父親偷聽後感到安慰。原來孝順的兒子不捨他離去。第二天醒來時發現全屋都是陌生老人和看護，原來兒子意思是要把自己家變成老人院，照顧父親同時又能賺錢。[10]

4

音樂專業出身、生活和工作於香港的楊嘉輝，不僅專精電子音效和影像製作技術，同時也是一位富哲學思辨力的表演者。他在澳洲和美國讀書時期，吸取了大量有關當代音樂——從流行音樂、實驗電音到文化史的豐富知識。他在世界各地旅行時，不斷研究和探索各種音樂和樂器背後的社會和政治內涵、其歷史發展，以及對人們生活的影響。後來，他將這些歷史參照轉化為多媒體裝置的「造型」元素，將展覽空間塑造為一個富詩性、甚至多愁善感的沈浸式聲音環境，並經常通過藝術家和觀眾參與的演出來加以凸顯。

楊嘉輝經歷過香港轉型以及近年來越來越受中國統治的經驗，使得他對聲音——從音樂到日常生活「噪音」——和政治環境變遷之間的張力格外敏感。他像一位獨行的游擊手，侵入和探索著從政治邊界到都市區劃分等各式各樣的政治空間。他在這些場域進行田野錄音，之後重新編排並運用在表演裝置當中，

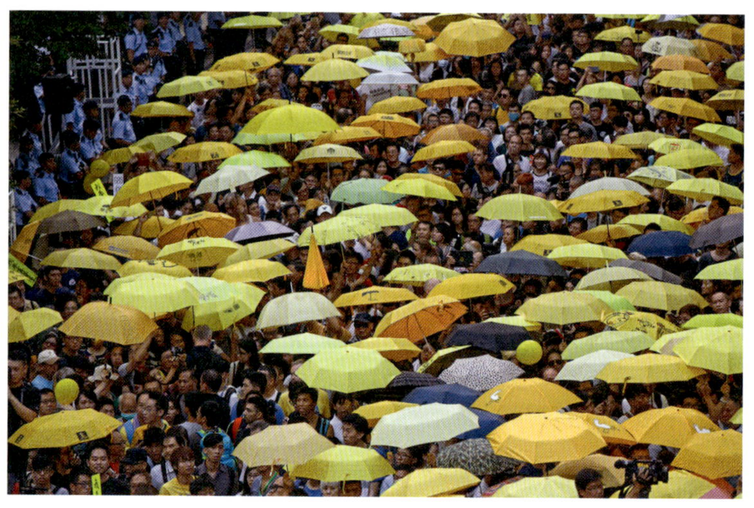

手舉黃色雨傘的抗議者聚集在香港政府總部周圍紀念「雨傘運動」一週年，2015年9月28日。
Protesters holding yellow umbrellas gather outside government headquarters in Hong Kong on the first anniversary of the "Umbrella Movement," September 28, 2015.

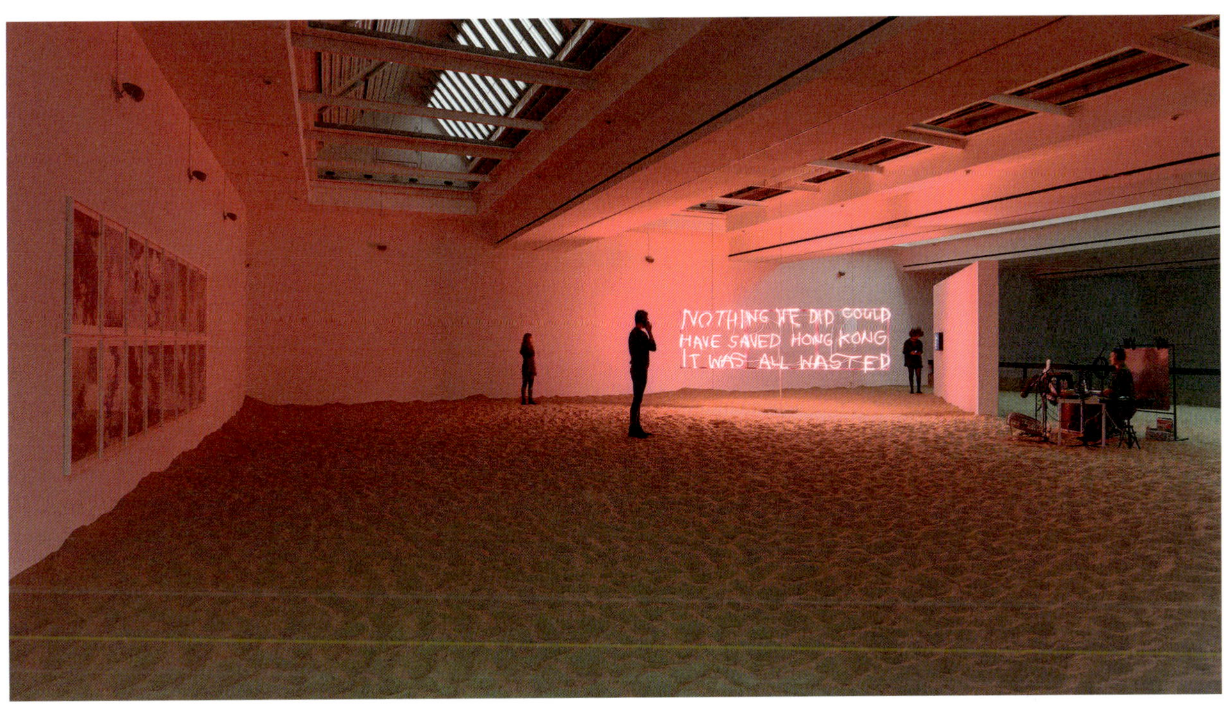

楊嘉輝，《Stanley》，2014，展覽現場
Samson Young, *Stanley*, 2014. Installation view

deals with the question of aging — an often ignored but increasingly urgent challenge, especially at a time when the digital economy and artificial intelligence threaten to deprive many people of the right to work. Even the young have to worry about their remote future. In his new animation on the subject, the artist warns us: the future is not what it used to be. Longevity is a crime. Then, a family story goes like this:

> The son says to his wife, "How could I ever have the heart to put Dad in a nursing home?" The father is eavesdropping and feels relieved: the filial son can't bear to have him leave. The next day the father wakes up to discover he is surrounded by elderly strangers and nurses. It turns out the son meant he would turn the house into a nursing home — he could make money while caring for his father.[11]

4

Trained as a musician, the Hong Kong–based Samson Young is a savvy technician of electronic sound and image production, as well as a committed performer with a philosophical intellect. Having studied in Australia and the United States, Young has acquired a rich knowledge of contemporary music — from pop songs to electronic experimentation — and cultural history. In his travels across the world, he constantly researches and explores the sociopolitical implications behind all kinds of music and instruments, their historical development, and their impact on people's lives. He then turns these historical references into "plastic" elements for multimedia installations that transform the exhibition space into a poetic and even melancholic immersive sonic environment, often highlighted by performances involving the artist and audience.

Young's experience of living through Hong Kong's transition and its increasing domination by China in recent years has made him particularly sensitive to the tension between sounds — from music to everyday "noises" — and changes in the political environment. Like a lone guerrilla, he invades and explores all kinds of political spaces, from national borders to the demarcations of urban zones. He conducts field recordings at these sites and then recomposes them for performative installations that reveal and amplify the traces of social, political, and geopolitical conflicts. In other cases,

揭露並放大了社會、政治和地緣政治衝突的痕跡。在其他情況下，他將關於戰爭、社會運動和人道主義援助等社會事件的現有歌曲重新編排。長期以來，音樂和歌詞的流通和翻譯，為楊嘉輝繪製出一條路徑，引導著他在聲音世界的冒險之旅。他的冒險旅程挑戰著歷史和現在、現實和虛構之間的界線，邀請我們重新定義如何在這個世界中共存共榮。這些冒險形成了一種協奏曲——不論和諧或嘈雜，表明了歷史和現實的矛盾本質，由此，權力和抵制、暴力和美、挫折和希望，本質上是緊密關聯的。這反映了人類征服世界的慾望——不論是以音樂、科學或政治之名的慾望，以及慾望根本上的不可能實現。在新作中，楊嘉輝製作了一系列「不可能的樂器」，以測試人實現「現實」的能力。最終，這項實驗就像現實生活一樣，同樣注定是一場致命的結局。一切都是動盪不定的。

在2016-2017年杜塞爾多夫美術館的個展上，楊嘉輝懸掛在其創作的聲音空間盡頭那個霓虹燈標示，格外耐人尋味。上面寫著：NOTHING WE DID COULD/ HAVE SAVED HONG KONG/IT WAS ALL WASTED（我們所做一切都無法/解救香港/一切全是徒勞）。

5

曹斐，1978年生於廣州，她的多媒體和跨領域創作體現了科技進步對人類感知和生活方式的衝擊。她的早期攝影和錄像捕捉了同儕——在千禧年之交不斷通過新的娛樂形式尋找新身份認同的青少年和年輕人，他們炫耀的生活方式和狂妄的想像。接著，她在網絡遊戲平台「第二人生」中繼續進行藝術冒險，設計了一個虛擬烏托邦：「人民城寨」，其中的建築環境反映、同時也超越現實世界。曹斐的創作結合了對科技創新的著迷以及對人類日益異化的生活「進步」的景況所提出的批判性審視——這甚至可能是我們所知的社會毀滅，因為人工智能技術的興起所重新定義的，不只是我們的社會關係，也包括我們對人性本身的理解！

十年前，曹斐受跨國企業西門子的委託，在廣州市附近的佛山一家工廠創作一件作品，開始研究新引進的資本主義工業製造模式和中國本地勞工之間的緊張關係。其成果《誰的烏托邦》(2006)是她和工人合作創造出的一個短暫但充滿樂觀的社會烏托邦願景。這個願景乃建立在個人對未來的夢想上，是作為面對全球化愈來愈多的壓力的一種抵抗行為。如今，她將探索延伸到受人工智能驅動的自動化所形塑的新現實中。她的新作品《Asia One》記錄了幾乎空無一人的自動化工廠的場景，讓我們看到即將到來的烏托邦，傑拉德·勞尼格稱之為「機器資本主義」：「自動化發揮到極致的結果，機器資本主義將不惜把人從社會生產中排除，以確保最大利潤；同時，一切有意義的事物正逐漸走向網絡、雲端和機器。」[11] 這個「進步」同時受到政治當權者的鼓勵，作為他們提升經濟競爭力和鞏固社會控制的手段。許多政府將新科技的發展——尤其是人工

he recomposes existing songs that relate to social events such as wars, social movements, and humanitarian actions.

Over time, the global circulation and continuous translation of musical and lyrical messages has charted a course that guides Young in his adventures in the sonic world. Challenging boundaries between history and the present, reality and fiction, these adventures invite us to redefine how we coexist in the world. Altogether, they form a kind of concerto — whether harmonious or cacophonic — that demonstrates the contradictory nature of history and reality, whereby power and resistance, violence and beauty, frustration and hope are intrinsically bound. This reflects the contradiction between the human desire to conquer the world — whether in the name of music, science, or politics — and the fundamental impossibility of ever realizing that desire. For his new project, Young has constructed an array of "impossible musical instruments" in order to test the human capacity to achieve "reality." Eventually, this experiment, just as in real life, is condemned to the same fatal end. Everything is precarious.

Tellingly, the neon sign Young hung at the end of the sonic space he created for his exhibition at Kunsthalle Düsseldorf in 2016–17 read: NOTHING WE DID COULD / HAVE SAVED HONG KONG / IT WAS ALL WASTED.

5

Born in Guangzhou in 1978, Cao Fei makes multimedia and transdisciplinary works that manifest the impact of technological progress on our perceptions and ways of life. Her early photography and video works captured the extravagant lifestyle and audacious imagination of her peers: teenagers and youths at the turn of the millennium continually searching for new identities through new forms of entertainment. She turned to the online platform of Second Life for her next adventure, designing the virtual utopia RMB City, which at once mirrors and transcends the built environment of the real world. Cao's central concerns combine a fascination regarding technological innovation with the critical examination of human conditions in our "progress" toward the further alienation of human life — and perhaps even the destruction of society as

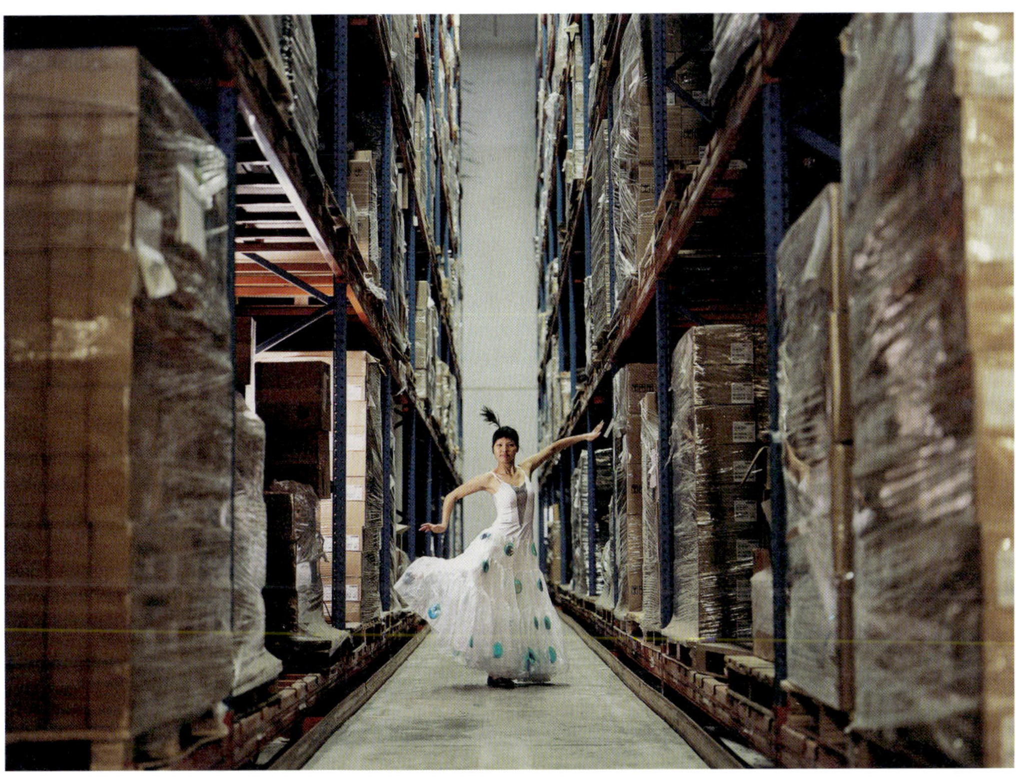

曹斐，《誰的烏托邦》，2006，錄像
Cao Fei, *Whose Utopia*, 2006. Video

we know it, as the rise of AI technology redefines not only our social relations, but also our understanding of humanity itself!

A decade ago, commissioned by the transnational corporation Siemens to produce a work at its factory in Foshan, outside Guangzhou, Cao began her research into the tensions between newly introduced modes of capitalist industrial production and the local labor force in China. For the resulting work, *Whose Utopia* (2006), she collaborated with the workers to create a vision of a temporary but optimistic social utopia based on individual dreams for the future as an act of resistance to the rising pressures of globalization. Now she has extended that exploration to the new reality shaped by AI-driven automation. Documenting scenes of automated factories that are almost entirely devoid of human presence, her new projects show us the coming utopia of what Gerald Raunig calls "machinic capitalism." Maximizing the use of automation, machinic capitalism does everything to exclude humans from social production so as to ensure maximum profits for capital, while increasingly "all that is relevant is appending to the networks, the clouds, the machines."[12] This "progress" is also encouraged by political power as a means for boosting economic competitiveness while consolidating control over society. Many governments see the development of new technologies, especially AI and robotics, along with the internet and big data, as their most vital economic, cultural, and political mission. To them, technology is not only a guarantee of state power but also a symbol of national glory. However, it will eventually lead to the technological singularity — a sci-fi scenario where humans are entirely surpassed by machines. Quoting the assertion of Stefano Harney and Fred Moten that "drones are not un-manned to protect American pilots. They are un-manned because they think too fast for American pilots,"[13] Raunig adds that "the drone is the machinic animal of the present, and at some point it will also unfold itself, multiply itself."[14]

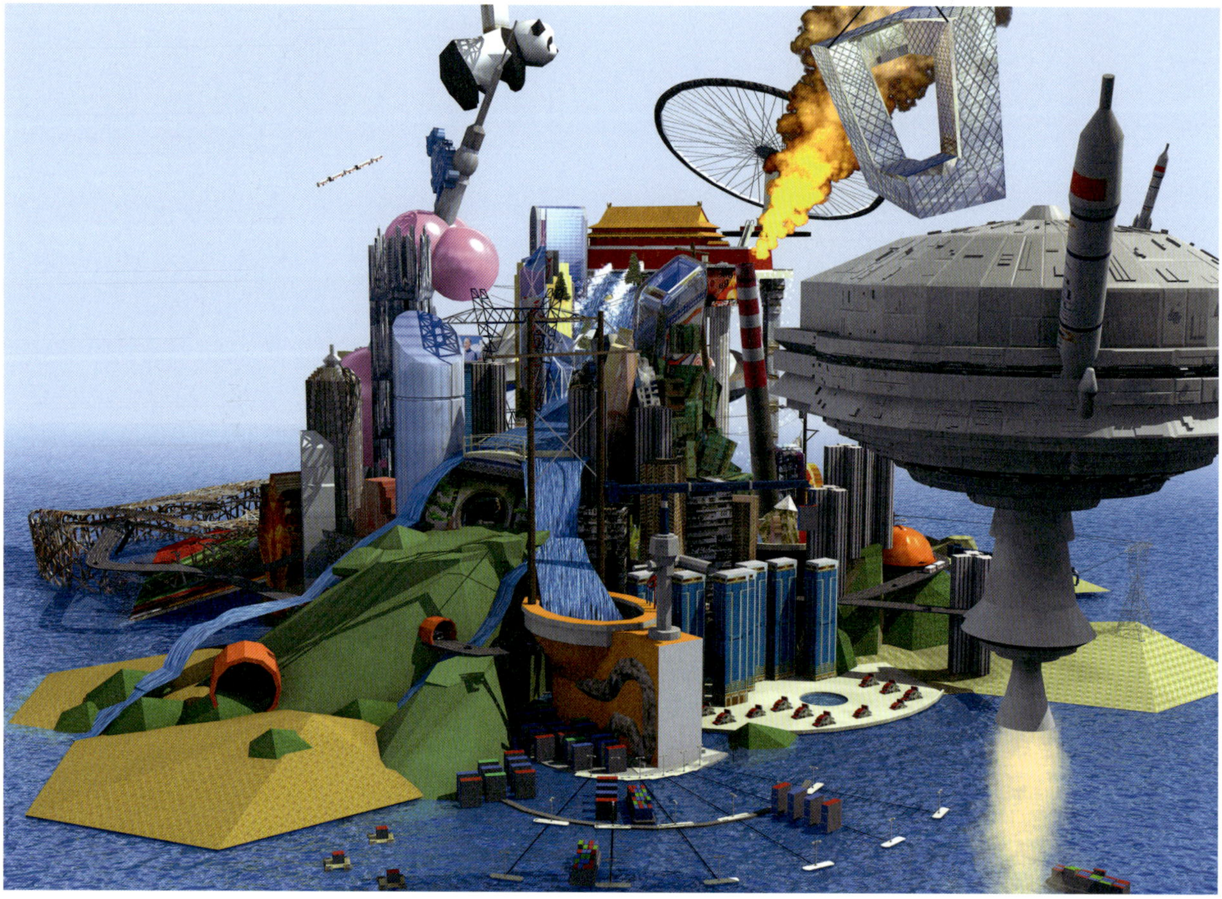

曹斐，《人民城寨：第二人生城市計劃（由曹斐化身「中國・翠西」創造）》，2007，錄像
Cao Fei, *RMB City: A Second Life City Planning by China Tracy (aka Cao Fei)*, 2007. Video

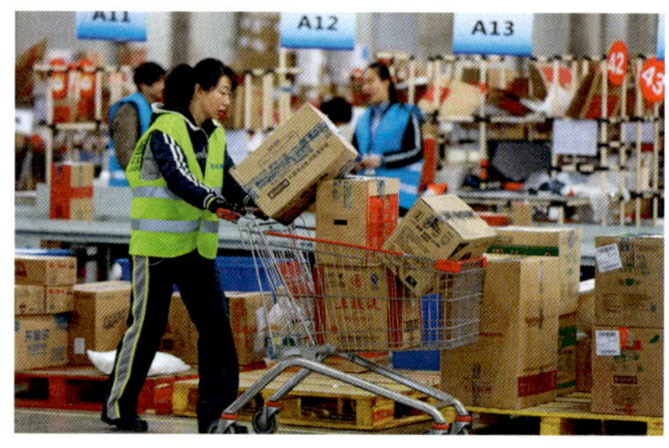

一個阿里巴巴在線零售倉庫的工人正在分類「雙十一」購物節的訂單，遼寧省瀋陽市，2017年11月11日。
A worker sorts Singles' Day shopping orders at online retailer Alibaba's warehouse in Shenyang, Liaoning Province, November 11, 2017.

智能和機器人技術，以及互聯網和大數據——視為他們最重要的經濟、文化和政治使命。對他們來說，科技不只是國家權力的保證，也是民族榮耀的象徵。然而，它最終將導致科技奇點——一個人類完全被機器超越的科幻情節。套用史蒂芬諾·哈爾尼（Stefano Harney）和弗雷德·莫頓（Fred Moten）的說法，「無人機不是為了保護美國飛行員而無人駕駛。它們之所以無人駕駛，是因為它們的思考速度對美國飛行員來說太快了。」[12] 勞尼格也寫道，「無人機是今天的機器動物，在某種程度上，它將逐漸自我發展，自我繁衍。」[13]

與此同時，許多人被困在另一個烏托邦之中：物質消費的狂熱，中國如今正「迎頭趕上」這波物質主義潮流。事實上，通過政府的積極推動，中國已成為全球最大的消費市場，其特點是瘋狂地動員大眾的購物熱情。對許多人而言，購買即生存。網購為這個「新的生命意義」添加了一股不可抗拒的推力。例如11月11日「光棍節」等打折促銷的節日，如今大受歡迎，並且創造驚人利潤。整個人口變成了全國性消費狂歡的顧客。在大型倉庫對這些商品的分揀和運輸是驅動自動化技術發展的一大因素，而這，反過來又進一步成為資本牟利機器的燃料和潤滑油……

然而，消費了一切包裝精美的商品之後，我們當真曾感到滿足嗎？眼前所見的是越來越多人面臨失業，人們在慶祝網上淘寶成功之後自己卻成了多餘的東西。成千上萬噸的包裝材料將郊區化為一望無盡的垃圾場。置身於這些即將到來的未來廢墟，我們怎能不再次感到孤獨？這一次，孤獨將為全人類所共享。

「單手拍掌的聲音是什麼？」

該是再次叩問「我們從何處來？」「我們是誰？」「我們將向何處去？」的時候了。

2017年11月17日，羅馬

At the same time, many people are trapped in another utopia: the frenzy of material consumption. China is now "catching up" with this materialism. In fact, through the government's active promotion, China has become the world's biggest market for consumer goods, characterized by the frantic mobilization of public zeal for shopping. For many, buying is living. Online shopping adds an irresistible push to this "new meaning of life." Festivals like the 11/11 Singles' Day (*Guanggun jie*) promotion are now hugely popular and generate staggering profits. The entire population is turned into the clientele for a nationwide carnival of consumption. The sorting and shipment of these goods at massive warehouses is one of the main factors driving the development of automated technology. And this in turn further fuels and lubricates the profit-making machine of capital.

Ultimately, after consuming all the beautifully packaged goods, can we really feel satisfied? It almost seems as though more and more people are losing jobs and being made redundant right after celebrating the success of their online bargains. The millions of tons of packing materials that pile up have transformed the suburbs into endless fields of trash.

Standing amid these imminent ruins of the future, don't we feel lonely again? This time, the loneliness is shared by the whole of humanity.

"What is the sound of one hand clapping?"

It's time to ask again: *Where Do We Come From? What Are We? Where Are We Going?*

Rome, November 17, 2017

1 《單手拍掌》，作詞林振強，作曲、原唱林子祥，由華納音樂香港發行，1994年。
2 G.W.萊布尼茨（G. W. Leibniz），《哲學原理，或單子論》（「The Principles of Philosophy, or, the Monadology」），收錄於《哲學文集》（*Philosophical Essays*），Roger Ariew和Daniel Garber翻譯，印第安納波斯利，Hackett出版社，1989年，第213–25頁。中文譯本參考《單子論》，選自《西方哲學名篇選讀》（上），翰水法、翰林合、張祥龍編，中國北京大學出版社，2014年，第229–49頁。
3 林一林發給作者的一封電郵，2017年10月23日。
4 禪學學者G. Victor Sōgen Hori將公案的廣泛應用比擬為「單手之聲」，他寫道：「一開始，和尚總以為公案是一個沒有生命的東西，必須把注意力集中放在上面，在很長一段時間的不斷反覆誦讀後，方才領悟公案其實充滿動能，是在不斷尋找公案的答案。公案既是被尋找的對象，也是持續不斷的自我尋找。在公案中，自我不是直接的自我，而是以藉由公案看到自我……一旦人領悟到（「實現」）這個身分性，此刻雙手合而為一。修行者成了他或她試圖理解的公案本身。那正是單手之聲。」G. Victor Sōgen Hori，《禪習語手冊翻譯》（「Translating the Zen Phrase Book」），《南山宗教文化研究所所報》（*Nanzan Bulletin*），1999年，23期，第50–51頁。
5 馬克・費舍（Mark Fisher），《資本主義現實主義：沒有別的選擇？》（*Capitalist Realism: Is There No Alternative?*），美國華盛頓，Zero出版社，2009年。
6 傑拉德・勞尼格（Gerald Raunig），《分人：機器資本主義與分子革命》，（*Dividuum: Machinic Capitalism and Molecular Revolution*），Aileen Derieg翻譯，美國加州南帕薩迪納，Semiotexte出版社，2016年，第19頁。
7 同前註。
8 段建宇和作者之間的微信對話，2017年6月18日。
9 白慧怡（Stephanie Bailey），《慾望在都市：對話黃炳》（「Sex in the City: Wong Ping in Conversation」），《Yishu》典藏國際版（*Yishu: Journal of Contemporary Chinese Art*），2017年9/10月，第48頁。
10 引自黃炳的「日記」，本畫冊第100頁。
11 勞尼格，《分人：機器資本主義與分子革命》，第111頁。
12 史蒂芬諾・哈爾尼（Stefano Harney）、弗雷德・莫頓（Fred Moten），《常識之下：逃亡計劃和黑人文化研究》（「The Undercommons: Fugitive Planning & Black Study」），美國紐約，Minor Compositions出版社，2013年，第88頁。引自勞尼格，《分人：機器資本主義與分子革命》，第114頁。
13 勞尼格，《分人：機器資本主義與分子革命》，第114頁。

1 From "Clapping with One Hand" [Danshou paizhang], lyrics by Richard Lam, music and vocals by George Lam, Warner Music Hong Kong, 1994. Author's translation.
2 G. W. Leibniz, "The Principles of Philosophy, or, the Monadology" (1714), in *Philosophical Essays*, trans. Roger Ariew and Daniel Garber (Indianapolis: Hackett, 1989), pp. 213–25.
3 Lin Yilin, email message to author, October 23, 2017.
4 Likening the broader practice of koan to "the sound of one hand," the scholar of Chan/Zen Buddhism G. Victor Sōgen Hori states: "In the beginning a monk first thinks a kōan is an inert object upon which to focus attention; after a long period of consecutive repetition, one realizes that the kōan is also a dynamic activity, the very activity of seeking an answer to the kōan. The kōan is both the object being sought and the relentless seeking itself. In a kōan, the self sees the self not directly but under the guise of the kōan. . . . When one realizes ('makes real') this identity, then two hands have become one. The practitioner becomes the kōan that he or she is trying to understand. That is the sound of one hand." G. Victor Sōgen Hori, "Translating the Zen Phrase Book," *Nanzan Bulletin* 23 (1999), pp. 50–51.
5 Mark Fisher, *Capitalist Realism: Is There No Alternative?* (Washington, DC: Zero Books, 2009).
6 Gerald Raunig, *Dividuum: Machinic Capitalism and Molecular Revolution*, trans. Aileen Derieg (South Pasadena, CA: Semiotexte, 2016), p. 19.
7 Ibid.
8 Duan Jianyu, statement to the author in WeChat conversation, June 18, 2017.
9 Stephanie Bailey, "Sex in the City: Wong Ping in Conversation," *Yishu: Journal of Contemporary Chinese Art* 16, no. 5 (September/October 2017), p. 48.
10 In Japanese, *otaku* refers generally to a person who has an obsessive interest or hobby, similar to the English "geek" or "nerd," but is especially associated with manga, anime, and video game enthusiasts. The term is rapidly gaining worldwide currency through the spread of Japanese fan culture. For further discussion of *otaku* in relation to contemporary art and culture, see Takashi Murakami, ed., *Little Boy: The Arts of Japan's Exploding Subculture* (New York: Japan Society, 2005), esp. pp. 112–34 and 165–85.
11 From Wong Ping's text on p. 100 of this volume, trans. Alvin Li.
12 Raunig, *Dividuum*, p. 111.
13 Stefano Harney and Fred Moten, *The Undercommons: Fugitive Planning & Black Study* (New York: Minor Compositions, 2013), p. 88, quoted in Raunig, *Dividuum*, p. 114.
14 Raunig, *Dividuum*, p. 114.

張䍦

Zhang Xiu

在沒有鳥以前〈11首〉

Before There Were No Birds (11 Poems)

Translated by Jennifer Feeley

Before There Were No Birds

The sky was empty
Nothing above the heavens except sky
As Heaven and sky were both empty
People often confused them
The emergence of birds marked an improvement
The sky was no longer empty (or became even emptier)
Heaven suddenly reigned supreme (perhaps it was just a whiff of air)
At the same time, people came to know all things
Could be translated, to sleep when tired

在沒有鳥以前

天空，空蕩蕩的
天上什麼都沒有除了天空
天和天空也因為空
常常被人搞混
鳥的出現是一種進步
它讓天空不再空蕩
(或更加空蕩)
讓天突然變得至高無上
(又可能只是一股氣)
同時也讓人認識到萬物
皆可翻譯，累了就要睡覺

Before There Were No Birds

Especially come September
Rain would fall from the sky
Someone seeking refuge from the rain
Stopped beneath a tree, completely still
As she hadn't seen any birds (she wanted to, but hadn't
seen any, certainly not)
The rain kept beating down
She felt empty, so much so that she began to suspect
She was about to get pregnant

Before There Were No Birds

Deeper in the sky
Even beyond the birds
Still deeper, in the deepest depths of sky
What are the secrets
That evade even the birds
This is what I'd like to know
But also what I fear

在沒有鳥以前

尤其到了九月
天空下著雨
避雨的人
停在樹下不動
因為沒見過鳥(想見,也沒有
見了,肯定也不是)
雨又老是下個沒停
她感到空虛,甚至起懷疑
自己是不是快要懷孕了

在沒有鳥以前

在更深的天空裏
甚至在有了鳥以後
在還要深、最深的天空
那裏有什麼
見不得鳥的東西
是我想知道的
但又怕

Before There Were No Birds

There was no wind, either. This conclusion is debatable
Even though it's true. But before there were no birds
How could anyone have believed such far-fetched nonsense
Even though the birds came in great numbers, hundreds of millions of years after the fact
There are only a handful of believers, and as for the nonbeliever
Even if the birds were to rebel and peck holes over and over in her dreams
After waking up, she'd still fall

Before There Were No Birds

As the fallen dragon
Had no strength
It couldn't return to the sky
From then on, left behind in the world
It was cursed
It's hard to say who was to blame
At first there were no birds
The dragon itself was a victim as well
The main thing to keep in mind is that people at the time
Hadn't eaten enough in days
Yet eagerly trekked down to the countryside
Out of blind adoration

在沒有鳥以前

也沒風。這個結論有待商榷
盡管它是事實。但在沒有鳥以前
一個人怎麼會相信這些，虛頭巴腦的
即使鳥大量出現，億萬年後的現在
信的人，總歸還是極少數幾個，不信的
即便鳥在她夢裏反覆打洞、造反
醒來後，她還是會接著墮落

在沒有鳥以前

掉下來的龍
因為沒有力氣
沒法再回去天空
從此遺留人間
成為禍害
這事不好怨誰
鳥，本來就沒有
龍，牠自己也是受害者
主要還是當時的人類
飯沒吃飽幾天
卻熱衷於上山下鄉
搞什麼偶像崇拜

Before There Were No Birds

Are there actually any birds in the sky?
There shouldn't be, if the sky predates birds
The *History of Birds* explains: *bird*—
The earliest thing in the sky; without birds
There'd be no sky. If this is true
Why have I been staring at the sky
For two minutes now and not seen any birds
The tried and true *History of Birds* can't be wrong
Okay, you say, that probably
Was before there were no birds

Before There Were No Birds

A seed fell to the ground
Three years later, it grew
Into a large, snow-white egg
Someone saw it, asked
What is this thing?
Someone knew, claimed it
Was an egg laid by the family dragon
No one knew how it flew here
For three years straight, it rained day after day
The egg went missing, it was rather quite sudden
Only then did people begin to think that perhaps slavery
Had become outdated

在沒有鳥以前

天空裏到底有沒有鳥
應該沒有，如果天空比鳥早
《鳥史》上的解釋是：鳥
最早是天空的事物，沒有鳥
就沒有天空。如果這說法沒錯
那我現在正看著天空
2分鐘了，為什麼不見鳥
經過證明的《鳥史》不可能出錯
好吧，你說，那大概
是在沒有鳥以前

在沒有鳥以前

一粒種子落到地上
三年後，它長大
長成一個雪白的大蛋
有人看見了，說
這是什麼東西
也有人知道，說它
是自己家的龍生的蛋
不知道怎麼飛到了這裏
再三年，還是雨天
蛋不見了，不見得很突然
人們這才想起奴隸制
可能已經落伍了

Before There Were No Birds

It's hard to narrate. A stone stopped in the sky
No one could see its beginning and development, climax and ending
The person looking at the stone waited three days, after three days
She was starving, looked for any reason she could find
To go home. From then on, she never went home again

Before There Were No Birds

Wind blew the leaves
It was only the wind that blew the leaves
Someone was walking alone on the road (in autumn)
But she didn't know what she was walking on
Daylight, soon the day would grow even lighter
Far off, she spotted fog
Her husband was also coming from afar

在沒有鳥以前

敘事還很難。一個石頭停在天空
看不出它的開始和發展、高潮以及結局
看石頭的人等了3天，3天後
她實在餓得不行了，便隨便找了一個理由
回到家中。從此，再也沒有回過家

在沒有鳥以前

風吹起樹葉
僅僅是風吹起樹葉
一個人在路上走（秋天）
卻不知道她在走什麼
天亮了，很快天變得更亮
遠處看見霧
丈夫也從遠處走來

Before There Were No Birds

We were drinking Pepsi
She stopped alone in the rain, completely still
We drank Pepsi and stared at her
Stopped alone in the rain
She was like a bird, the kind in the rain
Like that for an instant
And in another instant, nothing like that at all
Pepsi started out as a kind of American soft drink
Later it became popular in our village

Before There Were No Birds

A bird sailed through the air
No one knew it was a bird
Two, before there were no birds
There were no birds. In sum
Jimmy, you're already asleep
Let me tell you a secret: don't
Miss mankind (too much).

在沒有鳥以前

我們在喝百事
她一個人停在雨裏不動
我們喝著百事看她
一個人停在雨裏
她像鳥,雨裏的那種
像了一會兒
又哪裏都不像了
百事最開始是美國的一種汽水
後來在我們村也非常流行

在沒有鳥以前

鳥飛在空中
沒有人知道那是鳥
2、在沒有鳥以前
是沒有鳥的。作為總結
Jimmy,你已經睡了
告訴你一個祕密:不要
(過多的)想念人類。

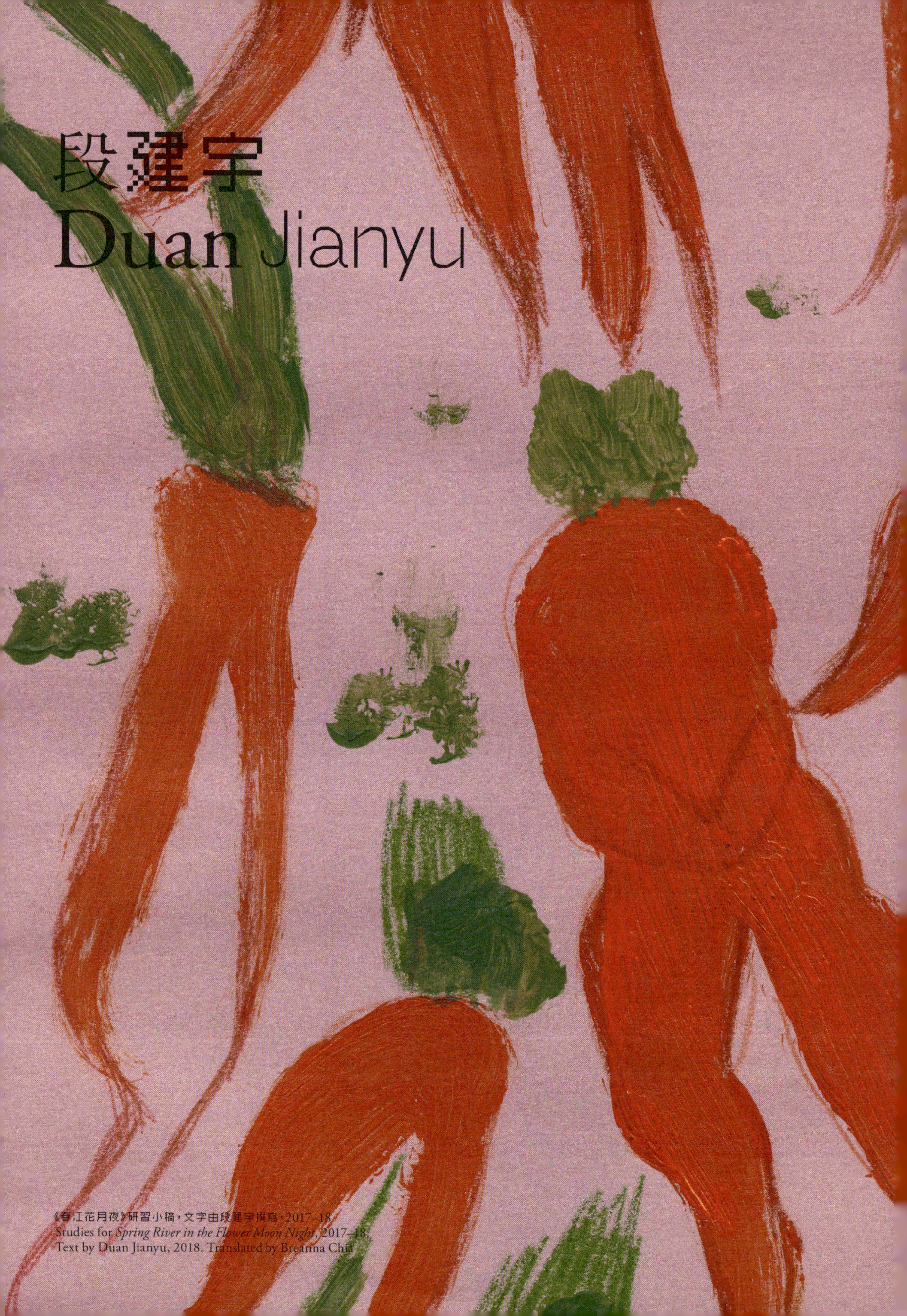

段建宇
Duan Jianyu

《春江花月夜》研習小稿，文字由段建宇撰寫，2017–18
Studies for *Spring River in the Flower Moon Night*, 2017–18.
Text by Duan Jianyu, 2018. Translated by Breanna Chia

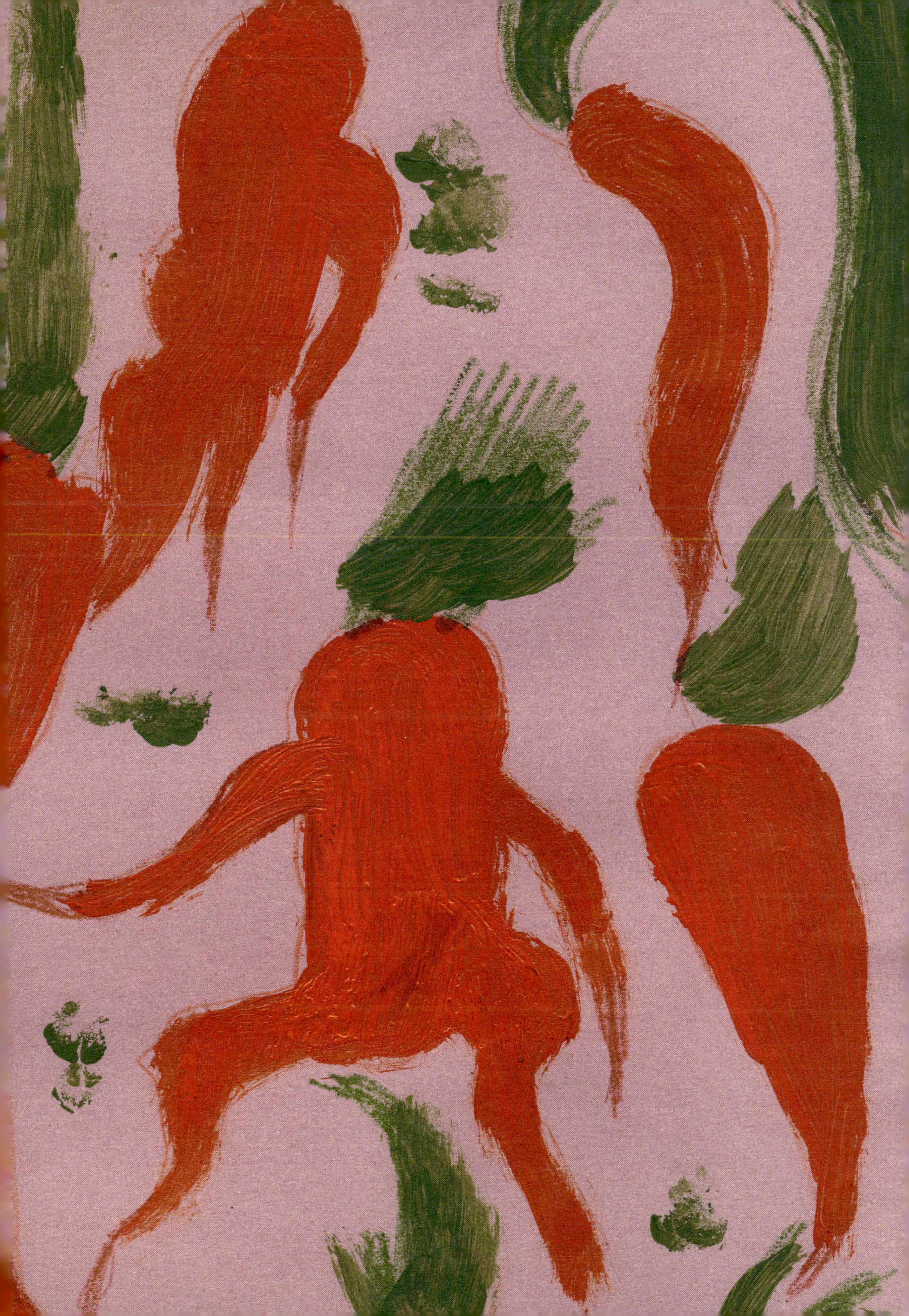

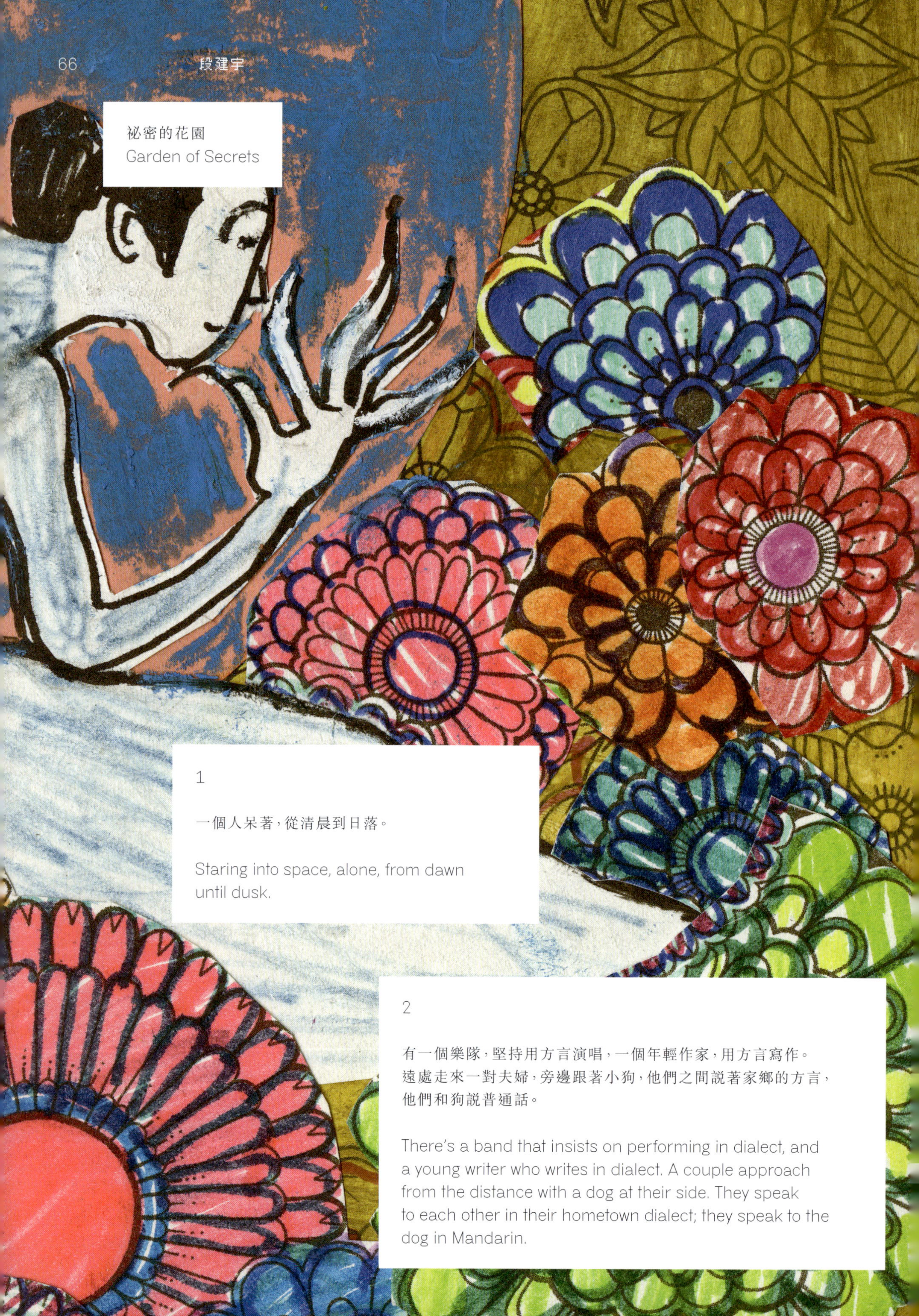

祕密的花園
Garden of Secrets

1

一個人呆著，從清晨到日落。

Staring into space, alone, from dawn until dusk.

2

有一個樂隊，堅持用方言演唱，一個年輕作家，用方言寫作。遠處走來一對夫婦，旁邊跟著小狗，他們之間說著家鄉的方言，他們和狗說普通話。

There's a band that insists on performing in dialect, and a young writer who writes in dialect. A couple approach from the distance with a dog at their side. They speak to each other in their hometown dialect; they speak to the dog in Mandarin.

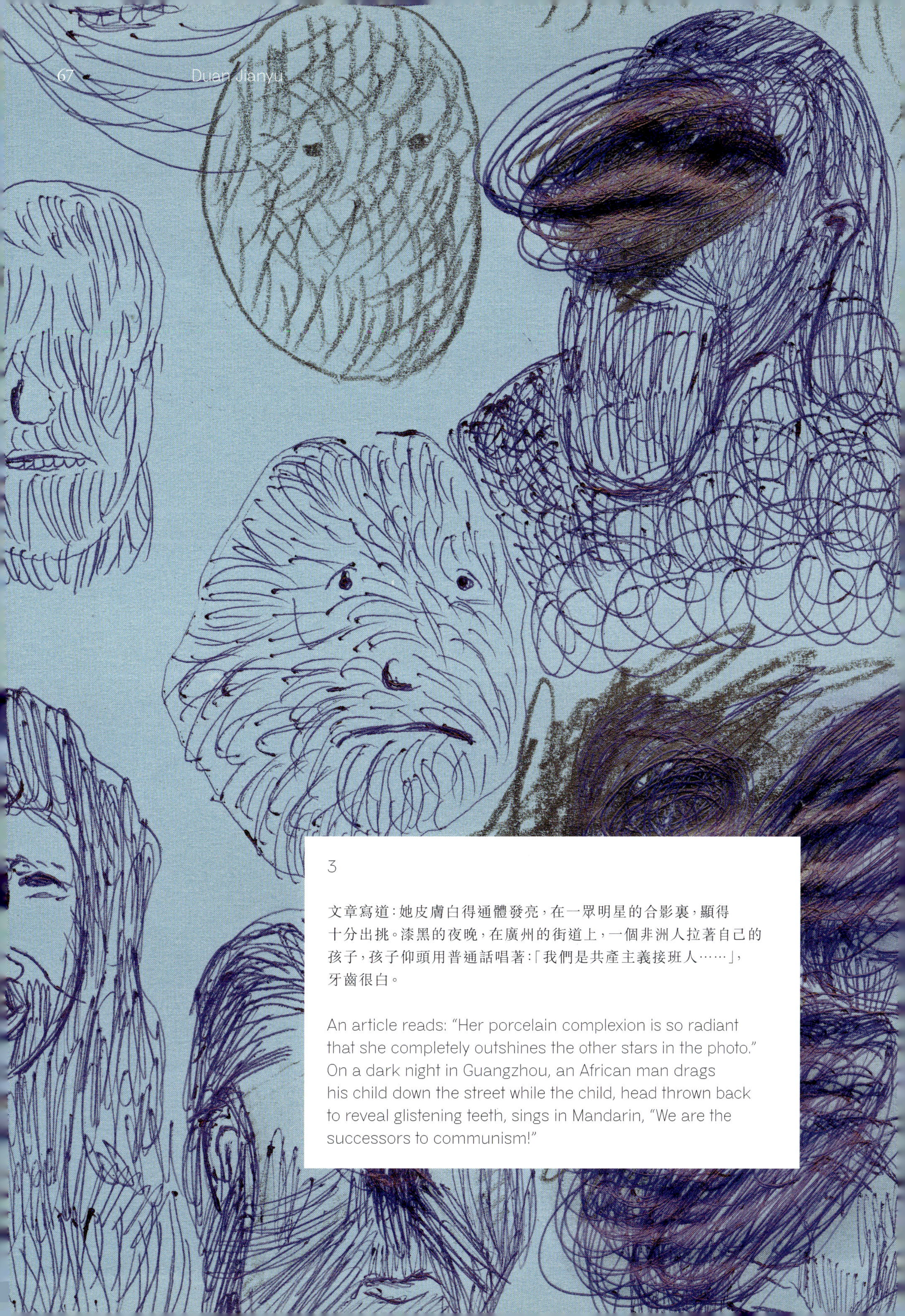

3

文章寫道：她皮膚白得通體發亮，在一眾明星的合影裏，顯得十分出挑。漆黑的夜晚，在廣州的街道上，一個非洲人拉著自己的孩子，孩子仰頭用普通話唱著：「我們是共產主義接班人……」，牙齒很白。

An article reads: “Her porcelain complexion is so radiant that she completely outshines the other stars in the photo.” On a dark night in Guangzhou, an African man drags his child down the street while the child, head thrown back to reveal glistening teeth, sings in Mandarin, “We are the successors to communism!”

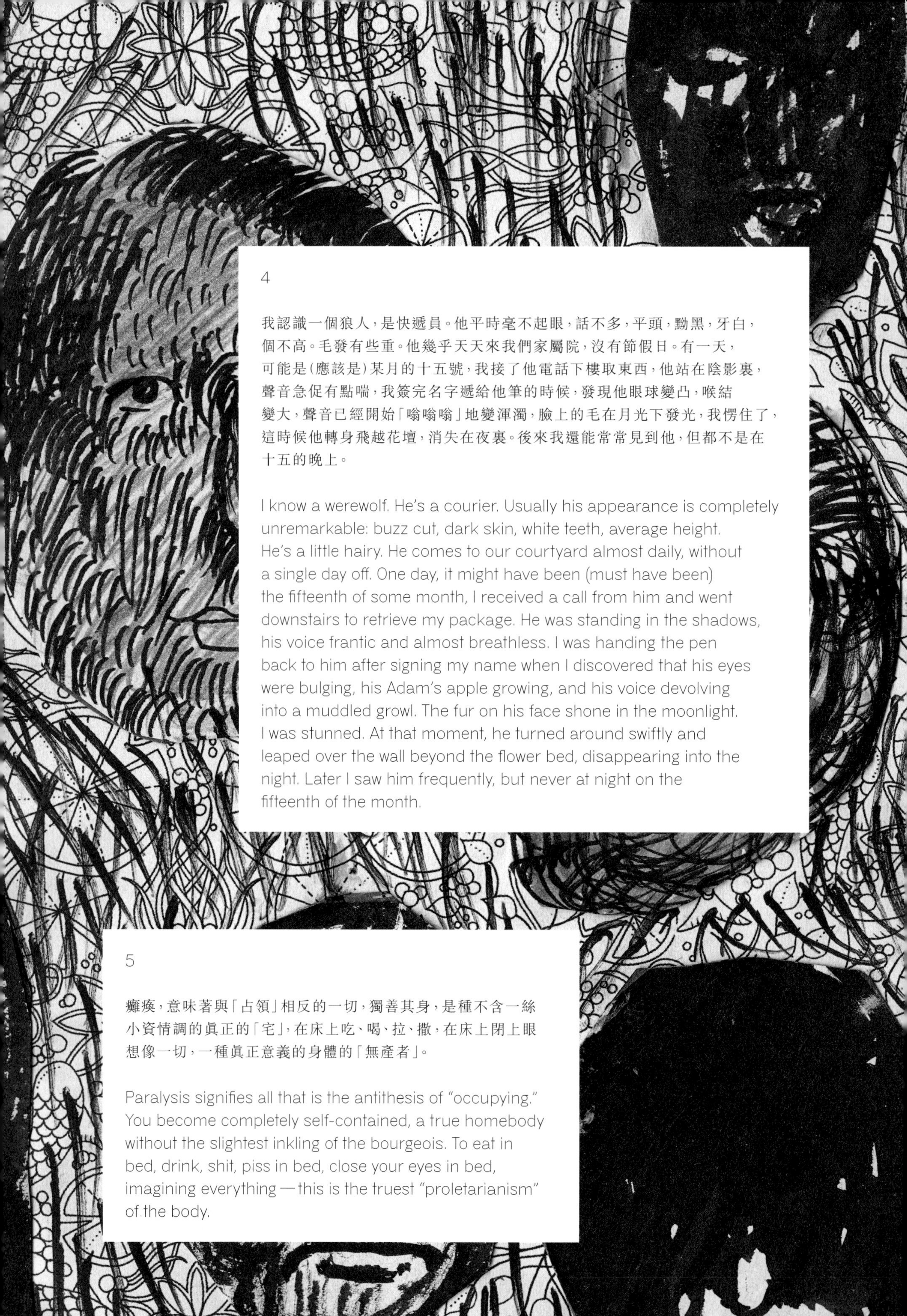

4

我認識一個狼人，是快遞員。他平時毫不起眼，話不多，平頭，黝黑，牙白，個不高。毛發有些重。他幾乎天天來我們家屬院，沒有節假日。有一天，可能是(應該是)某月的十五號，我接了他電話下樓取東西，他站在陰影裏，聲音急促有點喘，我簽完名字遞給他筆的時候，發現他眼球變凸，喉結變大，聲音已經開始「嗡嗡嗡」地變渾濁，臉上的毛在月光下發光，我愣住了，這時候他轉身飛越花壇，消失在夜裏。後來我還能常常見到他，但都不是在十五的晚上。

I know a werewolf. He's a courier. Usually his appearance is completely unremarkable: buzz cut, dark skin, white teeth, average height. He's a little hairy. He comes to our courtyard almost daily, without a single day off. One day, it might have been (must have been) the fifteenth of some month, I received a call from him and went downstairs to retrieve my package. He was standing in the shadows, his voice frantic and almost breathless. I was handing the pen back to him after signing my name when I discovered that his eyes were bulging, his Adam's apple growing, and his voice devolving into a muddled growl. The fur on his face shone in the moonlight. I was stunned. At that moment, he turned around swiftly and leaped over the wall beyond the flower bed, disappearing into the night. Later I saw him frequently, but never at night on the fifteenth of the month.

5

癱瘓，意味著與「占領」相反的一切，獨善其身，是種不含一絲小資情調的眞正的「宅」，在床上吃、喝、拉、撒，在床上閉上眼想像一切，一種眞正意義的身體的「無產者」。

Paralysis signifies all that is the antithesis of "occupying." You become completely self-contained, a true homebody without the slightest inkling of the bourgeois. To eat in bed, drink, shit, piss in bed, close your eyes in bed, imagining everything—this is the truest "proletarianism" of the body.

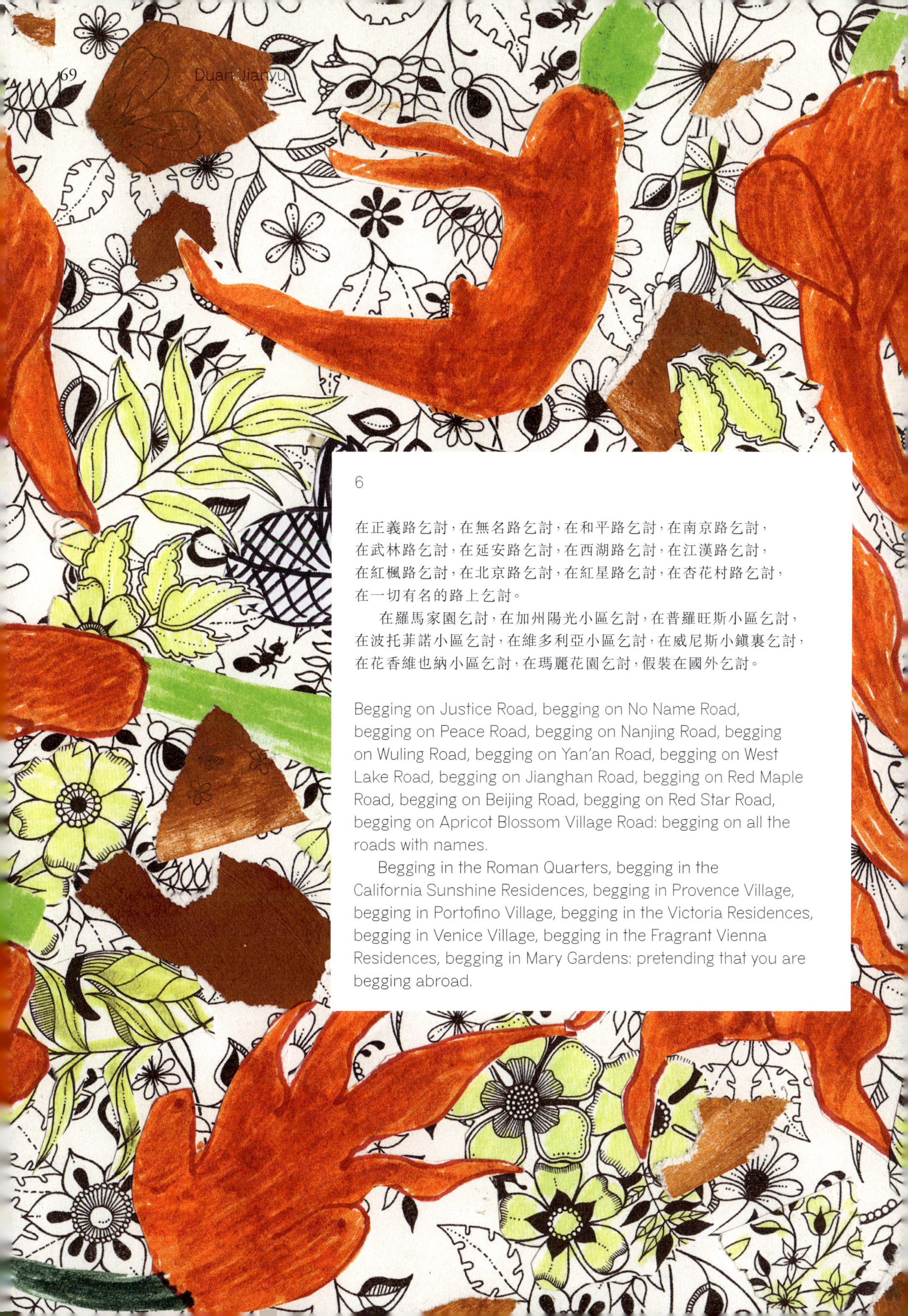

6

在正義路乞討，在無名路乞討，在和平路乞討，在南京路乞討，在武林路乞討，在延安路乞討，在西湖路乞討，在江漢路乞討，在紅楓路乞討，在北京路乞討，在紅星路乞討，在杏花村路乞討，在一切有名的路上乞討。

在羅馬家園乞討，在加州陽光小區乞討，在普羅旺斯小區乞討，在波托菲諾小區乞討，在維多利亞小區乞討，在威尼斯小鎮裏乞討，在花香維也納小區乞討，在瑪麗花園乞討，假裝在國外乞討。

Begging on Justice Road, begging on No Name Road, begging on Peace Road, begging on Nanjing Road, begging on Wuling Road, begging on Yan'an Road, begging on West Lake Road, begging on Jianghan Road, begging on Red Maple Road, begging on Beijing Road, begging on Red Star Road, begging on Apricot Blossom Village Road: begging on all the roads with names.

Begging in the Roman Quarters, begging in the California Sunshine Residences, begging in Provence Village, begging in Portofino Village, begging in the Victoria Residences, begging in Venice Village, begging in the Fragrant Vienna Residences, begging in Mary Gardens: pretending that you are begging abroad.

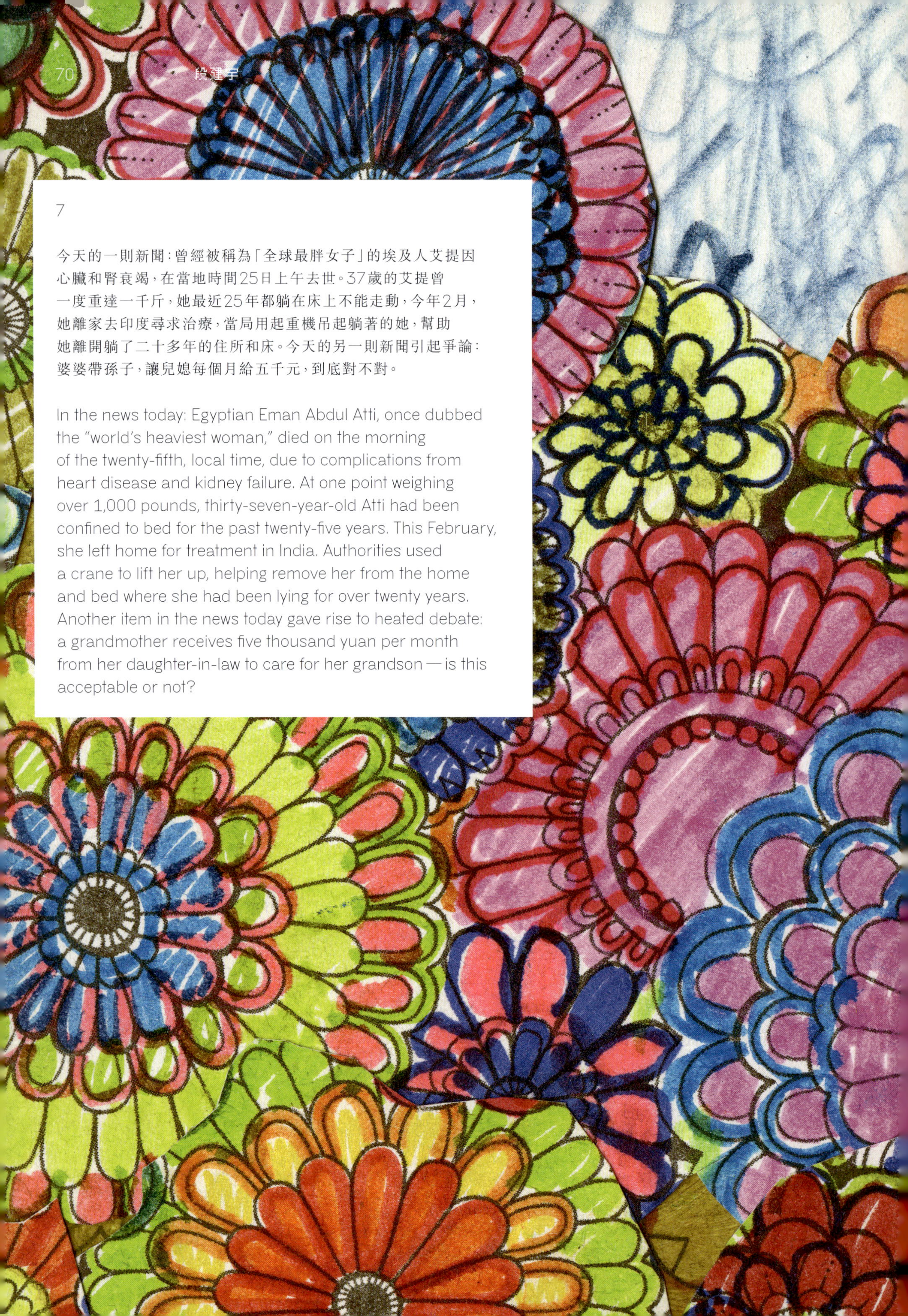

7

今天的一則新聞：曾經被稱為「全球最胖女子」的埃及人艾提因心臟和腎衰竭，在當地時間25日上午去世。37歲的艾提曾一度重達一千斤，她最近25年都躺在床上不能走動，今年2月，她離家去印度尋求治療，當局用起重機吊起躺著的她，幫助她離開躺了二十多年的住所和床。今天的另一則新聞引起爭論：婆婆帶孫子，讓兒媳每個月給五千元，到底對不對。

In the news today: Egyptian Eman Abdul Atti, once dubbed the "world's heaviest woman," died on the morning of the twenty-fifth, local time, due to complications from heart disease and kidney failure. At one point weighing over 1,000 pounds, thirty-seven-year-old Atti had been confined to bed for the past twenty-five years. This February, she left home for treatment in India. Authorities used a crane to lift her up, helping remove her from the home and bed where she had been lying for over twenty years. Another item in the news today gave rise to heated debate: a grandmother receives five thousand yuan per month from her daughter-in-law to care for her grandson — is this acceptable or not?

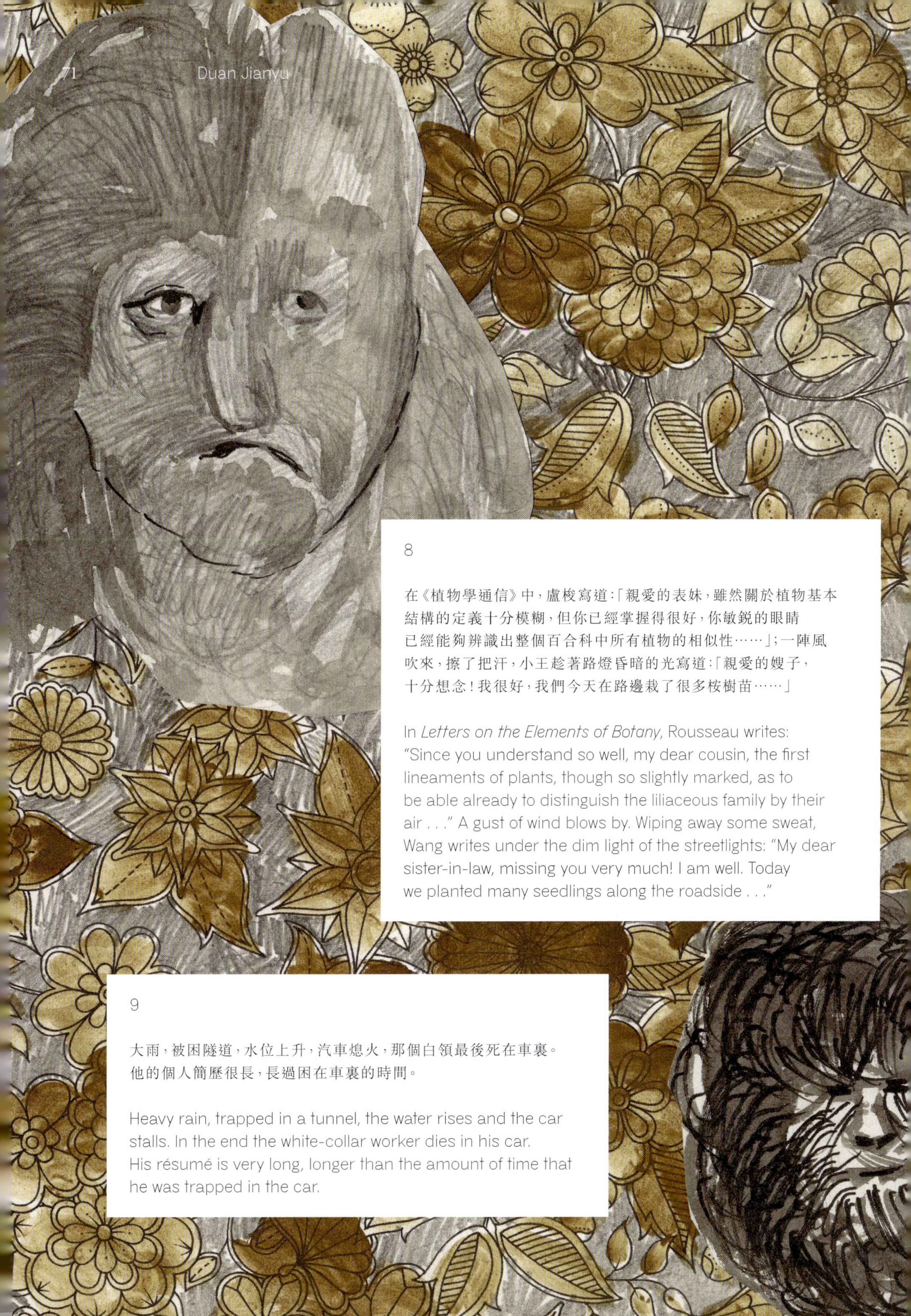

8

在《植物學通信》中，盧梭寫道：「親愛的表妹，雖然關於植物基本結構的定義十分模糊，但你已經掌握得很好，你敏銳的眼睛已經能夠辨識出整個百合科中所有植物的相似性……」；一陣風吹來，擦了把汗，小王趁著路燈昏暗的光寫道：「親愛的嫂子，十分想念！我很好，我們今天在路邊栽了很多桉樹苗……」

In *Letters on the Elements of Botany*, Rousseau writes: “Since you understand so well, my dear cousin, the first lineaments of plants, though so slightly marked, as to be able already to distinguish the liliaceous family by their air . . .” A gust of wind blows by. Wiping away some sweat, Wang writes under the dim light of the streetlights: “My dear sister-in-law, missing you very much! I am well. Today we planted many seedlings along the roadside . . .”

9

大雨，被困隧道，水位上升，汽車熄火，那個白領最後死在車裏。他的個人簡歷很長，長過困在車裏的時間。

Heavy rain, trapped in a tunnel, the water rises and the car stalls. In the end the white-collar worker dies in his car. His résumé is very long, longer than the amount of time that he was trapped in the car.

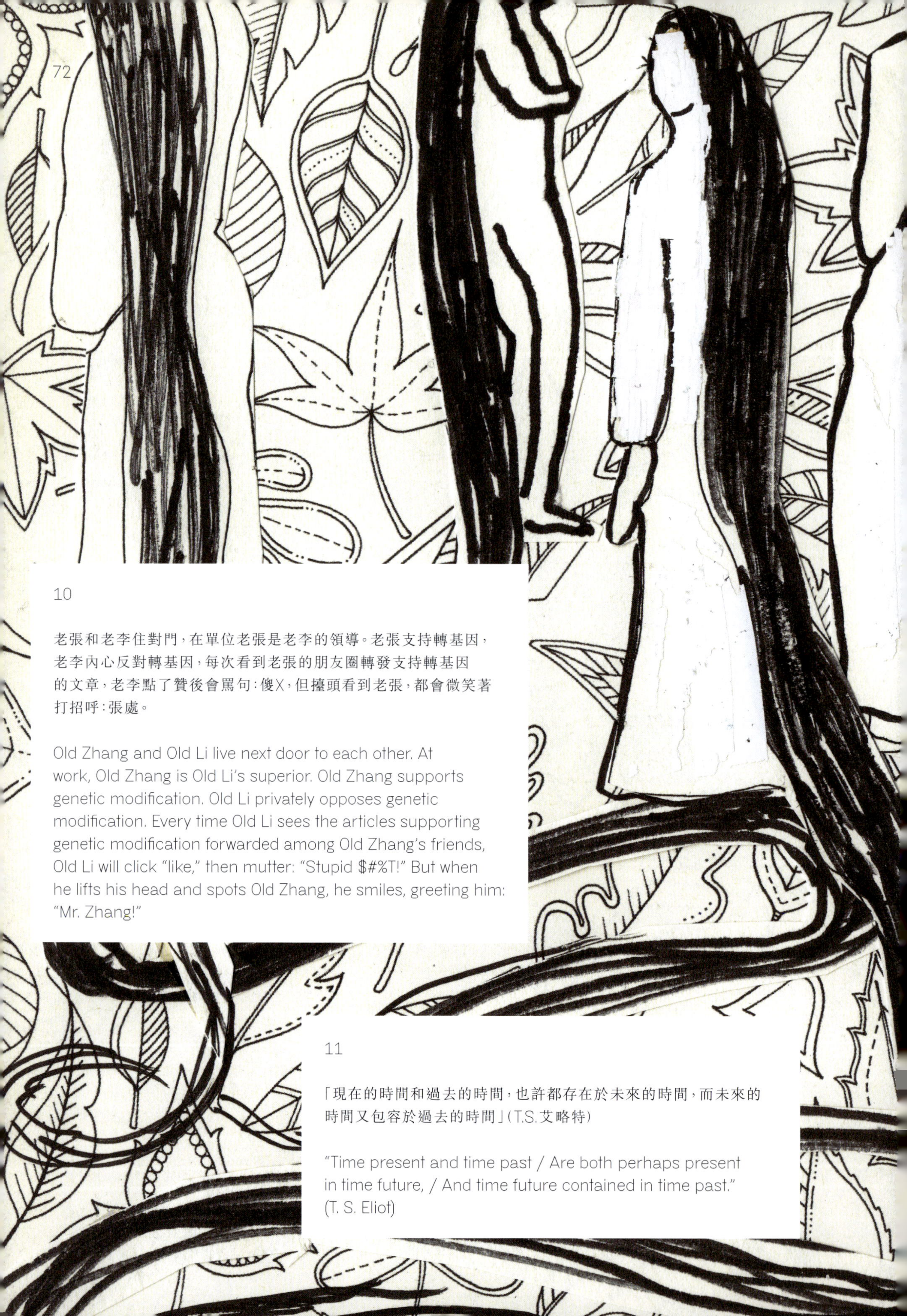

10

老張和老李住對門，在單位老張是老李的領導。老張支持轉基因，老李內心反對轉基因，每次看到老張的朋友圈轉發支持轉基因的文章，老李點了贊後會罵句：傻X，但擡頭看到老張，都會微笑著打招呼：張處。

Old Zhang and Old Li live next door to each other. At work, Old Zhang is Old Li's superior. Old Zhang supports genetic modification. Old Li privately opposes genetic modification. Every time Old Li sees the articles supporting genetic modification forwarded among Old Zhang's friends, Old Li will click "like," then mutter: "Stupid $#%T!" But when he lifts his head and spots Old Zhang, he smiles, greeting him: "Mr. Zhang!"

11

「現在的時間和過去的時間，也許都存在於未來的時間，而未來的時間又包容於過去的時間」(T.S.艾略特)

"Time present and time past / Are both perhaps present in time future, / And time future contained in time past." (T. S. Eliot)

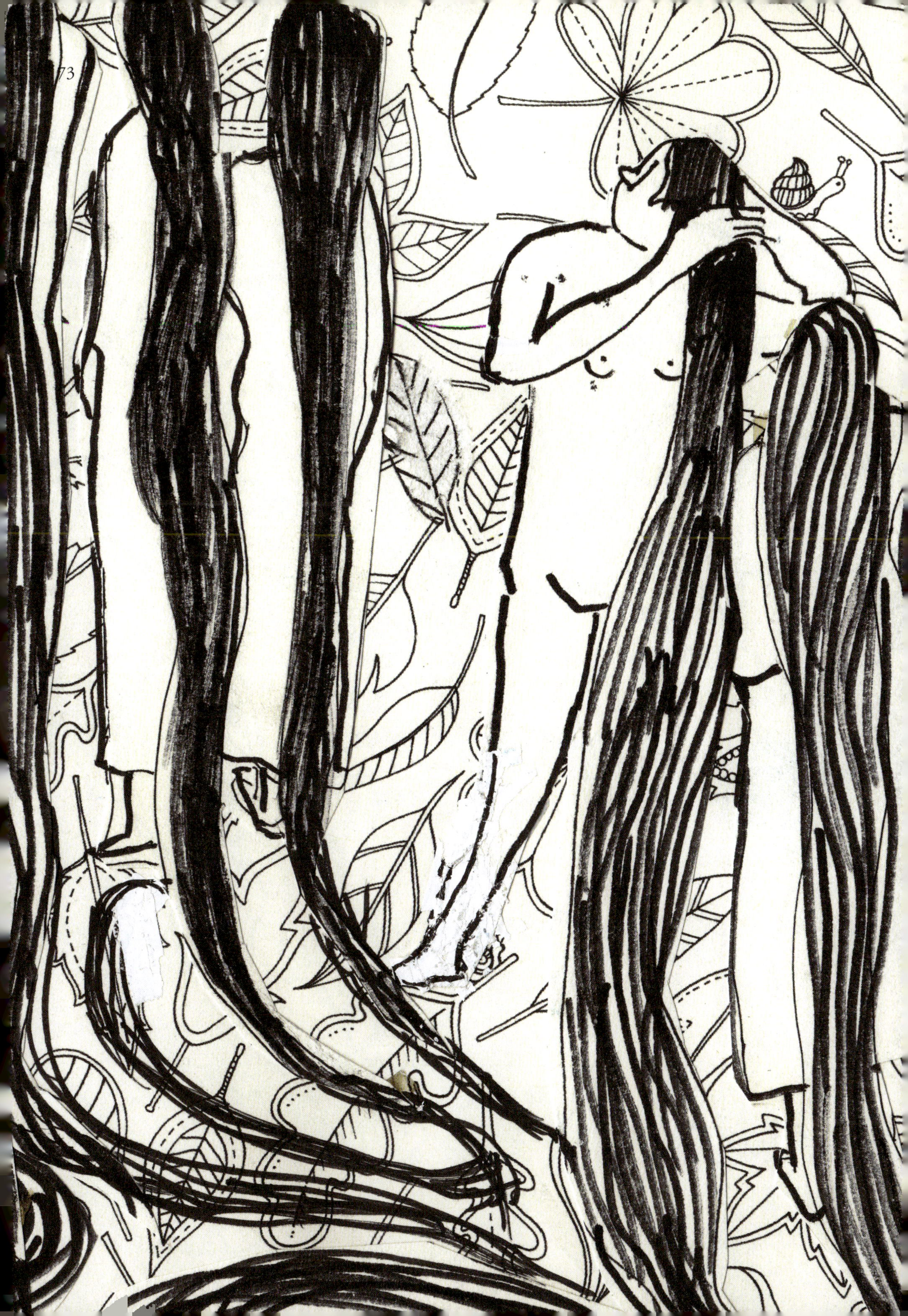

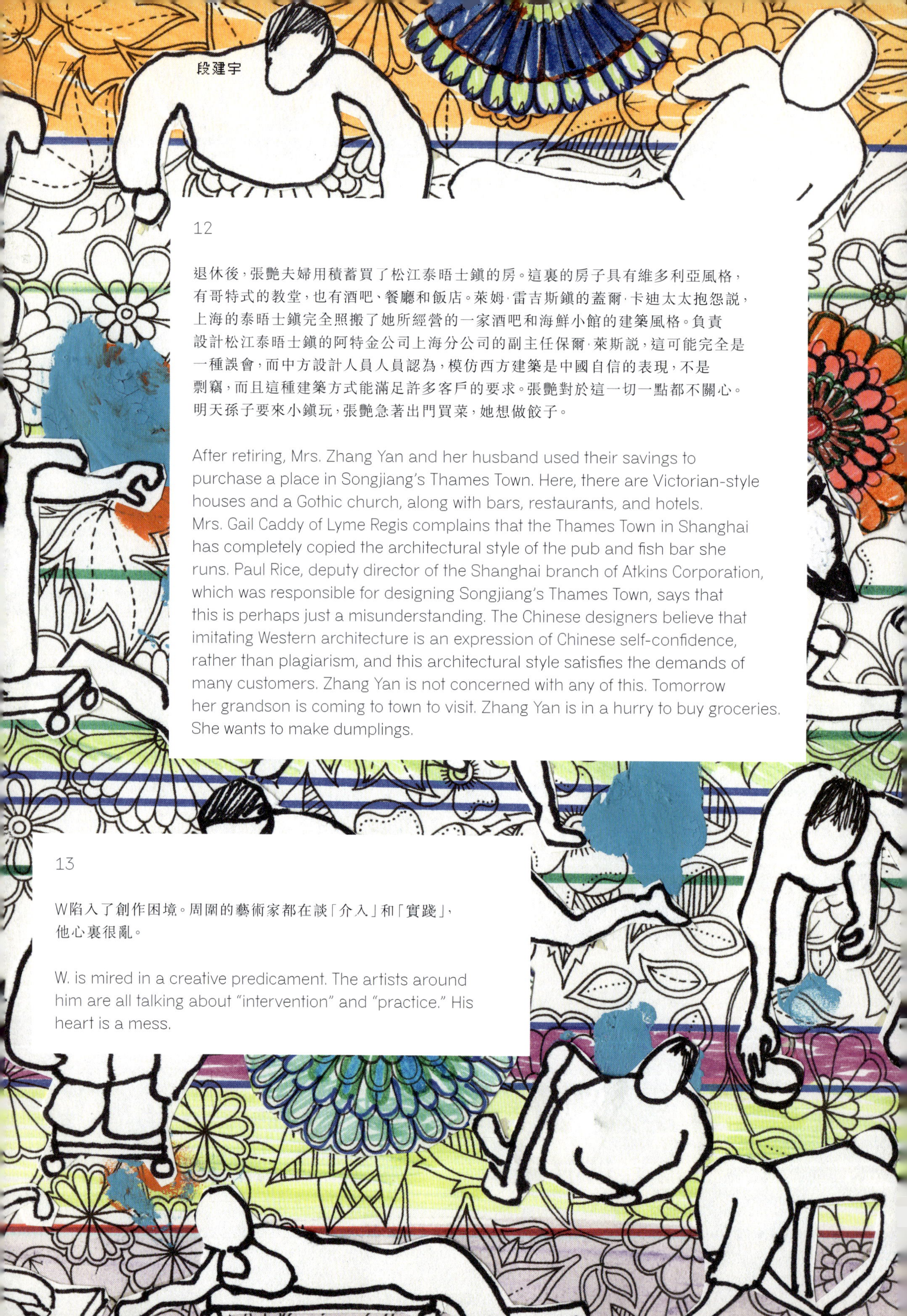

12

退休後，張艷夫婦用積蓄買了松江泰晤士鎮的房。這裏的房子具有維多利亞風格，有哥特式的教堂，也有酒吧、餐廳和飯店。萊姆·雷吉斯鎮的蓋爾·卡迪太太抱怨說，上海的泰晤士鎮完全照搬了她所經營的一家酒吧和海鮮小館的建築風格。負責設計松江泰晤士鎮的阿特金公司上海分公司的副主任保爾·萊斯說，這可能完全是一種誤會，而中方設計人員人員認為，模仿西方建築是中國自信的表現，不是剽竊，而且這種建築方式能滿足許多客戶的要求。張艷對於這一切一點都不關心。明天孫子要來小鎮玩，張艷急著出門買菜，她想做餃子。

After retiring, Mrs. Zhang Yan and her husband used their savings to purchase a place in Songjiang's Thames Town. Here, there are Victorian-style houses and a Gothic church, along with bars, restaurants, and hotels. Mrs. Gail Caddy of Lyme Regis complains that the Thames Town in Shanghai has completely copied the architectural style of the pub and fish bar she runs. Paul Rice, deputy director of the Shanghai branch of Atkins Corporation, which was responsible for designing Songjiang's Thames Town, says that this is perhaps just a misunderstanding. The Chinese designers believe that imitating Western architecture is an expression of Chinese self-confidence, rather than plagiarism, and this architectural style satisfies the demands of many customers. Zhang Yan is not concerned with any of this. Tomorrow her grandson is coming to town to visit. Zhang Yan is in a hurry to buy groceries. She wants to make dumplings.

13

W陷入了創作困境。周圍的藝術家都在談「介入」和「實踐」，他心裏很亂。

W. is mired in a creative predicament. The artists around him are all talking about "intervention" and "practice." His heart is a mess.

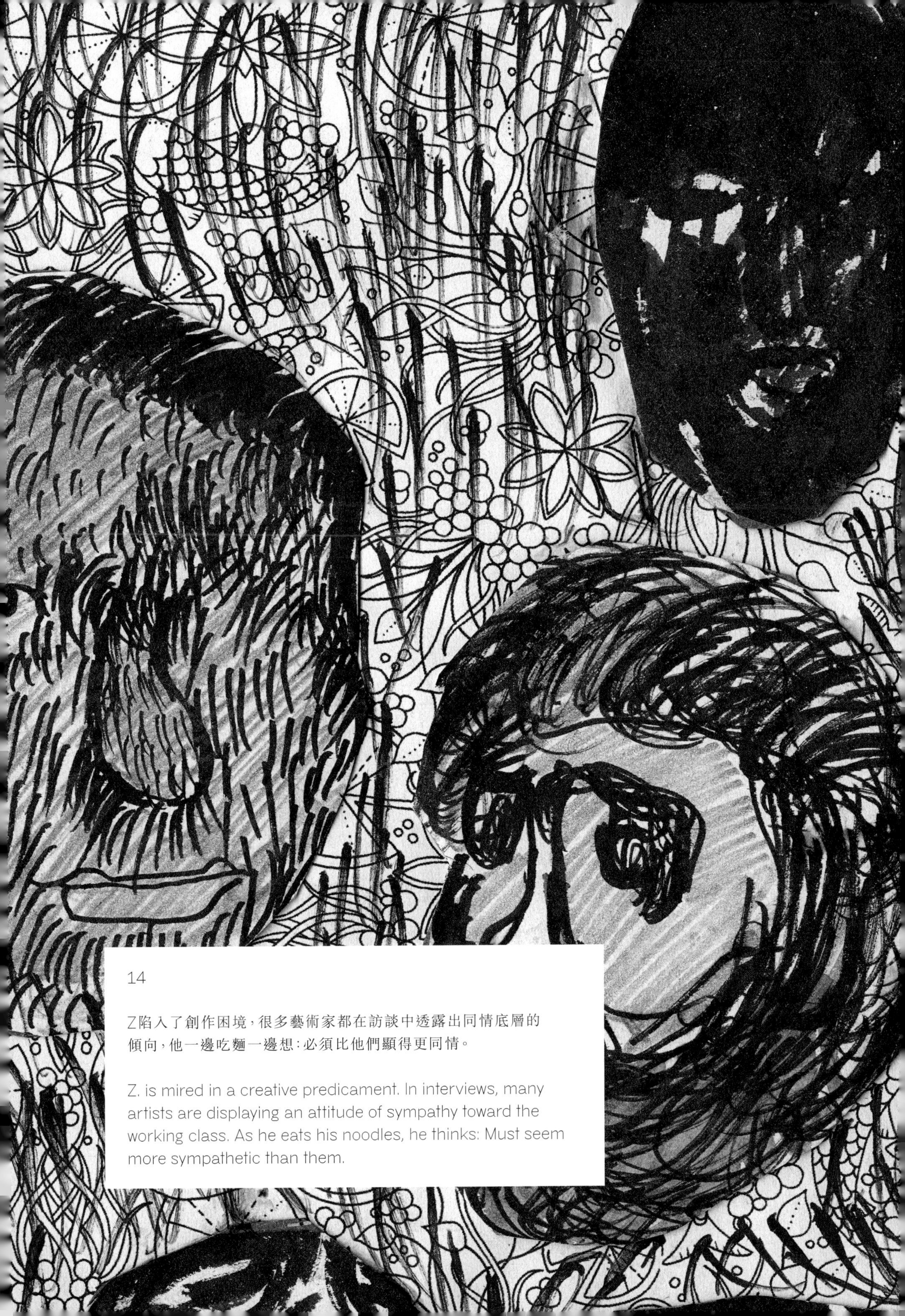

14

Z陷入了創作困境，很多藝術家都在訪談中透露出同情底層的傾向，他一邊吃麵一邊想：必須比他們顯得更同情。

Z. is mired in a creative predicament. In interviews, many artists are displaying an attitude of sympathy toward the working class. As he eats his noodles, he thinks: Must seem more sympathetic than them.

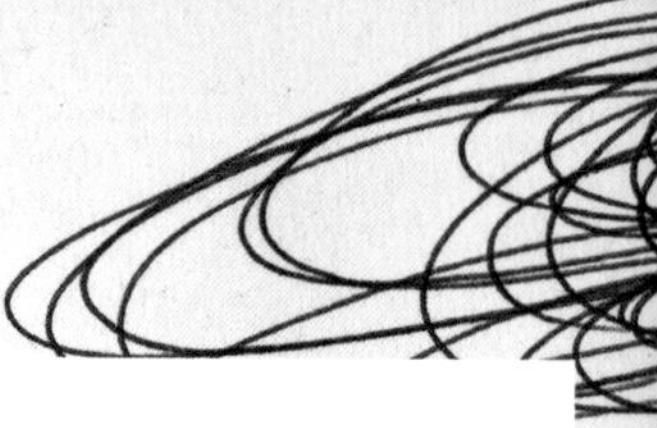

15

L陷入了困境，他昨天在微信朋友圈點了個贊，好幾個人罵他，那條微信是這樣的：福克納說，作家只需對他的藝術負責，如果他是一個優秀的作家，那他就會是完全無情的。他有一個夢想。這個夢想讓他備受折磨，他必須擺脱這個痛苦。但是在那之前，他是不會得到平靜的。為了完成寫作，榮譽、自尊、體面、安全、幸福等等一切都被拋在腦後。如果一個作家不得不搶劫自己的母親，他是不會猶豫的；一首《希臘古翁頌》比一打老婦人都來得有價值。(別人罵道：你媽他媽的很重要)

L. is mired in a predicament. Yesterday he "liked" something in a WeChat friend circle. Many people then berated him. The WeChat post went like this: Faulkner said that a writer is responsible only to his art. If he is a good one, he will be completely ruthless. He has a dream. That dream anguishes him so much that he must free himself from it. Until then, he will not have peace. Everything, such as glory, self-respect, dignity, security, and happiness, will be cast aside in service of his writing. If a writer has to rob his mother, he will not hesitate. The "Ode on a Grecian Urn" is worth more than a dozen old ladies. (Someone commented: Your mother, motherfucker, is important.)

16

一篇論文的題目《社會主義核心價值觀在精神病學教學中的功能初探》。

The subject of a dissertation: a first look at the function of socialism's core value system in the pedagogy of psychology.

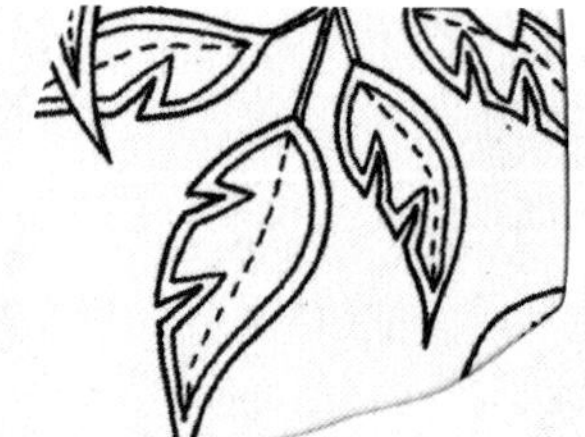

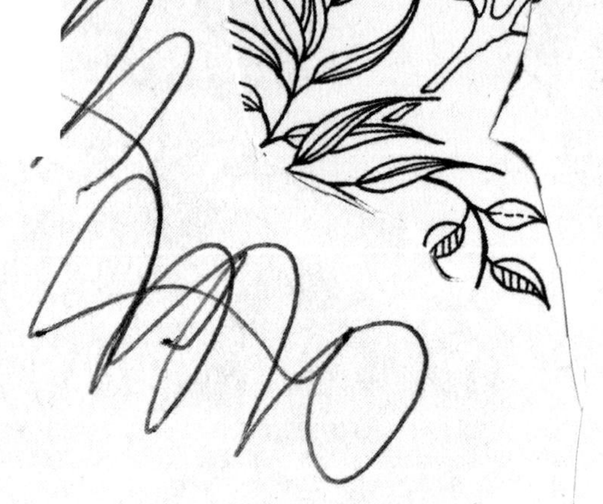

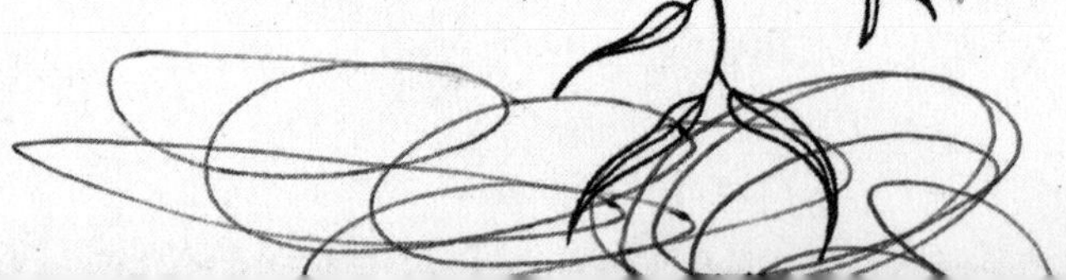

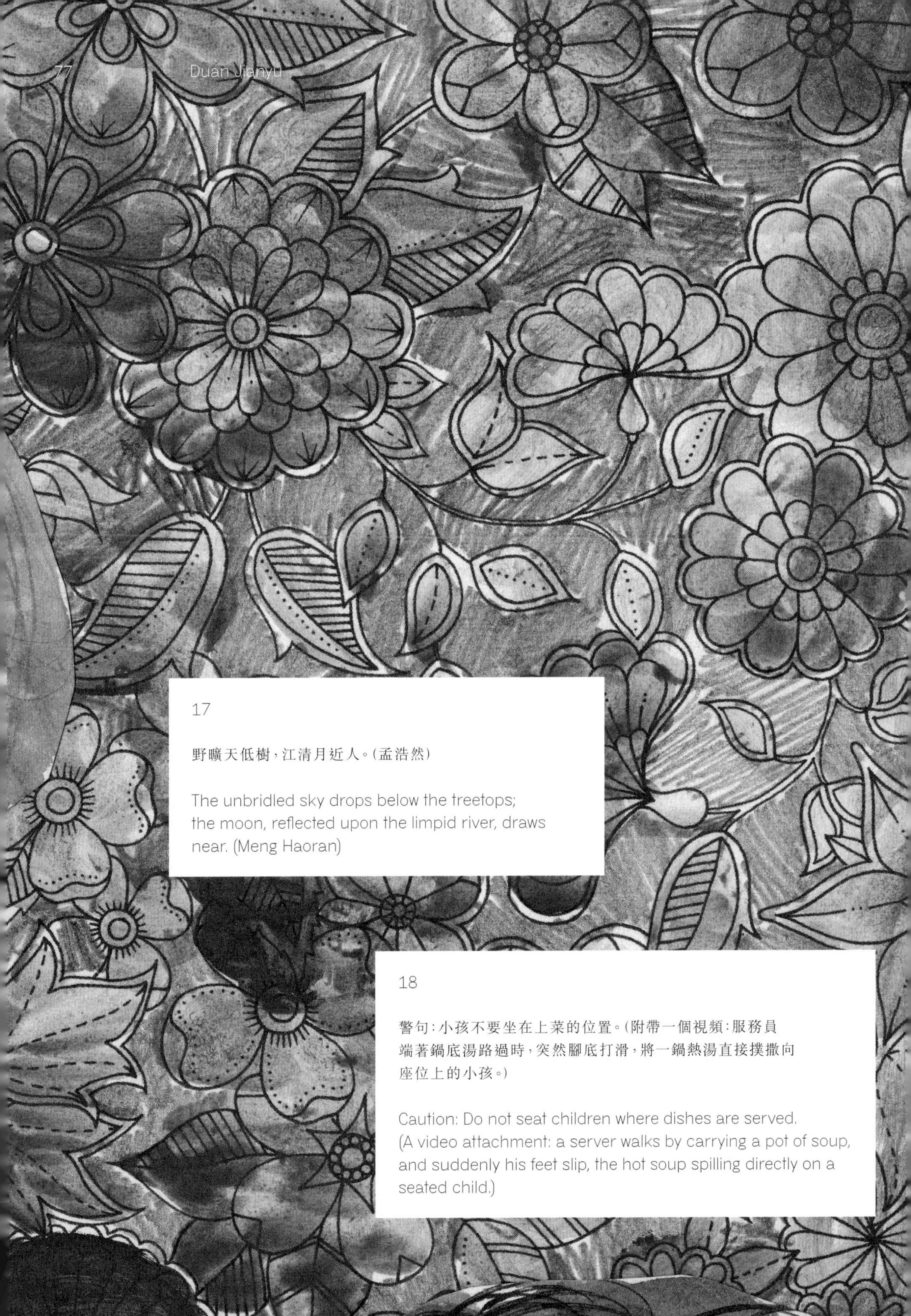

17

野曠天低樹，江清月近人。（孟浩然）

The unbridled sky drops below the treetops; the moon, reflected upon the limpid river, draws near. (Meng Haoran)

18

警句：小孩不要坐在上菜的位置。（附帶一個視頻：服務員端著鍋底湯路過時，突然腳底打滑，將一鍋熱湯直接撲撒向座位上的小孩。）

Caution: Do not seat children where dishes are served. (A video attachment: a server walks by carrying a pot of soup, and suddenly his feet slip, the hot soup spilling directly on a seated child.)

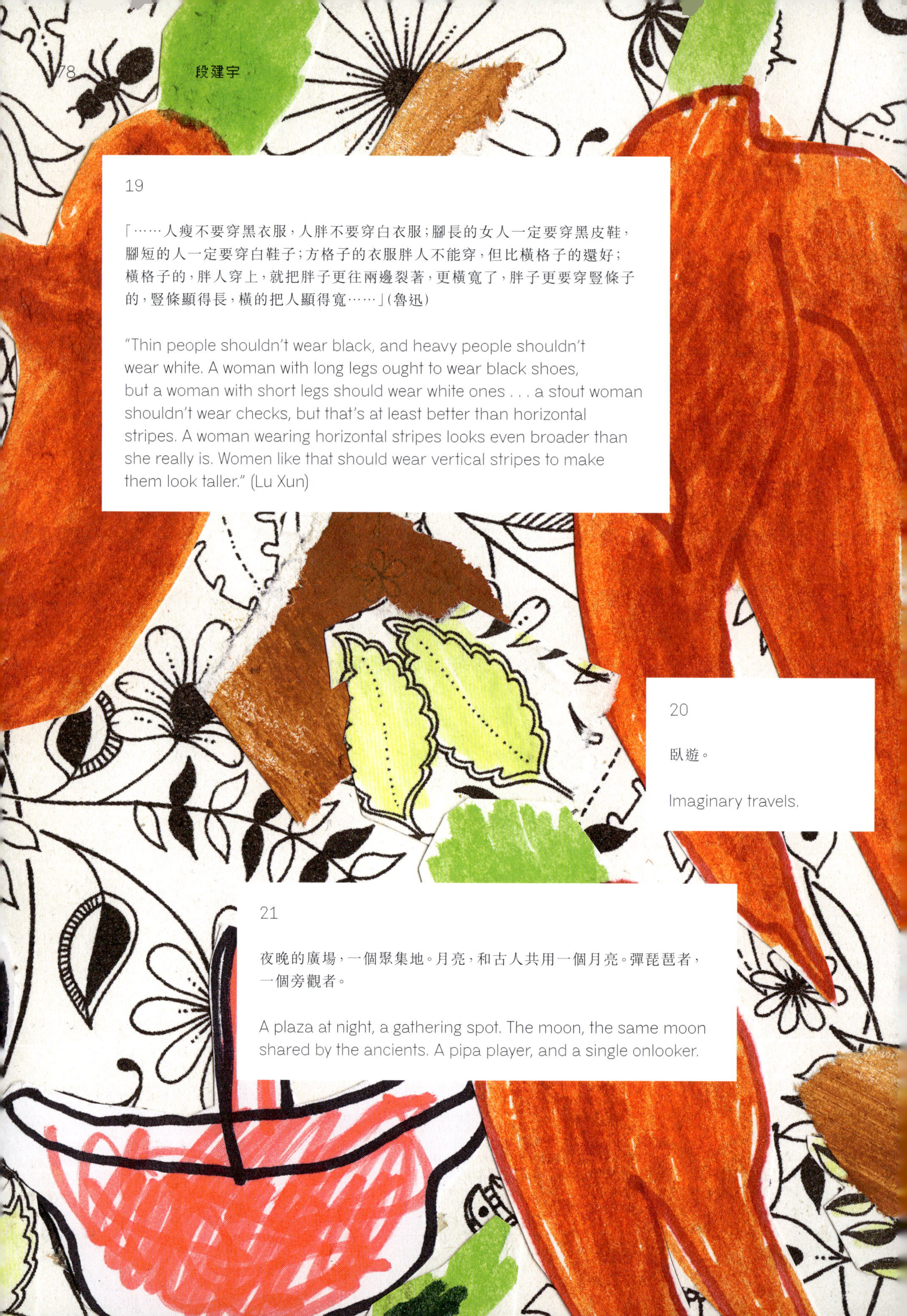

19

「……人瘦不要穿黑衣服，人胖不要穿白衣服；腳長的女人一定要穿黑皮鞋，腳短的人一定要穿白鞋子；方格子的衣服胖人不能穿，但比橫格子的還好；橫格子的，胖人穿上，就把胖子更往兩邊裂著，更橫寬了，胖子更要穿豎條子的，豎條顯得長，橫的把人顯得寬……」（魯迅）

"Thin people shouldn't wear black, and heavy people shouldn't wear white. A woman with long legs ought to wear black shoes, but a woman with short legs should wear white ones . . . a stout woman shouldn't wear checks, but that's at least better than horizontal stripes. A woman wearing horizontal stripes looks even broader than she really is. Women like that should wear vertical stripes to make them look taller." (Lu Xun)

20

臥遊。

Imaginary travels.

21

夜晚的廣場，一個聚集地。月亮，和古人共用一個月亮。彈琵琶者，一個旁觀者。

A plaza at night, a gathering spot. The moon, the same moon shared by the ancients. A pipa player, and a single onlooker.

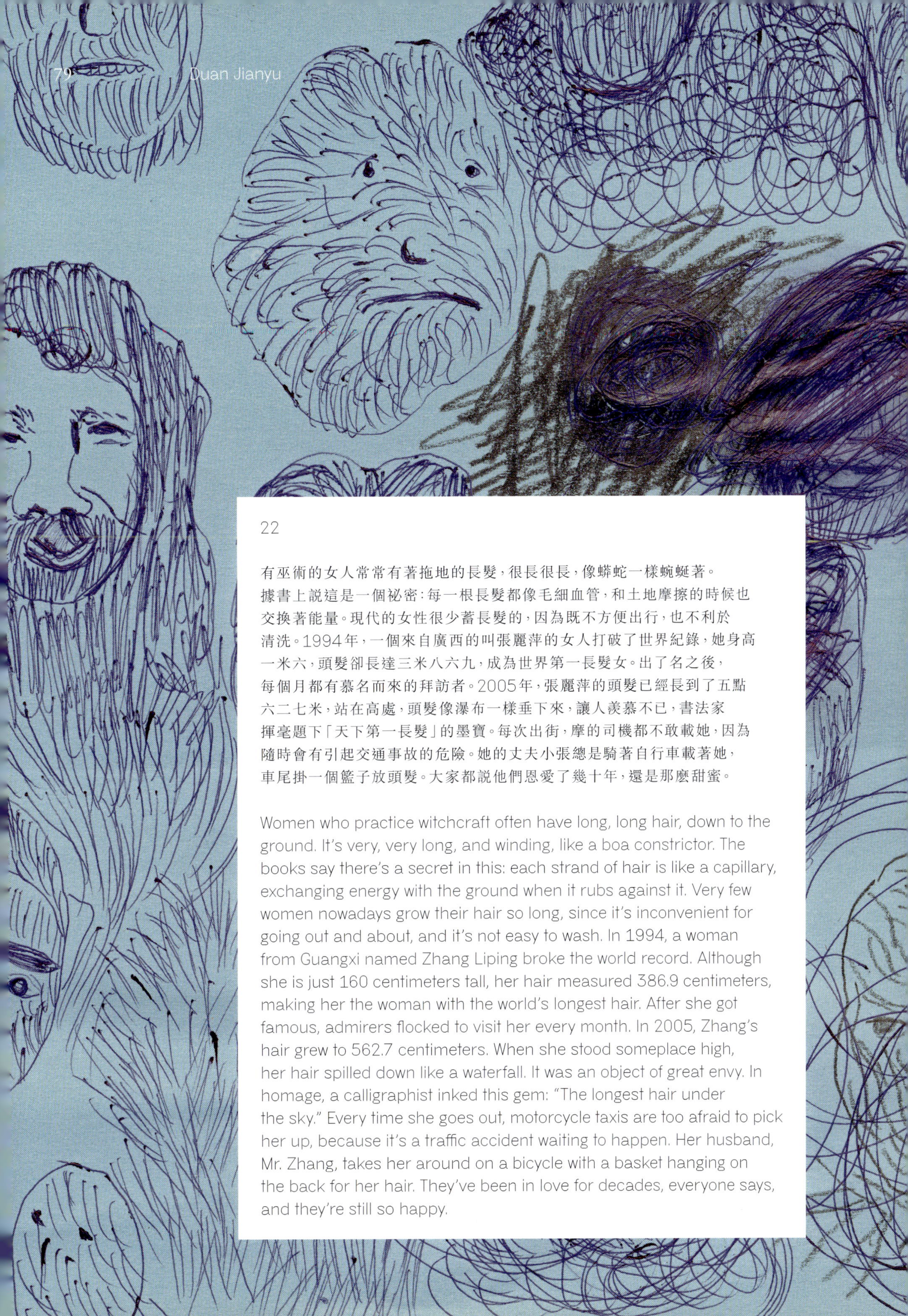

22

有巫術的女人常常有著拖地的長髮，很長很長，像蟒蛇一樣蜿蜒著。據書上說這是一個祕密：每一根長髮都像毛細血管，和土地摩擦的時候也交換著能量。現代的女性很少蓄長髮的，因為既不方便出行，也不利於清洗。1994年，一個來自廣西的叫張麗萍的女人打破了世界紀錄，她身高一米六，頭髮卻長達三米八六九，成為世界第一長髮女。出了名之後，每個月都有慕名而來的拜訪者。2005年，張麗萍的頭髮已經長到了五點六二七米，站在高處，頭髮像瀑布一樣垂下來，讓人羨慕不已，書法家揮毫題下「天下第一長髮」的墨寶。每次出街，摩的司機都不敢載她，因為隨時會有引起交通事故的危險。她的丈夫小張總是騎著自行車載著她，車尾掛一個籃子放頭髮。大家都說他們恩愛了幾十年，還是那麼甜蜜。

Women who practice witchcraft often have long, long hair, down to the ground. It's very, very long, and winding, like a boa constrictor. The books say there's a secret in this: each strand of hair is like a capillary, exchanging energy with the ground when it rubs against it. Very few women nowadays grow their hair so long, since it's inconvenient for going out and about, and it's not easy to wash. In 1994, a woman from Guangxi named Zhang Liping broke the world record. Although she is just 160 centimeters tall, her hair measured 386.9 centimeters, making her the woman with the world's longest hair. After she got famous, admirers flocked to visit her every month. In 2005, Zhang's hair grew to 562.7 centimeters. When she stood someplace high, her hair spilled down like a waterfall. It was an object of great envy. In homage, a calligraphist inked this gem: "The longest hair under the sky." Every time she goes out, motorcycle taxis are too afraid to pick her up, because it's a traffic accident waiting to happen. Her husband, Mr. Zhang, takes her around on a bicycle with a basket hanging on the back for her hair. They've been in love for decades, everyone says, and they're still so happy.

烏青
Wu Qing

Translated by Lucas Klein

父親說為什麼要聽音樂
我說我要陶冶情操
父親說陶個屁
我已經哭了
說我一定要陶

I Want to Buy an 800-Yuan Walkman

I woke up this morning
wanting to buy an 800-yuan Walkman
and also to call my father
A couple years ago
I said to him
Dad I want to buy a Walkman
He said What do you want to buy that for
I said To listen to music
He said What you want to listen to music for
I said So I can forge my character
He said Forge my ass
By that time I was crying
and said But I must forge

我想買一個800多元的隨身聽

今天醒來
我想買一個800多元的隨身聽
我還想給我的父親打個電話
一些年以前
我對父親說
爸爸我想買個隨身聽
父親說為什麼要買隨身聽
我說聽音樂

Before the Invention of the Washing Machine // The Hardworking Chinese Women

Before the invention of the washing machine
hardworking Chinese women
washed their laundry outside the home
by the river, by the stream, by the well
in the sunlight, washing together
they would pound the laundry with clubs
bang and *clang* peppered with laughter
Other times, hardworking Chinese women
would use wood basins and washboards
alone in their rooms
scrubbing in silence
tears dripping down

在發明洗衣機之前//勤勞的中國婦女

在發明洗衣機之前勤勞的中國婦女
她們在家以外的地方洗衣裳
她們在河邊，溪邊，井邊
在陽光下，一起洗衣服
她們使用棒槌紛紛敲打衣裳
霹哩啪拉，夾雜著歡笑聲
另外一些時候，勤勞的中國婦女
她一個人在房間裏
用木盆和搓衣板
默默地搓洗衣裳
眼淚咚咚滴

We're So Dark and Dense

We're not locusts
or sparrows
But still, thinking of that year
we're still so
dark and dense
Often we go by
darkly and densely
and darkly and densely come back
Little kids see us
and scream and shout
Mom, what is that?
We're not anything
We're just a dark and a dense
swarm

My Aunt's Death

Summer last year
my aunt was diagnosed with
late-stage lung cancer
When I went to see her
she was sitting on the floor
leaning over a chair coughing
thin and lean
no energy left even for spitting
In a low voice she said just one thing
"Grab some fruit"
I said "Okay"
and had a banana
then another banana
then I left
Not a month later
my aunt died
We went to the crematorium
where my aunt's body was laid out
We had boxed lunches
with canned winter melon tea
and then some pieces of candy
In the evening
my aunt's body was pushed inside
Not far from the crematorium was the sea
so when I got tired of waiting
I went to the sea

What Can We Do

I made a phone call, to Zhang Jianhua
but it was his mother
who answered
I asked: Is Zhang Jianhua there
His mother said, Yeah, he's taking a dump
I said, A dump eh
His mother said Yeah
I said to Zhang Jianhua's mother
Well then what can we do?

我們黑壓壓的

我們不是蝗蟲
也不是麻雀
但是，想當年啊
我們同樣是
黑壓壓的
我們經常
黑壓壓地過去
黑壓壓地回
小孩子看到我們
就會驚聲叫道
媽媽，那是什麼？
我們不是什麼
我們就是黑壓壓的
一片

小姨之死

去年夏天
我的小姨被查出得了
肺癌晚期
我去看她
她坐在地上
趴著凳子咳
瘦得很幹淨
吐痰的力氣都沒有了
她只低聲對我說了一句
「水果拿去吃」
我說「奧」
就吃了一根香蕉
接著又吃了一根香蕉
然後走了
不到一個月
小姨便死了
我們去了火葬場
小姨的屍體擺在那兒
中午我們吃盒飯
喝聽裝的冬瓜茶
後來我們還吃了幾顆糖
傍晚
小姨的屍體被推進去了
火葬場的不遠處是海邊
由於等待的無聊
我就一個人去了海邊

怎麼辦

我打電話，給張建華
接電話的是
他母親
我問：張建華在嗎
他母親說，在、在大便
我說，在大便啊
他母親說是的
我對張建華的母親說
那怎麼辦呢？

Praising White Clouds

The white clouds in the sky are really white
really, really very white
so white
so really very white
extremely white
damn white
I'm dying they're so white
wow —

Father and His Brothers

At evening, Father would say, Come,
Brothers, so
Father tossed me
and Second Uncle caught me
Second Uncle tossed me
and Third Uncle caught me
Third Uncle tossed me
and Little Uncle caught me
Little Uncle tossed me
and my father caught me
This was a common activity of theirs
at once a workout
and a way to bond
Until one day
I found I couldn't toss you anymore
Father said

對白雲的贊美

天上的白雲眞白啊
眞的，很白很白
非常白
非常非常十分白
極其白
賊白
簡直白死了
啊——

父親和他的兄弟們

傍晚，父親說，兄弟們
來一個，於是
我父親把我拋出去
我二叔把我接住
我二叔把我拋出去
我三叔把我接住
我三叔把我拋出去
我小叔把我接住
我小叔把我拋出去
我父親把我接住
這是他們的一項常規活動
既鍛煉了身體
又增進了情感
直到有一天
我發現拋不動你了
父親說

黃炳
Wong Ping

《親，需要服務嗎？》的旅行日記和概念手稿，文字由黃炳撰寫，2018
Travel notes and concept drawings for *Dear, can I give you a hand?*, 2018. Translated by Alvin Li

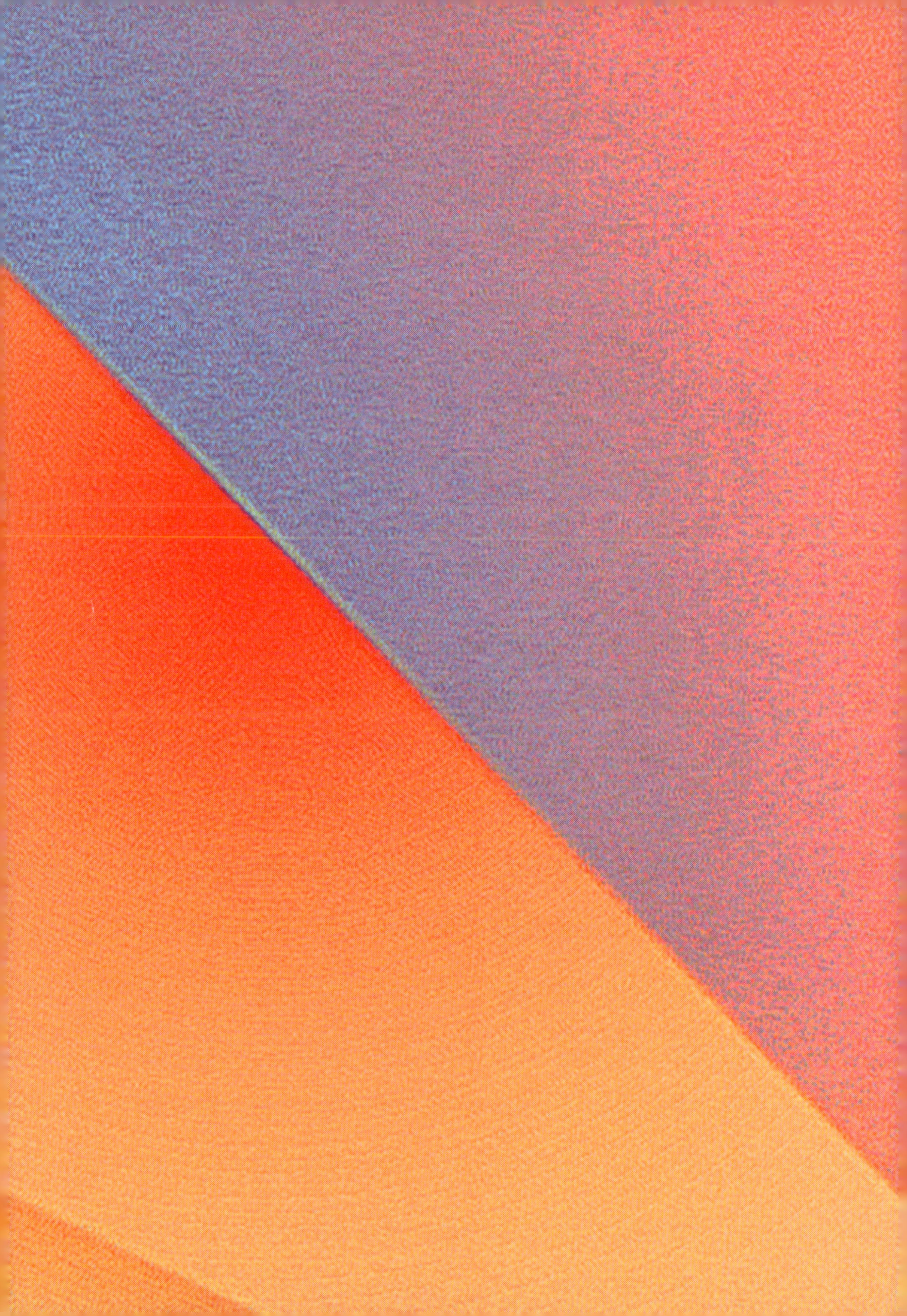

JUL 3

Thank you for your notes. Some years ago I had thought about writing a fantasy story, as I'm a big fan of Edogawa Ranpo's works.

For various reasons, I have become more concerned with elderly people in Hong Kong. There are more and more old people collecting garbage on the streets, walking back and forth pushing trash and paper scraps. Sometimes you'll see two grannies fighting over a scrap that's barely worth a dollar. They are like the fish that live off excrement and other refuse at the bottom of the tank.

Many of the young adults living with their parents and grandparents face problems sharing space. When I go to visit elderly relatives in nursing homes and am immersed in that inhumane environment and morbid atmosphere, I find it both terrifying and sad.

Following cremation, finding a place to inter the ashes can take over two years. Space is seriously crowded even after death, so price speculation over shrine plots has become common. Recently people have started promoting the idea of online tomb sweeping. The absurd almost seems practical. In the face of all this, people get discouraged about living long lives.

One afternoon a month ago, I was passing through a small park on my bicycle when I saw an old man carry a bag of objects to the recycling bin and dump them in. Just as the lid closed, I saw that he had stuffed the recycling bin full of pornographic VHS tapes. I turned around to see the man walking away dejectedly, and then, upon opening the bin to find several boxes of porn videos in perfect condition, without any yellowing in their pristine plastic packaging and covers, I realized that although VHS technology went obsolete long ago, he had been holding on to the tapes until that very day. Observing the past few years, I feel that average elderly people are suddenly being made obsolete faster

JUL 3

謝謝你的補充，早些年前有想過寫奇幻故事，因為十分喜歡江戶川亂步的作品。

最近因為種種原因，對存在於香港的老人家較為上心，街上收集垃圾紙皮、推來推去的老人越來越多，有時更看到兩個老婆婆為爭一塊紙皮打架，而那可能只值不夠一塊錢港幣，他們就好像那種專門吃排泄物和垃圾細菌而活的缸底魚一樣。

眾多年青人和上一代甚至乎上兩代共住的空間問題，又或是探望老人院時，被那種沒有人性的環境和等待死亡的氣氛包圍著我，很恐怖但又很難過。

就算火化後輪候安置骨灰龕大約都要兩年以上，死後空間都是嚴重擠迫，所以骨灰龕一直都炒賣成風，最近亦有提出上網掃墓，荒謬得來亦覺實用。面對種種都令人有不想活得長的想法。

月前的一個下午，我踏單車經過一個小公園，看見一個老伯伯拿著一大袋雜物放到環保回收箱中，剛巧經過看到回收箱的小門關上那一刻，裏面原來被他塞滿了色情錄影帶VHS Tape，我回頭看他垂頭喪氣地離開，我去打開回收箱的門，一盒盒保存得十分完美的色情錄影帶，那些精美的膠片包裝和封面一點都沒有發黃，知道VHS這科技早就被淘汰，他卻等到這一天才放手，而觀看這數年，基層的老人好像突然更快地被這城市淘汰到邊緣。為此寫下了一段小故事，想從此發展出一個荒誕的靈異故事。

than ever by a city that pushes them to the margins. For this reason, I wrote a short story, wanting to develop a fantastic supernatural tale that departs from this point.

Dear, can I give you a hand?

Ever since my son got married a few years ago and his wife moved into our home, they started bugging me to get rid of my junk, to make room for my daughter-in-law to live more comfortably. On the whole, I had no attachment to many of the things. I've always thought of memory as a sort of feeling, and it's fine if it just stays in your head. Wouldn't the dirty pictures you took with your ex leave a bad aftertaste now? So I listened to what they told me and threw out most of the stuff.

Recently, after my daughter-in-law got pregnant, they urged me to go through the remaining things and clean them all up bit by bit. At first this was a happy occasion, but there was nothing more for me to throw out, and so we started to argue. That made me terribly sad. My son angrily stormed into my tiny room and grabbed the old VHS player from under my bed, ready to throw it out. I held on to the door with all my might, and it was only when I looked as though I would faint from anger that he gave up.

The machine had been with me for more than twenty years. When making room previously, I had thought long and hard before deciding to keep it, throwing out some relics and keepsakes of my wife instead. When my wife passed away, the first thing I did was buy the player and bring it home. Back then there were no VCDs or DVDs; only videocassettes were widely available. In fact, I had wanted to try out this new technology early on, but unfortunately my wife's medical expenses were prohibitive. All we could do was save money. Sometimes, unable to bear it, I would still buy porn videos to add to my collection, hoping in my heart that one day I'd be doing well enough to afford the video player to watch them.

《親,需要服務嗎?》

自從幾年前兒子婚後和媳婦搬進來以後,家人就開始逼我拋棄我的雜物,騰出空間,好讓媳婦住得舒適。基本上很多雜物我都不會留戀,始終認為回憶是感覺,留在腦中就好了,你和前度的床上情慾淫照,又何曾拿出來回味過?所以我都聽聽話話地丟掉大部分東西。

最近家人又催促我把餘下的都逐一清理,因為媳婦懷孕了。本來是高興事,但我的東西真的不能再丟了,為此我們吵了一場,十分傷心。兒子衝進我細小的房間,在床下拉出一台舊式VHS錄影機,隨手就想拋掉,我用老命頂著房門搶過來,一時動氣差點暈倒他們才肯罷休。

這台錄影機伴著我廿十多年,之前為了騰出空間,想了很久才決定保留它而拋掉老婆的一些遺物和紀念品。當年老婆過身,第一件事就是把它買回家。那年代沒有什麼VCD呀,DVD呀,就只流行錄影帶。其實我一早就想試這個新科技,可惜老婆的醫療費用並不便宜,唯有一直省錢儲錢,有時候忍不住,會先買一些色情錄影帶作收藏,心想總有一天能發達買台錄影機來播放。還記得葬禮結束後,發現收到的帛金很多,扣除開支,餘下的我就拿去買了這台錄影機。因為那段時間一直照顧不能交合的病妻,到終於能實現願望播放那堆錄影帶時,我連續用它自瀆了兩星期。還記得第一次安坐家中,從視覺上得到肉體互相蠕動摩擦,愛液溫柔彼此交換的畫面,回放,慢鏡,快播等種種觀賞經驗,是何等新鮮刺激。那刻神佛都不能令我感恩,科技才能平撫我。

老實說,錄影機近年經已退役,長時間封印在我床下。一來是因為它被時代淘汰,難以接駁現代的電視。

I still remember how, when I discovered all the gift money after the funeral was over, I deducted the expenses and took the remainder to buy the video player. I had spent the whole time taking care of a sick wife who couldn't have sex, so once I finally fulfilled my dream of playing the videos, I used them to masturbate for two weeks straight. I remember the first time sitting contentedly at home, able to see with my own eyes the flesh wriggling and rubbing together, the love juices and tenderness being exchanged on the screen, while making use of instant replay, slow motion, fast forward, and all the other special viewing experiences. What a fresh stimulus it was! In that moment, not even all the gods and Buddhas could have taught me grace, only science and technology could soothe me.

To tell the truth, the video player has been retired for the past few years, sealed for a long time under my bed. One reason is that it's been made obsolete by the times: it's not compatible with modern televisions. But the main reason is because of my son's wife. After they got married, the pair moved in with me to save money, and my daughter-in-law is a freelancer who manages her Taobao online apparel shop from home every day. She has the hot blood of youth, and looks delicious: I wonder how could my son possibly be a good match for her? Since she moved in, I especially treasure the time before my son gets off work every day, because only the two of us are at home. The house is small, so she's forced to endlessly change clothes in the living room, snapping selfies and uploading the photos to her website. Sometimes for convenience and speed she wears no underwear as she tries on the clothes. So I also made it my habit to read in the living room more frequently, peeking out of the corner of my eye as I flip between pages, secretly waiting to catch a glimpse of her bouncy, half-exposed breasts.

I've actually seen similar plots in porn videos: they can be about old dudes

最主要原因卻是因為我的媳婦。婚後他們為了省錢搬來一起住，媳婦是自由工作者，每天在家經營自己的淘寶時裝店，她年青熱血，看起來美味可口，奇怪兒子怎配得上她。之後我每天都特別珍惜兒子下班前的時光，因為就只有我跟媳婦兩個在家。家裏小，她只好在客廳不停換裝自拍，再上傳到自己的網店，有時候求方便快捷，她都不會穿內衣去試裝，我亦習慣地更常坐在客廳看書，在翻頁之間用餘光去偷看她側身露出那半顆有彈性的乳房。

事實上我從色情錄影帶中早看過類似劇情，老爺與寂寞媳婦，又或是女朋友之母等家庭倫理片，但奇怪片中大多自自然然便從家中日常生活情節發展到做愛環節，在現實中卻從未發生過在我身上。雖然同住，但每天說話不到十句，色誘媳婦看來比影片中的示範難很多。我試過學片中橋段，借意打探她的經濟狀況，看看能否用金錢做點交易，可惜她早成為網紅網店大賣了，我的養老金根本付不起。又試過午飯時裝作不適嘔吐全身，期望她幫我抹身時的撫慰，可惜她沒有理會，後來她更嫌麻煩，請了一位男看護照顧我。

我不希望男看護介入我們之間競爭，只好離家流連於附近公園，那些地方總是坐滿無所事事的老人，我憎死那陣老人味。鳥語花香混雜著各人家庭問題是非對錯的討論噪音外，還會有很多中年以上的大嬸兜售服務，一次口交大約五十元，做愛要二百元。有一次我忍不住提醒她們收費比例的錯配，我認為口交收費應該要比做愛貴，嘴唇的吸啜一定比較爽，始終這把年紀，陰部肌肉定必易放難收，大家老人家，了解的。她們接納我的提議，結果生意好起來，慕名而來的人越來越多，她們想要向我報恩，但被我拒絕了。我腦中只煩惱著如何甩掉男看護，重投我與媳婦的二人世界。

有一晚，尿頻起床去廁所時聽見兒子跟媳婦在做愛，我很不高興的站在門外聽了四分鐘，他們便做完了，才四分鐘？好媳婦怎可能得到滿足呢？我兒子究竟怎配得上她呢？之後每晚我都失眠，在床上總是在留心著任何聲音，做假的呻吟聲，刻意的氣喘聲，刺耳的床褥彈簧聲，濕潤的吸啜聲，有節奏的玩具摩打聲，禪淨的手鏈珠碰撞聲等。有一次聽漏了，發現錯過旁聽的機會，因為早上我在洗衣籃裏發現媳婦濕濕的內褲，靠近聞一下，結果如我所料，內褲上沾滿了造假的潤滑劑。縱使是潤滑劑，我也決定把內褲收藏起來，等潤滑劑乾了，希望媳婦的味道會再一次湧出來。

第二天，我去老人社區中心報名參加電腦應用課程，導師對老人家很有耐性，我請他幫我在淘寶開個戶口，學會了購物。於是每當我把媳婦做完愛的內褲藏起後，便在她的網店向她購買同款內褲放回洗衣籃。每當她在網上對作為客戶的我說：「親，你好，需要什麼嗎？」，那種親上加親的感覺，總令我有力量活下去。

媳婦懷孕後，他們似乎不再做愛，我終於能放鬆入睡。孫女快要出世，兒子再一次要求我清理雜物，如今終於要和它們做個了斷，我爬高拿出藏在暗角熟識的色情錄影帶，膠盒都沒半點發黃污跡，來自日本的印刷包裝依然精美，我將老朋友一盒一盒的放到黑色大膠袋裏，走到垃圾房的每一步如巨石般重。放手那刻感覺很漫長，大膠袋像慢鏡般向下跌入垃圾桶的黑洞，賣仔勿摸頭，轉身便急步離去，邊走才發現雙手已不受控地抖震，眼淚熱呼呼地滾出來，我恨被新時代追殺，我恨我的家人，我恨我的子孫。

「伯伯，伯伯……」突然有把聲音從後把我叫住，我滿面淚光轉身，一位有朝氣的年青人拿著十秒前才被我狠心拋棄的黑膠袋追上來。

and their lonely daughters-in-law, or morality-themed situations that involve the girlfriend's mother. What's strange about these videos is how often these routine, everyday scenarios casually evolve into sex scenes, even though this has never happened to me in reality. Although we live together, my daughter-in-law and I never speak more than ten sentences per day to each other, and it certainly feels far more difficult to seduce her than how it's suggested in the videos. I tried replicating scenes from the videos, and also inquired about her financial situation to explore whether offering money to make a deal could be the solution; unfortunately, she already owned a hot online shop, and there was no way I could afford her with my savings. Then I tried pretending to get sick and throw up on myself during lunch, hoping she would help me clean my body, but she paid me hardly any attention. Growing more impatient, she soon hired a male caretaker for me.

Not wanting the male caretaker to come between us, I had to leave home and wander around the nearby park that was always filled with old people with nothing to do. I hated the smell of those old people. Aside from the birds, the scent of the flowers, and the family quarrels, there were also these middle-aged aunties selling blow jobs for around 50 HKD, and sex for 200 HKD. One day, I couldn't help but tell them how off their pricing was. A blow job should be more expensive than sex: getting sucked off would be the more pleasurable, because at that age a woman's pelvic muscles are only getting looser. I'm an old person too; I get it. They took my advice, and their business quickly took off. As more and more people flocked to them, the aunties wanted to return the favor, but I turned them down. All I could think about was how to get rid of the male caretaker so that I could return to the twosome of my daughter-in-law and me.

One night when I got up to go to the bathroom, I heard my son having sex with his wife. I was quite upset, so I stood outside the door and listened. They were done in just four minutes. Only four minutes? How could a good wife be satisfied by that? How does my son deserve her? Afterward, I couldn't sleep at night. Lying in bed, I was always alert to any sound: a fake moan, some calculated heavy breathing, an earsplitting squeak from the spring mattress, a slimy sucking sound, the rhythmic pulsing of the toys, the Zen sound of clattering Buddhist prayer beads, and so on. Once, not hearing them, I missed an opportunity for eavesdropping. The next morning when I discovered my daughter-in-law's wet panties in the laundry basket, I put my nose to them to sniff. Just as I expected, they were covered in fake lubricant. Even though it was only lube, I decided to keep the panties and wait for the lube to dry, hoping that the scent of my daughter-in-law would resurface.

The next day I went to the Community Center for Senior Citizens and enrolled in a computer skills course. The mentor was very patient with us. I asked him to help me set up a Taobao account, and learned how to shop online. Every time I stole my daughter-in-law's panties after she had sex, I bought the same type from her store and put them back in the laundry basket. Whenever she messaged me, believing I was a regular customer, she would say: "Dear, can I give you a hand?" The feeling of extra intimacy revitalized me.

After my daughter-in-law got pregnant, she and my son seemed to stop having sex, and I was finally able to relax and fall asleep. Once again, my son asked me to get rid of my junk. Now it was time to end it with "them." I climbed up the ladder and took out the porn videos hidden in the dark corner. The plastic boxes showed not the slightest yellowing, and their Japanese packaging was still pristine. I put my old friends one after another into a large black plastic bag, and as I walked to the garbage room, my every step felt weighted by stones. The moment of

「伯伯，錄影帶要先把磁帶和包裝膠分別拆開，再各自放進膠類和紙類回收箱，雖然你的生命快將完結，但地球還有很長的路要走，別累及下一代哦。」然後我們一起拆了半天磁帶和包裝盒。

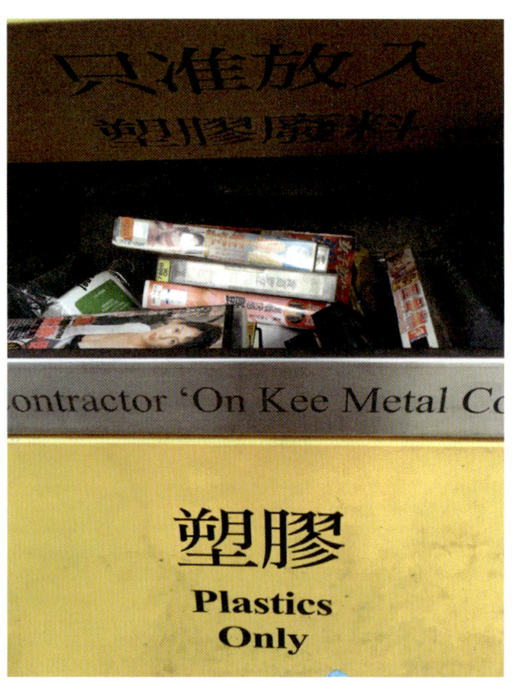

JUL 14

今天在紐約叫了Uber去古根海姆美術館，司機應該是新手，因為不停走錯路，到最後還誇張得要借我這個遊客的電話GPS去找，我有點不高興，想過要給她負評。直至到我看到她車前所顯示她的電話通話紀錄，見她不停地打給「My Life」，我擔心想，她人生是不是出現了什麼問題，但細想之下便十分羨慕她， 因為至少她知道Life的電話，知道有問題要問誰。

我拍拍她肩膀問：「你可以分享『My Life』的聯絡方法給我嗎，我都有很多問題想對人生發問呢。」

她說：「It's my life，你的人生自己找吧！」

下車後，我給了她負評。

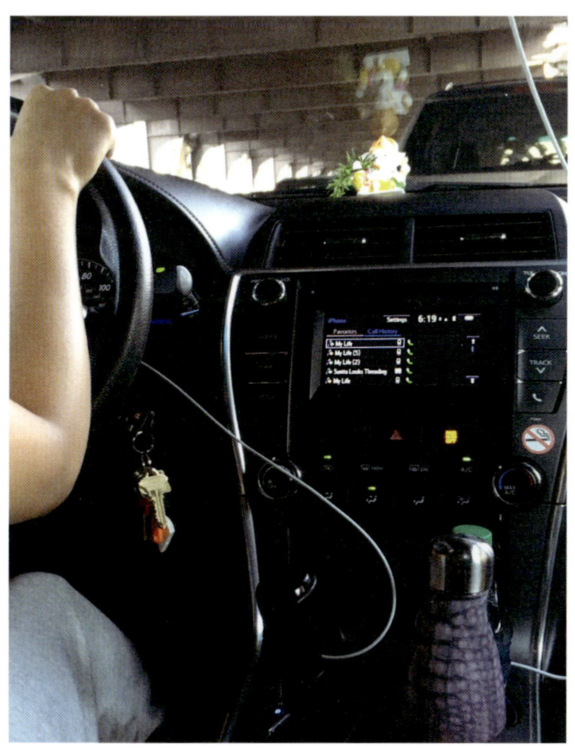

throwing the bag away felt excruciatingly long; the big plastic bag fell as though in slow motion into the black hole of the garbage bin. Well, there's no crying over spilled milk. I immediately turned around and scurried off. As I started walking, I noticed that my hands were shaking out of control, and my warm tears flowed out in a torrent. I hate being overtaken by the new era. I hate my family. I hate my descendants.

"Uncle, Uncle . . ." Suddenly a voice called me from behind. I turned around in tears. A lively young man was running after me, holding up the black plastic bag I had cruelly tossed away just ten seconds earlier.

"Uncle, you need to take the tapes out of their packaging cases, then put them in the different bins for plastic and paper recycling. Although your life is close to an end, the earth still has a long way to go. Don't burden the next generation!" We spent half a day together separating the tapes from their packaging cases.

JUL 14

Today I called an Uber to go to the Guggenheim. The driver must have been new, because she kept going the wrong way. In the end, she had to borrow my phone (from me, a tourist!) and use my GPS. I was a little upset, and wanted to give her a negative rating. Then I saw her phone call history on the monitor in her dashboard. I saw that she was always calling "My Life," and I worried that maybe something had gone wrong with her life. But after thinking about it, I grew jealous of her—at least she knows her life's number. If she has any problem, she knows who to call.

I tapped her on the shoulder and asked, "Could you tell me how to reach My Life? I've got a lot of questions for it."

She said, "It's my life. Find your own life yourself!"

After I got out the car, I gave her a negative rating.

JUL 16

昨天約了Airbnb女主人先在咖啡店見面，她說她
八年前從法國來到紐約，一直做自己音樂，又做不好，
很窮又不開心，所以將房間出租，她自己卻睡沙發。

到了她家門口，她向我介紹自己對New Age，光和
愛等的熱誠，指著大門貼著的一個中文字「細」，
她跟我說：「認著這個代表著光的字就是我們家了。」
我說這個字代表SMALL，她說怎可能呢，在Google
查light這個字是「細」呀，我說，可能light也可以
是輕的意思吧。

進到屋裏，發現周圍門，窗和牆都貼著「細」字，
她說八年後才知道真相好傷心，看著滿屋被SMALL
包圍著，我笑說怪不得音樂做得不順利，她說
她真有點想哭。

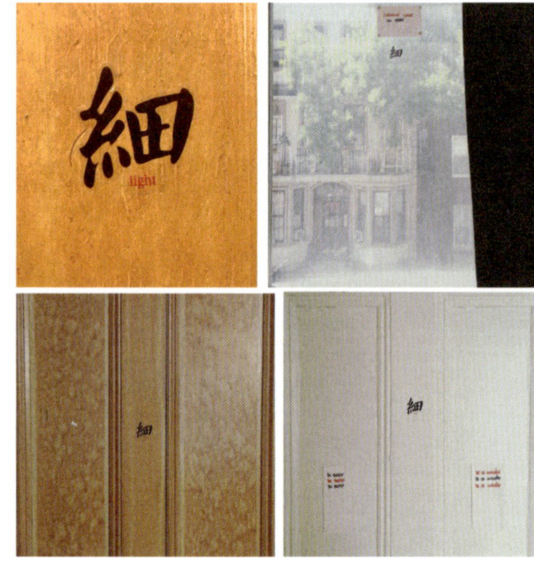

JUL 16

Yesterday I arranged to meet the Airbnb host at a coffee shop. She said she moved to New York from France eight years ago, and has been making her own music ever since. But she hasn't done well, and she's poor and unhappy, so she rents out her room and sleeps on the couch.

When we got to her door, she told me about her passion for New Age, light, and love. She pointed to a Chinese character pasted on the door, *xi*. She told me, "When you see the character for 'light,' you'll know it's our home." I told her the character means "small." She said, how is that possible? I Googled the character for light, and this is what came up! I told her that "light" could also refer to weight.

Upon entering her home, I discovered that all the doors, windows, and walls were covered in the character *xi*. She said she was sad to learn the truth after eight years. Seeing the room enveloped in "smalls," I laughed and told her, it's no wonder your music career hasn't gone well! She said she wanted to cry a little bit.

JUL 20

在紐約參觀古根海姆美術館這幾天，在想故事應該如何有趣地步向死亡，然後在街上留意到很多死了的動物都沒人理會。

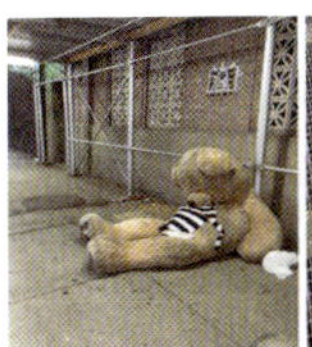
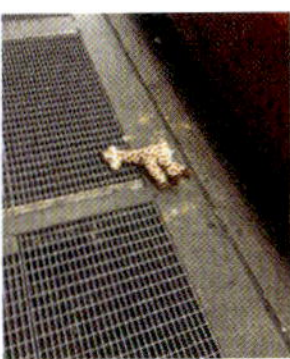
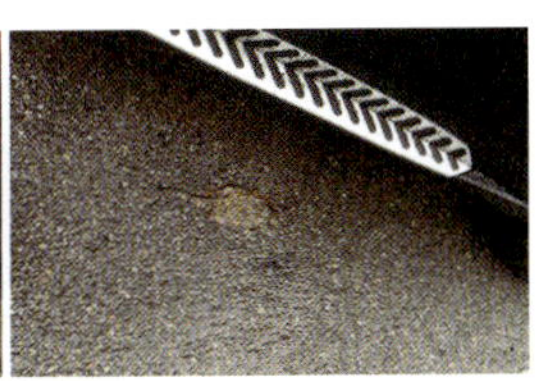

回港那天，在家中聽見一聲巨響，到露台一看發現一隻雀，好像沒有呼吸了，雖然看起來和我常吃的乳鴿很相似，但要觸摸牠還是感到害怕，我跑往廁所拿出長長的地拖，用捧端輕輕幫牠做心外壓，大約兩分鐘，牠有呼吸和打開雙眼，過了一會，牠站起來，但看上去像個老人一般閉眼氣喘。我跑去把剛買回來的葡萄和水給牠分享，但牠完全沒理會，沒多久就突然精神起來飛走了。我心想牠應該之後會帶著家人回來探我，可惜等了幾天都沒有，感到失望。

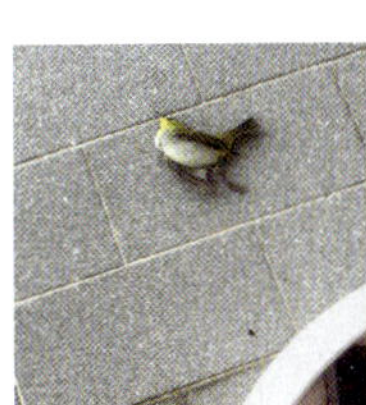
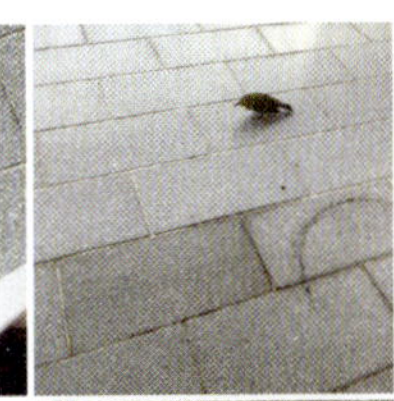
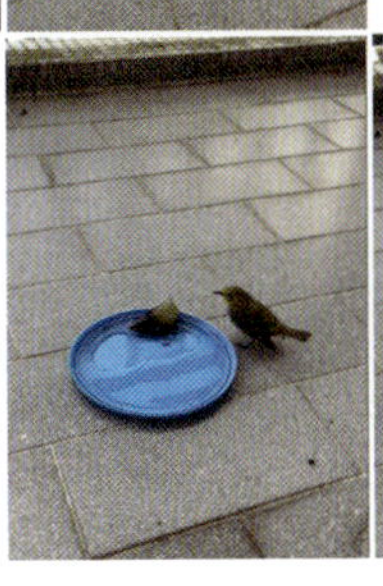
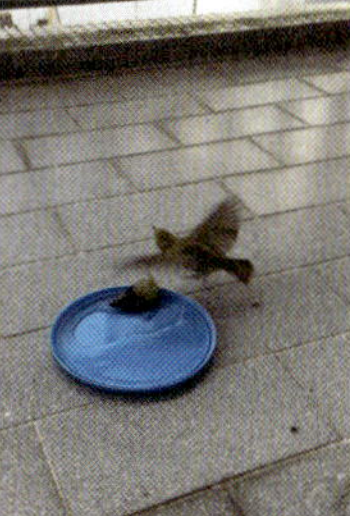

JUL 20

In New York, I visited the Guggenheim a few times, thinking about how to push the story toward death in an interesting way. Then I noticed so many dead animals on the street that no one seemed to care about.

The day I returned to Hong Kong, I heard a loud noise in my home and found a sparrow on the balcony. It didn't seem to be breathing. Although it looked a lot like the squabs I often eat, I was still afraid to touch it. I ran into the bathroom and grabbed a long mop, then used the end of the handle to lightly give it CPR. After about two minutes, it breathed again and opened its eyes. In a moment it stood up, but with its closed eyes and faltering breath, it reminded me of an old person. I ran to get the grapes and water I had just bought to share with it, but it ignored them. Shortly after, it suddenly perked up and flew off. I imagine it will come back with its family to visit me, but I've been waiting for days and it still hasn't shown up. I'm so disappointed.

AUG 2

有一天閉館時參觀古根海姆美術館，在螺旋型的斜坡走上去，發現牆的邊緣都是滑滑的圓角，感覺像是一個很安全的老人院設定，有衝動坐著輪椅由上往下衝，又或是把油從上層流下，我就可以脫光光的滑下去。

大約想像設定一個老人院廢墟的感覺，用有透明度的物料圍著。廣東話有一句，「推你出去曬太陽」，意思大約是要定期推著坐在輪椅上的長者，見見外面陽光，曬一曬，消消毒。香港有很多外地傭工，經常在街上見到的，都是幾個傭工隨便把長者推到某角落，然後傭工們趁這時間玩手機和聊天。

我在想未來如何能讓孝順更方便更無情。傭工們不用偷偷摸摸，長者們不用寂寞無聊，兒孫們又不用內疚。

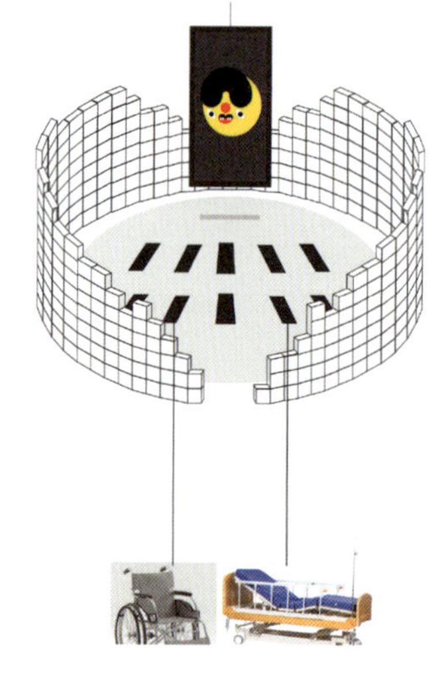

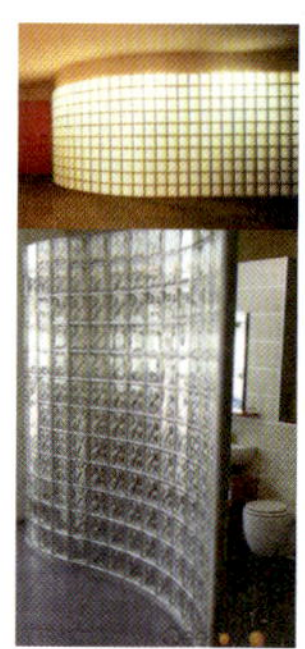

AUG 2

One day I visited the Guggenheim after hours. Walking up the spiral ramp, I discovered that all the walls were smooth and rounded, reminding me of the safety features of a nursing home. I had the impulse to speed down the ramp in a wheelchair, or pour oil from the top so I could slide down naked.

I imagine designing something that feels like the ruins of a nursing home, encased in a transparent material. There's a saying in Cantonese: "Push you outside to get some sun." It mostly means that you must regularly take elderly people in wheelchairs outside to see the sun—to bask in the light and air out. There are many foreign caretakers in Hong Kong. On the streets, you often see a few caretakers who have pushed some old people into a corner and then taken the opportunity to play on their phones or chat.

I'm thinking about how to make filial piety more convenient and detached in the future. Caretakers won't need to be so furtive, the elderly won't be so bored and lonely, and descendants won't feel so guilty.

孝順 beta 1.0

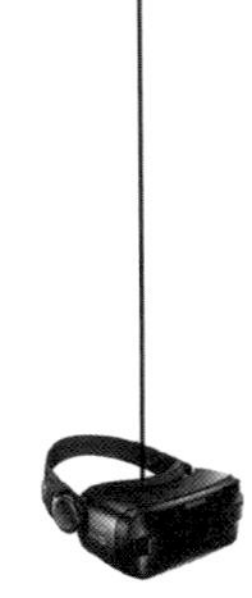

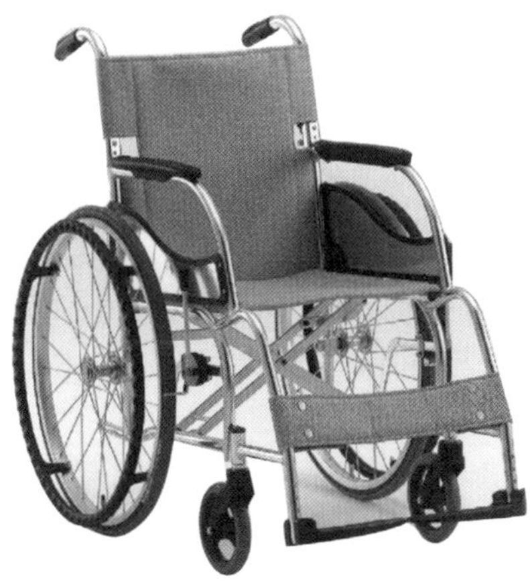

觀者在VR中看著前面一年四季的日落，兒孫數十人滿面笑容地排成一條長線推著觀者。

Filial Piety beta 1.0

The viewer sees four seasons' worth of sunsets in VR. Dozens of smiling descendants form a line to push the viewer.

AUG 3

一些念頭

- The Future Is Not What It Used To Be
- 孝順科技
- 清明節網上掃墓
- 婚姻制度更新的必要
- 長壽就是罪
- 道德文明越是進步，人性好像越被壓抑，快樂指數更是下降 :(
- 世界就是馬戲團，人同時是訓練員又是動物，世世代代訓練自己去除人性
- 人就像猴子模仿人一樣，模仿著做個沒人性的聖人，幸運地互聯網的出現，人們都走到裏面解放，甚至放大本來應有的人性黑暗小宇宙，終於能誠實地做回一個人了 :)
- 老人院
  兒子對妻子說：「我怎樣都不忍心把父親送到外面老人院去。」
  父親偷聽後感到安慰。原來孝順的兒子不捨他離去。第二天醒來時發現全屋都是陌生老人和看護，原來兒子意思是要把自己家變成老人院，照顧父親時又能賺錢。

AUG 3

Some Thoughts

- The Future Is Not What It Used To Be
- Filial Piety Technology
- Qingming Festival online tomb sweeping
- The necessity of updating the marriage system
- Longevity is a crime
- The more advanced morality and civilization are, the more repressed humanity is, and the more the happiness index drops :(
- The world is a circus, and we are both trainers and animals, disciplining the humanity out of ourselves for generation upon generation
- People are like monkeys imitating people, imitating a sage who lacks humanity. It's lucky the internet came about—everyone could enter it and be liberated. It even enlarges the small universe that is humanity's innate dark side. Finally, people can honestly be themselves :)
- Nursing Home
  The son says to his wife, "How could I ever have the heart to put Dad in a nursing home?"
  The father is eavesdropping and feels relieved: the filial son can't bear to have him leave. The next day the father wakes up to discover he is surrounded by elderly strangers and nurses. It turns out the son meant he would turn the house into a nursing home—he could make money while caring for his father.

AUG 8

一些念頭

今天在街上看到幾張咒罵某輪椅的街招，因為它張貼的高度很低，差點走漏眼。

我一直沿路跟著每一張街招走，發現可以跟上張貼者的路線，而且都是張貼在輪椅的高度。張貼者可能是行動不便的人，又或者，是一個很細心的健全人士，特意張貼在目標對象群的可視角度。

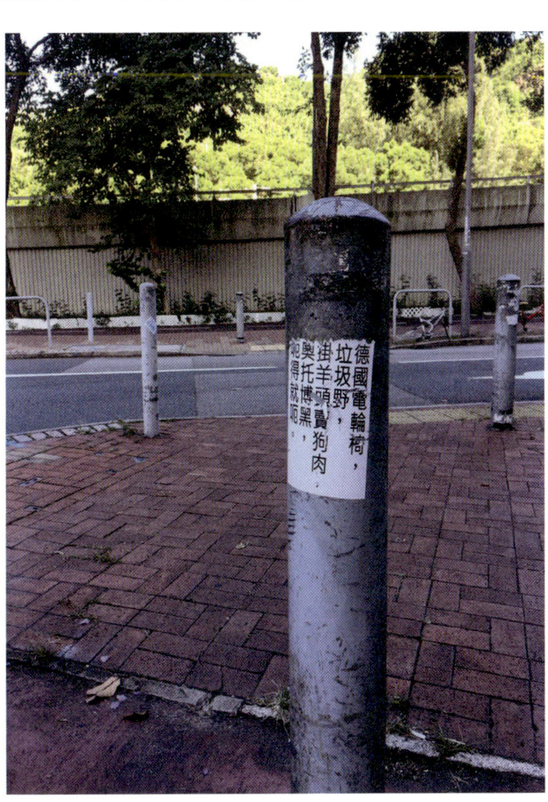

AUG 8
Some Thoughts
Today on the street, I saw some flyers cursing out a certain model of wheelchair. Because they were posted so low, I nearly missed them.

I kept following this particular flyer until I realized I could track the poster's route. Each flyer was placed at the height of a wheelchair. Maybe the person who posted them is disabled, or maybe the poster is a considerate able-bodied person who deliberately puts them where they can be seen by the target audience.

AUG 19

Some Thoughts

- The elderly continue to be a pillar of society.
- In Hong Kong, there's a TV ad that's been playing for years, in which the film star Simon Yam peddles the liver medication he endorses (the ad plays a few times a day). The ad boasts that you can still have a nightlife and feel young even when you're old. I think that it would be so funny if when Yam dies and they dissect his corpse, they find that all his internal organs are in extreme decline except for his liver, which is still beating along as healthily as that of a young man in his early twenties.
- One old man heard that if there's ever a day when you punch yourself and find it very painful, it proves your body is already quite weak, and you will soon die. From then on, he tested himself every day, until he beat himself to death.
- Another old man heard that if there's ever a day when you punch yourself and find it very painful, it proves you have a mean punch, and your body is still strong and healthy. From then on, he tested himself every day, until he beat himself to death.
- When I was young, my grandma and grandpa had mouths full of gold and silver teeth. At the time, I wasn't sure if it was real gold and silver. When I got older and saw the current fashion for gold teeth in the hip-hop subculture, and the street rappers with their fake gold grills, I remembered my dead grandma and grandpa, and thought those rappers were so tacky.

AUG 19

一些念頭

- 老人才繼續是社會的棟樑
- 香港有一個賣了多年的電視廣告，是電影明星任達華賣他代言的肝藥(每天播放幾次)，標榜年紀大了依舊能有夜生活，保持年輕。我在想，要是他死了，割開屍體一看，發現他的內臟全都嚴重衰退，就只有肝還像二十出頭的少年般健康紅潤地自己跳動，很有趣。
- 一位老人家聽說，當有一日用力打自己一拳的時候覺得很痛，證明你身體經已十分虛弱，快死了。他從此每天測試自己死期，結果把自己打死了。
- 另一位老人家又聽說，當有一日用力打自己一拳的時候覺得很痛，證明你出拳有力，身體還很壯健。他從此每天測試自己死期，結果把自己打死了。
- 我小時候，公公婆婆他們都滿口金牙銀牙，那時候不清楚是否真金真銀。長大了，看到現在hip hop subculture的gold teeth文化，滿街

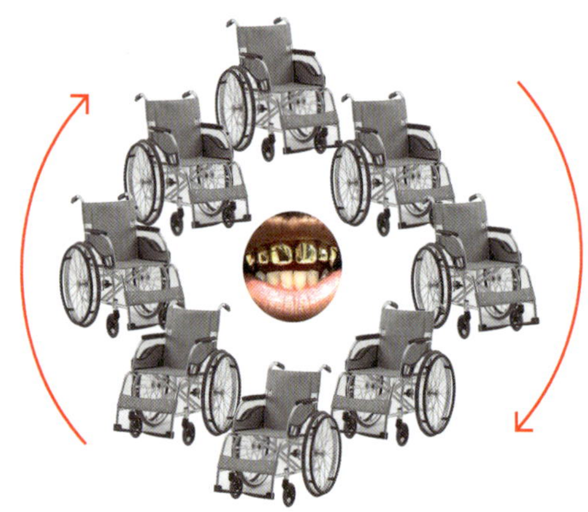

rapper戴著假金牙膠套，我想起了過身的公公婆婆，又覺得那些rapper很老土。

- 在未來，家人齊集家中，一起網上拜祭先人，竟然忘記了一年一次要登入的密碼和提示問題，最後更發現被黑客盜墓（網上），偷去了賠葬的眞金牙。
- 想像一班老人，住在一起，互相依靠，不再需要任何人。每日在老人院中央大家圍著圈，互相從後推動著前面的輪椅，慢慢加速直至形成一個輪椅漩渦，滿地都是被那離心力引至飛脫的假牙。

SEP 7

一些念頭

- 將假牙變成小時候的牙齒跳跳玩具，在場地中和周圍跳動。
- 上次提及老人們圍圈互相推著大家，最後形成一個輪椅漩渦，大家的金牙在旋轉中不停地往外飛，輪椅不停轉動在地下留下深深的坑，直至轉穿地板，輪椅和老人們都埋了一半在地板中，可能轉穿地板，直達地核……

這個畫面和我最近讀了談及沉默的螺旋Spiral of silence的社會現象文章很吻合，老人們所轉的就是沉默的螺旋。video想做正方型，插在地下一大堆假牙中，假牙讓人隨意踐踏或躺著，我喜歡古根海姆的高度，想在上空放些什麼，可能是個LED燈neon。做成一個未來感廢墟，亂中有序。

- In the future, families will gather at home to pay their respects to their ancestors online, only to forget the log-in passwords and backup questions that they use but once a year. In the end, they'll discover that hackers have robbed the (online) grave and made off with the real gold teeth buried with the dead.
- Imagine normal elderly people living together, relying on one another, no longer needing anyone. Every day they make a circle in the center of the nursing home. The one behind pushes the wheelchair of the person in front, slowly accelerating until they form a wheelchair vortex, and the floor is covered in dentures that have flown off from the centrifugal force.

SEP 7

Some Thoughts

- Take a pair of dentures and turn them into a child's chattering teeth toy, bouncing around the edge of the site.
- Last time, I mentioned elderly people pushing each other in a circle until they form a wheelchair vortex, gold teeth constantly flying out, wheelchairs spinning until they leave deep hollows beneath them, until they wear through the floor, and the wheelchairs and the old people are half-buried in the ground. Maybe they will break through the floor and reach the center of the earth . . .

This scene resonates with an article I read recently about the societal phenomenon of the "spiral of silence." The old people revolve in a spiral of silence.

想過輪椅們暗暗地在動畫下圍著轉圈，加上轉動時隆隆作響的環境配合。一直喜歡場地中除了動畫本身的聲音，還有點點雜聲，感覺很不安。

- 執拾時發現小時候的透明game boy，那時候覺得很潮很cool，很先進的未來感，奇怪反而現今很少科技用品例如電話會這樣處理。

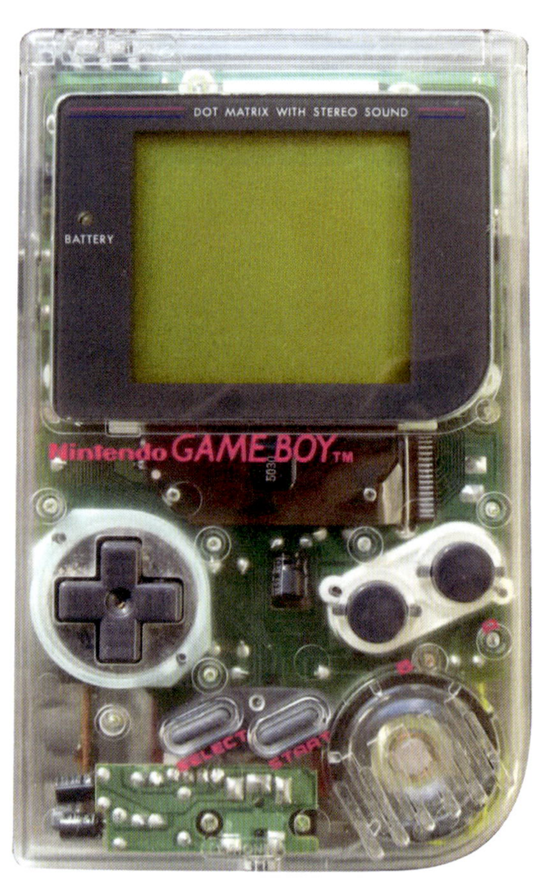

I want to make a square-format video and stick it in a big pile of dentures buried in the ground. People can tread or lie on the dentures at will. I like the height of the Guggenheim. I want to hang something overhead, possibly a neon LED light. Make it into a futuristic ruin, order within chaos.

I've thought that the wheelchairs might furtively revolve in a circle below the animation, accompanied by a rumbling noise as they rotate. I've always liked when, apart from the sound of the animation itself, a space also has a bit of white noise, where it feels unsettling.

- When I was packing, I found my clear Game Boy from when I was young. Back then I thought it was so hip and cool. It had a futuristic feeling, so technologically advanced. What's strange is that now there are so few technological items like phones that have this kind of design.

SEP 12

一些念頭

- 早前在圖書館借了兩本兒童書，《格林童話集》和《伊索寓言》，但因最近不在港而忘記歸還。直到今天已經遲了個多月，歸還時，圖書館職員告訴我，罰款是有上限的，意思是，遲還了一個月和一年的罰款是一樣的，因為已經到了上限。就好像一個殺了一個人的壞人和一個殺了一百個人的壞人所受的懲罰是一樣的。

  圖書館職員再告訴我，幸好我是借了兒童書籍，只罰$50，假如不是兒童書籍就要罰$130。我誠實地說，其實是我這個成人自己要看的，但他依舊只罰我$50。

  罰款當然是要懲罰不負責任的遲還者，但我認為不負責任沒分年紀，不論小孩或成年人，懲罰應該相同。

  又假如一位好學的小孩，借看在成人區的經典的文學小說，他就要有心理準備去承受成人的加倍罰款，縱使他還是一個小孩。再者，大部分小孩借還書籍的步驟，都是父母去處理，本來就是成人的責任。

  但更嚴重是，我一個成年人，卻不負責任地交著兒童罰款，感覺是自己借兒童去幫我運毒，被抓到都是兒童的錯，我可說是不負責任之中的不負責任，在圖書館想到這些時，有點腳軟。

SEP 12
Some Thoughts

- Some time ago, I borrowed two children's books from the library, *Grimms' Fairy Tales* and *Aesop's Fables*, but since I've been away from Hong Kong recently, I forgot to return them. Now they're several months overdue, but the librarian told me that there's an upper limit on the late fee. What this means is that returning a book a year late incurs the same fine as returning it a month late, because it's already reached the upper limit. It's like when someone who has killed one person and someone who has killed a hundred people receive the same punishment.

  The librarian told me I'm lucky I borrowed children's books—the fine is only 50 HKD. If they weren't children's books, the fine would have been 130 HKD. I was honest with the librarian and said that the books were for me, an adult, to read, but they still only fined me 50 HKD.

  The fine is, of course, a punishment for irresponsible borrowers. But I think that you can't sort irresponsibility by age. The punishment should be the same no matter whether it's a kid or an adult. Suppose a studious kid borrows a classic literary novel from the section for adults. He needs to psychologically prepare to take on the higher fine, even though he's still a kid. Moreover, it's usually the mom and dad who take care of borrowing and returning books. It's arguably an adult responsibility.

  But, more seriously, for an adult like me to pay a child's fine feels as though I'm using a child as a drug mule, and it's the child's fault that I've been caught. It's like I'm the most irresponsible of the irresponsible. I thought about this in the library, and felt a little wimpy.

許煜
Yuk Hui

走向技術未來的分支
For the Bifurcation of Technological Futures

> 「人類」這個概念是對帝國主義擴張特別有用的一件意識形態工具，而在其倫理-人道主義形態中，它又是經濟帝國主義的特定手段。這不禁讓我們想起從普魯東那裏稍微修改了的說法：誰提起人類，誰就想撒謊。
> ——卡爾·施密特，《政治的概念》[1]

> The concept of humanity is an especially useful ideological instrument of imperialist expansion, and in its ethical-humanitarian form it is a specific vehicle of economic imperialism. Here one is reminded of a somewhat modified expression of Proudhon's: whoever invokes humanity wants to cheat.
> — Carl Schmitt, *The Concept of the Political*[1]

正如卡爾·施密特所言，暗藏在「人類」這個詞背後的欺詐，在15世紀以來一直像幽靈侵擾著我們。「人類」最初是用來表示「人種，作為集體的眾人」。[2]「人類」這個詞的虛假之處不僅在於其充滿意識形態——施密特斷定它可以被工具化，用來指控敵方不是人，從而聲稱自己才是唯一的人類——就像特朗普和金正恩最近所做的那樣——而且還源於「人類」自身並不存在：以人類之名來講話即是行騙。我們今天回看施密特的這個主張，是因為不同的「x-人類主義」，不管這個x是「後」、「跨」、抑或是「超」，都爭先恐後地向我們呈現一種確定的人類未來。如果我們跟隨施密特，懸置「人類」這個用語，我們就需要思考其語義指稱瓦解會帶來的影響，並且，我們也需要從這個角度進一步地反思「人文科學」(humanities)的危機，因其在技術加速之下日益「落後」。

之所以說拒絕「人類」這個詞即拒絕人類的未來，正是因為，建基於幻象之上的這種未來比人類自身更加具有欺騙性。那麼，緊接著的問題便是：在拒絕了人類的未來以後，我們應該如何理解「未來」的問題？如果不能假裝現代化與全球化沒有發生過，不能回歸到非現代，我們還有怎樣的未來？這正是這篇文章的出發點：我嘗試理解超人類主義和技術奇點(singularity)的論述中(人類—機器混合、可增強智能、對情感的絕對操控、記憶移植、永生、人工智能、智能城市、太空移民等等)的未來性的問題。日本經典動畫《攻殼機動隊》(1995)向我們展示了這種不遠將來的景象：連通還是不連通(to plug in, or not to plug in)，這是個問題。未來，在其拉丁的詞源學中，指的是「尚未存在」，在中文裏表示「尚未到來」，然而，在技術決定論中或者壞的唯物主義(不管是新的還是舊的)中，「未來」都已經封存了。盡管尚未到達，但此「尚未」已經揭曉，未知再也不構成問題了。未知已被排除在這種未來之外，要麼就是一種對迫在眉睫的災難的預感，要麼就是尚未被科學技術(technoscience)證明或允可的神秘之物。而後者，正如馬丁·海德格爾(Martin Heidegger)所說，只能留待給詩人去處理了。

人類的未來是一種共時化的產物，這種共時化建基於由現代技術所實現的全球時間軸。我說的共時化，首先是指諸如鐘表如時間等等的統一諸生產過程和資本流動——施密特稱之為經濟帝國主義——的共同時間標準；其次，共時化指的是一種共同視野，

The deception hidden in the word "humanity," as articulated by Carl Schmitt above, has haunted us since the fifteenth century, when the word was first used to describe the "human race, humans collectively."[2] The word is illusory not only in that it is highly ideological — Schmitt asserts it can be instrumentalized to denounce the enemy as inhuman and claim the self as the only human, as Donald Trump and Kim Jong-un have demonstrated recently — but also because humanity as such doesn't exist: whoever speaks in its name is lying. If we recall Schmitt's assertion today, it is because different *x*-humanities, should this *x* be *post-*, *trans-*, or *super-*, are scrambling to present us a definite future of humanity. And if we follow Schmitt by suspending the term *humanity*, we will need to consider the consequences of the collapse of its semantic reference and, further, reflect on the crisis of the "humanities" in view of the term's increasing "backwardness" in relation to technological acceleration.

To refuse the term *humanity* is to refuse the future of humanity, precisely because, built as it is upon an illusion, such a future is even more deceptive than humanity itself. Then the immediate question is: having refused the future of humanity, how should we perceive the question of the future? What kind of future can we still have, other than returning to the nonmodern by pretending that modernization and globalization never happened? This is the point of departure of this essay, which attempts to understand what is at stake in the question of futurity described by the technological hype of transhumanism and singularity: human-machine hybrids, augmentable intelligence, perfect emotional control, memory transplantation, immortality, artificial intelligence, smart cities, space emigration, etc. The Japanese

即認為世界歷史只能如下的時間軸線展開：前現代–現代–後現代–末世。假如單一性意味著黑格爾意義下的歷史的終結，那麼「神人」（Homo deus）的出現則與作為歷史終結的神義論（theodicy）呼應。我們可以說，這種指向一個幻影般的神人的人類未來，是技術發展造成的共時化後果。而對其他諸未來的反思則被貶低為認識論人道主義（epistemological humanism）或保守主義的變體。以殖民化和現代化開始的共時化導致了今天的全球化——然而全球化也已經來到終點，因為如果（生產和資本流動的）共時化通過消除諸技術差異來獲得優化，那麼，辯證地，一旦所謂的南半球（Global South）在技術競爭中取得先機，北半球（Global North）在過去一百年獲得的優勢和特權就會被損害，結果貿易保護主義者、反動分子和極右分子就會蜂擁而至——正如我們最近所見的。[3]然而，如果我們將這種邏輯運用到國家之間的人工智能領域競爭，那麼情況就會像是普京所說的：「誰領先於人工智能將領先於世界。」[4]因為無論世界地圖如何劃分，我們仍留在同樣的全球時間軸上，朝著一樣的目的（telos）進發。問題在於，如果我們拒認這種人類的概念及其所聲稱的未來，那麼我們可以構想一個能夠分化出諸多樣性的世界歷史，一個新的世界歷史概念嗎？

———

只有在擺脱了上述的共時化，構想出各種不同的技術未來之後，諸未來的分支才能夠實現。這個推斷建基於我在新書《中國技術問題：論宇宙技術》提出的一個關於技術普遍性的二律背反[5]：

> 正論：技術是一種人類學普遍存在，理解為記憶的外置和諸身體器官的解放，正如一些人類學家和技術哲學家所闡述的那樣。
>
> 反論：技術不是人類學普遍存在，其可能性由諸特定宇宙論所給予和限制，這些宇宙論超出了諸功效的範疇。

康德式二律背反的特性在於，如果單獨地看，每個論題都成立，但它們本身卻互相對立；只有通過一種超越普遍性和特殊性的思考形式，二律背反才能消解。因為共時化依賴正論，削弱反論，所以我們只有在未來性的問題上闡明反論之後，一種可能的消解才會出現。正因如此，我提出各文化——因應著當前的歷史時刻——都應該系統地重新發現和闡述自身的認識論，追溯自身知識型（epistemes）歷史，以重塑出自己宇宙技術（cosmotechnics）的歷史。我將宇宙技術初步定義為：藉由技術活動來統一道德秩序和宇宙秩序。各文化都有其自身的宇宙技術，它們因為諸種

animation classic *Ghost in the Shell* (1995) has best shown us the scenarios of such an imminent future: to plug in, or not to plug in, that is the question. Future, which is the "yet to be" in Latin etymology, the "yet to come" (*weilai*) in Chinese, is already closed in a technological determinism, or bad materialism, whether old or new. Although not *yet* there, the "not yet" is *already* known, and what is unknown is no longer in question. Since the unknown is that which is excluded, either it is the feeling of impending catastrophe, or it is the mysterious that is not yet proved and endorsed by technoscience, and remains the task of poets, as Martin Heidegger suggested.

The future of humanity is the product of a synchronization based on the global temporal axis realized by modern technology; by synchronization, I mean first the sharing of a common temporal standard such as clock time that unifies all production processes and circulation of capital, as Schmitt calls economic imperialism; second, the common view of a world history in the process of making according to the following time axis: premodern — modern — postmodern — apocalypse. If the singularity signifies the end of history in the Hegelian sense, the emergence of *Homo deus* coincidentally corresponds to theodicy as the end of history. We could say that the future of humanity is a synchronized effect produced by technological development that points toward a phantasmal *Homo deus*, while reflections on other *futures* are discredited as being variants of epistemological humanism or conservatism. The synchronization that commenced with colonization and modernization gave rise to the globalization of today — a globalization that is, however, already at an end, since if synchronization (of production and capital flow) attains optimization by eliminating technological differences, then dialectically, once the so-called Global South takes the lead in technological competition, the advantage and privilege enjoyed by the Global North for the past century will be jeopardized, and consequently protectionists, reactionaries, and the extreme right will surge in popularity, as we have seen recently.[3] However, if we follow this logic regarding the competition between countries over the development of AI, then it will be as Vladimir Putin told the Russian children, "Whoever leads in AI will rule the world,"[4] since no matter how the cartography is divided, we are still on the same global temporal axis and therefore moving toward the same telos. Would rejecting this concept of humanity and its claims to the future allow us to conceive a new concept of world history that is able to bifurcate into diversities?

The bifurcation of futures can only be achieved by breaking away from the synchronization described above to envisage different technological futures. This speculation is based on an antinomy of the universality of technology addressed in my recent book, *The Question Concerning Technology in China: An Essay in Cosmotechnics*,[5] which could be stated:

> Thesis: technology is an anthropological universal, understood as the exteriorization of memory and liberation of bodily organs, as some anthropologists and philosophers of technology have formulated.
>
> Antithesis: technology is not anthropologically universal; it is enabled and constrained by particular cosmologies, which go beyond functionalities and utilities.

The peculiarity of the Kantian antinomy is that each thesis holds on its own but opposes the other; such an antinomy must be resolved by a form of thinking beyond universality and particularity. Synchronization relies on the thesis and undermines the antithesis. To answer the question concerning futurity, we must clarify the antithesis before a resolution can emerge. This is why I propose that each culture should develop its own history of cosmotechnics by systematically rediscovering and formulating its epistemologies and tracing the history of its epistemes in response to the current historical moment. Here is a primary definition of cosmotechnics: the unification of the cosmic and moral orders through technical activities. Every culture has its own cosmotechnics, each differing from the other in terms of relations and the dynamics of these relations. The aim of conceptualizing cosmotechnics is to reopen the question of technics that was unfortunately closed down in past centuries. Following the analysis in Heidegger's 1949 lecture later published as "The Question Concerning Technology," we find two concepts and essences of technics. The first is the Greek *technē*, which means "poiesis" or "bringing forth" (*Hervorbringen*), and the second is modern technology, the essence of which is no longer the Greek technē, but rather enframing (*Gestell*), meaning that everything is considered calculable and exploitable as resources (*Bestand*); while it is difficult, if not impossible, to position other kinds of technics — for example, the Chinese, Indian, or Amazonian — without reducing them to Greek technē, it is self-evident that they are not "modern" technologies.

The question of technological futures must be approached through historical and metaphysical investigations of cosmotechnics: I have suggested carrying out this task by reconstructing a Chinese technological thought. I attempted to do so by tracing the relation between *dao* and *qi* (器) in Confucianism, Neo-Confucianism, and New Confucianism through a characterization of the dynamics between these two metaphysical categories as different epistemes. Dao literally means "path," and qi, "utensils" (not to be confused with the *qi* or *ch'i* [氣] usually translated as "energy"[6]). Dao is a moral cosmological thinking that situates humans as cosmological beings, and leads them toward the good. Dao is eternal but not static; the search for the unification between dao and qi reflects the episteme of the epoch. Here I understand the question of episteme in terms of sensibility, instead of "knowledge" or "science" as described in Aristotle's *Nicomachean Ethics*, since episteme in the Foucauldian sense is not knowledge per se, but rather the condition under which such-and-such knowledge emerges. Epistemic ruptures are responses to crisis that must be resolved by inventing new sensibilities corresponding to new social, political, and aesthetic life, as seen in Chinese history, for example, in the decline of the Zhou dynasty, the impact of Buddhism during the late Tang dynasty, and modernization after defeat in the mid-nineteenth-century opium wars.[7]

This qi–dao relation is no mere intellectual conceit; it is also reflected in artistic creation, technical invention, and everyday life. We can say

關係及這些關係間的相互作用而相異。但遺憾地，關於技術問題的探討在過去數個世紀終止了，而我將宇宙技術概念化的目的正在於重啟這種追問。根據海德格爾在1949年演講之後出版的《論技術問題》(The Question Concerning Technology)，我們可以得到兩種對技術的概念和本質的定義。第一種是古希臘語的technē，意思是poiesis，即「有詩意地帶到跟前(Hervorbringen)」，第二種是現代科技，其本質再也不是希臘語中的technē，而是(技術背後的)座架(Gestell)，也就是說所有的存在都被視為可支配的資源(Bestand)；然而我們很難，如果不是完全不可能的話，用古希臘的technē來理解諸如中國的、印度的或者是南美部落的技術；而且顯而易見，這些技術不可能是「現代」科技。

技術未來的問題必須經由對宇宙技術的歷史和形而上學調查來展開——我曾嘗試重構一種中國技術思想史來進行這項工作。我試圖將「道」和「器」的相互作用的動態發展理解成不同的知識型，從而追溯這兩個形而上學範疇在儒家、宋明理學和新儒家思想中的關係變遷。「道」的字面意義為「路」，而「器」則表示「用具」(勿與通常翻譯為energy的「氣」混淆[6])。「道」是一種道德宇宙思想，人是一種宇宙存在(cosmological beings)，而知「道」則能向善。「道」是永恆而非靜止的，對「道」和「器」的統一追尋反映了每個時代的知識型。我視知識型問題為感知性(sensibility)問題，而不是亞里士多德在《尼各馬可倫理學》(Nicomachen Ethics)中描述的「知識」或者「科學」，因為福柯意義下的知識型並不是知識自身，而是各種知識得以出現的條件。知識型斷裂是對危機的回應，而這些危機必須通過發明契合於新的社會、政治和美學生活的感知性來解決。我們可以在中國歷史上找到很多這樣的例子，例如周朝衰落、晚唐時期佛教的沖擊以及在18世紀中期鴉片戰爭落敗後的現代化運動。[7]

器道關係並不僅僅是理智上的構想，它同時也反映在藝術創作、技術發明和日常生活上。我們可以說中國傳統藝術宗旨即求道，這既不是柏拉圖對話錄中的美德(arēte)，也不是斯多噶學派中自然的理性。在這個意義上，藝術也是一種宇宙技術。以六朝時期的畫家和哲者宗炳(375-443)所著的中國最早的山水畫理論著述《畫山水序》為例，裏面開篇寫道：

> 聖人含道暎物，賢者澄懷味像。至於山水，
> 質有而靈趣……夫聖人以神法道，而賢者通；
> 山水以形媚道，而仁者樂。不亦幾乎？[8]

繪畫技術的完美並不體現在精確性或幾何透視上，而在於作品能否讓「道」作為可知的本體向觀看者顯現自身[9]，盡管此道並「不可道」。我們也可以在《莊子》中著名的「庖丁解牛」的故事中看到這種對道的追尋，庖丁在解剖牛的時候就像在跳舞一樣。他說自己所好的是「道」，掌握了「道」，刀進入牛身就像穿透虛空一樣，刀刃無須碰撞筋骨。誠然，我們不能僅僅著眼於這些古舊的例子而無視歷史的進程；我純粹想要表明，還存在著其他技術歷史，這些技術不能被簡化為當今科學和技術研究中所持有的技術概念，這些技術不僅僅是自然法則的應用。這也並不是要復興「過時」和神祕的知識，而是提議重新發現其他技術思想和認識論。而困難在於：諸宇宙技術歷史的重新發現如何能夠促成未來的分支？

———

當然，篇幅所限，我無法在這裏回答這個問題，但我在此想強調的是重啟技術問題的緊迫性，並對一種同質的技術未來提出質疑。每種文化都必須調查自身宇宙技術的歷史，因為在過去一個世紀，它們均被同質化，作為特定的技術或技術系統，例如冶金術、造紙或鐵路技術等，在同一歷史時間軸上被拿來比較誰比誰先進。而要讓這些調查得以展開，我們必須擯棄由「神人」的實現或現代性的進步所主導的人類未來概念。這並不是說要像勒德份子(Luddite)一樣拒絕運算機器和現代科技，而是通過重新發現宇宙技術，重新居有(reappropriate)這些技術，以克服它們加之於我們身上的局限性。擯棄了線性技術進步的圖景，也就擯棄了把加速主義政治視為解決社會和政治問題的唯一方法的這種妄想。因為，如果諸未來的分支是可能的，衡量加速的將不再是各種量——即自動化或生產力總量的程度。衡量加速的將會是技術的分支能力(the capacity of technology to bifurcate)。這種分支將導向異質的宇宙技術，轉而促使我們離開自歐洲現代性以來被視為世界歷史的全球時間軸，走向多元的未來。

that the objective of art in the Chinese tradition is the pursuit of dao, which is neither the *arēte* of Plato's dialogues, nor the Stoic rationality of nature. Art was also a cosmotechnics in this sense. Consider the first theoretical writing on *shanshui* landscape painting, by Zong Bing (also Tsung Ping, 375–443), a painter and philosopher of the Six Dynasties period. The text begins:

> Sages, possessing the Dao, respond to things. The virtuous, purifying their thoughts, savor [the phenomenon]. As for landscape, it has physical existence, yet tends toward the spiritual. . . . Now, sages follow the Dao through their spirits, and the virtuous comprehend this. Landscapes display the beauty of the Dao through their forms, and humane men delight in this. Are these not similar?[8]

The perfection of the technique of painting is not about exactitude or geometrical perspective but rather about whether dao manifests itself as a knowable noumenon for the viewer,[9] even though it cannot be reduced to any discourse. This pursuit of dao is also evident in the famous story of the butcher and his knife in the *Zhuangzi*, in which the butcher dissects the cow as if he were dancing. The butcher says that what interests him is dao, and that by knowing dao, he can penetrate the cow as though entering the void, without needing to confront bones or tendons. To be sure, limiting ourselves to such antic examples and disregarding the progress of history is insufficient; what I suggest is simply that there are other histories of technology that cannot be reduced to the application of the laws of nature as currently conceived in science and technology studies. This is not an attempt to revive "outdated" and mythical knowledge, but rather a proposal to rediscover other technological thoughts and epistemologies. The challenge is: how can these rediscoveries and histories of cosmotechnics contribute to the bifurcation of futures?

It is of course impossible to answer this question in such limited space. What I want to emphasize here is the urgency of reopening the question of technology, and thereby putting a homogeneous technological future into question as well. Every culture will have to investigate its histories of cosmotechnics, which in the past century have been reduced to *one* history of technology measured by the advancement of particular techniques or technical systems, from metallurgy to papermaking or railways. To prepare for these investigations to emerge, we must reject the notion of the future of humanity presented as the realization of *Homo deus* or the progress of modernity. This is no Luddite refusal of computational machines and modern technologies, but rather a matter of reappropriating these technologies through the rediscovery of cosmotechnics so as to overcome the limits they impose on us. By rejecting the linear path attached to the image of technological progress, we also reject the politics of acceleration as the only option available for resolving social and political problems, since if the bifurcation of futures is possible, acceleration can no longer be measured by quantities, e.g., degree of automation or amount of productivity. Instead, it will be measured by the *capacity of technology to bifurcate* into heterogeneous cosmotechnics, which in turn allows multiple futures to emerge and remain irreducible to the global axis of time perceived as world history since European modernity.

1 卡爾·施密特,《政治的概念》,美國芝加哥大學出版社,2008年,54頁。
2 「人類」詞源學在線字典,2017年10月10日訪問,http://www.etymonline.com/word/humanity。
3 有關單邊全球化之終結的詳細分析,見許煜《新反動主義者的苦惱意識》,*e-flux Journal* #81,2017年4月,http://www.e-flux.com/journal/81/125815/on-the-unhappy-consciousness-of-neoreactionaries。
4 出自總統普京在2017年9月1日對小朋友的知識日演講,https://www.rt.com/news/401731-ai-rule-world-putin。
5 許煜,《論中國的技術問題》,美國法爾茅斯,Urbanomic出版社,2016年12月。
6 「器」和「氣」同音異義,在英文中用qi和ch'i來加以區分。關於「道」、「器」和「氣」的關係,見許煜《中國技術問題:論宇宙技術》,第12、13、134–47頁。
7 見許煜和洛文克(Geert Lovink),《追求一個中國技術哲學:洛文克訪談許煜》,(*Parrehsia: A Journal of Critical Philosophy*)期刊,27期,2017年,第60頁:「我想在中國哲學史中區別出三種知識型:一、先秦哲學的出現以及周朝結束後儒學逐漸占據統治地位,它在天人之間建立了、也正當化了道德感知性,因為天提供正當性給政治行動、社會行動、個人行動;二、晚唐佛學占據統治地位後,11世紀出現了新儒學,它重建道德宇宙論,重新把宇宙生成學引入儒家思想,來重申宇宙和道德之間的統一;三、中國在鴉片戰爭被英國擊敗後,被迫尋求新的知識型,來處理西方科學和科技,可是卻失敗了,因為中國嚴重缺乏理解科技的知識,也嚴重缺乏掌握這種物質轉型的經驗。對我來說現在似乎剛好又能認真考慮這個對認識論和知識型的探求了,因為全球化現在已經走到極限了,回應人類紀變得越來越迫切了。」
8 宗炳(375–443),《畫山水序》,南朝,宋,被認為是中國第一本畫論。
9 新儒家學派哲學家牟宗三(1909–1995),康德三大批判的中文翻譯者,認為中國哲學著重於智的直覺(intellectual intuition)。康德將其定義為認識本體的可能性條件(正如感性直覺對應著現象),然而他也否定人擁有智的直覺。牟氏將對於智的直覺的不同理解劃分為中西哲學的根本性差異。

1 Carl Schmitt, *The Concept of the Political* (Chicago: University of Chicago Press, 2008), p. 54.
2 "Humanity," the Online Etymological Dictionary, accessed October 10, 2017, http://www.etymonline.com/word/humanity.
3 For a more detailed analysis on the end of unilateral globalization, see Yuk Hui, "On the Unhappy Consciousness of Neoreactionaries," in *e-flux Journal,* no. 81 (April 2017), http://www.e-flux.com/journal/81/125815/on-the-unhappy-consciousness-of-neoreactionaries.
4 "'Whoever Leads in AI Will Rule the World': Putin to Russian Children on Knowledge Day," RT.com, September 1, 2017, https://www.rt.com/news/401731-ai-rule-world-putin/.
5 Yuk Hui, *The Question Concerning Technology in China: An Essay in Cosmotechnics* (Falmouth, UK: Urbanomic, 2016).
6 The homophones 器 and 氣 can be distinguished here by differing romanizations, qi and ch'i, respectively. For more on the relations between dao, qi, and ch'i, see Hui, *The Question Concerning Technology in China*, § 12, § 13, pp. 134–47.
7 See Yuk Hui and Geert Lovink, "For a Philosophy of Technology in China: Geert Lovink Interviews Yuk Hui," in *Parrhesia: A Journal of Critical Philosophy* 27 (2017), p. 60: "I am tempted to distinguish three epistemes in the Chinese history of philosophy: first, the emergence of pre-Qin philosophy and the gradual dominance of Confucianism after the fall of the Zhou dynasty which established and legitimated the moral sensibility between humans and the heavens, for the latter provides the legitimacy for political, social and individual actions; secondly, after the dominance of Buddhism in the late Tang dynasty, the emergence of neo-Confucianism in the 11th century re-established a moral cosmology by reintroducing cosmogonies into the Confucian doctrine in order to reaffirm the unity between the cosmic and moral orders; and third, after the defeat by Britain in the opium wars, China was forced to search for a new episteme to cope with Western science and technology, but it has failed because there was a serious lack of knowledge and understanding of technology throughout the experience of dealing with such a material transformation."
8 "The Significance of Landscape Painting," in *Early Chinese Texts on Painting*, ed. Susan Bush and Hsio-yen Shih (Cambridge: Harvard University Press, 1985), p. 36, translation modified. Regarding the last sentence, François Jullien proposed another translation in *Vivre de paysage ou l'impensé de la raison* (Paris: Gallimard, 2014), p. 138: "Le Sage par son esprit donne forme à la Voie, tao. Les montagnes par leur forme actualisée rendent attirant la Voie et les eaux." (The sage by his spirit gives form to the way, dao; the mountains, by their actualized form, render dao and water attractive.) Although this translation is unusual, Jullien is right to note that 像 (*xiang*) and 形 (*xing*) should be more carefully distinguished.
9 The New Confucian philosopher Mou Zongsan (1909–1995), Chinese translator of Kant's three *Critiques*, argued that Chinese philosophy centers on the cultivation of intellectual intuition—defined by Kant as the condition of possibility of knowing the noumenon (as what sensitive intuition is to phenomenon)—despite Kant's claim that intellectual intuition is actually beyond human faculty. Mou sees these different emphases as the fundamental difference between Chinese and Western philosophy.

林一林
Lin Yilin

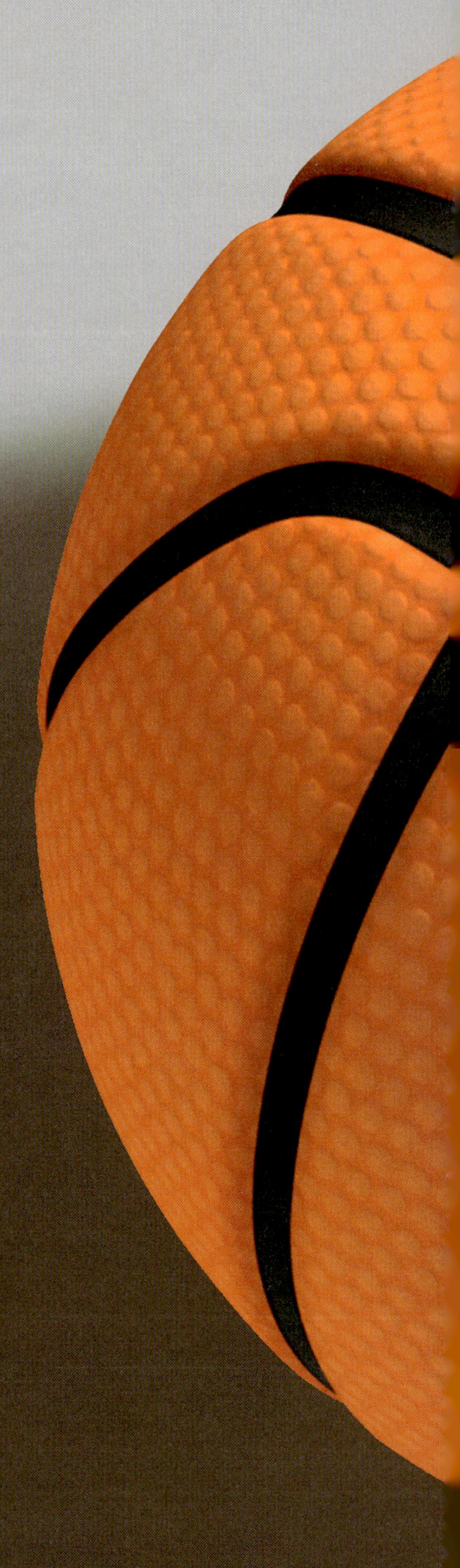

《單子》的創作手稿和方案效果圖，2018
Preparatory drawings and digital renderings for *Monad*, 2018

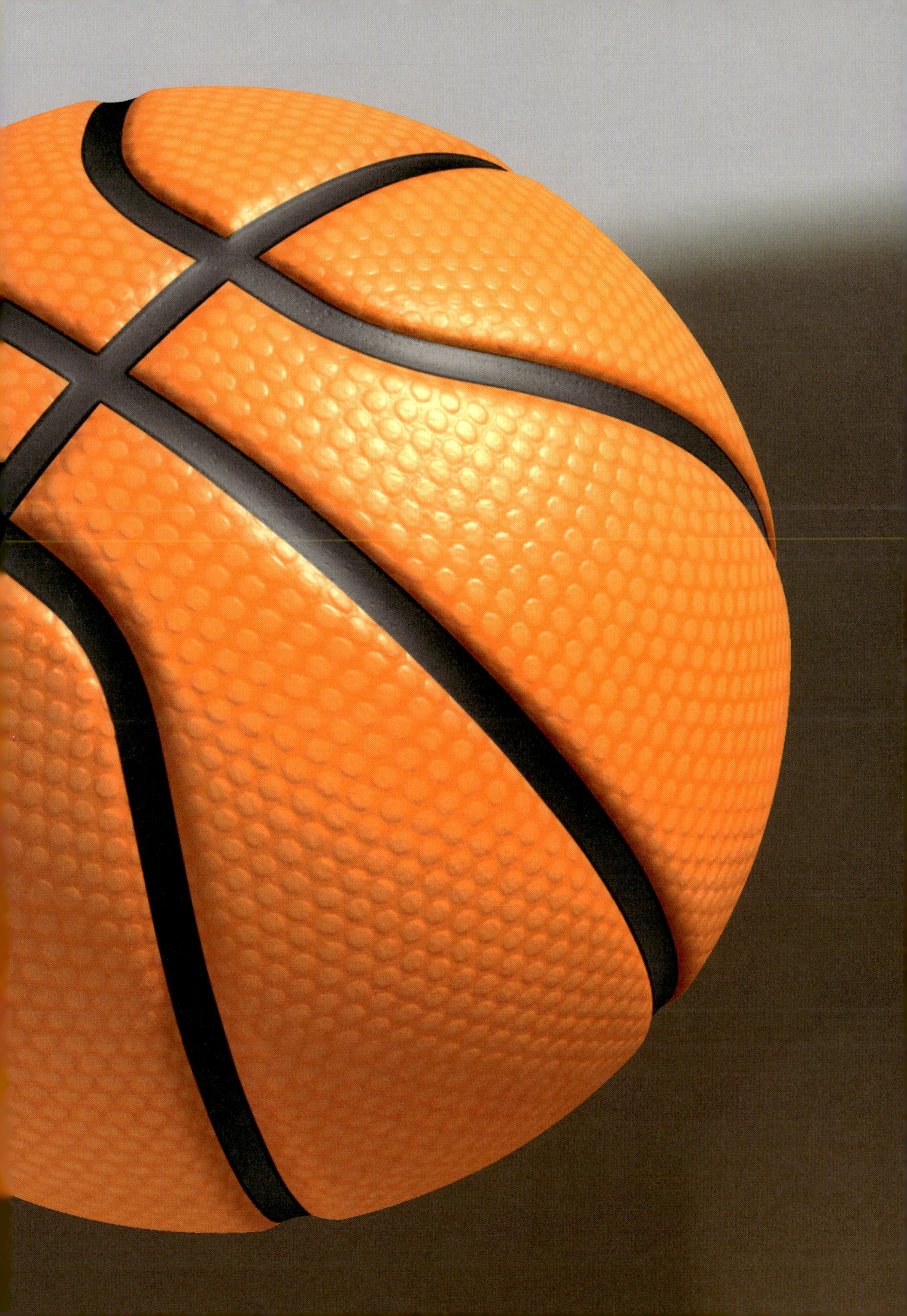

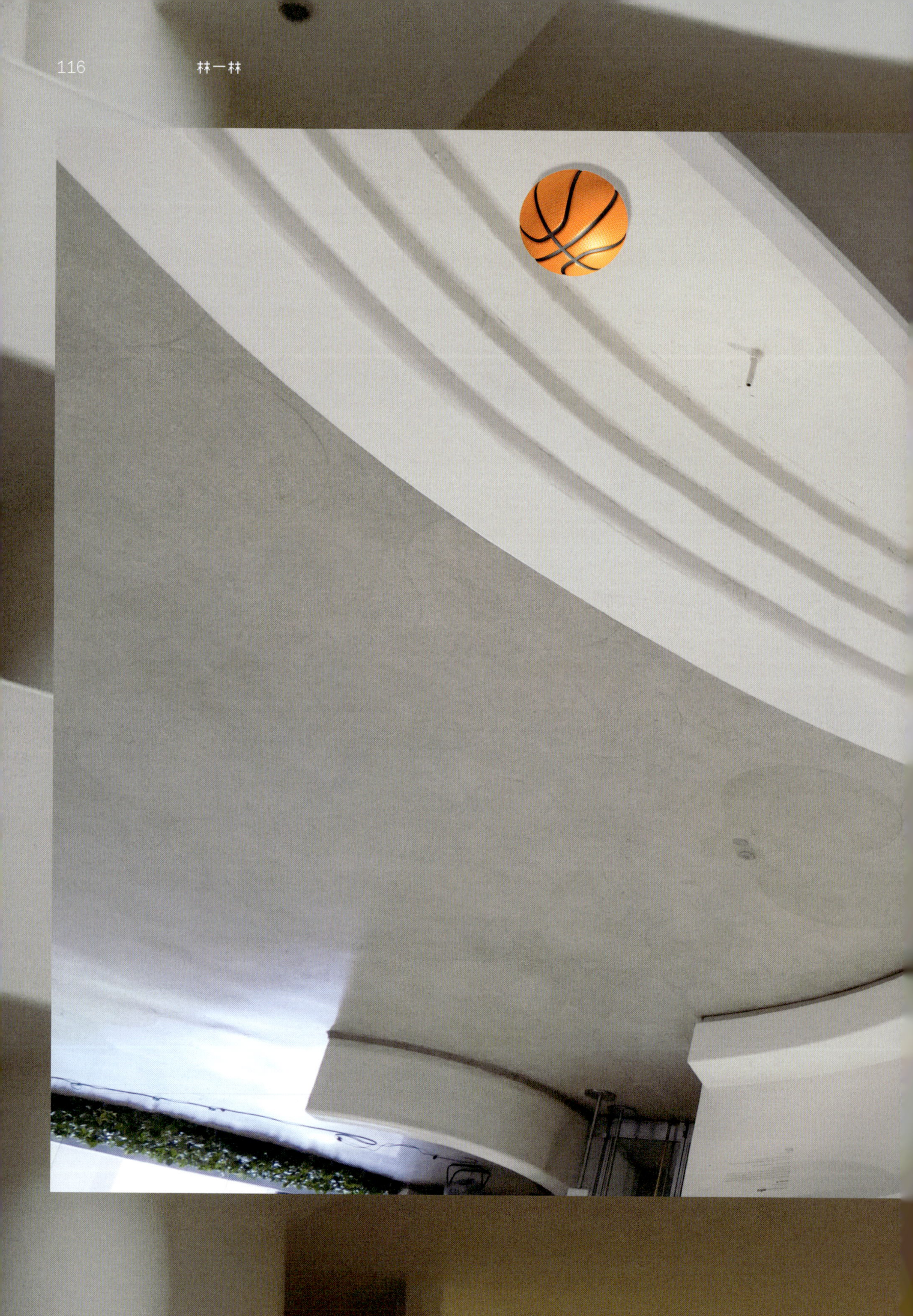

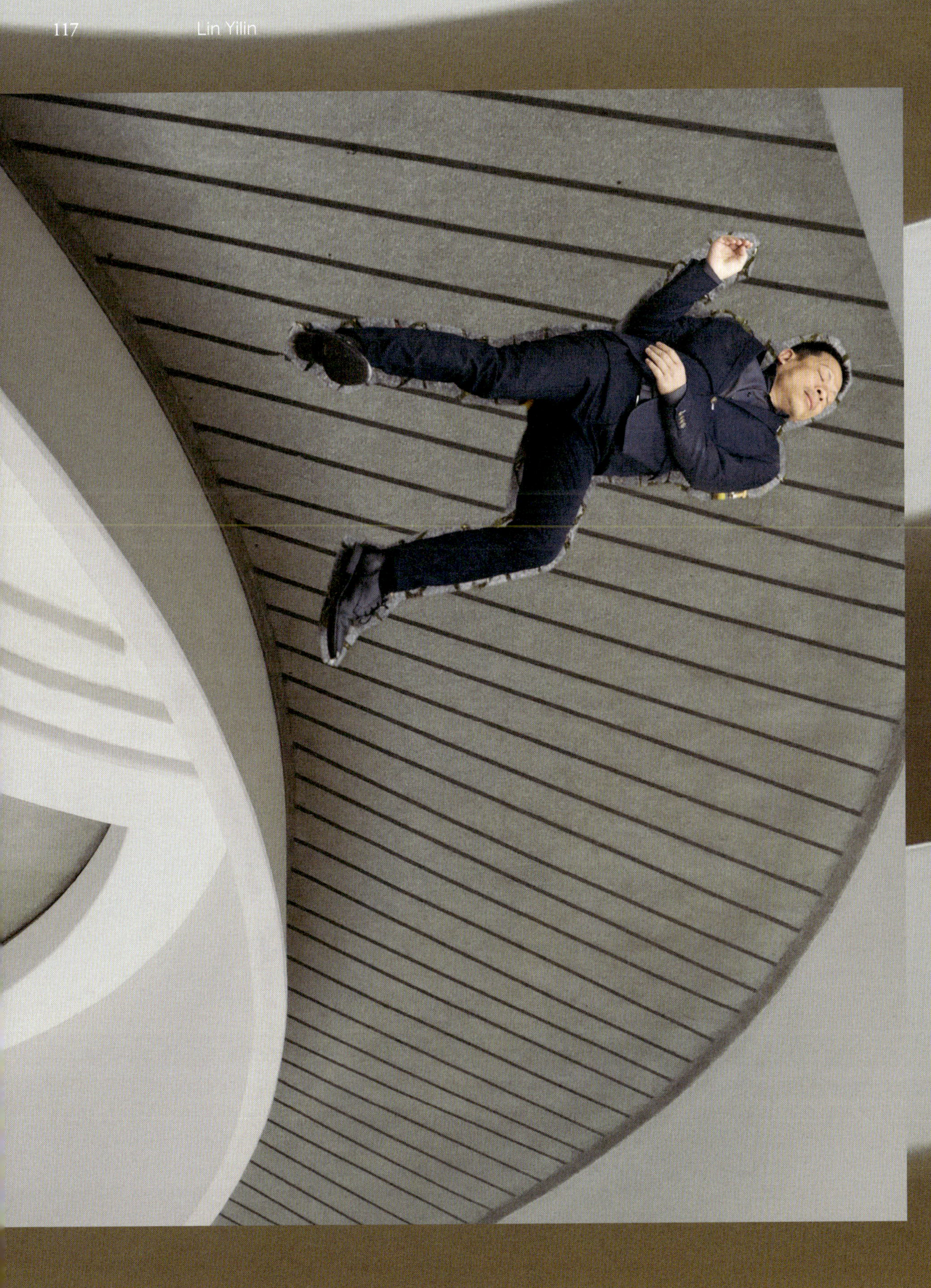

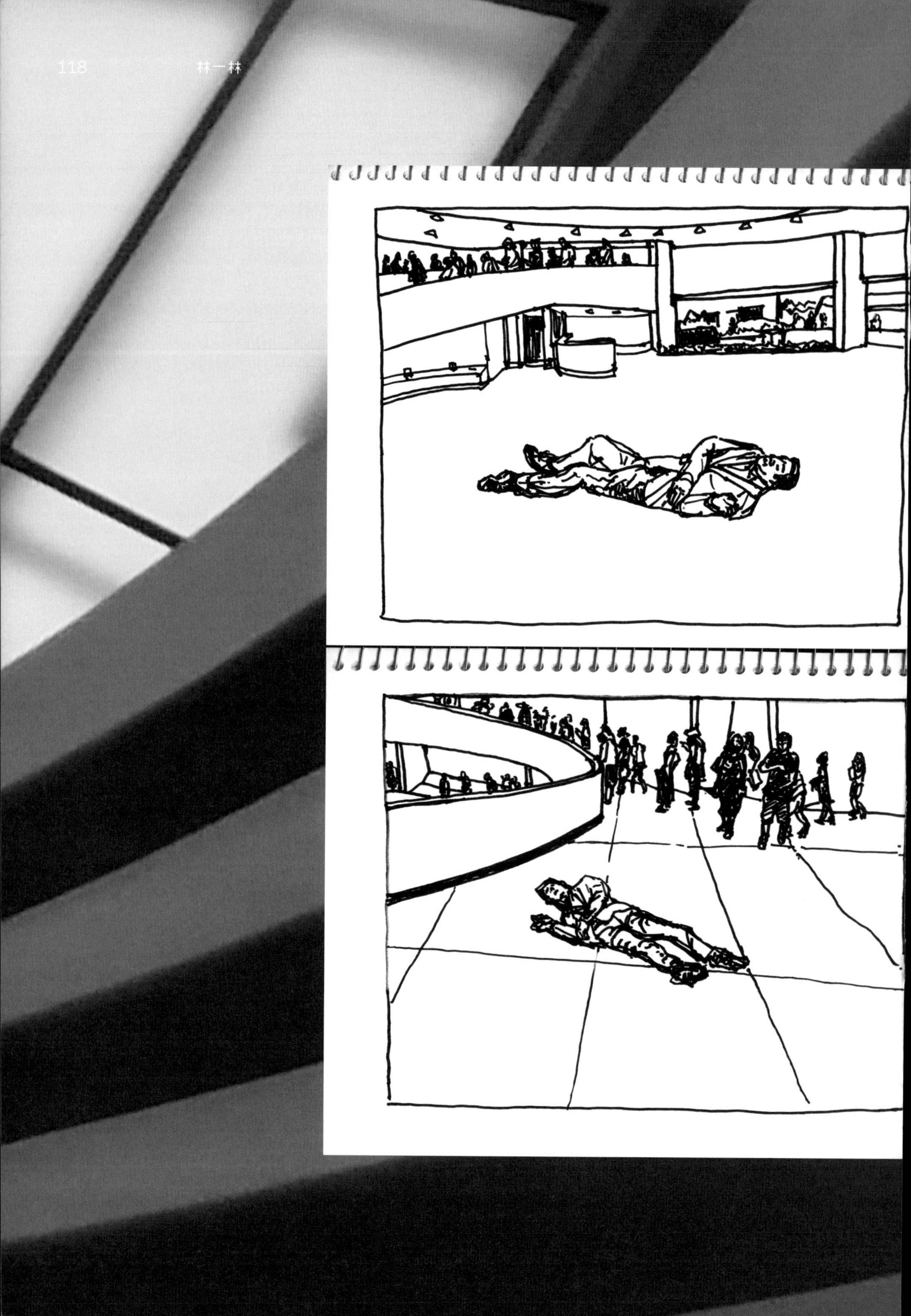

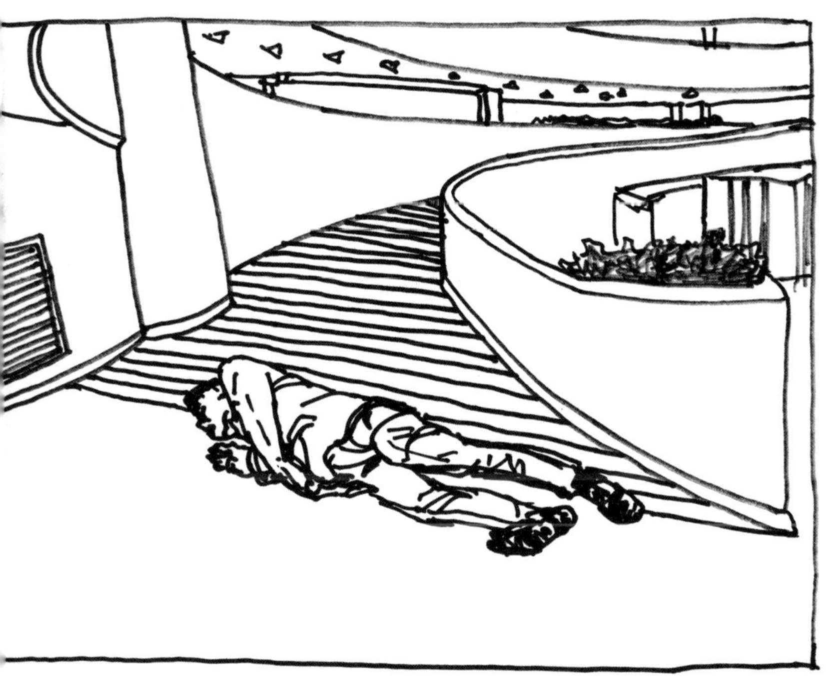

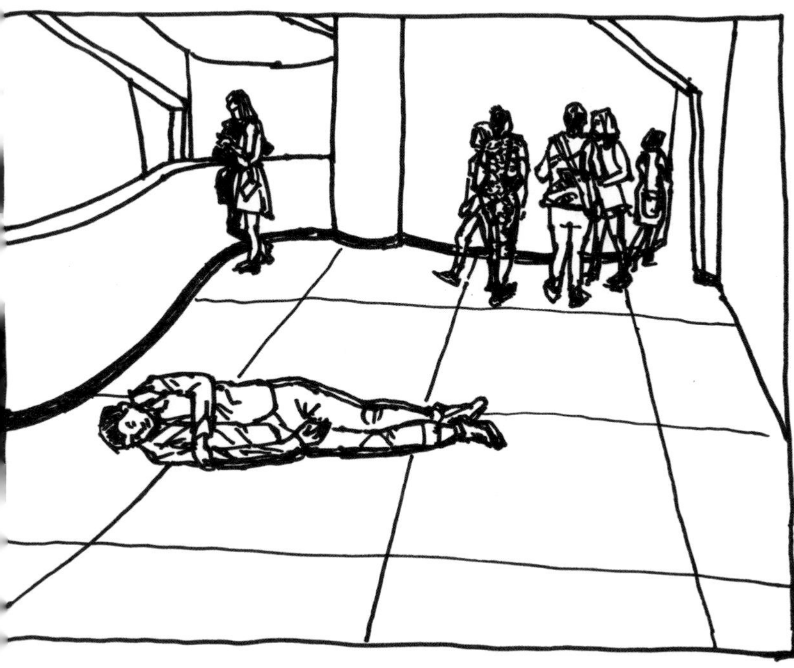

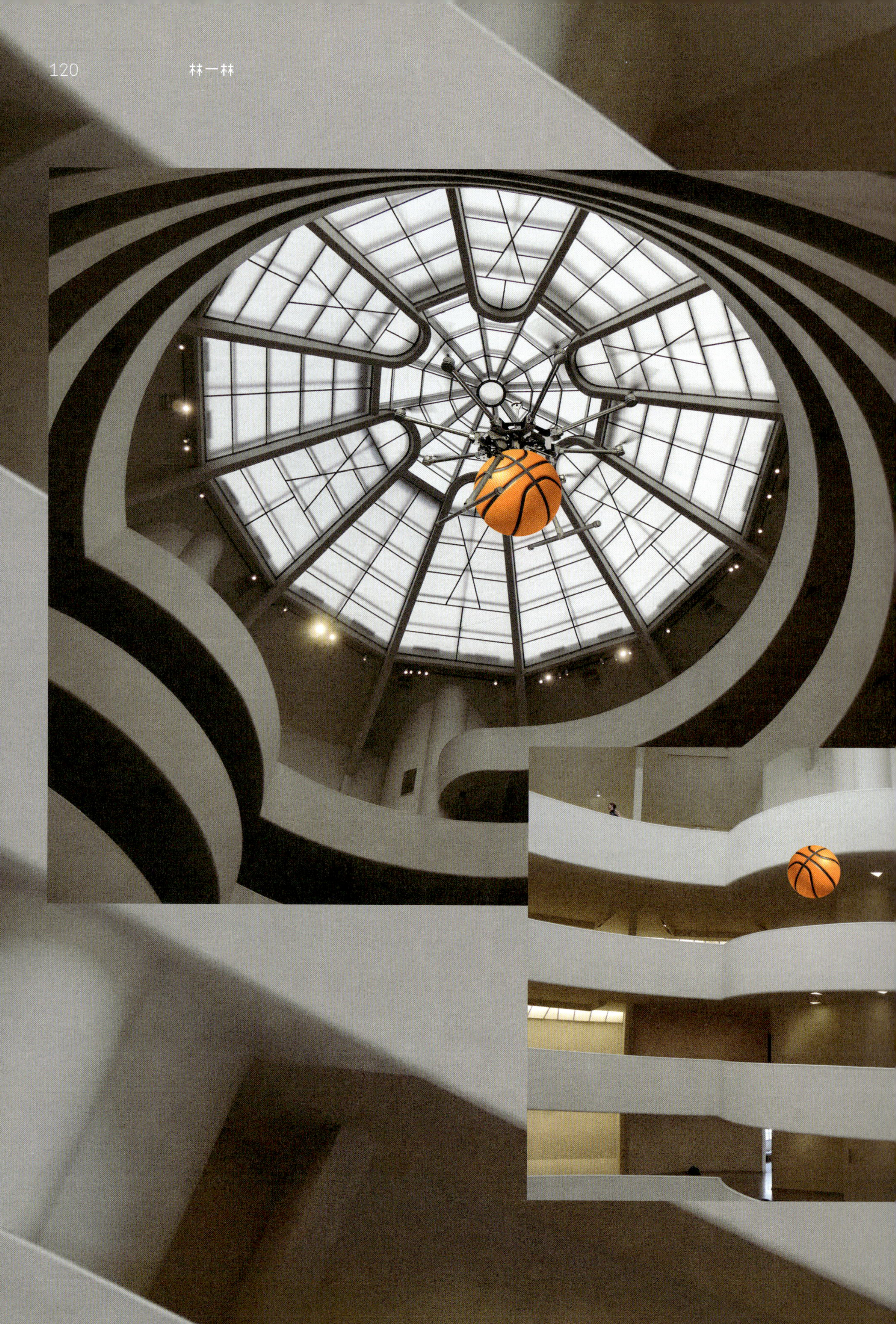

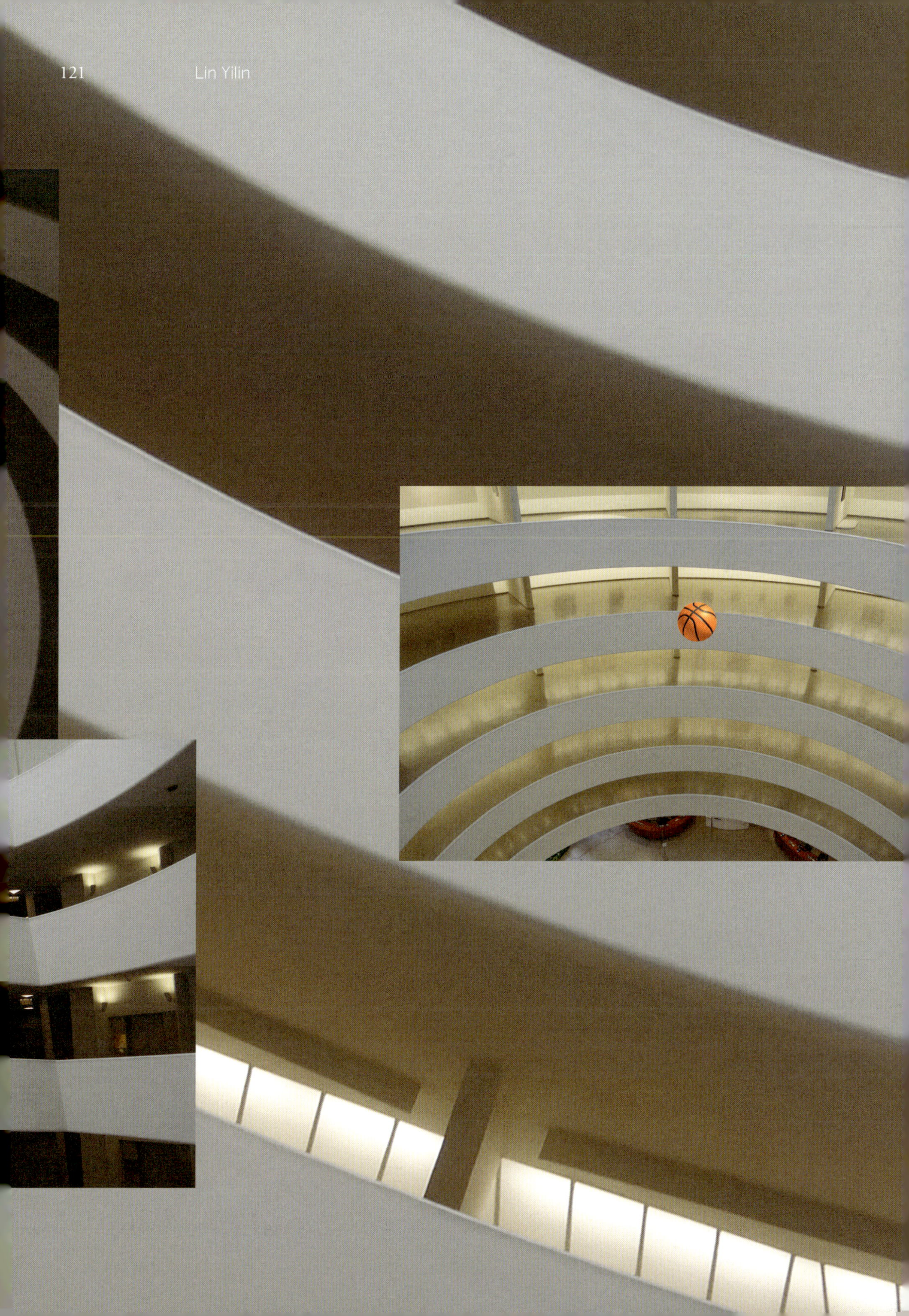

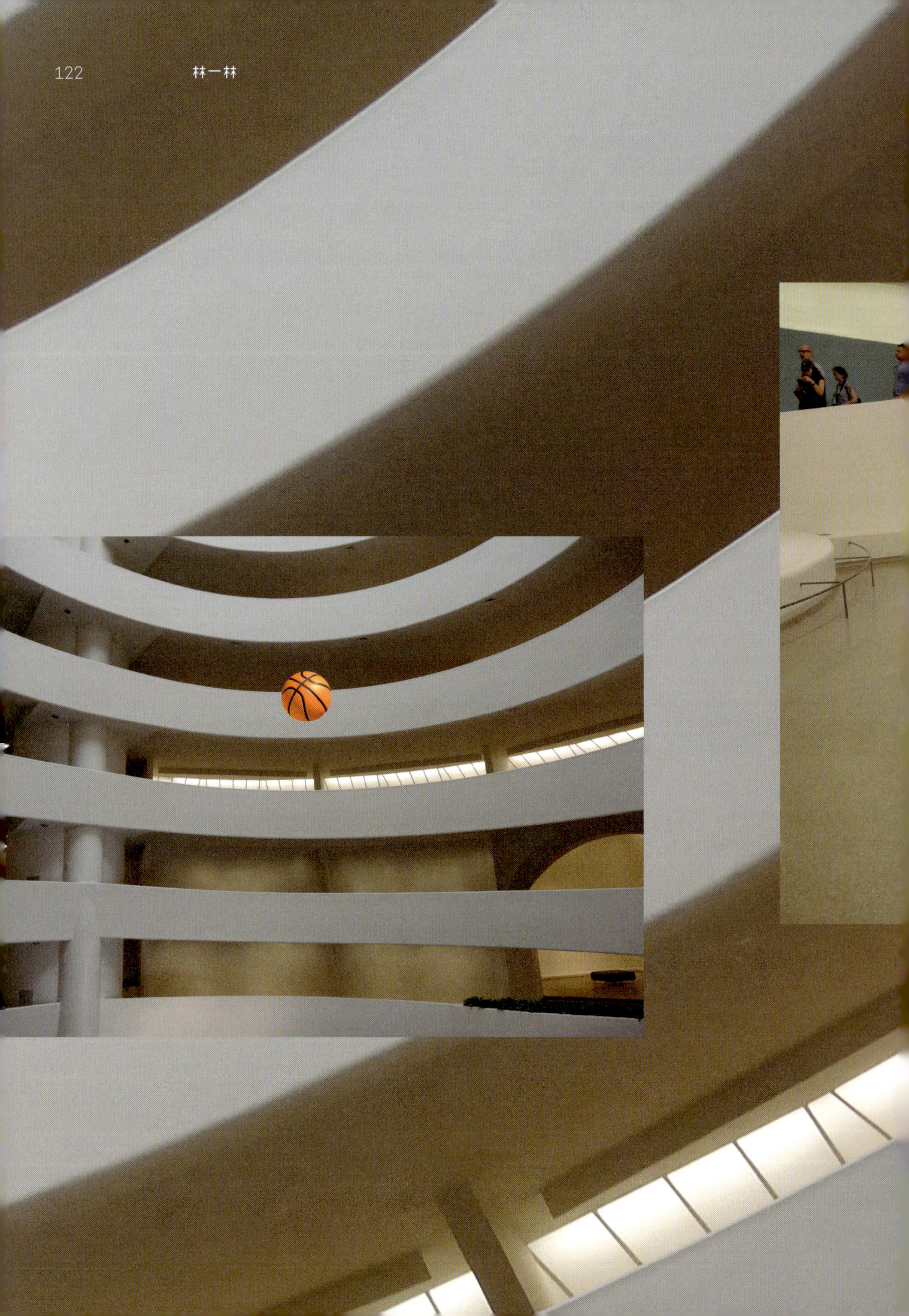

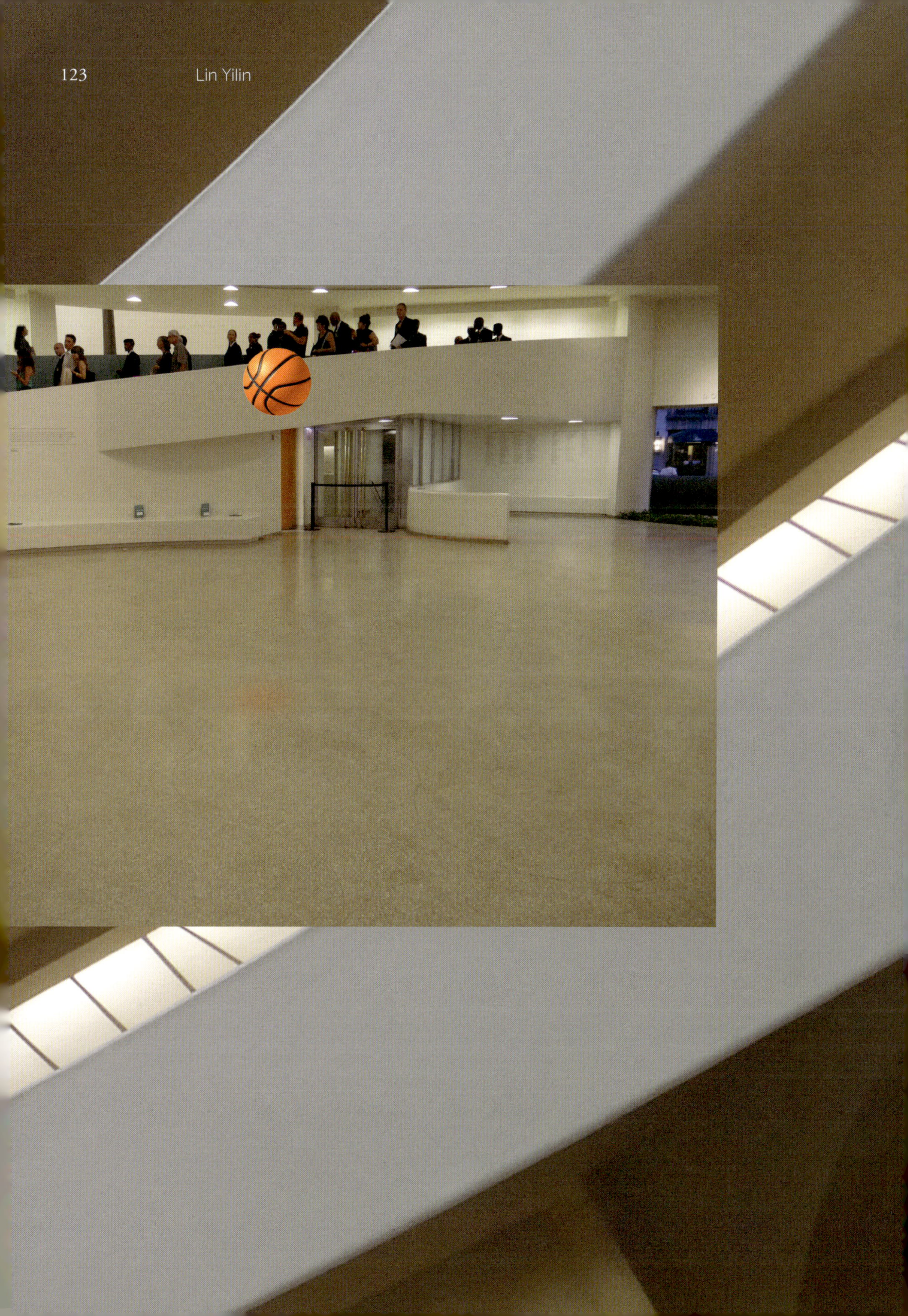

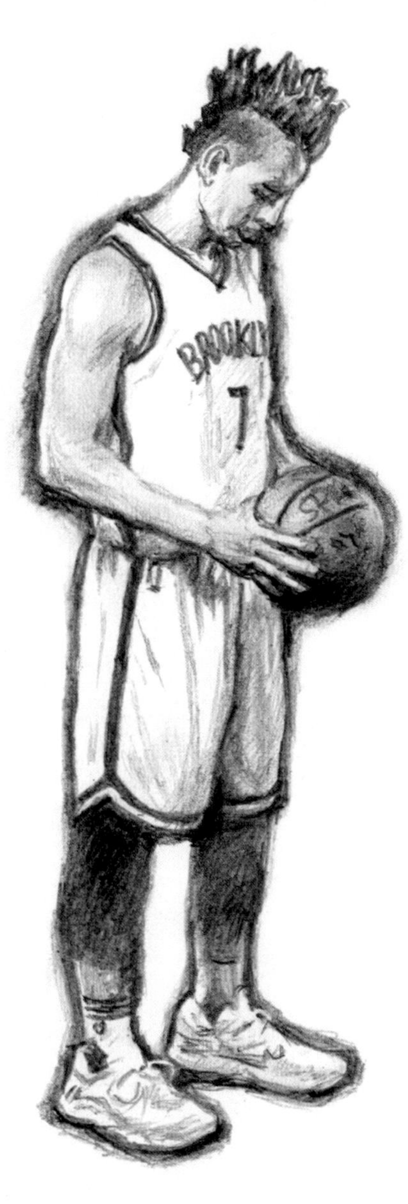
7

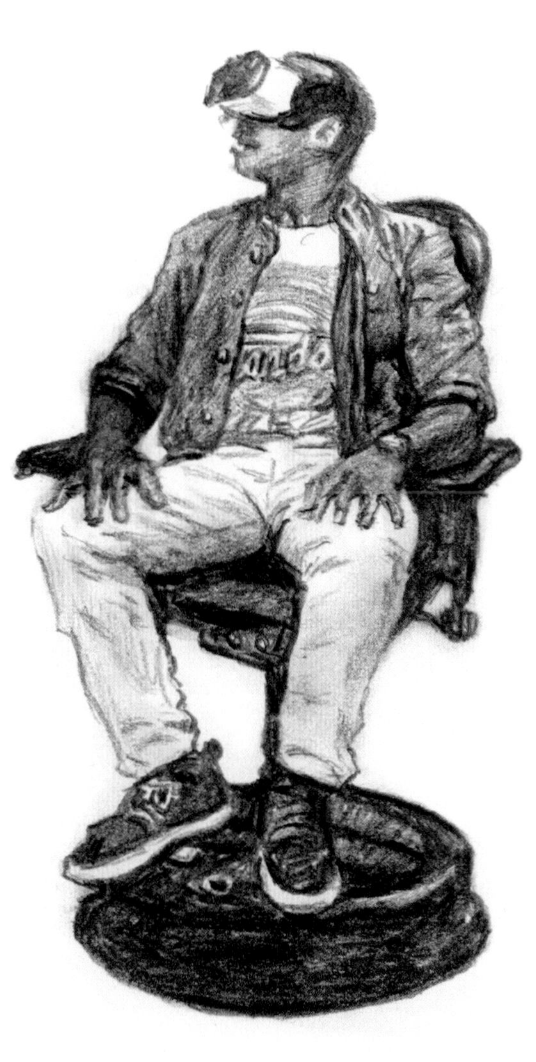

許立志
Xu Lizhi

Translated by Eleanor Goodman

我願在海上獨自漂流
I Long to Float Alone on the Ocean

朝著流水線的方向
Along the assembly line
我的愛恨時緩時急
my love and hate alternate speeds
手上，握著電批的顫抖
the shudder of the electric screwdriver
clenched in my hand
把一顆顆螺絲打入無底黑洞
drives screws one by one into bottomless dark holes
讓它銜接電板與主體
each linking an electric plate to a main component
猶如銜接未來與過去
like linking the future to the past
日光燈高懸，照亮我身體黑暗的部分
fluorescent lights hang overhead, illuminating the dark
parts of my body

它們已漫漶成咳嗽，喉痛，腰弓
they've blurred into coughing, a sore throat,
    a hunched back
我的心跳還跟不上生產的節奏
my heartbeat can't keep up with the pace
    of production
那些莫名的情緒，一閃一閃
inexpressible emotions, flashes
讓我擡頭，低頭，盼望，流淚
that make me look up, look down,
    look forward to, cry
時間匯聚成海，我沈湎其中
past evenings offer succulent seductions
往夕有著饞人的魅惑
time gathers into an ocean, where I lose myself
讓我一再回頭，品嘗孤獨，成長
drawing me back again to the taste of
    loneliness and age
年歲如片帆飄遠
my years drift far as a sail
我願在海上獨自漂流
I long to float alone on the ocean

2011-9-9

發展與死亡
Development and Death

流下絲綢般的血，橫亙著哭泣的失業
Blood flowing like silk,
unemployment spreading
like tears
我心臟裏彎曲的兩岸，溢出的都是傷
the curved banks of my heart
overflow with wounds
工業區呼吸粗礪疆域擴張，無視工人
集體爆發
the industrial zone breathes with
rough expansion, ignoring the
collective explosions
of workers
集體失眠集體死亡一樣活著
a life of collective insomnia and
collective death
保質期內的棺材，在GDP懷裏腐爛
an unexpired coffin rots in the
bosom of the GDP
像二奶在官員床上側躺
like a mistress reclining on an
official's bed
他們尋找退役的蛆蟲，發展的軌跡用
血書寫
they search for retired maggots,
and the orbit of development
is written in blood
愛的墓碑刻滿兒孫的詛咒，媽媽末日
的叫喊
love's gravestones are covered in
the curses of children,
a mother's doomsday cries

2011-12-20

私人收藏
Private Collection

三天前洗的被單
The sheet I washed three days ago
至今天還沒乾
is still damp today
其間我曾多次動用吹風機
I used a hairdryer on it a few times
沒想到結局還是一樣
never thinking it wouldn't make
any difference
煩躁之下
fidgety and annoyed
我索性將它扔到空中
I might as well just throw it over
the edge
就當是為天空貢獻了一朵
a contribution to the sky
私人收藏的白雲
a cloud from a private collection

2013-5-13

懸疑小說
Suspense Novel

去年在網上買的花瓶
The vase I bought last year online
昨天晚上才收到
finally arrived last night
實事求是地説
and honestly
這不能怪快遞公司
I can't blame the delivery service
怪只怪
I can only blame the fact
我的住處太難找
that my address is so hard to find
因此當快遞員大汗淋漓地
and so when the delivery man appeared
出現在我面前時
dripping with sweat
我不但沒有責備他
Not only did I not reprove him
還向他露出了
I even gave him
友好的微笑
a friendly smile
出於禮貌
out of courtesy
他也對我點頭哈腰
he groveled a little
為了表示歉意
to express regret
他還在我的墓碑前
and presented a fresh bouquet
遞上一束鮮花
to my tombstone

2013-6-6

逃
Escape

繞了一圈
Going around full circle
我悲哀地發現
I realize to my distress
我終究還是
in the end I still can't
逃不出地球
escape this earth

2013-6-8

一個人的手機史
Cellphone History of a Person

索尼愛立信K510c（2009.1.29——2011.2.1）
Sony Ericsson K510c (1.29.2009-2.1.2011)
諾基亞5230（2011.2.1——2012.3.10）
Nokia 5230 (2.1.2011-3.10.2012)
中興U880（2012.3.11——2013.6.11）
Zhongxing U880 (3.11.2012-6.11.2013)
小米2S（2013.6.11——）
Xiaomi 2S (6.11.2013-)

2013-6-11

移民
Emigration

我移民月球了
I've emigrated to the moon
你們誰也不用羨慕我
but none of you need envy me
這事表面看來風光無限
it might seem everything is great on the surface
其實也有讓我頭疼的問題
but there have also been some problems
比如到底坐什麼交通工具
like what's the best form of transportation
到月球比較方便
to get to the moon
是自行車還是公交車
bicycle or bus
是輪船還是飛機
steamship or airplane
是火箭還是神十
rocket or the Shenzhou spacecraft
無奈之下
left without a choice
我索性把手伸向天空
I might as well reach up
採下白雲一朵
and grab a cloud
學電視裏的齊天大聖
I should learn from the Monkey King on TV
幾個筋鬥翻到了月球
and somersault all the way to the moon
成功著陸的那一刻
and the instant I touch down
竟還收到
I'll even receive
習總發來的賀電
a message of congratulations from President Xi

2013-7-17

深圳深圳
Shenzhen Shenzhen

世界之窗　歡樂谷　東部華僑城
Window to the World　Happy Valley　Overseas Chinese Town East
海洋世界　大小梅沙　仙湖植物園
SeaWorld　Dameisha Beach　Xianhu Botanical Garden
地王大廈　京基100　寶安機場
Diwang Tower　KK100 Tower　Bao'an Airport
深圳中心書城　深圳圖書館
Shenzhen Book City　Shenzhen Library
深圳音樂廳　深圳少年宮
Shenzhen Concert Hall　Shenzhen Children's Palace
深圳大劇院　深圳大學　深圳北站
Shenzhen Theater　Shenzhen University　Shenzhen North Station
鞋材廠　電鍍廠　模具廠
shoe factories　electroplate factories　die mold factories
電子廠　塑料廠　造紙廠
electronics factories　plastics factories　paper factories
線材廠　家具廠　磚頭廠
wire rod factories　furniture factories　brick factories
玩具廠　五金廠　印刷廠
toy factories　hardware factories　printing factories
電器廠　馬達廠　服裝廠
appliance factories　motor factories　clothing factories
針織廠　製品廠　肉聯廠
knit products factories　manufactured goods factories
　meatpacking factories

2013-12-4

流水線下的女工
Woman Worker on the Assembly Line

她蹲在流水線下
She kneels by the assembly line
低著頭，把玩一顆鋥亮的螺絲
head down, fondling a shiny screw
她嘴唇微微抖動
her lips tremble a bit
雙手微微抖動，兩個膝蓋微微抖動
her hands tremble a bit, her knees
tremble a bit
肩膀微微抖動，微弓的背微微抖動
her shoulders tremble a bit, her slightly
hunched back trembles a bit
借著靜電衣與工衣的雙重掩護
behind her double camouflage of
uniform and electrostatic suit
她藏起一頭青絲，藏起身體的海岸線
she hides her dark hair, hides the
coastline of her body
藏起青春藏起愛情，藏起名字藏起夢想
hides her youth and her love, hides
her name and her dreams
在這個無人入眠的冬夜
on a winter night when no one sleeps
我猜想，她還偷偷藏起
I think she may also secretly hide
體內剛剛綻放的
a few plum blossoms
兩三朵梅花
just blooming inside her body

2014-1-5

一顆螺絲掉在地上
A Screw Falls to the Ground

一顆螺絲掉在地上
A screw falls to the ground
在這個加班的夜晚
tonight on the night shift
垂直降落，輕輕一響
it drops straight down, with
a faint sound
不會引起任何人的注意
that won't draw anyone's
attention
就像在此之前
just as before
某個相同的夜晚
on the same kind of night
有個人掉在地上
a person fell to the ground

2014-1-9

絕句
Broken Verse

總要有人撿起地上的螺絲
There must always be
someone to pick screws up
off the ground
這廢棄的生活才不至於生銹
so all these discarded lives
won't just turn to rust

2014-1-15

曹斐
Cao Fei

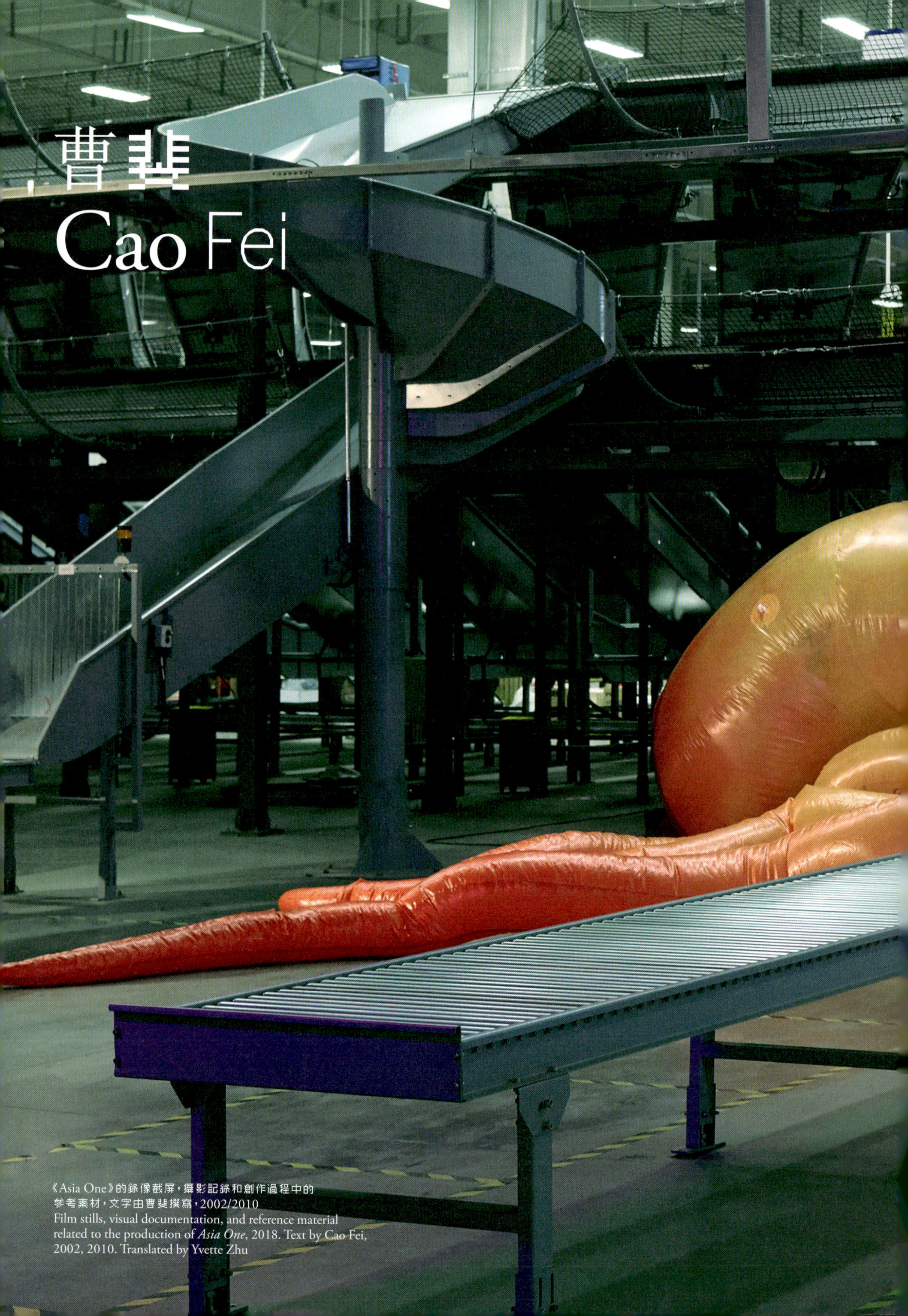

《Asia One》的錄像截屏，攝影記錄和創作過程中的參考素材，文字由曹斐撰寫，2002/2010
Film stills, visual documentation, and reference material related to the production of *Asia One*, 2018. Text by Cao Fei, 2002, 2010. Translated by Yvette Zhu

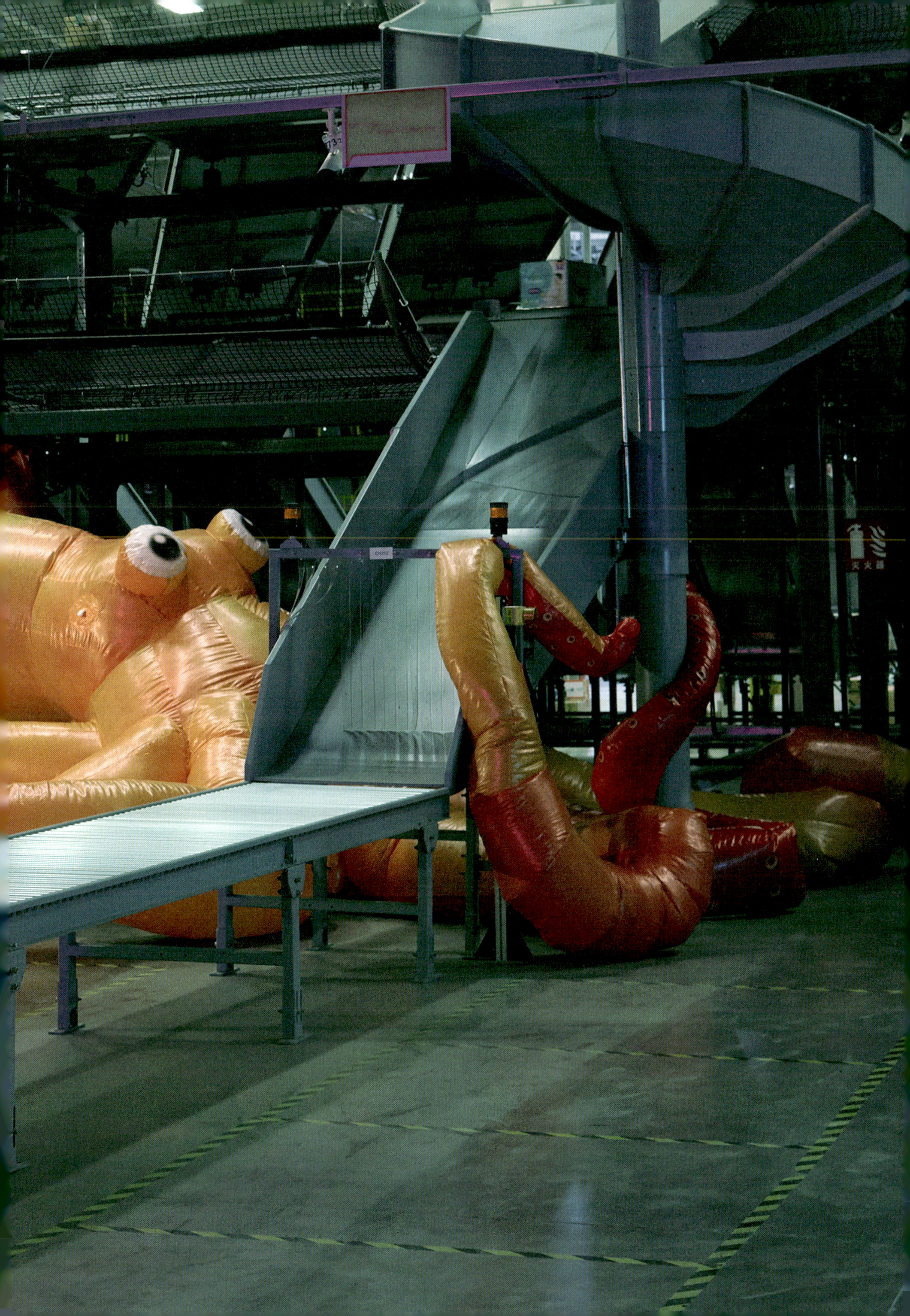

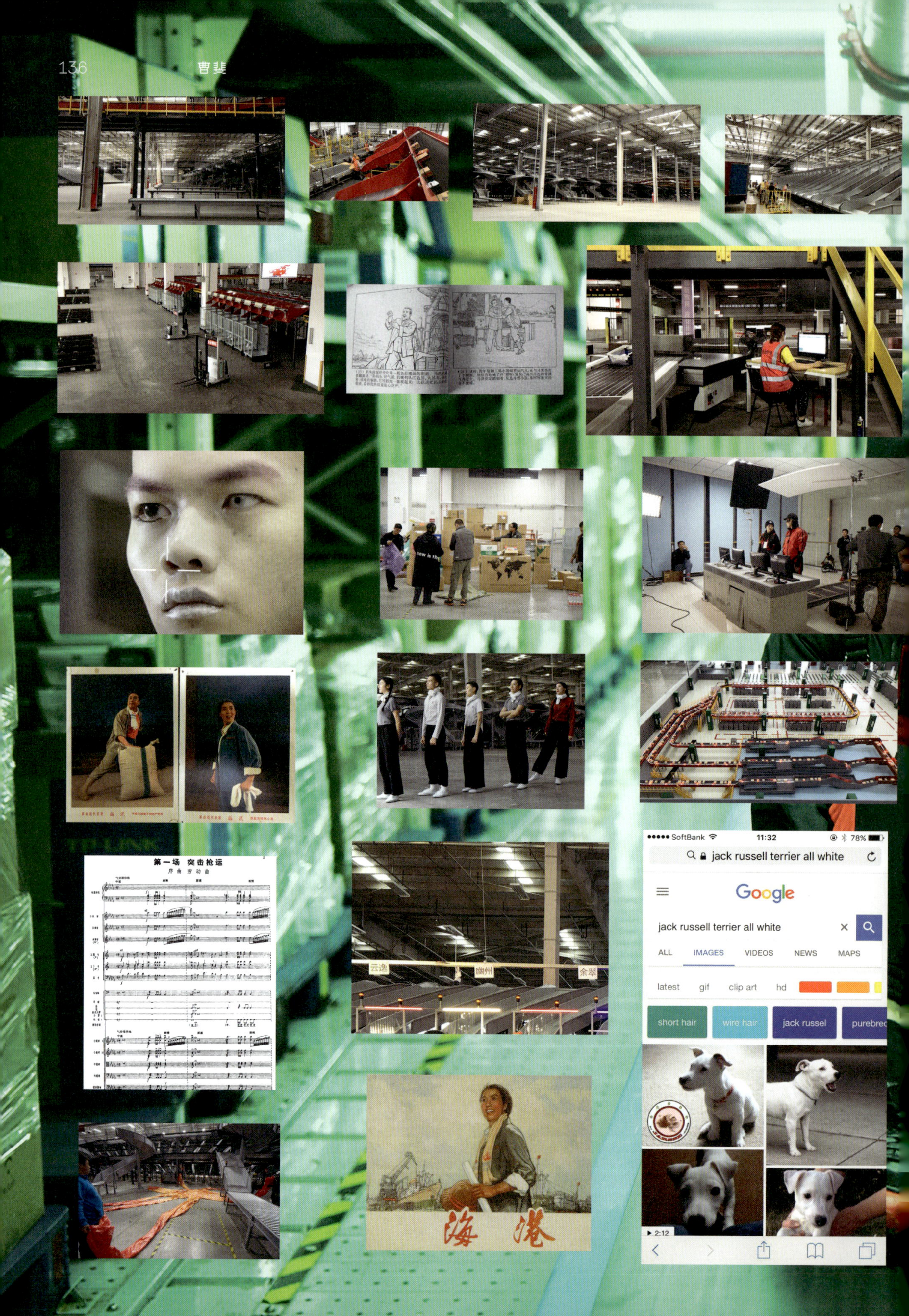
第一场 突击抢运
序曲 劳动曲
海 港
SoftBank
11:32
78%
jack russell terrier all white
Google
jack russell terrier all white
ALL
IMAGES
VIDEOS
NEWS
MAPS
latest
gif
clip art
hd
short hair
wire hair
jack russel
2:12

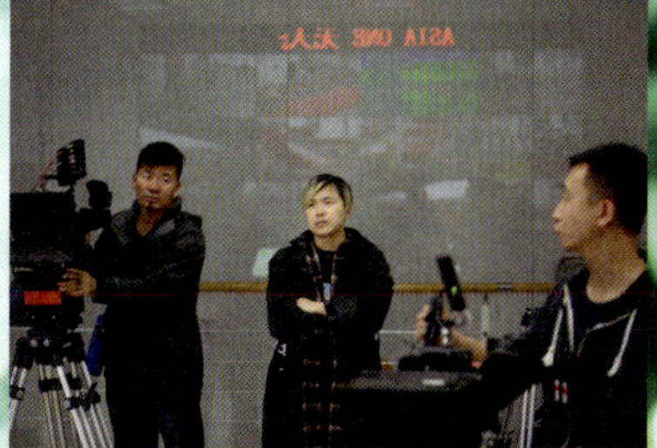

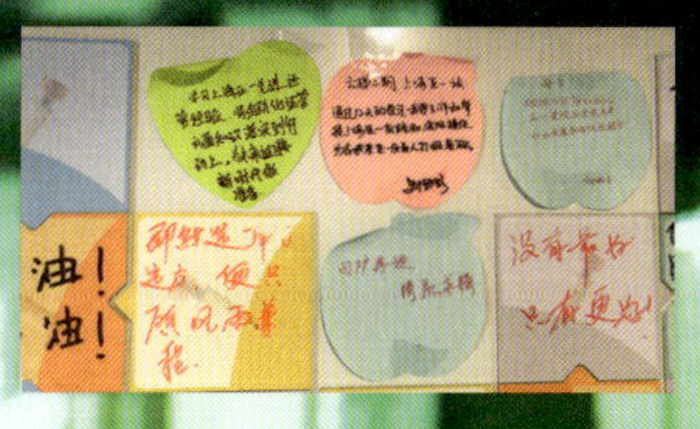

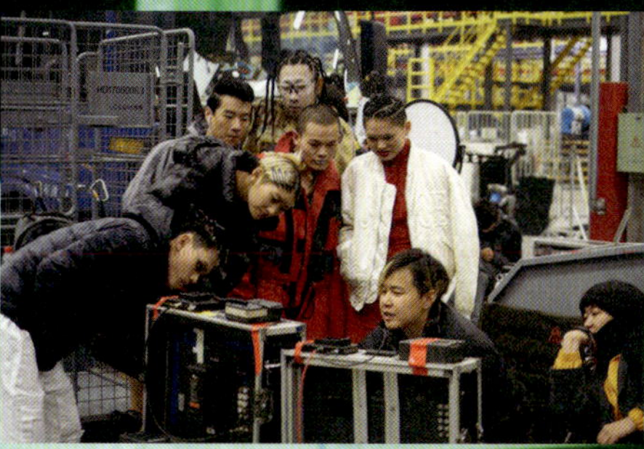

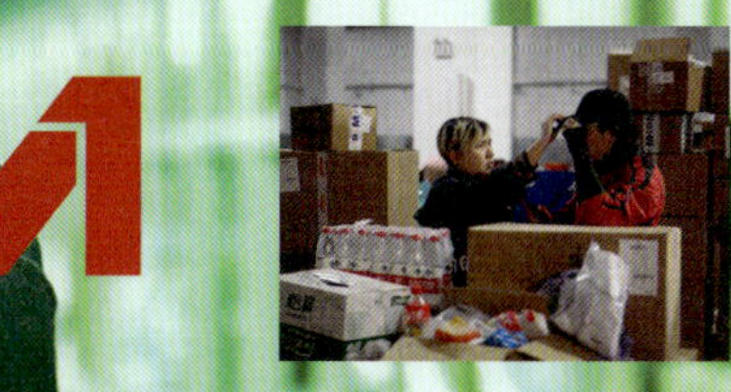

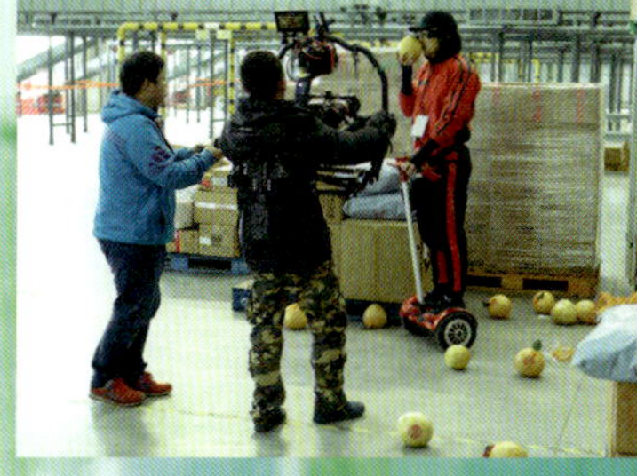

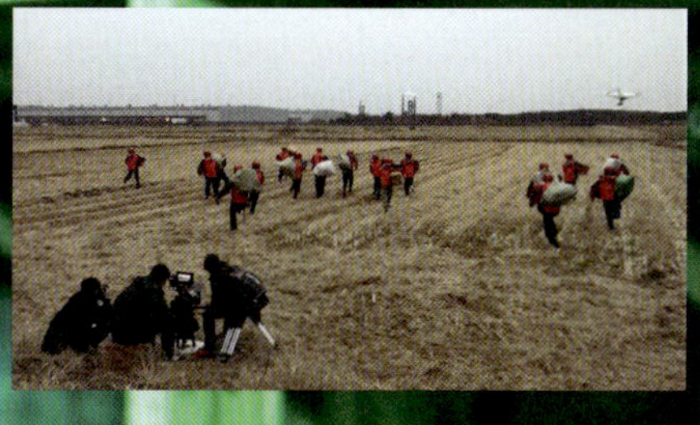

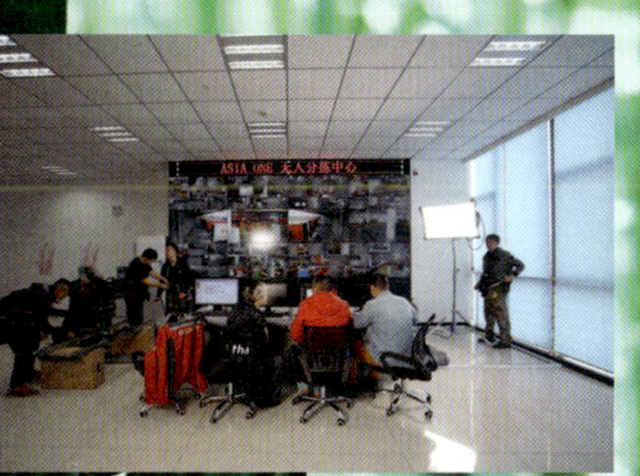

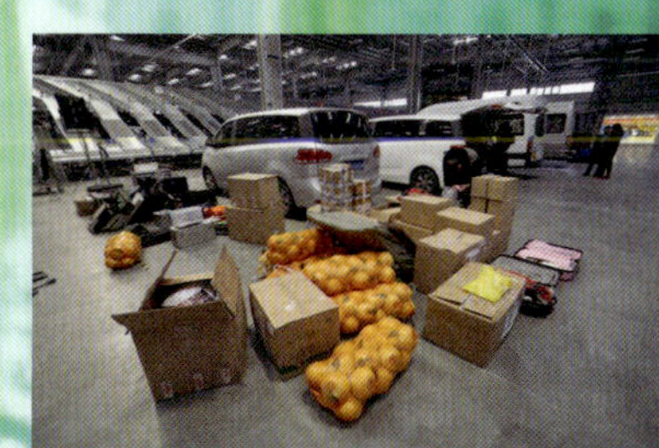

海港 大跃进把码头的面貌改

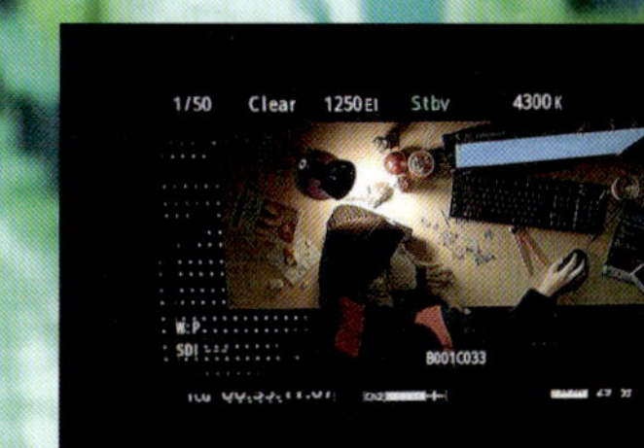

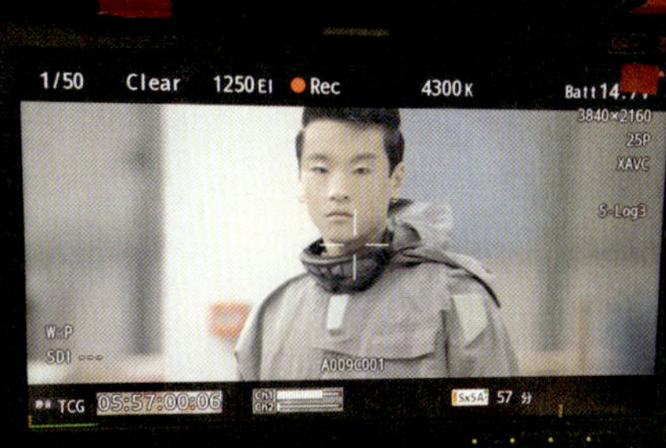

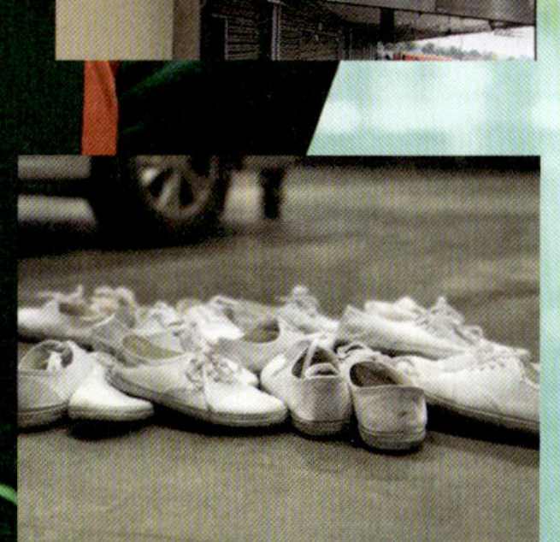

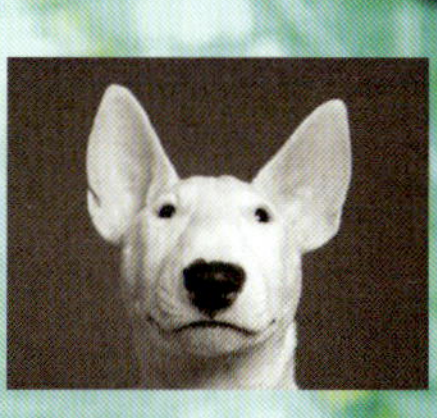

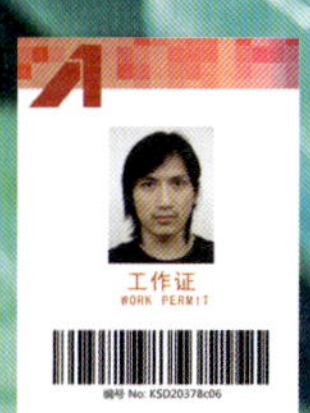

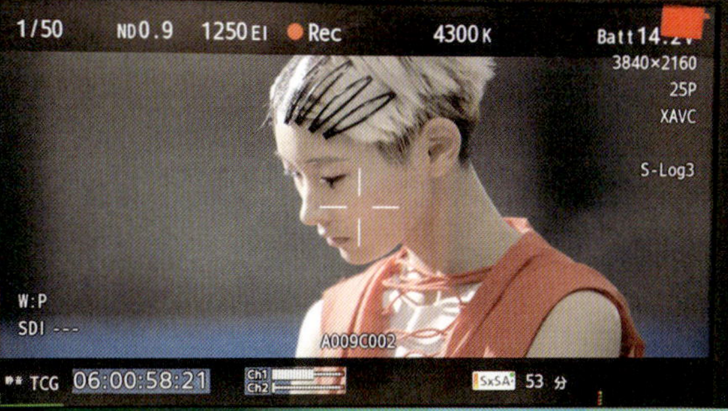

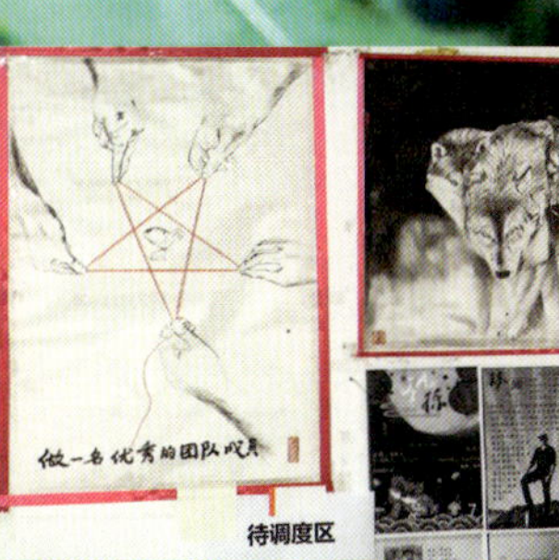

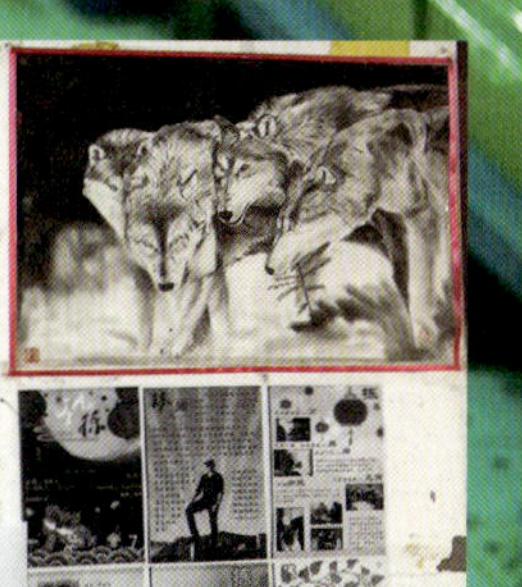

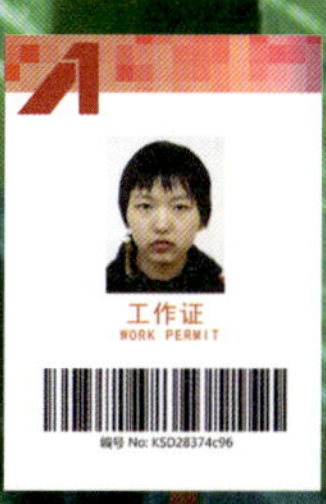

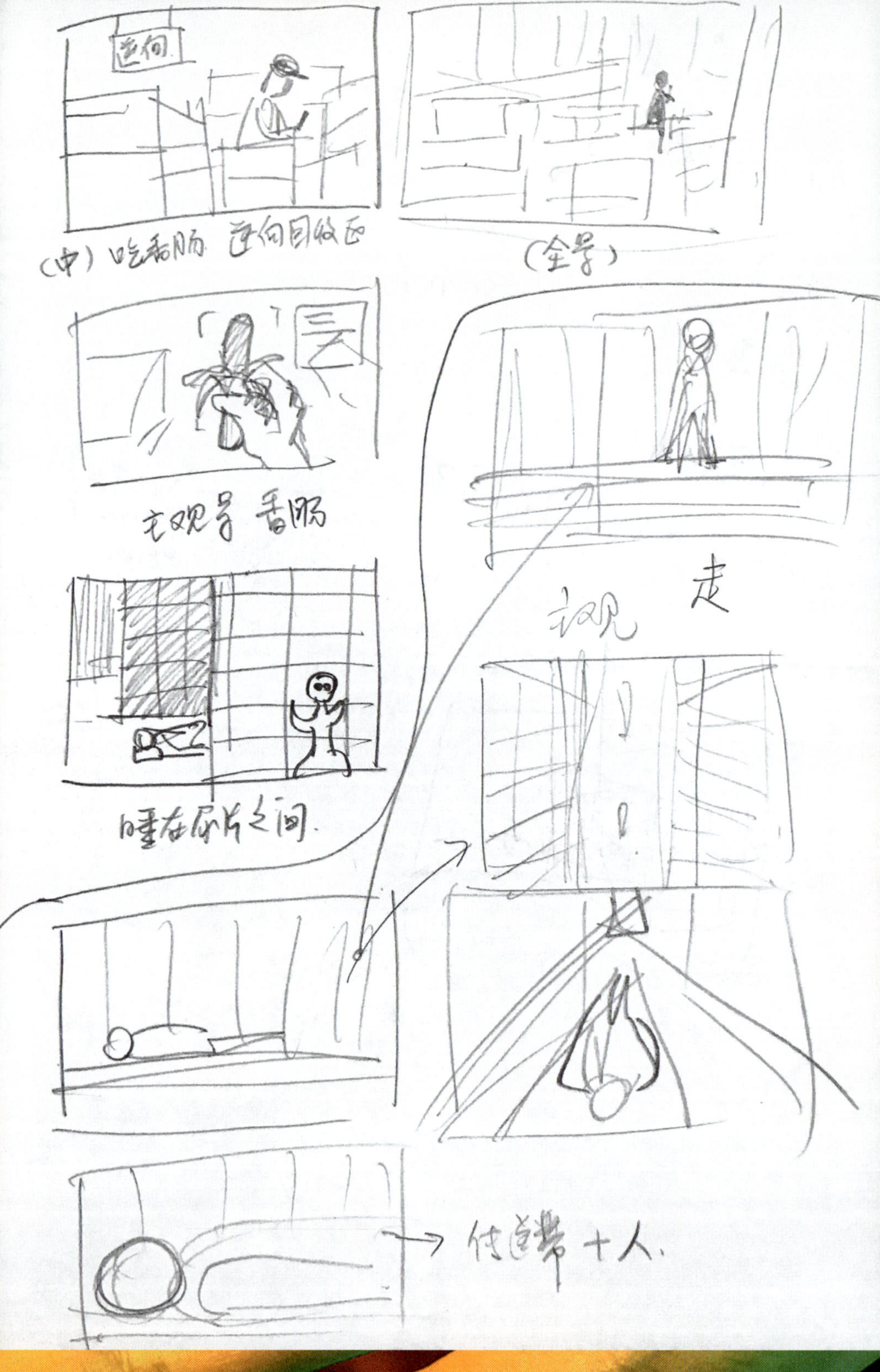
逆向
(中) 吃香肠 逆向回收区
(全景)
主观镜 香肠
睡在废片之间.
主观
走
传送带 十人.

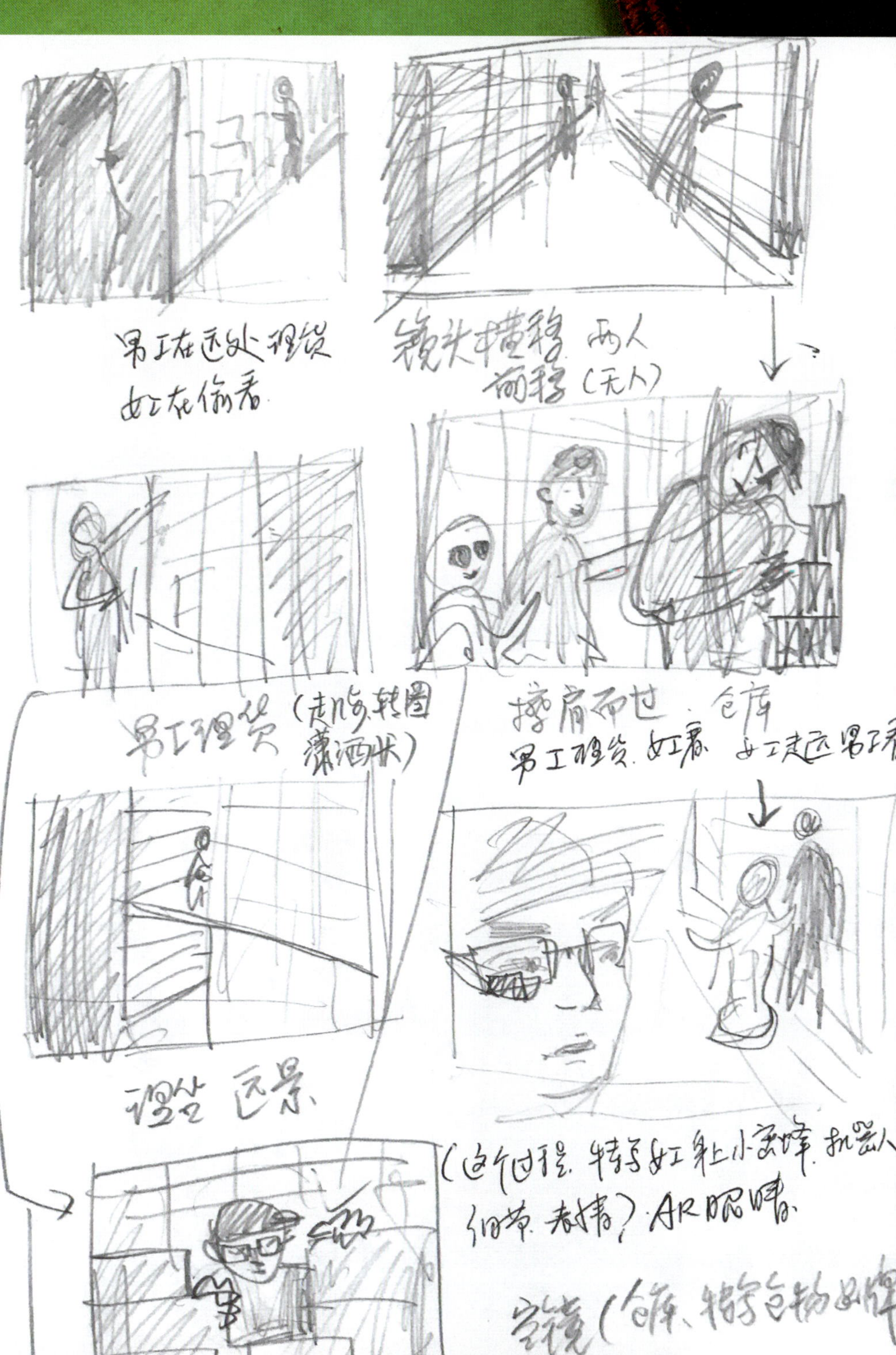
男工在远处理货
女工在偷看
镜头横移 两人
前移（无人）
擦肩而过 仓库
理货 远景
理货

Express Delivery

A dim, somber room. A girl hides crying in the comforter on the bed, weeping and falling quiet from time to time while channel surfing. A beautiful, expansive seascape appears on the TV screen.

The girl finds a cardboard box. She combs her hair before the mirror.

She makes a call. Then she calmly lies down in the box and waits.

The courier from the express delivery company arrives. He seals the box with tape and carries it out of the room.

The box is thrown onto the delivery truck, where it sits among the other items (a bamboo basket full of chicken eggs, a birdcage, a cured pig's head . . .).

The courier arrives at a company. When he opens the door, out flows the sound of Western opera music. The staff sing with mouths wide open. Their loud singing traces the undulating curve of a graph depicting the yearly sales figures. Off to the side, a dismissed male employee is stuffed into a cardboard box.

Through the holes of the two boxes (only their eyes are visible), the male employee and the girl stare at each other wordlessly.

A bumpy, rugged road. The cardboard box with the girl inside tumbles off the express delivery truck. A farmer on a chicken transport motorcycle who has been tailgating the truck picks up the package and ties it to the top of his chicken cage. He chases after the truck.

A migrant worker peddles a foam delivery tricycle across the road in front of the chicken transport motorcycle. The farmer broadsides the tricycle. Foam spills all across the road. The cardboard box with the girl inside flies from the motorcycle onto the roadside. The chicken cage falls down and is thrown open. Some chickens escape, others die. The motorcycle farmer dies on the spot while the migrant worker lies unconscious. The police come rushing to the accident scene on motor scooters and begin investigating. They

快遞

在昏暗的房間裏，她躲在床上的被褥裏哭，哭哭停停，一邊按遙控選電視台，畫面出現美麗的海洋風景。

她找來一個紙皮箱，對鏡梳理一番。

她打了個電話，然後安靜地躺在箱子裏面等待。

快遞公司的人上門，用封條封好箱子，把箱子搬走。

箱子被扔上貨車車廂，和其他物件擺放一起，（一籮筐雞蛋，一籠鳥，臘豬頭……）

快遞員到了一家公司，進門時就听到西洋歌劇的聲音，職員們都在張口歌唱，（看著年度銷售曲線圖，隨著曲線高低縱聲歌唱）。一名被辭退的男職員被裝進箱裏。

透過兩個箱子的孔（只能看見眼睛），他們互相對望，一言不發。

在崎嶇的公路上，汽車的顛簸把裝女孩的那個箱子抖了下去，被在後面開摩托運雞的村民拾到。他把箱子綁在雞籠上，追趕快遞公司的汽車。

摩托車撞上橫過馬路運泡沫的三輪車民工，泡沫倒一地，箱子飛到路邊上，雞籠跌開，一些雞死了，

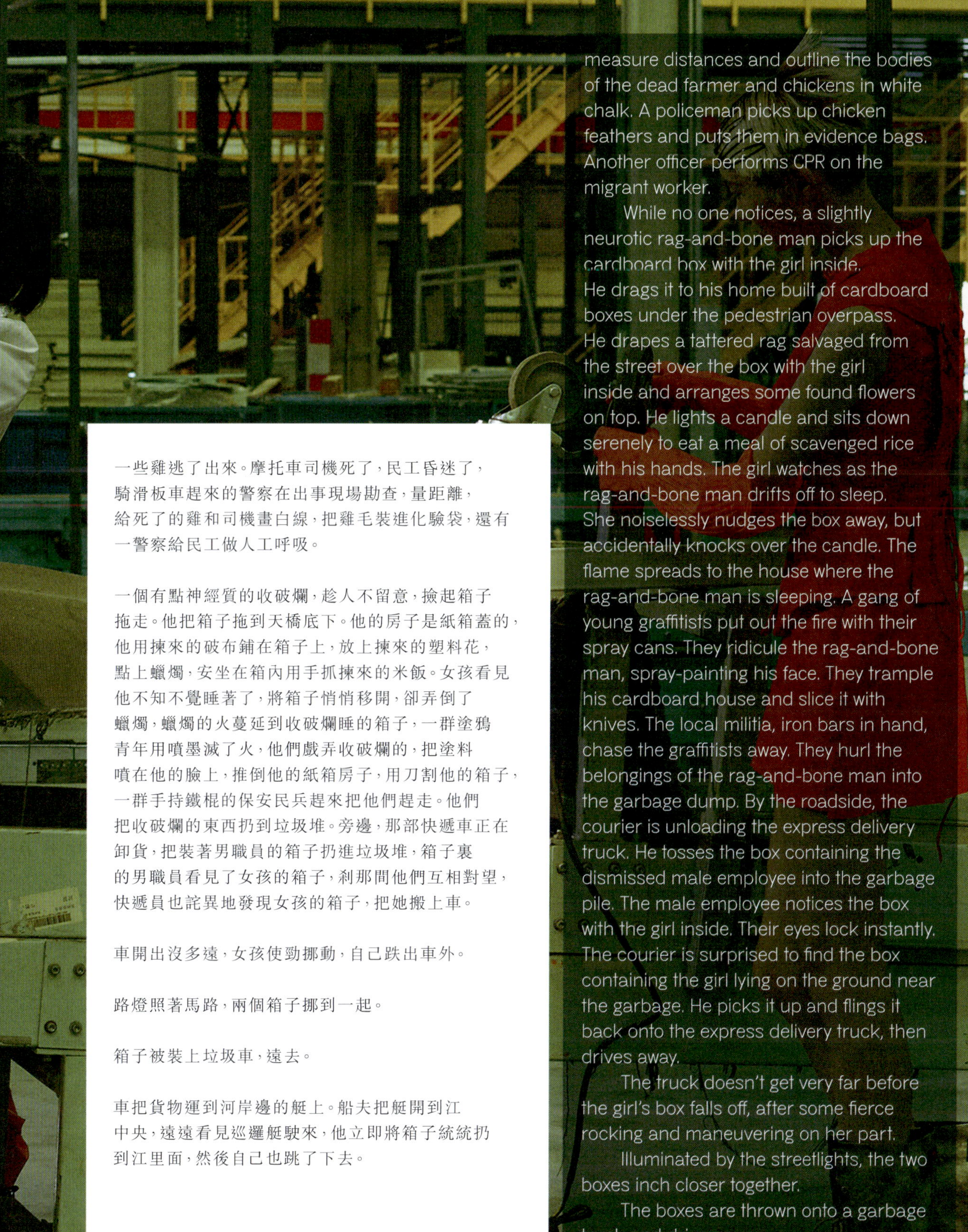

一些雞逃了出來。摩托車司機死了，民工昏迷了，騎滑板車趕來的警察在出事現場勘查，量距離，給死了的雞和司機畫白線，把雞毛裝進化驗袋，還有一警察給民工做人工呼吸。

一個有點神經質的收破爛，趁人不留意，撿起箱子拖走。他把箱子拖到天橋底下。他的房子是紙箱蓋的，他用揀來的破布鋪在箱子上，放上揀來的塑料花，點上蠟燭，安坐在箱內用手抓揀來的米飯。女孩看見他不知不覺睡著了，將箱子悄悄移開，卻弄倒了蠟燭，蠟燭的火蔓延到收破爛睡的箱子，一群塗鴉青年用噴墨滅了火，他們戲弄收破爛的，把塗料噴在他的臉上，推倒他的紙箱房子，用刀割他的箱子，一群手持鐵棍的保安民兵趕來把他們趕走。他們把收破爛的東西扔到垃圾堆。旁邊，那部快遞車正在卸貨，把裝著男職員的箱子扔進垃圾堆，箱子裏的男職員看見了女孩的箱子，剎那間他們互相對望，快遞員也詫異地發現女孩的箱子，把她搬上車。

車開出沒多遠，女孩使勁挪動，自己跌出車外。

路燈照著馬路，兩個箱子挪到一起。

箱子被裝上垃圾車，遠去。

車把貨物運到河岸邊的艇上。船夫把艇開到江中央，遠遠看見巡邏艇駛來，他立即將箱子統統扔到江里面，然後自己也跳了下去。

measure distances and outline the bodies of the dead farmer and chickens in white chalk. A policeman picks up chicken feathers and puts them in evidence bags. Another officer performs CPR on the migrant worker.

While no one notices, a slightly neurotic rag-and-bone man picks up the cardboard box with the girl inside. He drags it to his home built of cardboard boxes under the pedestrian overpass. He drapes a tattered rag salvaged from the street over the box with the girl inside and arranges some found flowers on top. He lights a candle and sits down serenely to eat a meal of scavenged rice with his hands. The girl watches as the rag-and-bone man drifts off to sleep. She noiselessly nudges the box away, but accidentally knocks over the candle. The flame spreads to the house where the rag-and-bone man is sleeping. A gang of young graffitists put out the fire with their spray cans. They ridicule the rag-and-bone man, spray-painting his face. They trample his cardboard house and slice it with knives. The local militia, iron bars in hand, chase the graffitists away. They hurl the belongings of the rag-and-bone man into the garbage dump. By the roadside, the courier is unloading the express delivery truck. He tosses the box containing the dismissed male employee into the garbage pile. The male employee notices the box with the girl inside. Their eyes lock instantly. The courier is surprised to find the box containing the girl lying on the ground near the garbage. He picks it up and flings it back onto the express delivery truck, then drives away.

The truck doesn't get very far before the girl's box falls off, after some fierce rocking and maneuvering on her part.

Illuminated by the streetlights, the two boxes inch closer together.

The boxes are thrown onto a garbage truck and driven away.

The garbage truck arrives at a riverbank; its contents are offloaded onto a boat. The boatman steers the boat to

the middle of the river. From the distance comes a police patrol boat. The boatman dumps all the boxes into the river, then jumps in himself.

Inside the courtyard of the police station, a policeman plucks a chicken; to his side are a few hens. Some policemen are carrying the body of the motorcycle driver, while others escort the rag-and-bone man inside. Members of the egg-throwing audience squat in a row on the floor, as if in a police lineup, while the egg-pelted musician laments tearfully to the police. An old man yells that his bird is missing, while another policeman performs CPR on the boatman, who spits up a lungful of water. A few soaked boxes are strewn around. A policeman writes in his notebook.

The receiver's address on the soaked box is illegible.

The courier from the express delivery company returns the box to its sender.

A disheartened middle-aged man opens the door. He unwraps the box, and is shocked to find his long-lost wife. They hug, cry, kiss.

Suddenly, noises pour out from the box. The man looks and discovers their child inside.

警察局大院裏，旁邊是幾隻母雞，一個警員在拔雞毛，有的警員搬運摩托車司機的屍體，有的警員押送收破爛的進來，扔雞蛋的觀眾一字排開蹲在地上，被扔的那個音樂家在向警員哭訴，一個老頭在嚷嚷他的鳥不見了，那個船夫在警察的人工搶救下，吐出吞進的水，幾隻濕透的箱子放在地上，一個警員在作登記。

箱子上的收貨地址模糊了。

快遞公司的人員尋著地址將箱子送回原點。開門的是個沮喪的中年男人。男人將箱子打開，驚奇地發現他失踪多時的妻子，他們哭著擁抱、親吻。

突然，箱子里傳來聲音，男人一看，原來是他的孩子。

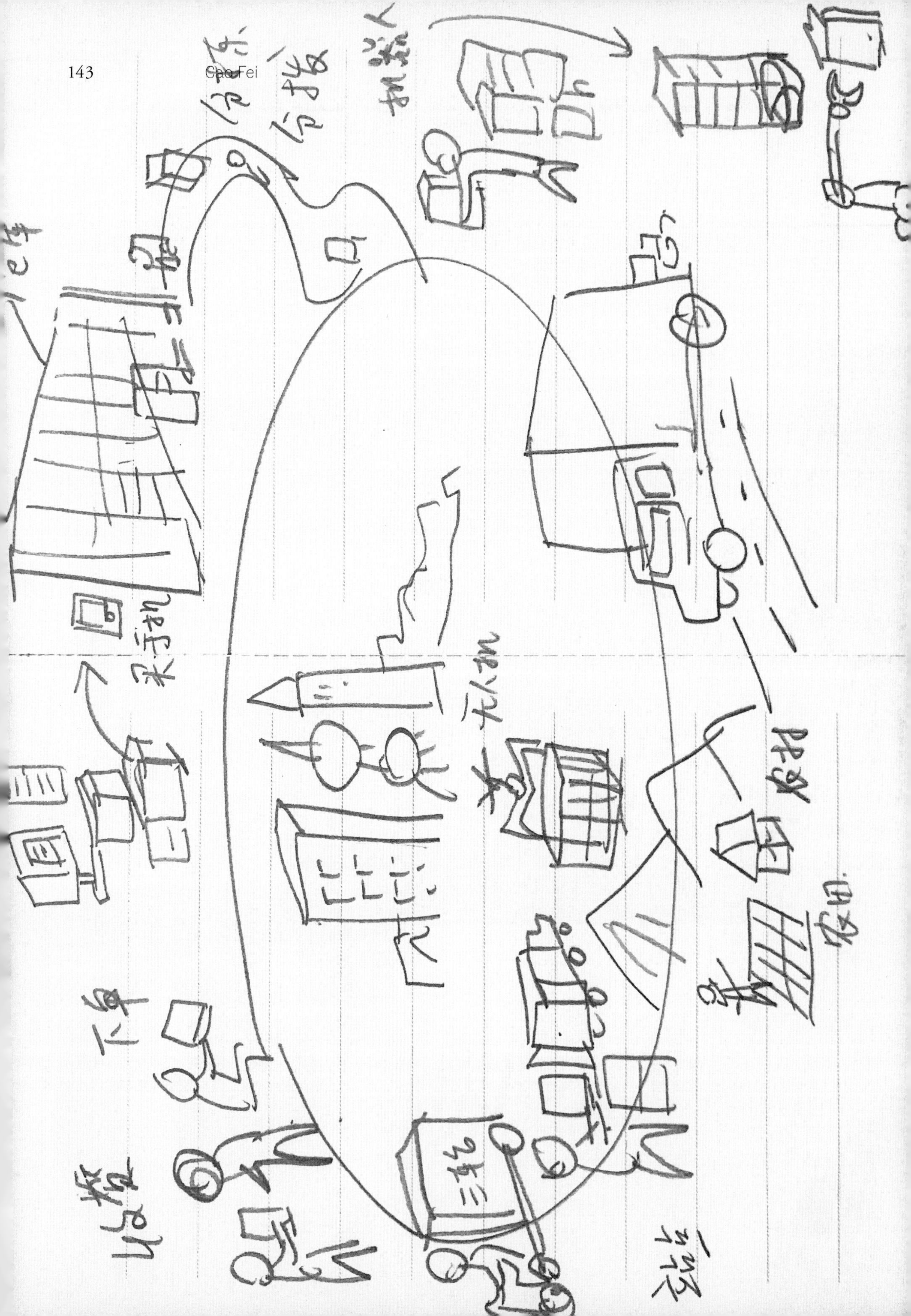

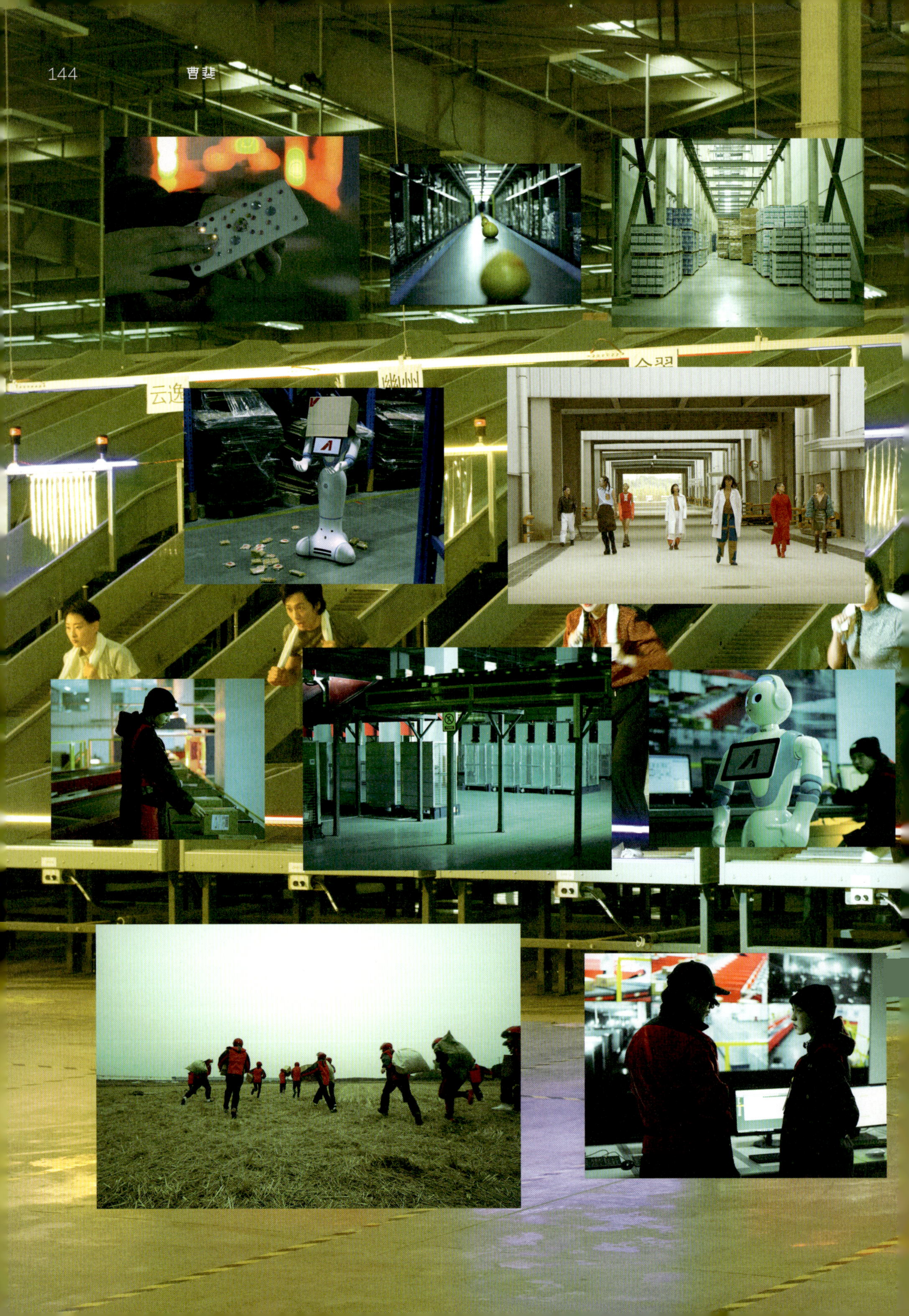

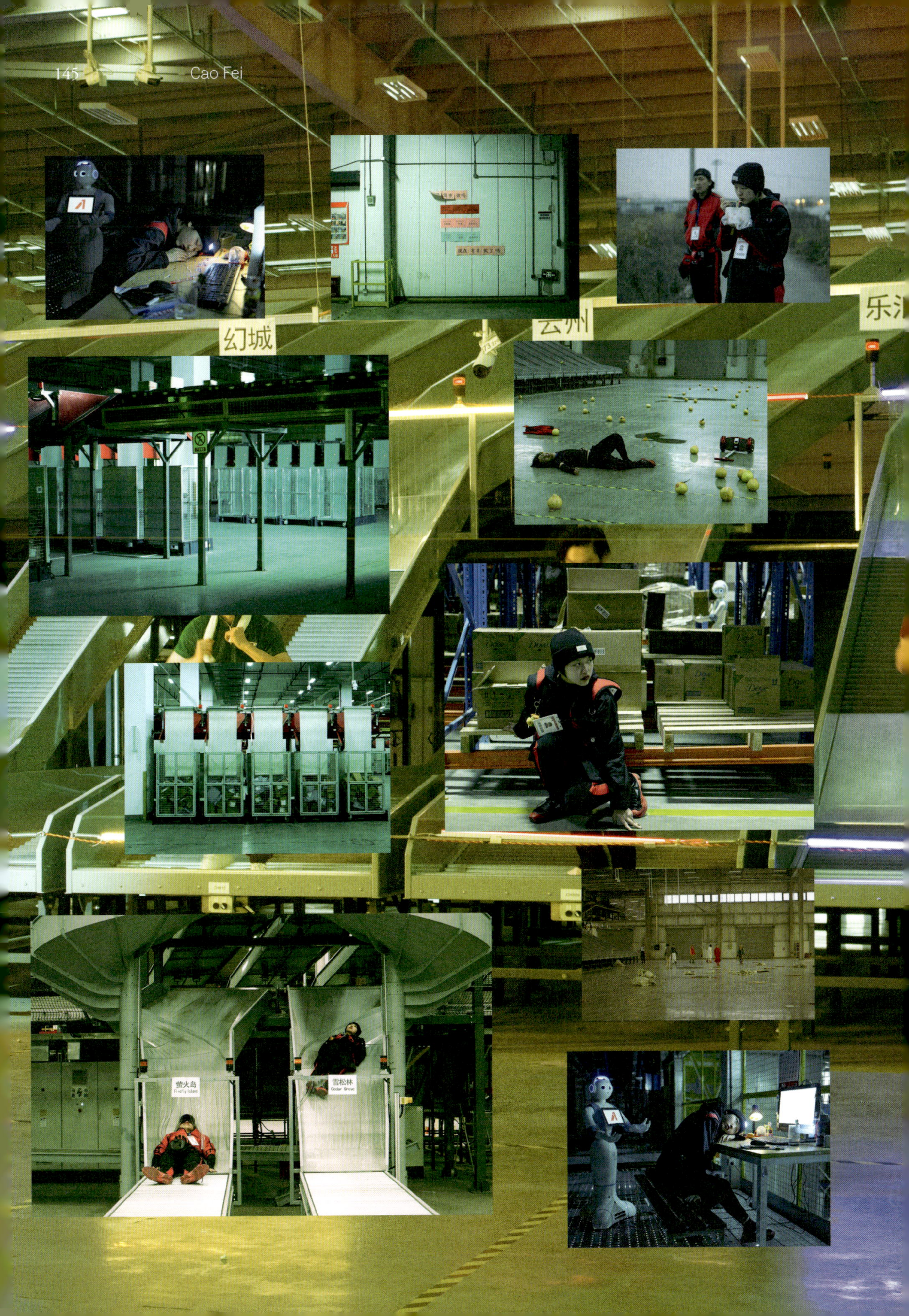
幻城
云州
萤火岛
Firefly Island
雪松林
Cedar Grove

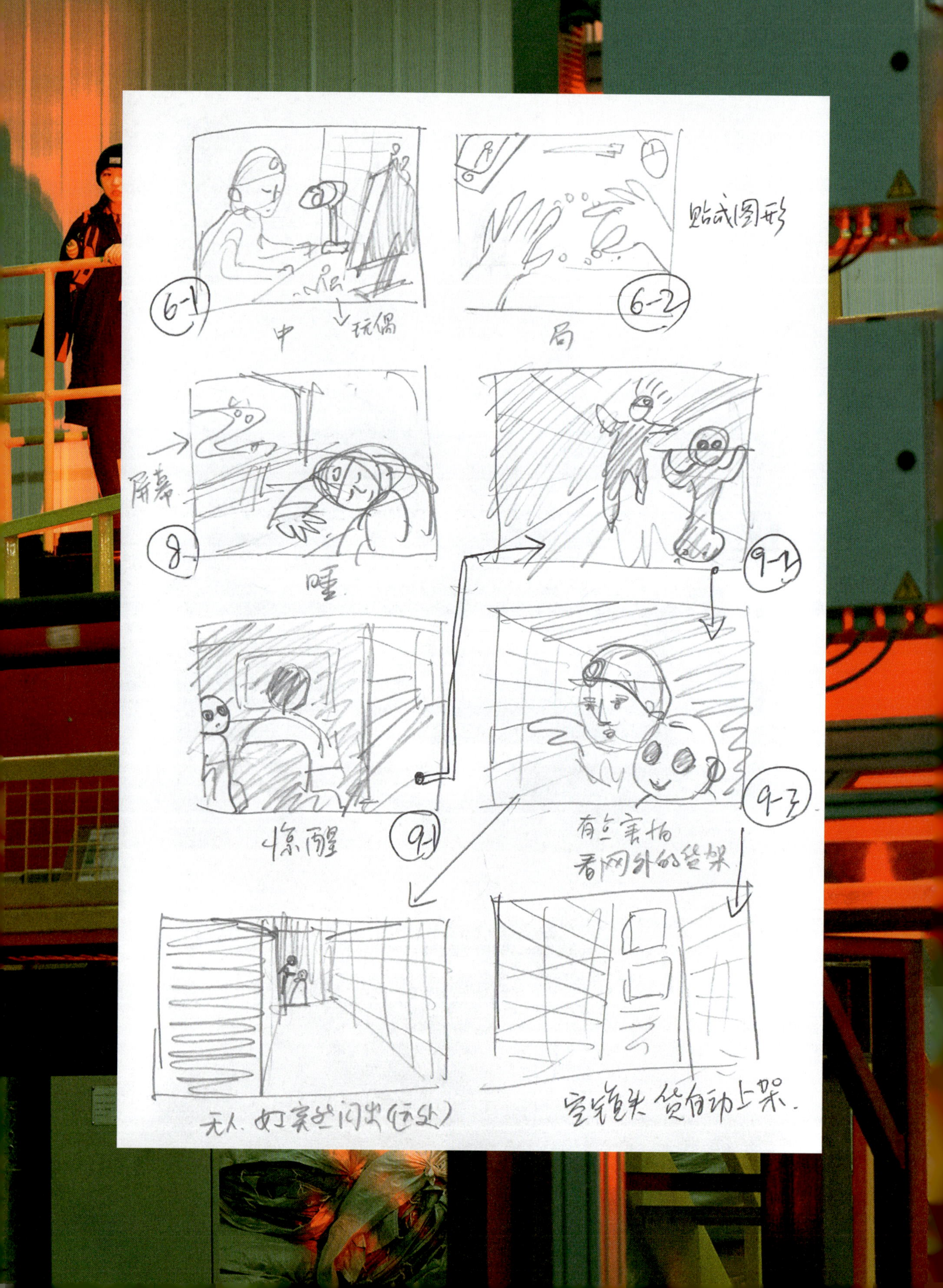

贴式图形

6-1

中 玩偶

6-2

局

屏幕

8

睡

9-2

9-1

惊醒

9-3

有点害怕
看网外的货架

无人. 女工突然闪出(远处)

空镜头 货自动上架.

淘寶

她忘記從什麼時候迷上了淘寶，其實她什麼都不缺了，但她習慣性的每天打開淘寶網頁，源源不斷的輸入各種物品的名稱，試圖再淘出個什麼，而每個東西都有使她有放入購物車的理由，每個物品都會相聯繫到其他各種物品，因此那個商品汪洋不斷擴張她無窮的慾望。她習慣在高級商場或者在時尚雜誌裏看到什麼，手機拍下來，方便在淘寶裏找到更廉價的同類產品，從瘦腹霜到大閘蟹，最近是湖南的辣蘿蔔乾和香港的出前一丁快餐面，更甚是她老公的痔瘡膏，而且是民間赤腳醫生的偏方，因為她也會依據大眾評論來判斷商戶的可信度。她還嘗試過搜索「A片」或者「AV」字眼，但看來早被淘寶設定為敏感詞了。淘寶的快遞員隔個兩三天總會按響她家的門鈴，最高紀錄是一天之內不同快遞公司為她送了十二件大小包裹。她喜歡購買，但不喜歡快遞員總在不恰當的時間打擾她，比如中午休息時打她手機，她沒穿內衣只穿睡裙的時候要去接包裹，有些快遞員不帶筆，有些甚至已經記住她的容貌和姓名，甚至攀談般聊起她屋裏煲的湯很香。她討厭這些經常上門的陌生人，但她喜歡訂購和打開包裹的過程，她是宅在家裏購買整個世界的那種。

Taobao

She doesn't remember when she became addicted to Taobao, the eBay of China. It's not like she needs anything. She logs on every day, and out of habit types in product names one after another as if panning for gold; she always finds a reason to add them to the shopping cart. One item leads to another, and the sea of merchandise only expands her bottomless appetite. If she sees something she likes in a shop or magazine, she'll use her phone to take a picture so she can find a similar item at a cheaper price on Taobao.com — from body-firming creams to Chinese mitten crab. Recently, she found Hunan spicy pickled radishes and Hong Kong Demae Itcho instant noodles. She even found a special hemorrhoid ointment for her husband; it was a folk remedy developed by a barefoot doctor. Of course, she relies on buyers' feedback and customer comments to determine the seller's reputation before purchasing. One time, she even tried searching "adult pictures" and "AV" for adult videos, but Taobao must have long since classified them as "sensitive words." Every two or three days, a Taobao courier rings her doorbell. Her record is twelve deliveries in one day. She loves shopping but hates to be disturbed at naptime — especially when she has to get up to receive a package in her nightgown with nothing else on underneath. Some couriers come without a pen, some know her by name or looks, some even strike up a conversation and remark on the delicious aroma of the soup she's making. She loathes these strangers who frequent her doorway, but she loves shopping and opening packages. She's the kind who buys the whole world while staying at home.

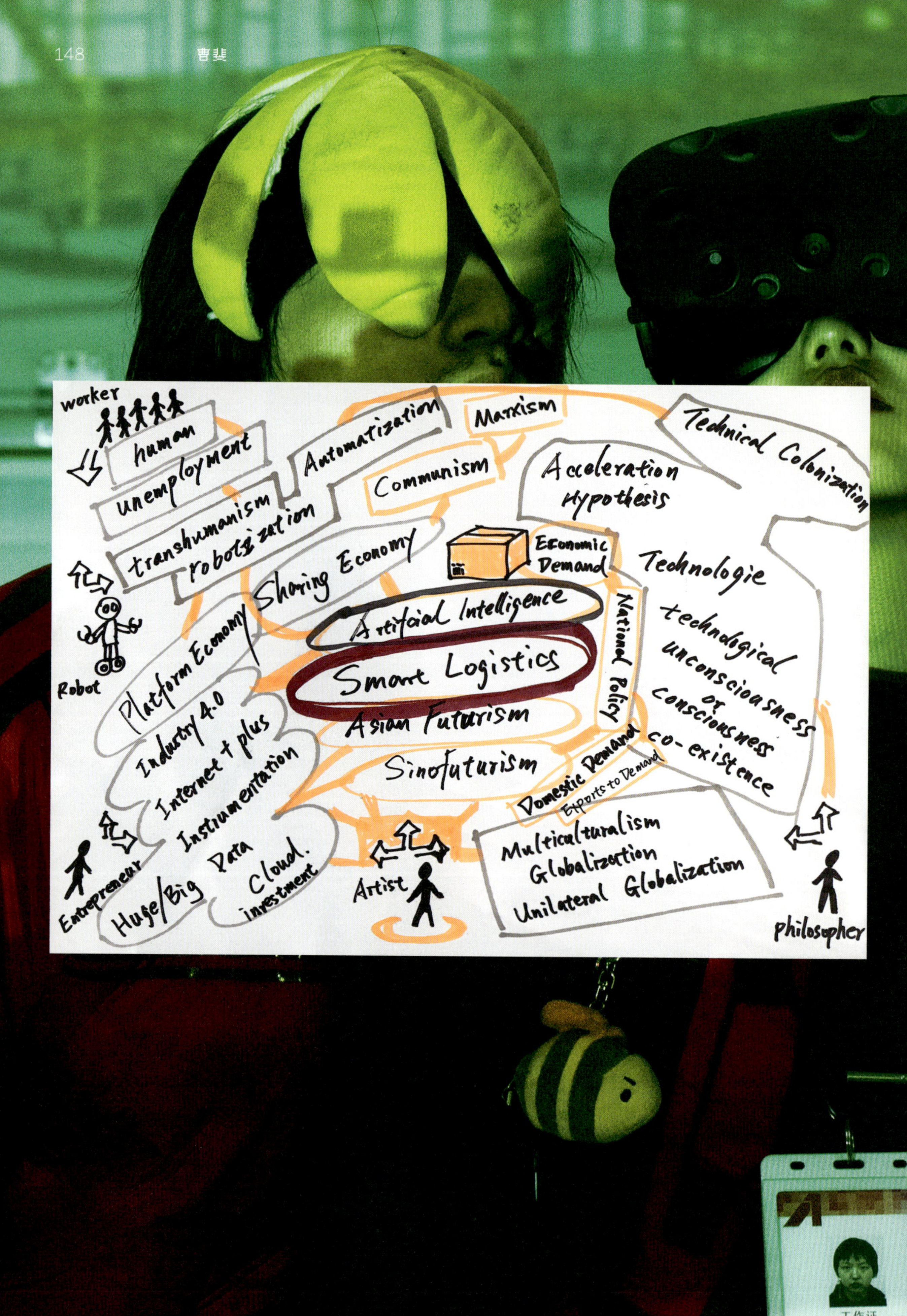
worker
human
unemployment
Automatization
Marxism
Technical Colonization
transhumanism
robotization
Communism
Acceleration Hypothesis
Sharing Economy
Economic Demand
Technologie
Robot
Artificial Intelligence
National Policy
technological unconsciousness or consciousness co-existence
Platform Economy
Smart Logistics
Industry 4.0
Asian Futurism
Internet + plus
Instrumentation
Sinofuturism
Domestic Demand
Exports to Demand
Multiculturalism
Globalization
Unilateral Globalization
Entrepreneur
Huge/Big Data
Cloud.
investment
Artist
philosopher
工作证
WORK PERMIT

JD.

9月14日 — 10月7日. 构思/准备

中间参观. 上海昆山. 北京站点 广东麻涌

站点
地理: 送货

1. 新疆: 阿克苏/喀什
2. 西藏 ②
3. 北京门头沟
4. 湖南凤凰古城

仓储

1. 上海昆山 ③
2. 广东麻涌

无人机

1. 江苏宿迁 ①
2. 陕西

双十一 爆仓

北京

拍摄时间

1. 11月中旬 — 12月中旬

黃裕邦
Nicholas Wong

黑暗改編
Dark Adaption

翻譯:徐晞文

到了2052年,詩人在香港將會非常渴市,因為文化大革命2.0將剷除粵語及其流行文化作品。一群雙語詩人在地下展開祕密合作,在一連串由壓力引發的情緒性愛行為之後,展開了保存粵語流行歌行動。政治意涵濃厚,或宣稱政治意涵濃厚的作品將獲優先處理。詩人們在一部配備英語人工智能的機器上朗讀粵語歌詞,讓機器按照讀音將歌詞謄錄成同音的英文,然後運用詩意的干預方式,把這些「誤」譯本修改成表面看來既無政治含意,亦無緬懷殖民地時期之意的詩作,最後,由眞人譯者將之譯回中文。在吃喝過期三文治和威士忌之後,詩的由來也隨之忘卻。

In 2052, poets will be in great demand in Hong Kong because of Kultural Revolution 2.0, which will eliminate the Cantonese language and popular cultural texts produced in it. A number of bilingual poets will collaborate underground, after much stress-induced emotional sex, to preserve Cantopop songs. They will start with the highly political ones, or those allegedly labeled so. They will read the lyrics in Cantonese to a machine equipped with English artificial intelligence and have it homophonically transcribe the lyrics into English, then revise the "falsely" translated versions through poetic intervention into poems that carry, on the surface, no political connotations or nostalgia for the colonial period. A human translator will then be asked to convert the texts into Chinese, and forget their origin over expired sandwiches and whiskey.

改編自《皇后大道東》(1991)

正如題目完全沒有提到
任何人、任何名銜或城鎮，然後
有座短命城鎮呼喚一首曲子，
如果非如此不可，曲子只唱一件事——
幸運的年輕人數着
蟋蟀，被不明物體噎住。
他們的靴子佈滿孔洞，眉宇間
暗藏緊繃，繃緊得
眼睛已經拿去
維修了。就像聲稱
只要某個洞穴是法律的玩物，
在洞裏殺死一個男孩也沒有問題。
暗紅的夜低鳴；所有人
都在尋找一種聲音，好去談妥
事情，講最差勁的無害
笑話，比方說，對Calvin Klein講一聲拜拜，
在海邊嘲笑一隻手的
措辭，一排排整齊的船
無法抹掉風，好去明白
那些關於離開家園的笑談，
明白到歸航有時純屬意外。

Based on "Queen's Road East" (1991)

Like how the whole title says no
one, says no title & no town, then
a town, outlasted, calls for a tune
that sings, if you must, one thing—
young men of luck counting
crickets & choked on unknowns.
Their boots full of holes & tension
hides between eyebrows, so much
so that their eyes have been taken
to maintenance. Like claiming
it's okay to kill a boy in a hole, so
long as that hole is a toy of the law.
The night hisses in red; everyone
looks for a sound to talk things
out, to tell the worst harmless
jokes, like saying bye-bye to Calvin Klein
& to taunt a hand's phrasing
by the sea, when neat rows of boats
can't wipe off the wind to understand
the cackling of leaving home & that,
sometimes, their return happens by mistake.

改編自《海闊天空》(1993)

請代表光填滿所有空格。
它辦不到的事情那麼多:它若不灌
醉你,不無視陰影的反對,
揭露某隻手上的
噬痕,不勾勒你
那電單車後座的
空虛——你認為它總在駛向更美好的地方,
就無法講述一段愛情故事。
但時間很有名,沒有道理
像芫荽一樣激進。有一次,
時間帶你去見一本書,然後是一具軀體,
你知道兩者都噁心。
有一次,它先是帶你來到那些手面前,
他們要你像新聞般即時在場時,
你咬過那些手,
然後時間又帶你遇上那些把你像衞星般
擲出去的手,你自己的手則逐漸
發現要掙脫束縛,
發現並不是每一滴水都為沸騰而生。
有些空間永遠如此年輕,使你
習慣懲罰自己,
比方說,在商場裏嗅聞
小鮮肉的肌膚,他們揉合了香水試用裝
與橫衝直撞的青春。

Based on "The Boundless Oceans, Vast Skies" (1993)

Complete all blanks on behalf of the light.
So much it can't do: it can't narrate
a love story without drinking
you down, without revealing the bite marks
on a hand against the shadow's
consent, without outlining the emptiness
of the pillion behind you, the one,
you believe, steering always to a better place.
But time is famous & it's pointless
to be radical like coriander. Once,
time carried you to a book, then a body
& you knew there's repulsion in both.
Once, it carried you first to hands you'd bite
when they made you present like the nowness
of the news, then to those that cast
you away like a satellite, when yours, little
by little, have learnt the need to let loose
& not all water exists for boiling.
Some space is forever so young that it puts
you in the habit of punishing yourself,
like smelling in a mall the skin
of twinks, who mix perfume samples
with youth that works & wrecks.

[中場註解]

1. 羅蘭·巴特會因為寫過以下句子而遭封禁。他寫下的這句話，多年後奇跡地與2014年一場社會運動吻合。然而，這場運動於2039年被政府正式易名為「社會動亂」：黃色雨傘的風尚。──眞荒唐！── 如果每個人都有一把……下雨就不那麼令人沮喪了。

2. 政府還會發表公開聲明，譴責這座城市的年輕人像芫荽一樣過份大膽，因此禁止三十歲以下市民在超市購買芫荽。

3. 參與「黑暗改編」行動的部分詩人將被捕或被消失（注意：被動語態刻意與主動動詞連用，表示行動並非自願）。由於（土地短缺導致）監獄囚室不足，他們不會被控叛國或煽動顛覆政府。取而代之的是，他們將被控未有履行作家的責任。按照政府的定義，所謂作家責任，就是提供意義封閉的說教文字。以下這首詩是一眾詩人被消失前寫下的最後一首詩。他們希望讀者代表光去填滿空格。

起初是這樣的：有些雞蛋知道，
它們要怎樣應對____如果____沒有打碎它們

這一直是____
與____之間背後反覆冒起的戰鬥

一條關於____的重要法律趕得及出爐，
但更快犯眾怒

你醒來時，給掏空了____
A. 雞 B. 雞 C. 雞

你希望贏得完美難題的是____
而不是____

當時有人在談論A. ____
B. ____ C. 路牌的情緒教學燃燒着

____的火焰就是好的火焰
任何開端都不在意命運或持久性

水倒進一個沒有挖出來的____
人們得____

____是四處漂泊的靈媒
你在城裏指着城市

──就是那座被某些人的____拳頭清空的城市
在那裏有人教你不要____

你是____裏的時鐘，走過
從「只管去做吧」到「你辦到了」之間的許多年

[mid-notes]

1. Roland Barthes will be banned for having written the following sentence, which years later, miraculously, aligned with a social movement that happened in 2014, which, however, was officially renamed by the Government in 2039 as "a movement of social unrest": *The Fashion for yellow umbrellas.—Quite ridiculous!—If everyone had one . . . it would make the rain less depressing.*

2. The Government will also make a public statement condemning the youths in the city for being too daring like coriander, thus banning citizens below age thirty from purchasing it in supermarkets.

3. Some of the poets involved in the "Dark Adaptation" project will be arrested, or *be disappeared* (note the passive voice intentionally used together with an active verb to suggest involuntary behavior). They will not be charged with treason or advocating overthrow of Government, because of the lack of vacant cells in prisons (due to the land shortage). They will, instead, be charged for not complying with the duty of being writers, which, in the Government's sense, is to provide closed yet didactic meanings. The following poem is the last piece the poets write before they *are disappeared*. They want their readers to complete the blanks on behalf of the light.

This is how it was in the beginning: some eggs knew
what to do with _______ if _______ did not break them

It was always a battle between the _______
and the _______ that kept rising behind the door

A grand law about _______ was hatched fast
enough but was hated even faster

You woke up emptied of _______
A. Chicken B. Chicken C. Chicken

You hoped _______, not _______, could win
a perfect problem

Someone was saying something about A. _______
B. _______ C. Emotional pedagogy of road signs

A flame burning with _______ was a good flame
No beginning cared about destiny or duration

Water poured into a _______ that had not been dug
One had to _______

_______ was a psychic on the road
In a city you pointed from you pointed at the city

—the one that was emptied in someone's fist of _______
the one where you had been taught not to _______

You were a clock in a _______, walking
through years between just do it and you did it

改編自《雞蛋與羔羊》(2014)

一個洞在家裏挖掘自己;它知道你想要第二個家
在洞的深處,你找到一個兒子。他並不等於你,你一向把他綁起來
他看來像個破損的鐘,經常斜靠着風
風調音調得很差
主要是早晨與天殘地缺的聲音
不像你的名字般天殘地缺。你後來發現,名字不過是加諸你身上的聲音
世界就是這樣認識你的
再也沒有人唱歌了。等待取代了歌唱,等待第二個家、另一個空間
等待已成一門專業
對於世界,你總在猜測
無人可以在談論祕密時說拇指紋
每隻手都有五根針,碰到會痛
世界就是這樣認識你的
你抱起兒子讓他看看天際線時弄痛了他

Based on "Eggs and Lamb" (2014)

A hole digs itself at home; it knows you want a second home
Deep in it, you find a son that's not you, but one you've always tied up
He looks like a damaged chime, often leaning toward the wind
The wind that does a bad job in tuning
There're mostly mornings and imperfect sounds
Not imperfect like your name that you later know is just sounds
    imposed onto you
That's how the world's known you
No one sings anymore. Singing is replaced by waiting for a second home,
    a different space
Waiting has become an expertise
About the world, you always second-guess
No one can say *thumbprints* when he talks about secrets
Each hand has five pins, and touching hurts
That's how the world's known you
How you hurt your son when you hold him up to let him see the skyline

楊嘉輝 Samson Young

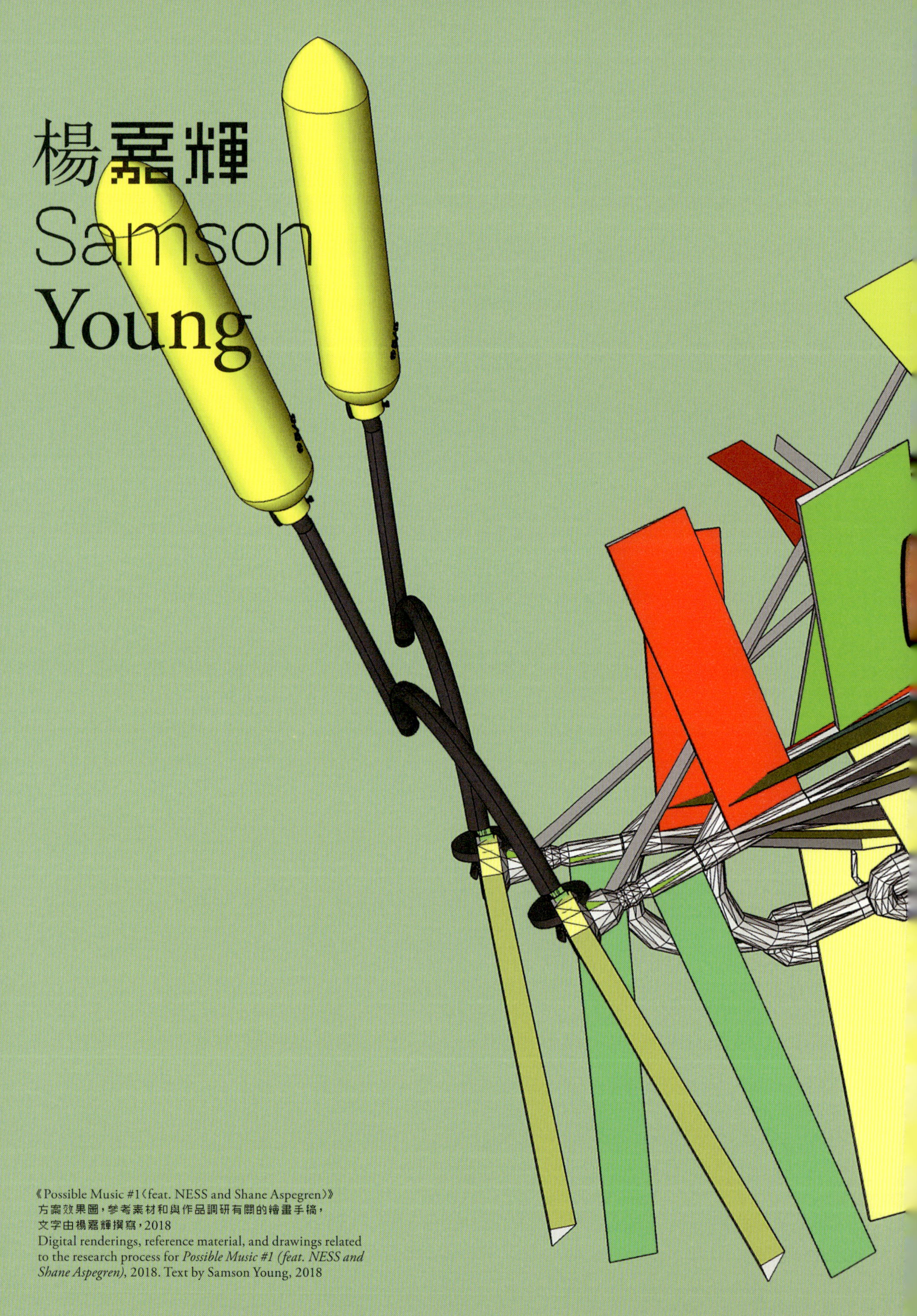

《Possible Music #1〈feat. NESS and Shane Aspegren〉》
方案效果圖，參考素材和與作品調研有關的繪畫手稿，
文字由楊嘉輝撰寫，2018
Digital renderings, reference material, and drawings related to the research process for *Possible Music #1 (feat. NESS and Shane Aspegren)*, 2018. Text by Samson Young, 2018

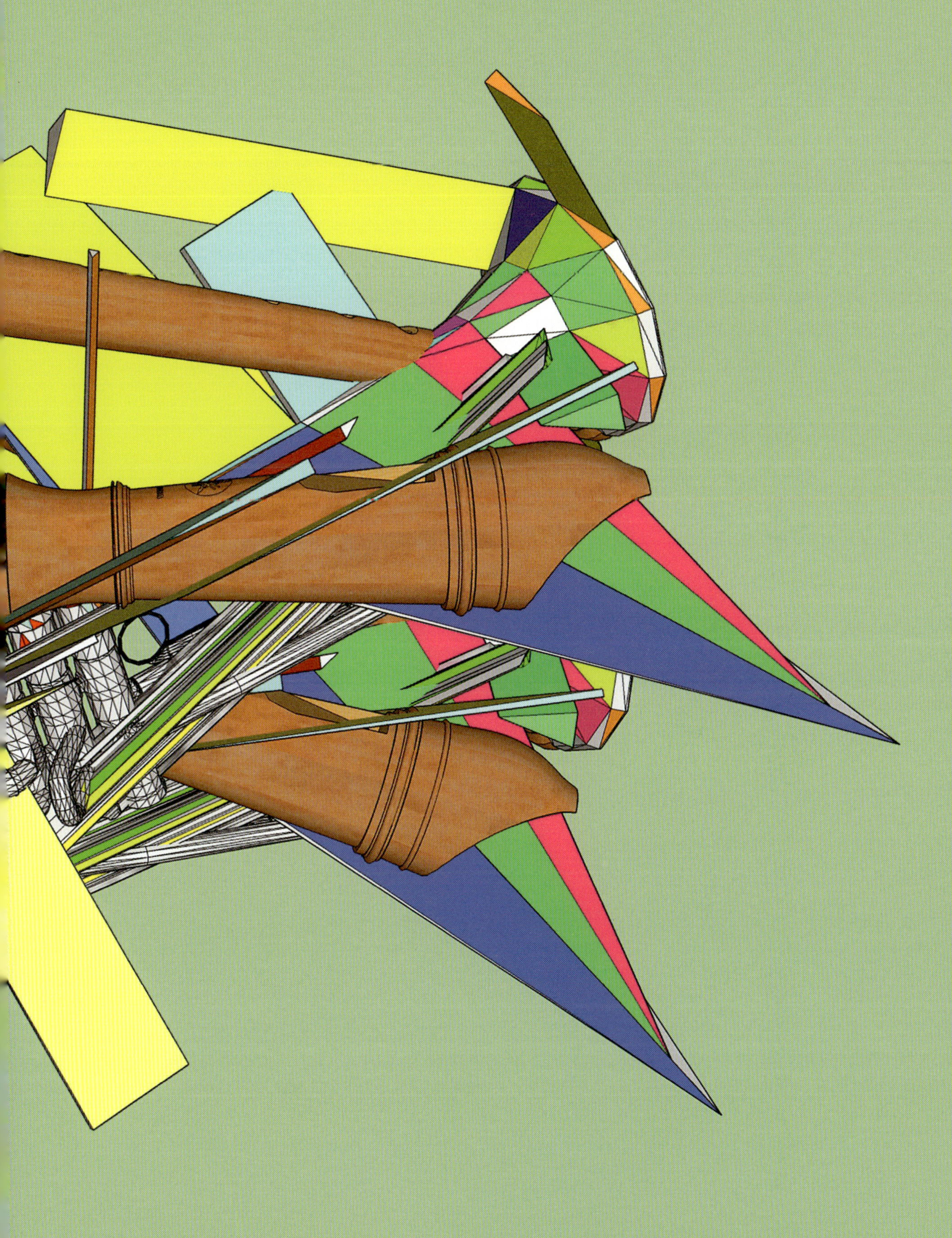

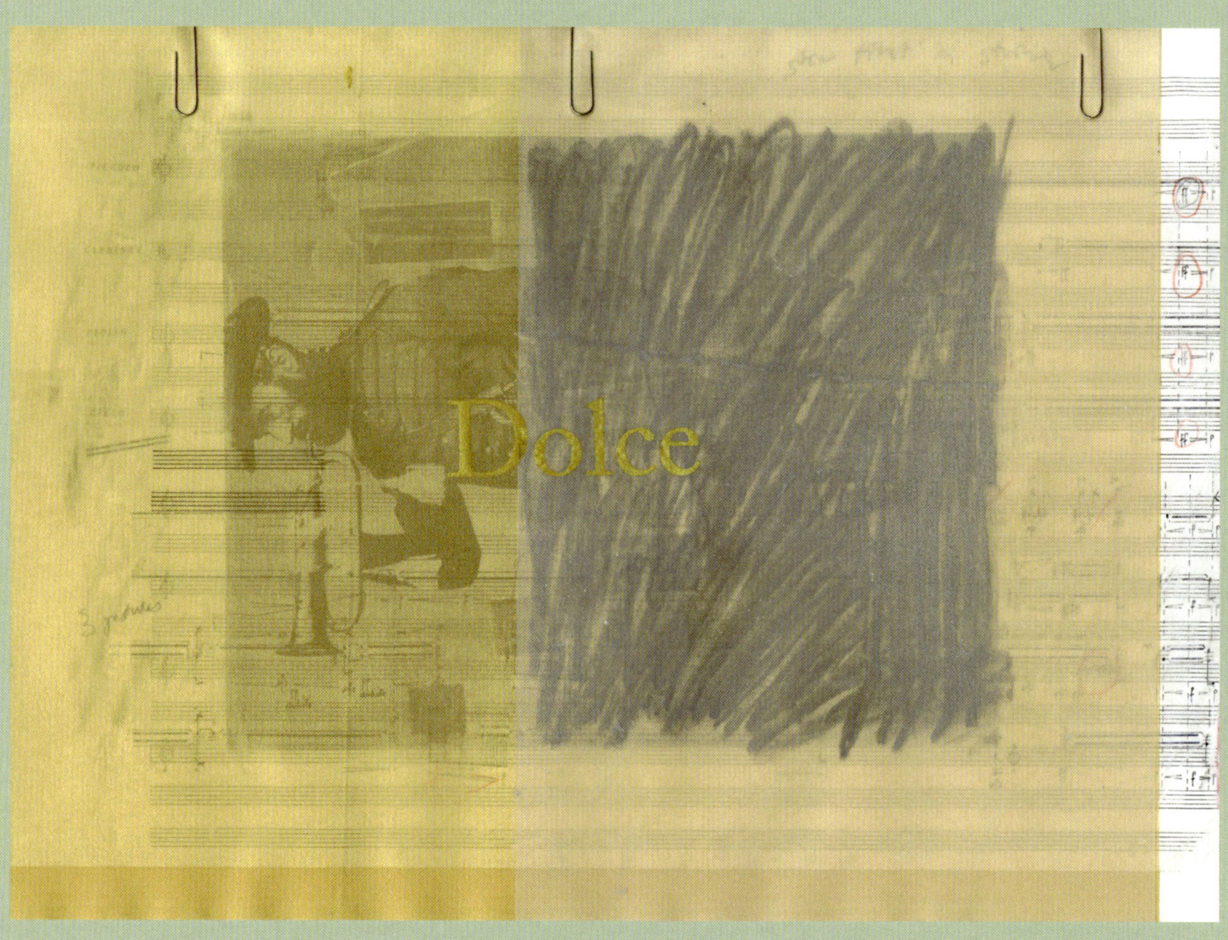
Dolce

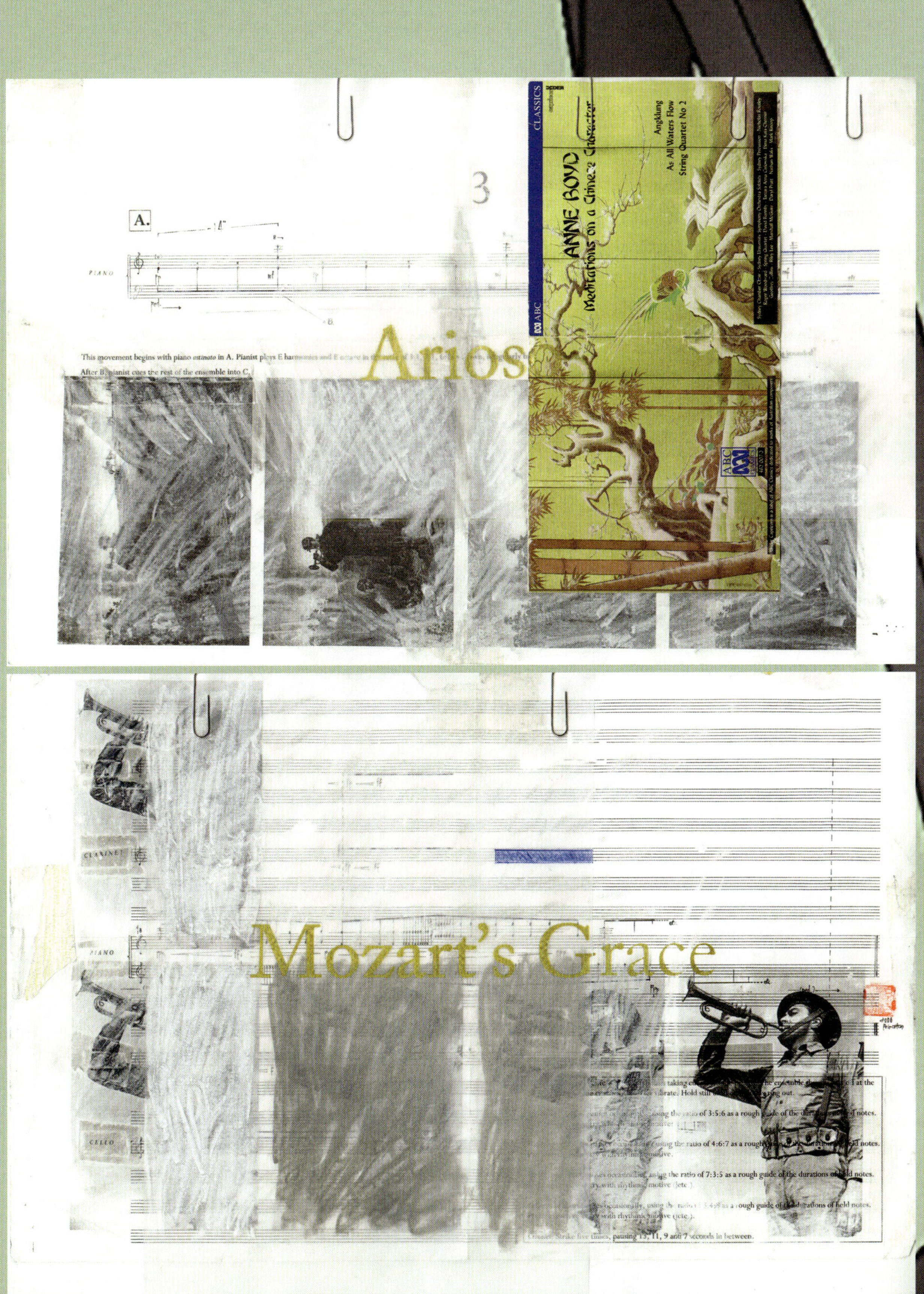
A.
PIANO
This movement begins with piano ostinato in A.
After B, pianist cues the rest of the ensemble into C.
Arioso
CLASSICS
ANNE BOYD
Meditations on a Chinese Character
Angkuklung
As All Waters Flow
String Quartet No 2
ABC
CLARINET
PIANO
CELLO
Mozart's Grace
Crotale: Strike five times, pausing 13, 11, 9 and 7 seconds in between.

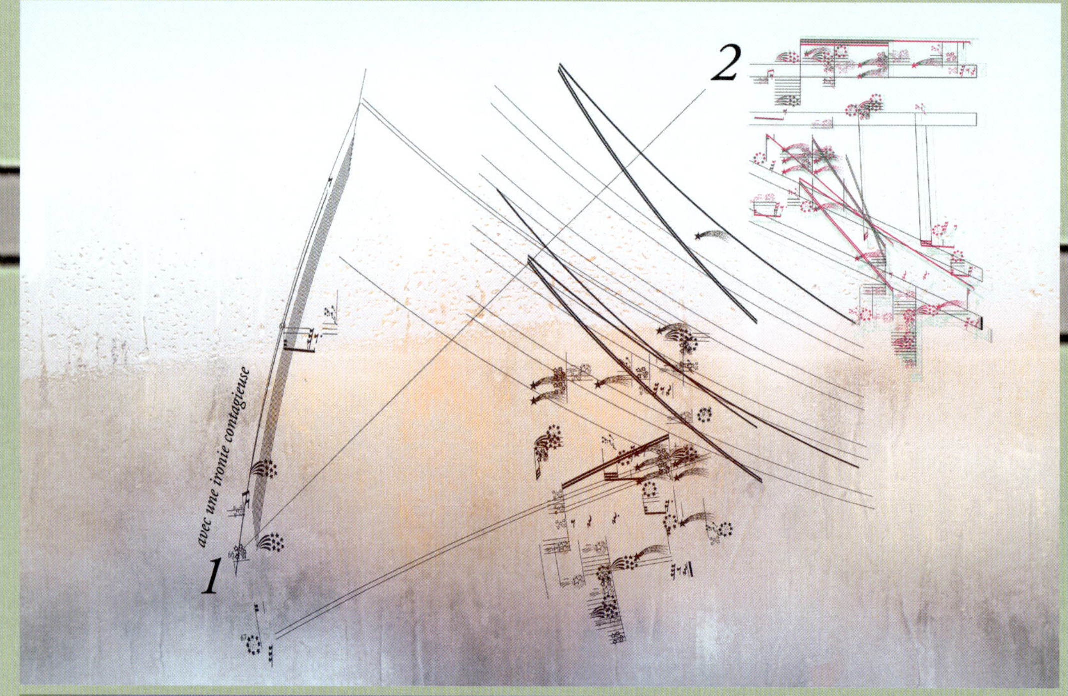
2
avec une ironie contagieuse
1

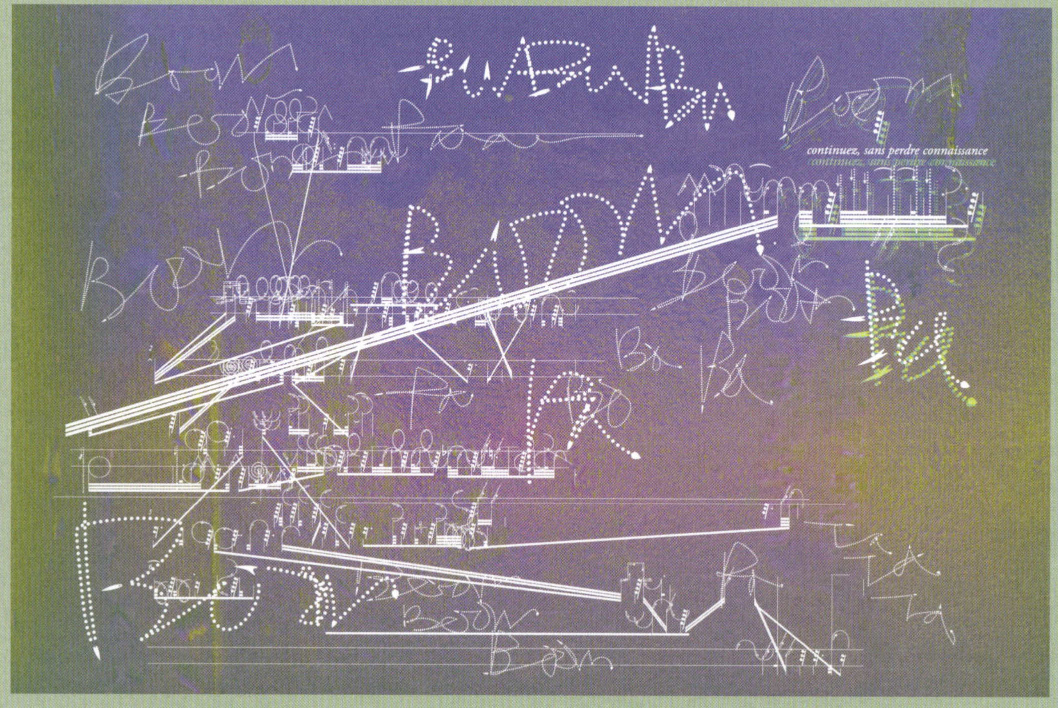
continuez, sans perdre connaissance

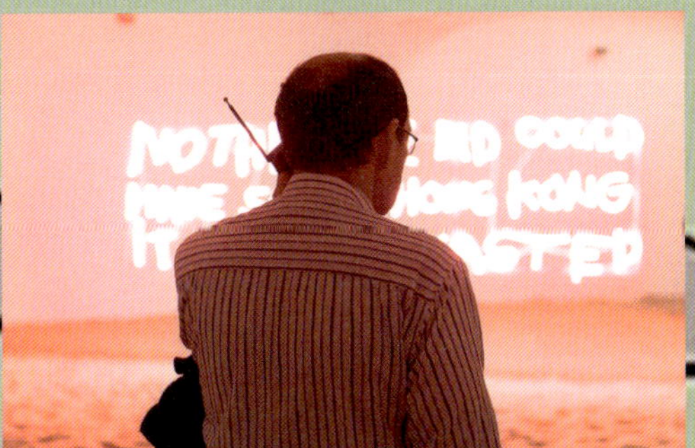

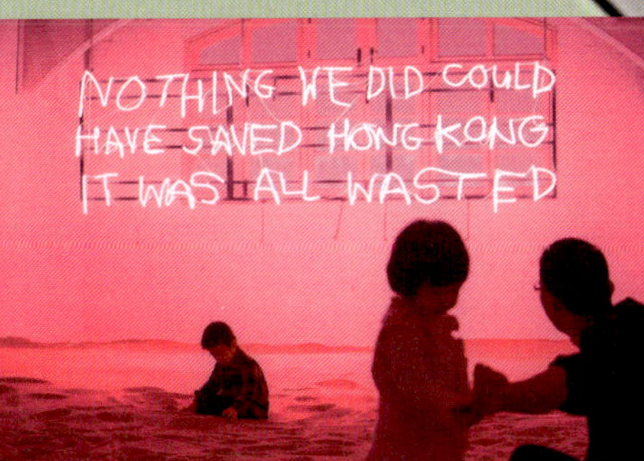
NOTHING WE DID COULD
HAVE SAVED HONG KONG
IT WAS ALL WASTED

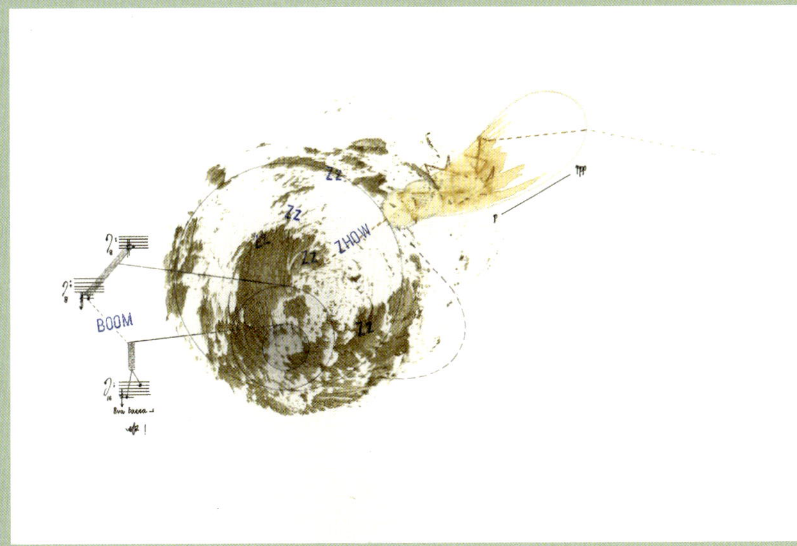
ZHOW
BOOM

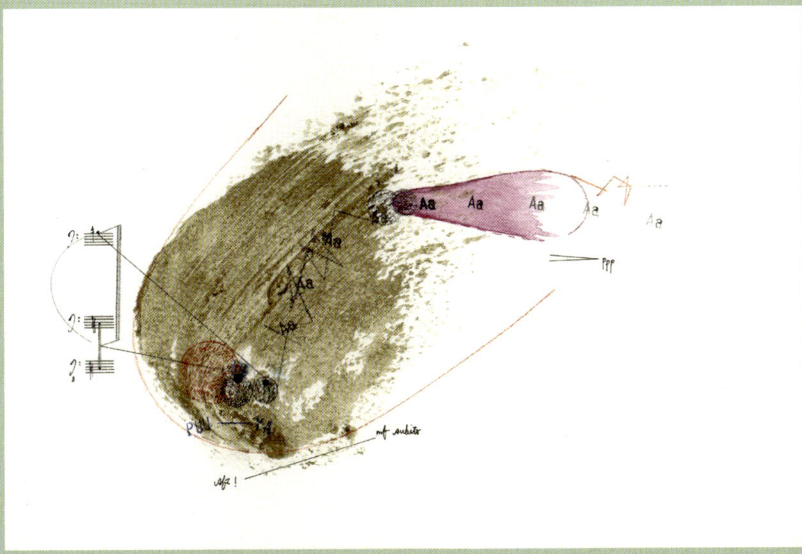
Aa

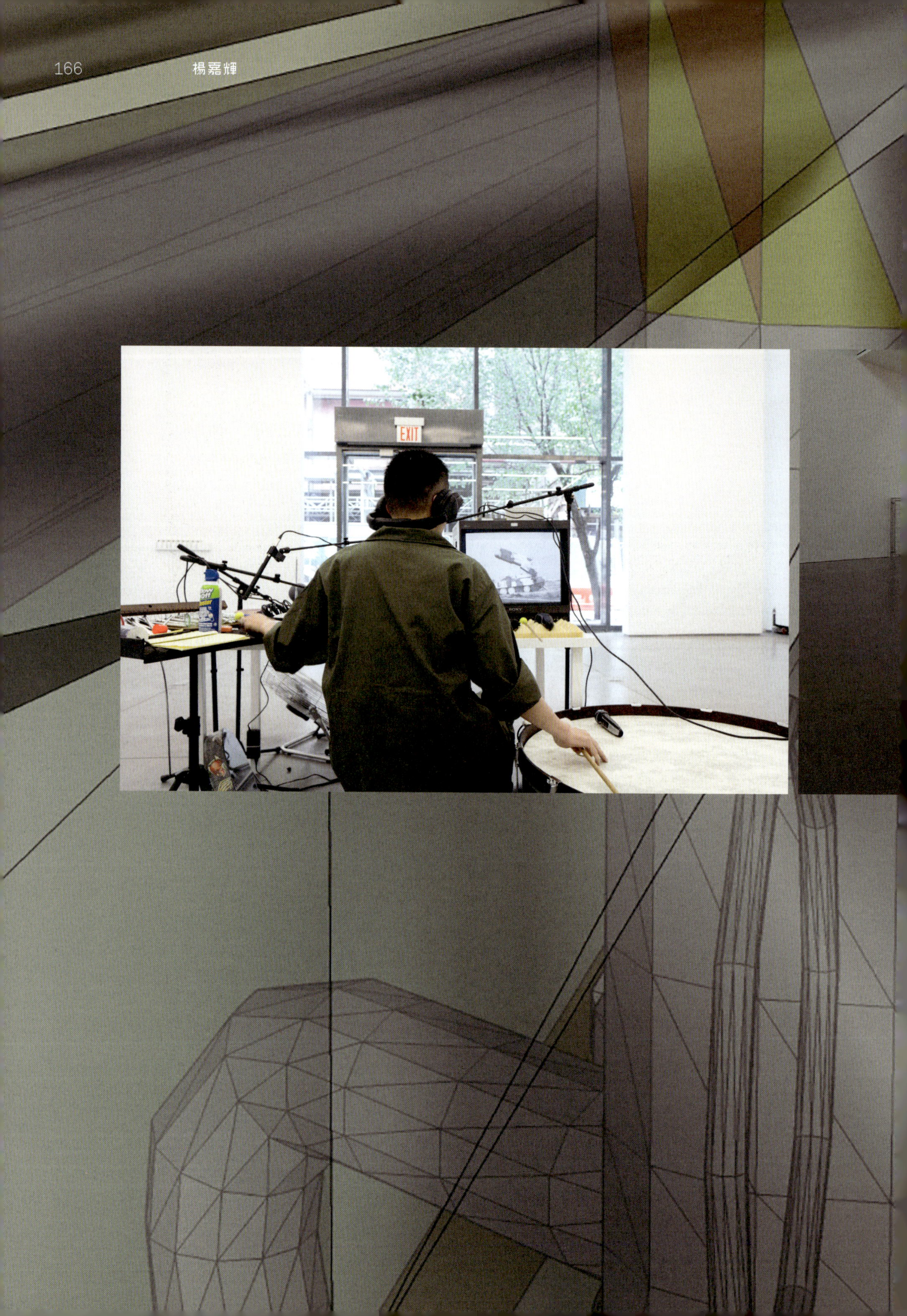
EXIT

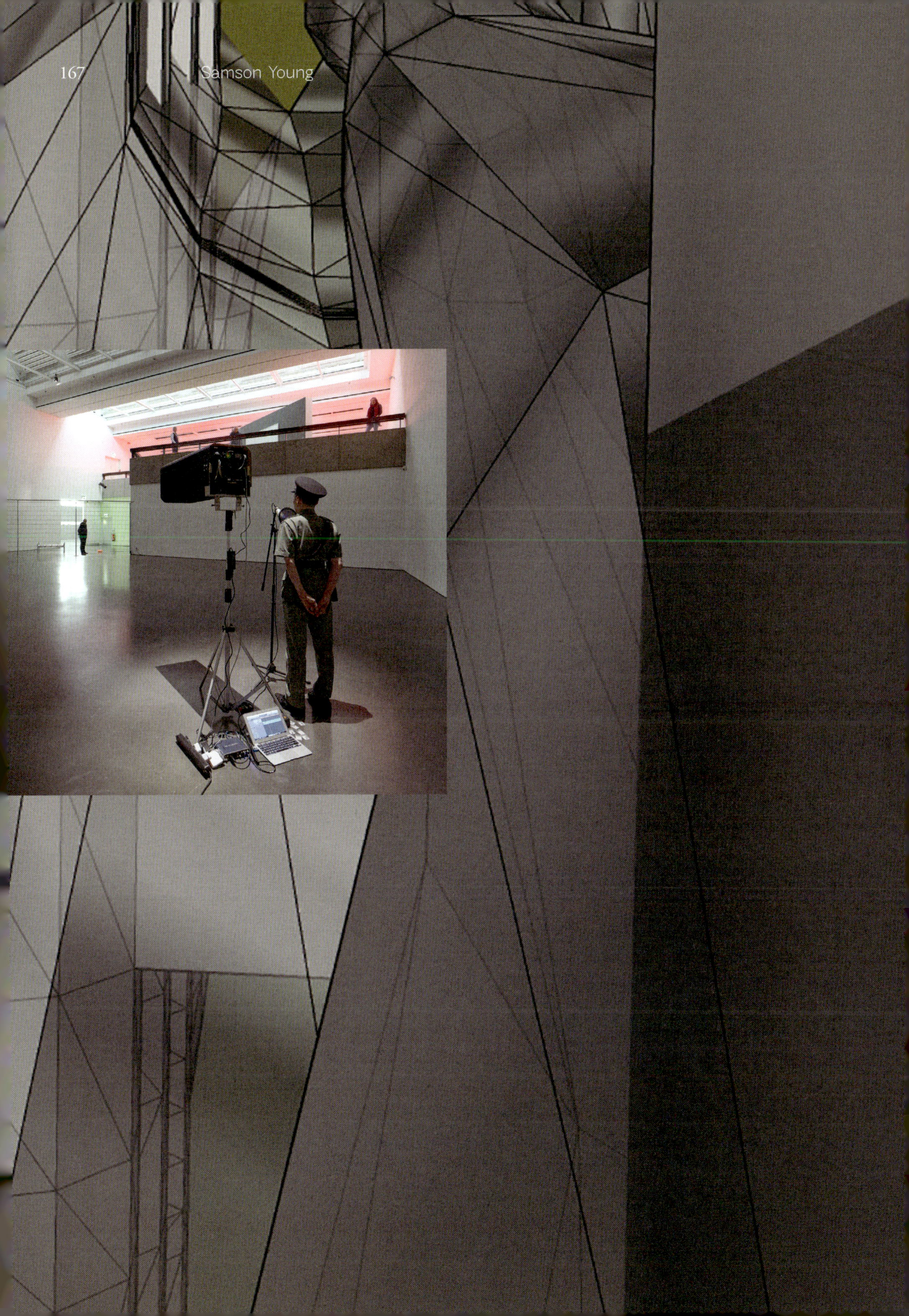

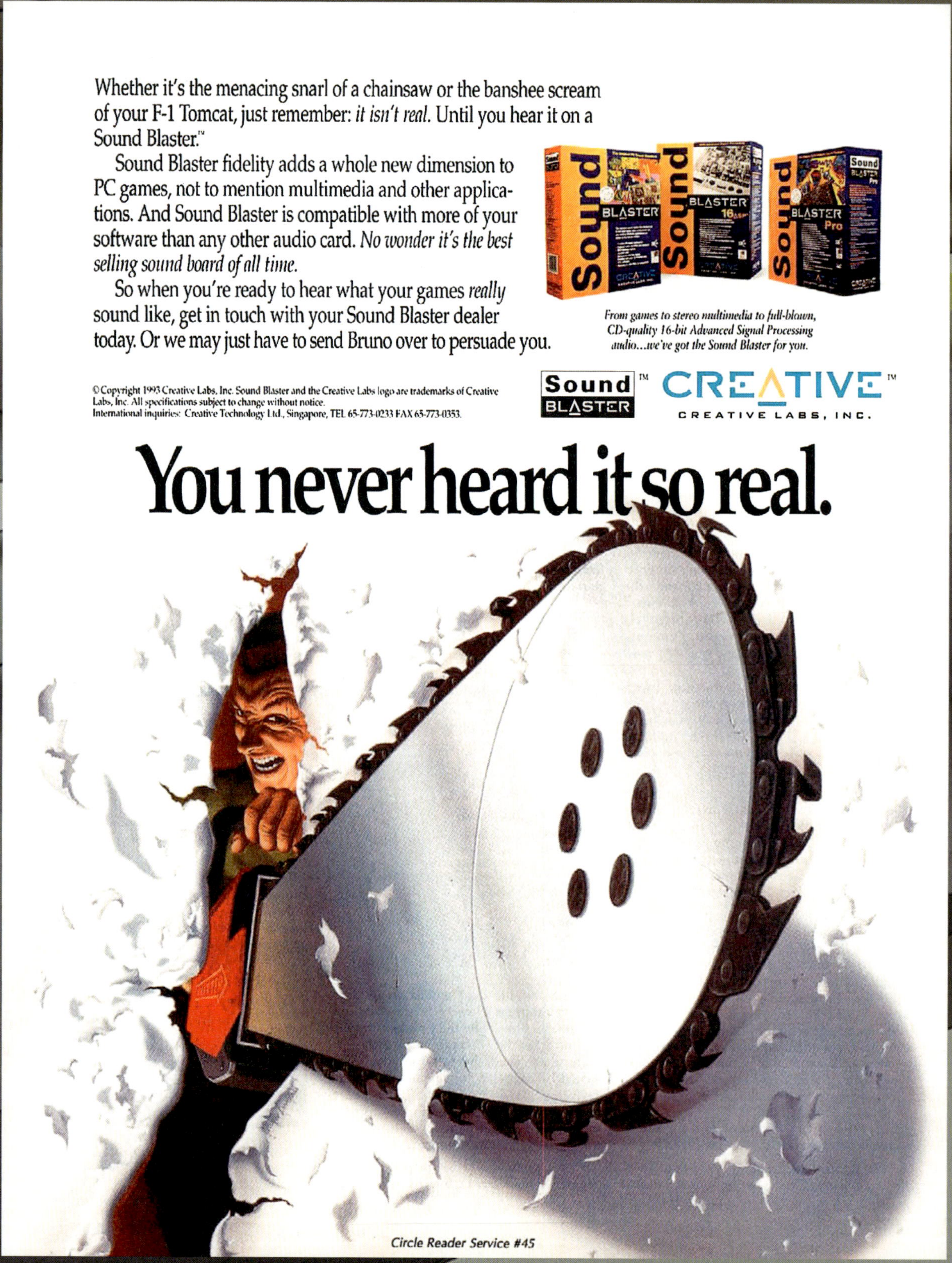

Whether it's the menacing snarl of a chainsaw or the banshee scream of your F-1 Tomcat, just remember: *it isn't real.* Until you hear it on a Sound Blaster.™

Sound Blaster fidelity adds a whole new dimension to PC games, not to mention multimedia and other applications. And Sound Blaster is compatible with more of your software than any other audio card. *No wonder it's the best selling sound board of all time.*

So when you're ready to hear what your games *really* sound like, get in touch with your Sound Blaster dealer today. Or we may just have to send Bruno over to persuade you.

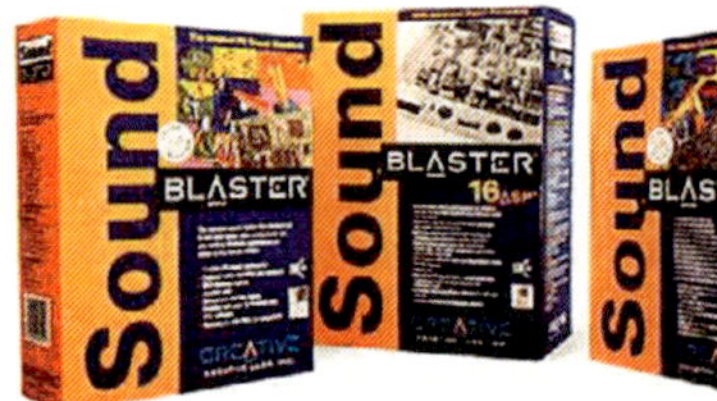

From games to stereo multimedia to full-blown, CD-quality 16-bit Advanced Signal Processing audio...we've got the Sound Blaster for you.

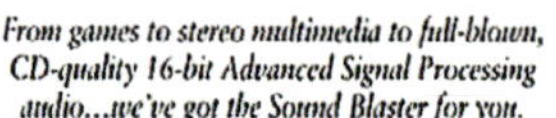

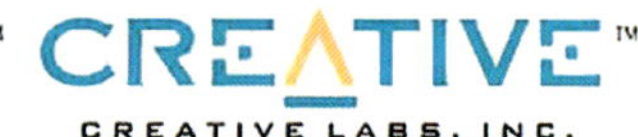

You never heard it so real.

Circle Reader Service #45

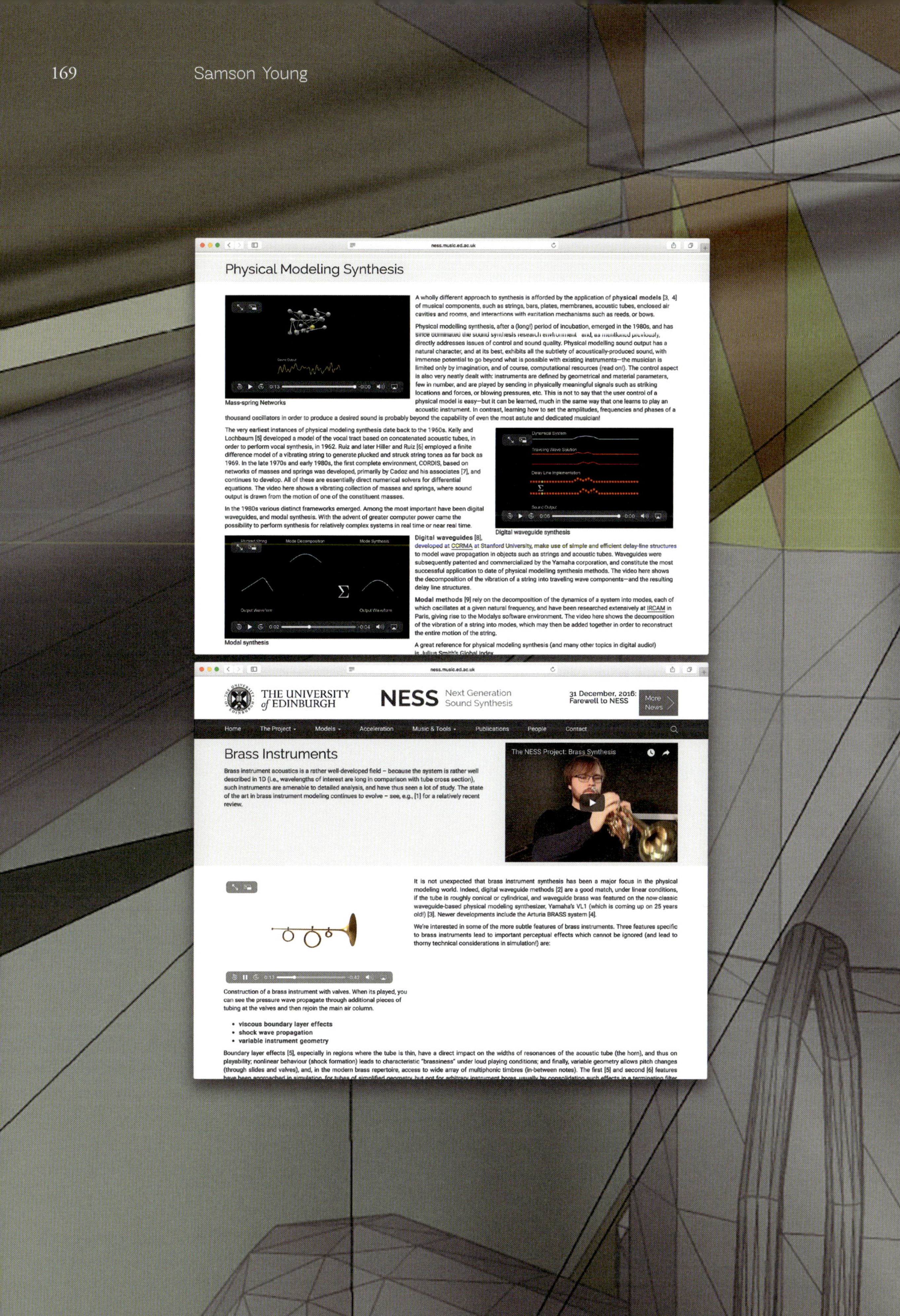

ness.music.ed.ac.uk

Physical Modeling Synthesis

A wholly different approach to synthesis is afforded by the application of **physical models** [3, 4] of musical components, such as strings, bars, plates, membranes, acoustic tubes, enclosed air cavities and rooms, and interactions with excitation mechanisms such as reeds, or bows.

Physical modelling synthesis, after a (long!) period of incubation, emerged in the 1980s, and has since dominated the sound synthesis research environment—and, as mentioned previously, directly addresses issues of control and sound quality. Physical modelling sound output has a natural character, and at its best, exhibits all the subtlety of acoustically-produced sound, with immense potential to go beyond what is possible with existing instruments—the musician is limited only by imagination, and of course, computational resources (read on!). The control aspect is also very neatly dealt with: instruments are defined by geometrical and material parameters, few in number, and are played by sending in physically meaningful signals such as striking locations and forces, or blowing pressures, etc. This is not to say that the user control of a physical model is easy—but it can be learned, much in the same way that one learns to play an acoustic instrument. In contrast, learning how to set the amplitudes, frequencies and phases of a thousand oscillators in order to produce a desired sound is probably beyond the capability of even the most astute and dedicated musician!

Mass-spring Networks

The very earliest instances of physical modeling synthesis date back to the 1960s. Kelly and Lochbaum [5] developed a model of the vocal tract based on concatenated acoustic tubes, in order to perform vocal synthesis, in 1962. Ruiz and later Hiller and Ruiz [6] employed a finite difference model of a vibrating string to generate plucked and struck string tones as far back as 1969. In the late 1970s and early 1980s, the first complete environment, CORDIS, based on networks of masses and springs was developed, primarily by Cadoz and his associates [7], and continues to develop. All of these are essentially direct numerical solvers for differential equations. The video here shows a vibrating collection of masses and springs, where sound output is drawn from the motion of one of the constituent masses.

In the 1980s various distinct frameworks emerged. Among the most important have been digital waveguides, and modal synthesis. With the advent of greater computer power came the possibility to perform synthesis for relatively complex systems in real time or near real time.

Dynamical System
Traveling Wave Solution
Delay Line Implementation
Sound Output

Digital waveguide synthesis

Digital waveguides [8], developed at CCRMA at Stanford University, make use of simple and efficient delay-line structures to model wave propagation in objects such as strings and acoustic tubes. Waveguides were subsequently patented and commercialized by the Yamaha corporation, and constitute the most successful application to date of physical modelling synthesis methods. The video here shows the decomposition of the vibration of a string into traveling wave components—and the resulting delay line structures.

Mode Decomposition
Mode Synthesis
Output Waveform
Output Waveform

Modal synthesis

Modal methods [9] rely on the decomposition of the dynamics of a system into modes, each of which oscillates at a given natural frequency, and have been researched extensively at IRCAM in Paris, giving rise to the Modalys software environment. The video here shows the decomposition of the vibration of a string into modes, which may then be added together in order to reconstruct the entire motion of the string.

A great reference for physical modeling synthesis (and many other topics in digital audio!) is Julius Smith's Global Index

ness.music.ed.ac.uk

THE UNIVERSITY of EDINBURGH

NESS Next Generation Sound Synthesis

31 December, 2016: Farewell to NESS

More News

Home | The Project | Models | Acceleration | Music & Tools | Publications | People | Contact

Brass Instruments

Brass instrument acoustics is a rather well-developed field – because the system is rather well described in 1D (i.e., wavelengths of interest are long in comparison with tube cross section), such instruments are amenable to detailed analysis, and have thus seen a lot of study. The state of the art in brass instrument modeling continues to evolve – see, e.g., [1] for a relatively recent review.

The NESS Project: Brass Synthesis

It is not unexpected that brass instrument synthesis has been a major focus in the physical modeling world. Indeed, digital waveguide methods [2] are a good match, under linear conditions, if the tube is roughly conical or cylindrical, and waveguide brass was featured on the now-classic waveguide-based physical modeling synthesizer, Yamaha's VL1 (which is coming up on 25 years old!) [3]. Newer developments include the Arturia BRASS system [4].

We're interested in some of the more subtle features of brass instruments. Three features specific to brass instruments lead to important perceptual effects which cannot be ignored (and lead to thorny technical considerations in simulation!) are:

Construction of a brass instrument with valves. When its played, you can see the pressure wave propagate through additional pieces of tubing at the valves and then rejoin the main air column.

- **viscous boundary layer effects**
- **shock wave propagation**
- **variable instrument geometry**

Boundary layer effects [5], especially in regions where the tube is thin, have a direct impact on the widths of resonances of the acoustic tube (the horn), and thus on playability; nonlinear behaviour (shock formation) leads to characteristic "brassiness" under loud playing conditions; and finally, variable geometry allows pitch changes (through slides and valves), and, in the modern brass repertoire, access to wide array of multiphonic timbres (in-between notes). The first [5] and second [6] features

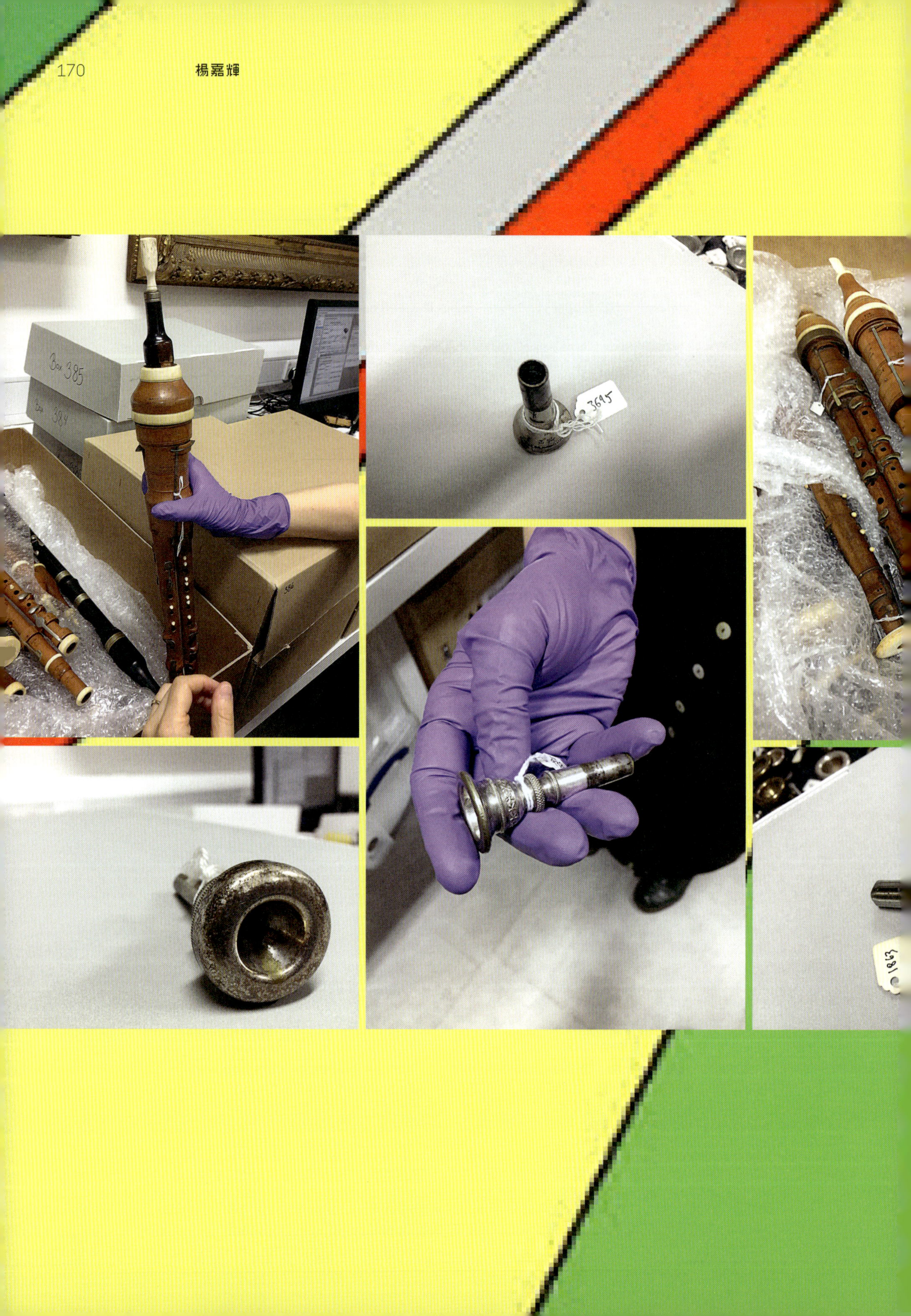
Box 385
3695

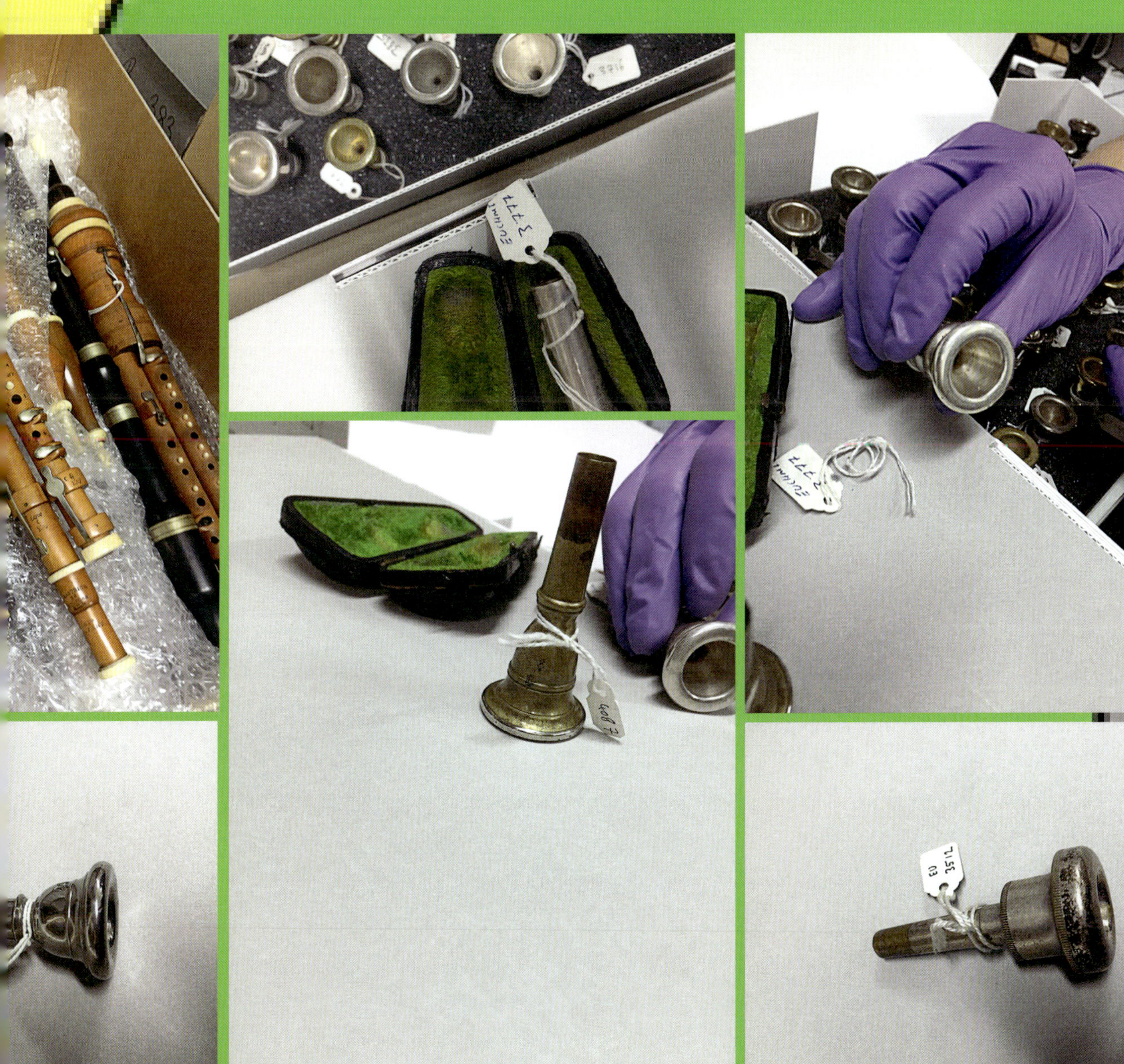

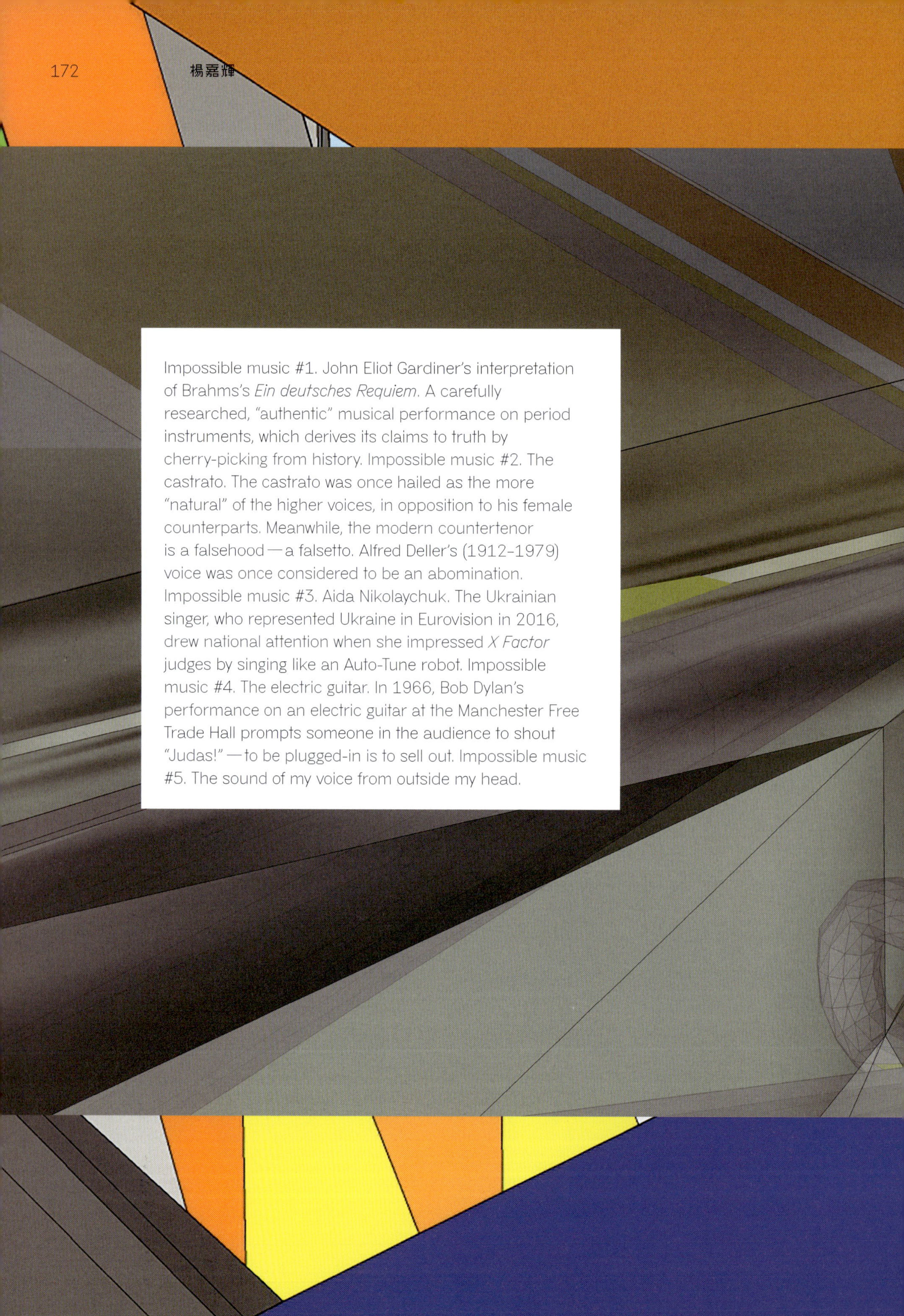

Impossible music #1. John Eliot Gardiner's interpretation of Brahms's *Ein deutsches Requiem*. A carefully researched, "authentic" musical performance on period instruments, which derives its claims to truth by cherry-picking from history. Impossible music #2. The castrato. The castrato was once hailed as the more "natural" of the higher voices, in opposition to his female counterparts. Meanwhile, the modern countertenor is a falsehood—a falsetto. Alfred Deller's (1912–1979) voice was once considered to be an abomination. Impossible music #3. Aida Nikolaychuk. The Ukrainian singer, who represented Ukraine in Eurovision in 2016, drew national attention when she impressed *X Factor* judges by singing like an Auto-Tune robot. Impossible music #4. The electric guitar. In 1966, Bob Dylan's performance on an electric guitar at the Manchester Free Trade Hall prompts someone in the audience to shout "Judas!"—to be plugged-in is to sell out. Impossible music #5. The sound of my voice from outside my head.

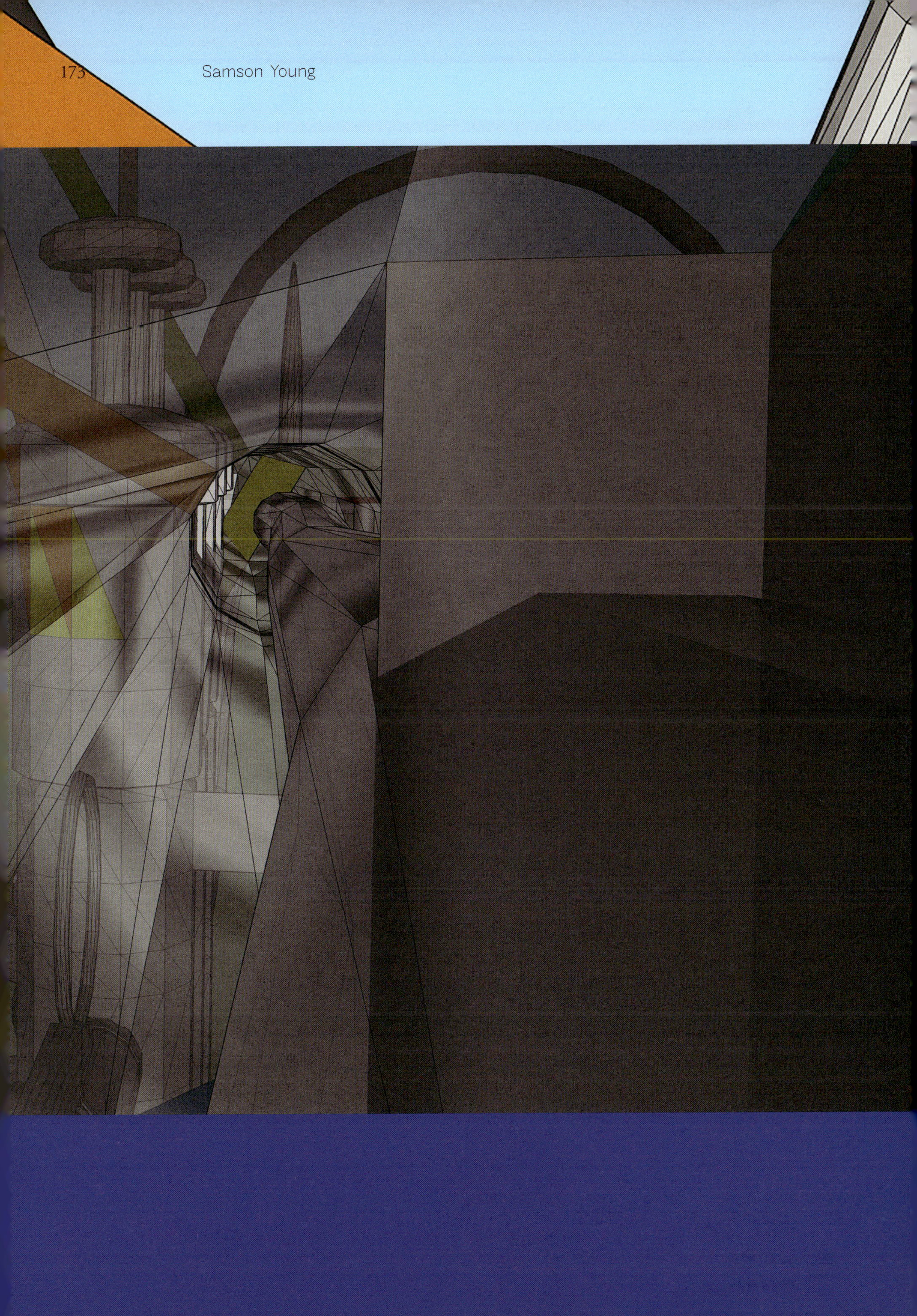

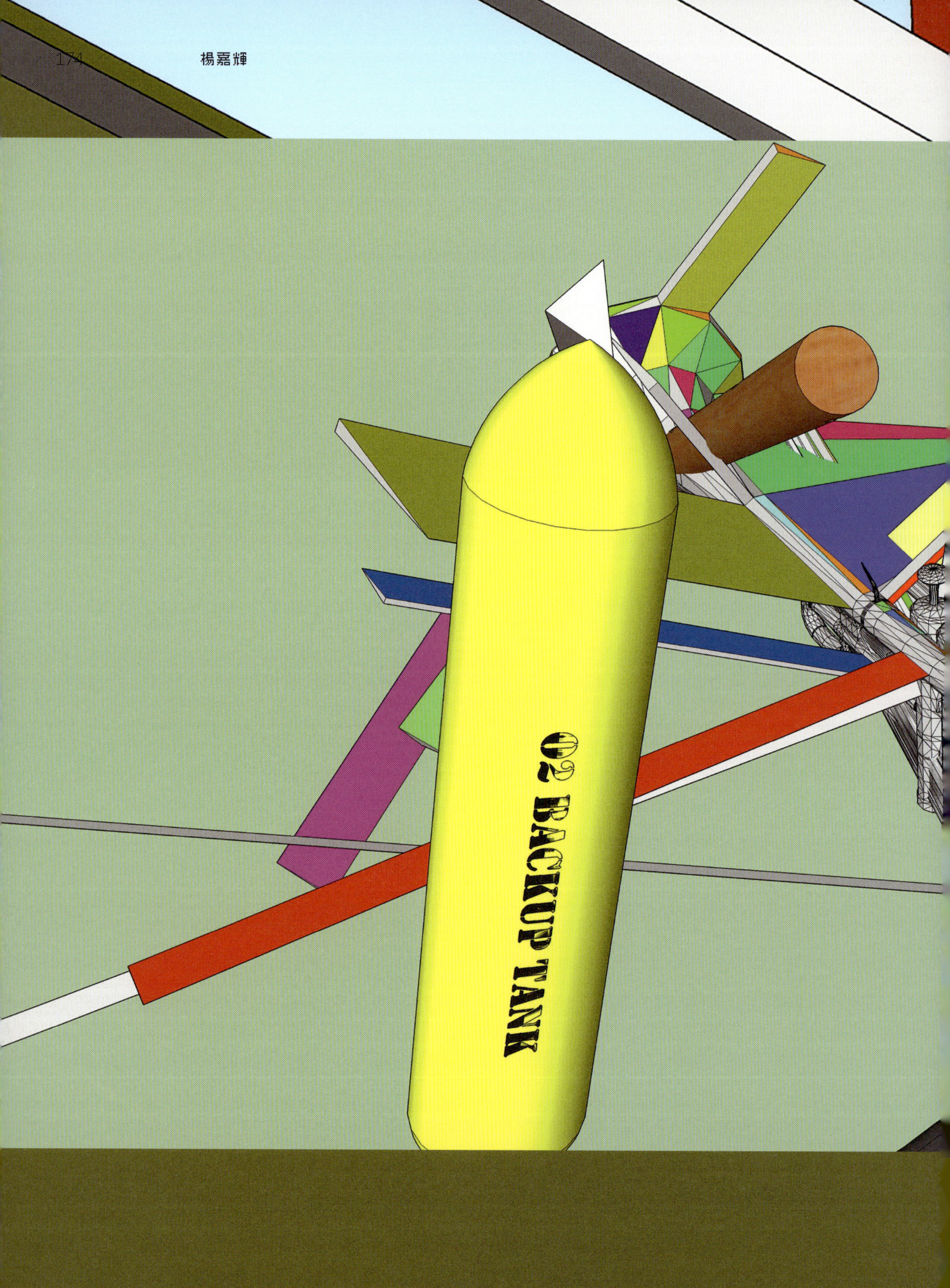
O2 BACKUP TANK

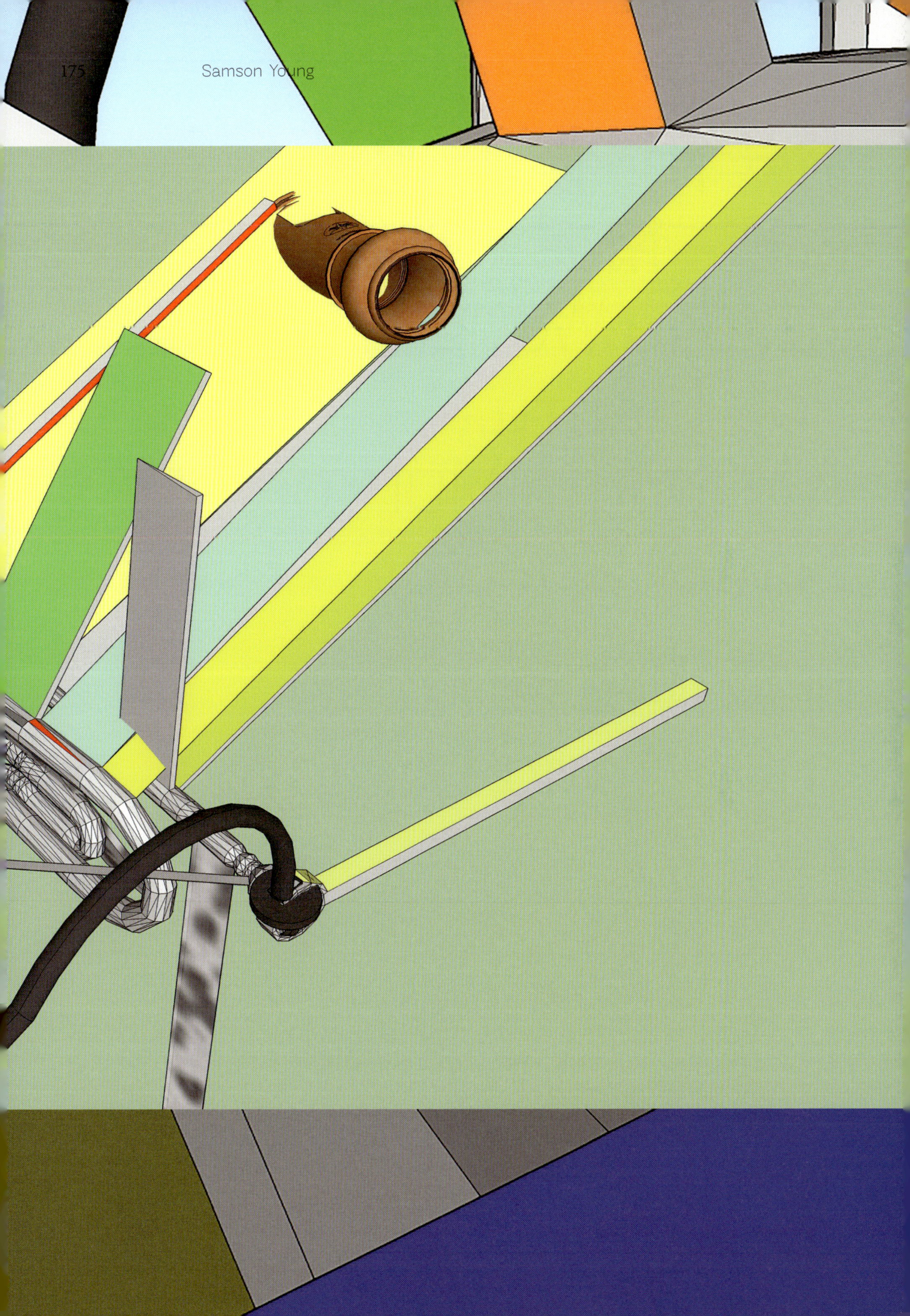

翁笑雨、侯瀚如、孟璐、南希・斯佩克特
Xiaoyu Weng, Hou Hanru, Alexandra Munroe, Nancy Spector

碰撞與生產
Impact and Legacy

古根海姆美術館的何鴻毅家族基金中國藝術計劃
The Robert H. N. Ho Family Foundation Chinese Art Initiative at the Guggenheim

作為一項以構建館藏為目的的多年策展項目，「何鴻毅家族基金中國藝術計劃」於2013年啟動，以委任新作品呈現了三個展覽：「汪建偉：時間寺」（2014–15年）、「故事新編」（2016–17年）以及「單手拍掌」（2018年）。該計劃更延伸和支持了策展駐留以及諸多公共項目，並出版了有關三場展覽的中英雙語出版物。在湯偉峰完成首個展覽的策劃之後，何鴻毅家族基金副策展人翁笑雨接手了該項目主持的工作，此後的兩個展覽由翁笑雨與何鴻毅家族基金策展顧問侯瀚如共同策劃。

以下內容來自一次閉門圓桌討論，翁笑雨，侯瀚如，監督該藝術計劃的三星亞洲藝術高級策展人及全球藝術高級顧問孟璐以及藝術總監、詹妮弗與大衛·斯多克曼首席策展人南希·斯佩克特（Nancy Spector），共同藉「何鴻毅家族基金中國藝術計劃」最後一次展覽的契機進行了相關討論。

翁笑雨：孟璐，能不能和我們簡單談一下設立「何鴻毅家族基金中國藝術計劃」的初衷是什麼？通過委任作品、舉辦展覽以及建設館藏，你本人以及何鴻毅家族基金希望達成哪些目標？

孟璐：古根海姆美術館的亞洲藝術計劃於2006年創立，第一個由其主辦的展覽是2008年蔡國強的回顧展「我想要相信」。自創立之始，中國一直是亞洲藝術計劃及古根海姆致力關注的中心。中國當代藝術領域代表了、甚至主導了人們對於亞洲當代藝術的普遍認知。但借助「何鴻毅家族基金中國藝術計劃」，我們希望挑戰這一既定觀念，跳出地域的框架，更加強調個體的創作。我們希望揭示個體的態度，在觀念、智性、文化以及哲學層面上的態度，尤其是在大中華地區工作的重要藝術家，他們的創作和思考能以何種方式進入古根海姆美術館與全球當代藝術之間更廣闊的對話之中。

我認為在很多方面，我們都已經趨近於這一目標。「何鴻毅家族基金中國藝術計劃」的第一個展覽聚焦了頗具資歷的藝術家汪建偉，此前，他在國際範圍內並未獲得與其成就匹配的認可。群展「故事新編」則介紹了如闞萱、周滔和陽江組等較年輕藝術家的創作，他們的作品此前並未在美國廣泛展出過。這些藝術家從自身的經歷與處境出發，對世界現實進行回應，而不是作為什麼民族代表來解答中國當代藝術到底是什麼。

翁笑雨：瀚如，我有一個大膽的問題：你認為人們對中國藝術仍抱有興趣嗎？

侯瀚如：我認為對中國藝術的興趣仍舊是存在的，好消息是人們對中國藝術的興趣與之前感興趣的點不一樣了，人們開始關注具體的藝術家及作品。這也是我們如何

Launched in 2013 as a multiyear collection-building project at the Solomon R. Guggenheim Museum, The Robert H. N. Ho Family Foundation Chinese Art Initiative encompasses three exhibitions of newly commissioned works: *Wang Jianwei: Time Temple* (2014–15); *Tales of Our Time* (2016–17); and *One Hand Clapping* (2018). Additionally supporting a curatorial residency, public programming, and the production of bilingual publications to accompany each exhibition, the initiative is led by Xiaoyu Weng, The Robert. H. N. Ho Family Foundation Associate Curator of Chinese Art, who succeeded Thomas J. Berghuis in that capacity after the latter organized the first exhibition by Wang Jianwei. Weng has organized the subsequent two exhibitions in collaboration with Hou Hanru, Consulting Curator, The Robert H. N. Ho Family Foundation Chinese Art Initiative. The following text developed out of a closed-door roundtable discussion held on the occasion of the initiative's final iteration by Weng and Hou with Alexandra Munroe, Samsung Senior Curator, Asian Art, and Senior Advisor, Global Arts; and Nancy Spector, Artistic Director and Jennifer and David Stockman Chief Curator.

Xiaoyu Weng: Alexandra, what was the original intent behind the establishment of The Robert H. N. Ho Family Foundation Chinese Art Initiative, and what were some of the goals that you and the foundation set out to achieve through this commissioning, exhibition, and collection-building program?

Alexandra Munroe: The Guggenheim's Asian Art Initiative was created in 2006, and the first exhibition presented under its auspices was the Cai Guo-Qiang retrospective held in 2008, *I Want to Believe*. From day one, China has been central to the ideas that the initiative and the Guggenheim have sought to engage. The field of contemporary Chinese art overwhelmingly represents, if not dominates, the general perception of Asian contemporary art. But with The Robert H. N. Ho Family Foundation Chinese Art Initiative, we wanted to explode that concept, to get out of a regional framework and address

可以講述「我們這個時代的故事」*的出發點。這些「故事」提供了另一種敘述，這一敘述跳脱出了傳統的史實構架，或是被意識形態所投射的歷史，特別是在西方語境下，有關他者的歷史，當然這也就包括中國的歷史。我們試圖以個體的軌跡來構建時間線，每個個體的自身經歷都能折射出一段共同經驗，而這也在某種程度上對線性時間進行解構。這是一種對所謂中國當代藝術的實驗性探索，其所強調的並非僅是國家或個體，還有在個體及強加於其上的身份之間的張力，以及去重新定義我們認知中「他者」的身份，甚至歷史的可能性。就像是德勒茲(Gilles Deleuze)與加塔利(Felix Guattari)將人與自然的互動、地質及化學條件等因素引入歷史的敘述中，這些因素橫貫了經驗的諸多層次，使得其獨特性，而非主觀性，得以形成——也就是德勒茲與加塔利所描述的「千高原」。這讓我們在宏大敘事及地域變遷的背景下得以從另一層面思考個體。

因此，我們並非對中國藝術避而不談，而是試圖以中國的特定情況出發來看待藝術，作為理解世界複雜性的一條通路。我們希望能夠從陽江組飲茶這樣的日常活動，或闖萱於幾乎被官方歷史遺忘或抹去的邊疆地區非官方考古中，發現某種不確定、不可控甚至不可知的可能性。最後一次展覽我們探討的是這個時代所面臨的挑戰，即技術及其影響給人類的身份所帶來的轉變。其實這一主題在孫原&彭禹於「故事新編」中創作的機械裝置作品中已經有所體現。

我認為「何鴻毅家族基金中國藝術計劃」提供了一個令人興奮的平台，能夠讓我們思考如何為古根海姆美術館，這座具有全球影響力的美術館「量身定做」出一個項目，在某種程度上這個項目也可以進一步拓展這座美術館本身的視野。通過展出與收藏技術複雜且豐富多樣的作品，也促使我們重新思考美術館如何能夠繼續作為實驗場。這是當今所有機構所面臨的問題，一方面我們必須應對日益增加的來自市場的壓力，另一方面則需對抗普遍存在的社會不安全感。一個機構如何能成為臨時的烏托邦，讓我們實驗或者體驗生活中一些不失有趣的挑戰？

翁笑雨：南茜，你在古根海姆就職期間已經主持了多項藝術計劃，包括柏林德意志古根海姆美術館的委任項目。你認為我們這項藝術計劃與美術館的使命和主旨如何對接？

南希・斯佩克特：「何鴻毅家族基金中國藝術計劃」進行的期間，我們手上有多項工作也正在開展。在這項計劃啟動時，我們也在準備「古根海姆瑞銀聯合擴大推進全球藝術倡議」計劃，而德意志古根海姆的工作則在最後的收尾階段。德意志古根海姆項目的初衷是我們把建設紐約美術館的館藏作為前提來挑選藝術家。也就是説，我們委任藝術家創作新作品，這些作品會在柏林展出，

individual creative practices. We wanted to reveal the individual positions — conceptual, intellectual, cultural, and philosophical positions — of key artists working in the sphere of Greater China whose work, and whose brilliance, could be integrated into a larger conversation in the context of the Guggenheim and global contemporary art.

I think in many ways we have come close to achieving the goal. The Wang Jianwei exhibition featured a senior artist who until then had not received the international recognition he deserved, while *Tales of Our Time* introduced younger artists, like Kan Xuan, Zhou Tao, or even the Yangjiang Group, whose works had not been presented extensively in the United States. These artists all respond to the world through the lens of their own experiences and conditions, without trying to represent an entire national construct of what contemporary Chinese art might mean.

XW: Hanru, let me ask you a provocative question. Do you think people are still interested in Chinese art?

Hou Hanru: I think there is still interest in Chinese art, but the good news is that people are less interested in Chinese art *as such*; they are interested in specific artists and artworks. That's the starting point for how we tried to tell the "tales of our time." These tales offer an alternative narrative to traditional frameworks of historicity and the projection of ideology onto history — especially the history of the other, including China, in the Western context. We are exploring how to build a timeline through the trajectory of each individual, each with their own story that reflects a common experience, and this entails deconstructing the linear timeline to an extent. It is an experiment in approaching so-called Chinese contemporary art by emphasizing not only the national or the individual, but also the tension between the individual and the imposed identity on the one hand, and the new possibilities for redefining what we call identity, and even history, on the other. Think about how Gilles Deleuze and Felix Guattari have introduced into historical narratives factors such as the interaction between man and nature or geological and technological conditions.

These factors traverse the multiple levels of experience across which singularity, rather than subjectivity, is formed — what Deleuze and Guattari wrote about as the "mille plateaux." This enables another level of thinking about individuals in the context of the "grand narrative" or shifts in geographical territory, and so on.

So it's not that we are avoiding talking about Chinese art, but rather that we are exploring how to look at art using the Chinese situation as a means for understanding the complexity of the world. We want to push toward the unpredictable and uncontrollable, the unknown possibilities to be found in anything from everyday activities such as tea drinking with the Yangjiang Group to the unofficial archaeology Kan Xuan performs when she travels around border areas that have been forgotten or erased from official history. Then the next step is to address the challenges of our time — primarily, the question of technology and its impact on the transformation of human identity. This was already suggested by Sun Yuan & Peng Yu's robot installation in *Tales*, and the topic will feature prominently in the upcoming exhibition.

Let me add that The Robert H. N. Ho Family Foundation Chinese Art Initiative has provided an exciting platform for thinking about how to conceive a project specifically for the Guggenheim — an institution with a global reach — in a way that can further expand the perspective of the institution. The introduction of diverse and technically challenging works in this context prompts us to reconsider how institutions can continue operating as sites for experimentation. This is an issue all institutions face today, at a time when we must navigate the increasing pressure of the market on the one hand, and a pervasive sense of social insecurity on the other. How can an institution provide a temporary utopia for us to experiment with or experience something that makes our lives a bit more challenging, yet also playful?

XW: Nancy, you've led many initiatives over the course of your career at the Guggenheim, including the commissioning program at the Deutsche Guggenheim in Berlin. How do you see the current initiative connecting with the institution's broader mission?

Nancy Spector: A number of strands came together around The Robert H. N. Ho Family Foundation Chinese Art Initiative. When we launched the initiative, we were simultaneously developing The Guggenheim UBS MAP Global Art Initiative and also wrapping up our work with the Deutsche Guggenheim. The whole premise with the Deutsche Guggenheim was that we would select artists whose work we prioritized for the New York collection. Essentially, we would commission them to make new works of art for an exhibition in Berlin, and then the work would enter our collection. This became a model for subsequent initiatives.

But as we come to the conclusion of the Ho Family Foundation and UBS MAP initiatives, I've been reflecting on how to approach geographic specificity within the mission of the Guggenheim. Whereas the Ho Family Foundation Initiative concentrates on Chinese art, the UBS MAP Initiative surveyed broad regions: South and Southeast Asia; North Africa and the Middle East; and Latin America. With each iteration, we found that each of the curators who were tasked with creating a thematic exhibition and building a collection of regional art essentially broke down the notion of region and problematized it for us. They all argued that instead of carving the world into sections, we should look at geographic, national, religious, and ethnic borders in a more holistic way. As important as these initiatives have been for the Guggenheim, that experience has also raised provocative questions for me. Should we be so singular in dealing with other cultures? What about artists who don't want to be labeled as coming from any specific country?

Regarding the practice of commissioning — and speaking as the curator who is ultimately responsible for the collection — I believe that museums should actively participate in producing new art. I'm excited by the idea that museums can step up in this way.

AM: Hanru and Nancy both touch upon discussions that we had from the start of the Asian Art Initiative twelve years ago. The field has changed rapidly since then, thanks in large part, I would argue, to the exhibitions, scholarship, programs, and publications we've presented at the Guggenheim. Initially, the idea was not so

展覽結束後進入我們的館藏。之後的兩個藝術計劃也延續了這一模式。

當「何鴻毅家族基金中國藝術計劃」和「古根海姆瑞銀聯合擴大推進全球藝術倡議」接近尾聲，我一直在思考如何在古根海姆的機構願景和宗旨之下考量有關地理地方性的問題。「何鴻毅家族基金中國藝術計劃」聚焦中國藝術，而「古根海姆瑞銀聯合擴大推進全球藝術倡議」則縱覽多個地域：南亞及東南亞，北非與中東，還有拉丁美洲。在組織三次展覽的經歷中，我們發現每位負責其特定地區藝術的策展人，在組織專題展並發展館藏時，都拆解了「地域」的概念且將有關這樣概念所帶來的問題呈現我們。策展人們認為，與其將世界分割成為不同的部分，我們更應以整體性的眼光來看待地理、國家、宗教及民族的分野。這幾項藝術計劃對於古根海姆至關重要，這些經驗也給我帶來了頗具挑戰的問題：我們是否應該以特殊性的眼光看待其他文化？如果藝術家們並不願將自己標籤為來自某個國家呢？

作為最終對館藏負責的策展人而言，在委任作品方面，我相信美術館應該始終積極致力於生產新的藝術。美術館能夠在這方面添磚加瓦，我感到十分興奮。

孟璐：瀚如和南希都提到了我們在十二年前啟動亞洲藝術計劃時所進行的討論。這一領域如今發生了翻天覆地的變化，我認為在很大程度上，我們在古根海姆所呈現的展覽、學術研究、公共項目和出版物對此貢獻了很多。最初，我們便無意將這些藝術家放在地域性的框架內進行理解，而是試圖構建理論方法，將這些來自或身處歐洲藝術生產中心區域以外的藝術家融入到我們的展覽議程之中。為實現這一遠見，委任和購藏作品是至關重要的。在舉辦蔡國強、李禹煥，以及日本藝術團體具體派的展覽時，我們意識到，作為一個收藏型的機構，只有通過購入作品、將其變成機構基因的一部分，才會更有意義和持久的影響力。如果光有展覽，其本身並不能有效地助推未來的研究，也不能驅使機構眞正地重新思考其在當今世界的位置，它只會讓幾個策展人，在特定的時間裏，局限於和幾位藝術家一起工作。我認為美術館的職責是在新的語境下始終保持反思的態度，不斷重新生產、呈現新的學術研究，這些工作是與策展人一同進行的，無論他們是否熟悉中國、印度尼西亞或南亞藝術、文化或政治。只有為這樣的目標打好基礎，我們才能為美術館未來的發展注入新的可能性。

翁笑雨：我們似乎一直在探討這個項目如何啟發我們思考關於地方性及全球化的觀念。當我們在呈現一個明確以身份、國籍，甚至民族國家作為基礎的藝術計劃時，如何同時強調藝術家作為個體的敘述方式，如何權衡其中的關係？在這樣的語境下，「何鴻毅家族基金中國藝術計劃」的參與藝術家無不明顯地在作品中探討作為中國藝術家，或來自中國的藝術家，到底

much to contextualize these artists in a regional framework, but rather to build a theoretical approach for integrating into the program artists who were coming from and working outside the Eurocentric boundaries of art production. The commissioning and acquisition of works is essential to that vision. We realized that for all that goes into organizing exhibitions for Cai Guo-Qiang, or Lee Ufan, or for the Gutai group, there would be no residue unless we, as a collecting institution, brought in works to be part of what we consider the DNA of the institution. Exhibitions alone do not compel future scholarship, or compel the institution to truly rethink its position in the world in the twenty-first century. It would be limited to a specific band of curators working with those specific artists at that specific time. I think it is the museum's responsibility to keep rethinking and re-presenting and regenerating new scholarship in new contexts, with curators who may or may not be familiar with Chinese art or culture or politics, or with Indonesian or South Asian perspectives. Creating the groundwork for that to happen is how we inject future possibilities into the museum.

XW: We seem to be circling around the question of how this project makes us rethink our notions of the local and the global. How do we negotiate those relationships when we present something that is clearly identity-based, nationality-based, or even nation-state-based, versus discourses that address what artists are thinking about as individuals? As is evident in the works they produced in this context, the artists of the Ho Family Foundation Initiative all question the concept of what it means to be a "Chinese" artist or to be from China. Hanru already mentioned how some artists address China as a territory while others approach it from the viewpoint of identity, and each has its own problematics. I think that in terms of both production and exhibition making, the museum can think together with the artists about these issues of representation.

This is not just about how we conceive history, but also how we imagine the future—one of the main themes of the current exhibition. The two concepts are deeply interconnected. There has been speculation over the years about whether the transition from modernity to postmodernity has already occurred, and if so, what it portends for the future. In response, some theorists have proposed the idea of the singularity. They claim that instead of achieving a utopic society of the future, we will end up with a more or less neoliberal social structure that focuses on individual identity. The various modes of social media networks are a good example of this. Paradoxically, the more we connect through social networks, the more it seems that notions of collectivity are dissipating, and we are moving away from grand historical narratives. So when artists say that they don't want to be labeled as anything, that they want to be taken solely as individuals, what does that say about our current concepts of collectivity?

Developing out of the genealogy of European modernism, the concept of the artist as the ultimate individual shapes how we understand the uniqueness of each artist's practice. But this individualized or autonomous mode of working has now penetrated into many different industries and fields of activity, as seen in the case of tech start ups, for instance. I think an important distinction is that artistic production in some way has a utopic dimension. It doesn't necessarily aim at generating profit or providing concrete and immediate solutions to social problems. The gesture of working individually stays within the bounds of individual interactions. But for the tech industry, the individualized mode of working has the explicit goal of generating profits, and it is exploitative. This is the contradiction inherent to neoliberal values.

HH: The museum itself is a key node for thinking about the connections between history and future. I'm learning to build a collection in a museum context now as artistic director of MAXXI (Museo nazionale delle arti del XXI secolo) in Rome, and it reinforces for me that we need to continue thinking about how to define what a "collection" is. What does it mean, materially? It's a system that is constantly evolving in a living process as it responds to changes in society, technology, and of course art itself. It would be easier to say, this is not a museum or a collecting institution, it's a production institution, and be done with it.

NS: Well, it's both. I think one outgrowth of the Ho Family Foundation Initiative model that has been really interesting is that when the artists have made works in editions, some of those editions have also gone to other institutions. I've never seen that before, where one museum produces the work, and then there are donations to other museums. I think it's admirable. That way, in terms of building a legacy or the outreach of the program, it's not just Guggenheim-centric. It allows the artist to make an imprint at select institutions around the world. That's a significant innovation.

AM: I'd love to hear everyone's thoughts on the whole idea of commissioning work, which is something that has been challenging for us to communicate to the public, and yet is integral to the realization of the Ho Family Foundation Initiative. What is the difference between commissioning new work for a specific context and acquiring work that already has currency and status in a particular art history? What do we learn about the artist through the commissioning process, and what is its significance to the initiative?

HH: The practice of institutional commissions has a fascinating history that relates to shifts in contemporary art in the postwar period. I'm thinking in particular of the 1960s, when site-specific art became an aesthetic regime — not simply an approach or physical frame — that redefined the role of artists in the world, and brought them out of their studios to engage with context. Many institutions followed this direction, and opened themselves up to it by redefining their own identities. A generic museum could turn itself into a specific museum by commissioning new works or site-specific interventions. This is an important tradition or legacy of the last fifty years that has fundamentally transformed how at least two or three generations of artists work. And today we are facing another interesting moment with the rise of the global contemporary art market, which threatens to undermine site-specificity, pushing artists back into their studios, and institutions back to the pattern of collecting and displaying "dead objects" — in other words, commodities. As Xiaoyu mentioned, neoliberalism

意味著什麼。瀚如已經提到，一些藝術家思考「中國」作為領土的概念，另一些則以身份為出發點，抱有各自的反思和叩問。我認為從藝術創作及展覽制作角度看來，美術館應該與藝術家以合作的方式一起來思考如何呈現這些問題。

這不僅是關於我們如何理解歷史，也是如何想像未來，而這也正是當前展覽的主題之一，兩個概念是緊密相連的。近些年，關於我們是否已經完成了從現代時期進入後現代時期的轉型(不僅是理論上，而是實際上)，及其對未來啟示的討論不絕於耳。部分理論家提出了「奇點」的概念作為一種回應。他們宣稱，我們的未來並不會是烏托邦式的集體社會，而是更接近新自由主義的社會形態，強調個體的身份。當下複雜多樣的社交媒體網絡模式便是一個很好的例子。比較荒謬的是，當我們通過社交網絡更為頻繁地聯繫時，集體的觀念反而消失殆盡，更是與宏大的歷史敘述背道而馳。所以值得思考的是，當藝術家們不願被打上任何標籤，而希望僅僅以個體的狀態被接納時，這又如何體現了我們對當下有關集體觀念的理解呢？

藝術家作為終極個體的概念其實是從歐洲現代主義傳統裏來的，而這種觀念其實支配著我們為何會去理解每一位藝術家的創作都是獨特的。但是這種本來較為藝術所特有的，個體化、獨立的工作模式已經滲入到不同行業和領域的活動中，例如科技創業公司。我認為其中重要的差別是，藝術生產存在一個理想化的維度。它並不直接指向利益的牟取，或是為社會問題提供快速有效的解決方案，獨立工作的行為僅僅限定在個體互動的範圍內。但對於科技行業而言，個體工作的模式帶有明確的盈利目的，因此也帶有剝削的性質。這體現了新自由主義的價值觀內部存在的本質矛盾。

侯瀚如：美術館本身就是思考歷史與未來聯繫的重要關節點。作為羅馬國立二十一世紀藝術博物館的藝術總監，我正在學習如何站在美術館的角度建立館藏，而這也提醒我如何不斷思考「收藏」的定義到底為何。在物質的層面上，它意味著什麼？這是一個有生命的、不斷發展的系統，它回應社會、科技及藝術自身的變化。但有些機構如果只是說自己不是美術館、不是收藏機構，而是生產機構的話、並對此就滿足的話，這就把事情想得太簡單了。

南希・斯佩克特：可以說生產、收藏其二者兼備。我認為「何鴻毅家族基金中國藝術計劃」的模式帶來的一個有趣的事是，當藝術家創作的作品有版本時，其中一些作品的其他版本也會進入其他機構。這是前所未見的方式：一個美術館所「生產」的作品，它的其他版本可以通過捐贈的方式進入到其他美術館的館藏。這個模式不免令人欽佩。如此，無論是建立館藏還是作為計劃的延伸，這個藝術計劃都不只是以古根海姆為中心的。這也讓藝術家得以在全球範圍內的一些機構留下印記。這是一個了不起的創新和突破。

孟璐：我希望聽聽大家對委任作品這一構想的看法，對我們而言，向公眾清楚有效地傳達關於「委任」的概念一直不是很容易，但這同時也是「何鴻毅家族基金中國藝術計劃」得以實現的關鍵構成部分。從某個具體的語境出發委任新的作品，與購藏那些在特定的藝術史時期已經取得成就的作品，當中有何分別？在委任的過程中，我們從藝術家那裏學到了什麼？這對於這次藝術計劃的重要性又是什麼？

侯瀚如：機構委托藝術家創作這一行為在戰後的當代藝術變遷中有著一段引人入勝的歷史。我尤其想到的是上世紀六十年代，當時場域特定作品大行其道，其「美學政權」，不僅僅是一種方法或框架，它甚至重新定義了藝術家在世界中的位置，讓他們從工作室中走出來，與環境產生互動。很多機構都跟隨了這個潮流，通過敞開美術館的大門來重新定義身份。通過委任新作品或場域特定的介入，一座普通的美術館可以搖身一變成為一個特別的機構。這在過去的半個世紀間成為了重要的傳統或思想遺產，從根本上改變了兩到三代藝術家的創作方式。而我們當今正在面臨著另一個有趣的時刻，全球當代藝術市場的興起正從中瓦解場域特定創作的基礎，從而把藝術家們再度逼回到工作室中，機構因而也不得不循規蹈矩，退回到收藏和展示「死物件」的模式，換言之，這些「死物件」即是商品。正如笑雨提到的，新自由主義強加給我們一種特定的生活方式，讓我們再一次面臨藝術生產、流通、市場與收藏等環節的根本性轉變。

通過「何鴻毅家族基金中國藝術計劃」，我們對過去三十年的中國藝術構建了一種場域特定的敘述，從而抵制當中國藝術進入全球市場及媒體視野之後所形成的某種既定觀念。我們所生產是有關計劃的、過程的、干預的、小姿態的，以及對不會停頓事物之即時反應的展覽。並且它們持續著自己的生命，它們無法被定性為某種最終的物質產出。如此看來，我認為在討論未來美術館應為怎樣時，機構的獨特性是一個關鍵因素。

南希・斯佩克特：在我親身參與的委任作品計劃中，最根本的理念一直是：美術館可以為藝術家們提供條件，讓他們實現在其他情況下他們無法實施、甚至無法想像的一些想法。「贊助人」這個詞或許不夠準確，我認為委任者應該被視作經紀人或聯合制作人：他們挑戰藝術家，讓藝術家踏出舒適圈之外進行思考。在柏林，德意志古根海姆的空間成為了藝術家們試圖回應的場所。例如威廉・肯特里奇(William Kentridge)將他在南非的經歷與德國在非洲的殖民歷史相連接，創作了《黑箱子》(2005)。這件作品現在是古根海姆館藏的一部分，它的重要性在於它讓藝術家跳脫出了他慣常的創作主題。杉本博司以蠟像為拍攝對象的《肖像》(2000)系列攝影作品也同樣出自於德意志古根海姆項目的委任。在一次會面中杉本博司提出：「我正在考慮做這個」，

has imposed a particular mode of living on all of us, and we are once again facing fundamental changes in the relations of art production and circulation, the market, collecting, and so on.

I would say that through the Ho Family Foundation Initiative we are building a site-specific narrative of the past thirty years of Chinese art that rejects the clichés that have been consumed since Chinese art entered the global market and media. We are producing exhibitions of projects, processes, interventions, small gestures, timely responses to things that cannot be stopped. And they continue to live—they cannot be formulated as a final material product. In this way, I think the specificity of the institution is a key element in discussions of how museums of the future should be.

NS: In my involvement with commissioning works, the basic idea was always that the museum would provide a means for artists to achieve something they wouldn't otherwise be able to do or even think of, necessarily. I don't think *patron* is the right word, but I'd say the commissioner could be considered an agent or coproducer: someone who challenges artists to think beyond their comfort zones. In Berlin, the location became a site that artists responded to. For example, William Kentridge brought together his experiences as a South African with the history of German colonialism in Africa to make a piece that now lives in the Guggenheim collection, *Black Box/Chambre Noire* (2005). That is an important work that resulted from the artist branching out beyond his usual subject matter. Hiroshi Sugimoto's *Portraits* (2000) series of wax-figure photographs also emerged from a Deutsche Guggenheim commission. In an early meeting Sugimoto said, "I'm thinking of doing this," to which we immediately replied, "Go for it," and then provided the time and the means to produce the new work and, ultimately, the venue in which to exhibit it. In the best case with commissions, you really are in a dialogue with the artist. And the notion of venue is as important a factor as time or support. It doesn't have to be just one venue. I'm still hoping to tour *Tales*, because it should be out in the world continuing to circulate.

XW: Another important aspect of commissioning work for me is that it encourages artists to respond to current events. We are living in a world that is hyper-accelerating due to the proliferation of new technologies of communication and interaction. How can contemporary art stay relevant amid all that? This is not to say that commissioning is the only answer, but to echo Hanru, we should support artists who are eager to get out of the studio and participate in world events, especially in China, where the market pushes even young artists toward factory-type situations for churning out commodities. Of course, such social engagement would have to operate on a different level than, say, an Instagram post or Twitter feedback. This is the key for me: how can artists make works that respond to the important events we're experiencing right now, and yet how can we free the artistic voice from being instrumentalized, or otherwise differentiate it from the information that circulates around us? Commissioning artworks is one way to add criticality to these ongoing discourses.

AM: This reminds me of the original threshold of our thinking, as a curatorial department and as an institution, in engaging with these initiatives—both The Robert H. N. Ho Family Foundation Chinese Art Initiative and The Guggenheim UBS MAP Global Art Initiative, as well as the work we've done with the Asian Art Initiative. From the beginning, the intention was to activate an international network and a conversation with communities that were living, thinking, and working in Hong Kong, or in Bangkok, or in Delhi, so that we could engage voices from beyond the normally prescribed boundaries or playground of the established art world. I remember that in one of our first Asian Art Council meetings, Arjun Appadurai said, "It's not just about integrating works from artists who are living and working from these other positions. It's also about interrogating our own position." And I think that the goal of these initiatives was also to project the curators into those cities and the places where works are being made, to stimulate conversations there, and to bring those experiences back to stretch our own thinking about the world. When we assess the efficacy of all these initiatives, I think

我們立即回應道:「那就去做」,然後為其提供了創作這件新作品的時間和條件,以及最終展示這件作品的場地。作品委任的最好狀態是你與藝術家產生真正的對話。而對於展覽場地的考量,與時間和所得到的支持同樣重要。展覽場地未必限於一處。我非常希望能夠巡展「故事新編」,它應該在全球範圍內繼續傳播。

翁笑雨:對我而言,委任作品的重要性還在於,它鼓勵藝術家對當下的事件進行回應。由於通訊和互動類新科技的激增,我們所生活的世界正在瘋狂加速。當代藝術如何能與之保持相關?當然這並不意味著委任是唯一的答案,我們應該支持那些急於跳出工作室,希望設身參與世界進程中的藝術家們,特別是在中國,市場正逼迫著年輕藝術家們走向工廠化制造產品的境地。當然,這裏所提到的社會參與是在非常不同的層面上的,肯定不是簡單地往Instagram上傳自拍,或是在Twitter上發發牢騷。藝術家們應當如何創作作品,以回應當下我們正在經歷的重要事件?而與此同時,這樣的社會介入又不去被意識形態化?並且使這些藝術表達區別於我們身邊所流通的信息?這些問題對我而言至關重要。委任作品是讓這些正在進行的論述變得更加重要的、具有批判性的方式之一。

孟璐:這讓我想起了我們初始的思考,作為一個機構的策展部門,主動參與到這些藝術計劃之中,包括「何鴻毅家族基金中國藝術計劃」與「古根海姆瑞銀聯合擴大推進全球藝術倡議」,以及我們的亞洲藝術計劃所開展的工作。一開始,我們的目的是啟動一個國際網絡,與生活、思考和工作在香港、曼谷或新德里的文化社群展開對話,以此來介入所謂藝術中心之外的聲音和討論。我記得在亞洲藝術委員會初創之時的某次會議上,Arjun Appadurai說道:「這不光意味著吸納那些生活或工作在別處的藝術家們的作品,更是檢視我們自身所處的位置。」我認為這些藝術計劃的目的同樣在於將策展人帶到作品所實際產出的城市或地方,以激發在地的對話,並且將這些經驗帶回來,以豐富我們對當下世界的思考。在評估所有這些計劃的效能時,我認為需要謹記的是那些我們所構建的社群,那些我們所發展的研討會方式,以及我們所給予彼此的考驗。前來觀展的公眾,或是予以評論的藝評人都不是我們唯一的觀眾。通過這些計劃的意義被帶到世界各地不同的生產中心的過程中,我們的觀眾便遠遠地延伸到紐約之外。

此次圓桌於2017年10月3日在紐約古根海姆美術館舉行,此處發表的內容經過精簡與編輯。

*** 展覽題目「Tales of Our Time」直譯為「我們這個時代的故事」,而展覽的中文題目「故事新編」既借用了魯迅的同名著作,也是一種意譯。**

it's important to keep in mind the communities we've built, the workshop approaches we've developed, and the mutual testing we've given each other. The public who come to see the show are not our only audience, and neither are the critics who review it. The public extends beyond New York through the way the meanings of these projects ricochet back to different production centers around the world.

This discussion was conducted at the Solomon R. Guggenheim Museum, New York, on October 3, 2017, and has been edited and condensed for this publication.

藝術家簡介 Artist Biographies

由安輝景整理
Compiled by Kyung An

曹斐

2001年從廣州美術學院畢業之後，曹斐突破性的多媒體創作享譽國際。作品探究了虛擬和真實世界、烏托邦和異托邦以及身體和科技之間的互動等等。1978年出生於廣東廣州，曹斐在當代生活不穩定的社會經濟狀況中尋找刺激，她的作品一直都是中國劇烈的經濟增長、城市開發和失控的全球化對個體沖擊的批判性見證者。

早期作品如《角色》(2004)中的年輕人，通過打扮成幻想中遊戲角色，探索了疏離和對逃離的渴望。曹斐在佛山一個照明工廠六個月的駐地創作《誰的烏托邦》(2006)，記錄了工廠工人在他們的夢中脱離了自身原來的角色，化身為芭蕾舞者、太極拳師或是音樂人。在《人民城寨》中，曹斐將她的觀察領域轉移到「第二人生」上——在這個虛擬平台中，用戶可以通過虛擬替身一起建造一個想像中的烏托邦。曹斐在遊戲中扮演的「中國·翠西」花了幾年時間開發了一個虛擬城市：一只漂浮的大熊貓、北京奧林匹克體育館「鳥巢」、底朝天的CCTV大樓和上海東方明珠塔，這些亂糟糟的後現代城市景觀，一方面反映了今天快速城市發展的奇觀，另一方面也成為了追尋新世界秩序的實驗室。

2006年，曹斐從廣州搬至北京，奇妙的大都市成為她作品的重要主題。《霾》(2013)探討了中國對市場資本主義和消費主義之追逐引發的精神不適。在影片中，一種精神狀態的「霾與霧」也使人聯想到北京的空氣污染。城市的混凝土高架橋和無名的住宅樓成為一個懸浮現實的背景，或是曹斐所稱的「喪屍文化」：「喪屍文化反映了一種全球情境——麻木、野蠻且失控……在中國，魔法就發生在真實生活中。」在她最新的影像作品《La Town》(2014)中，曹斐回顧了具體時間或文化之外的超現實都市主題。伴隨著法國戰後經典電影《廣島之戀》(1959)中的對話，她的鏡頭緩慢地在一個末日之後的城鎮日常生活裏穿梭，而這個城鎮是用藝術家網上購買的微縮模型搭建的。

曹斐的個展包括「角色」，Para Site藝術空間，香港，2006年；「烏托邦」，現代藝術研究所，澳大利亞布里斯班，2009年；「霾與霧」，當代藝術中心，特拉維夫，2016年；「曹斐」，MoMA PS1，紐約，2016年。部分群展和雙年展包括廣州三年展，2002年，2005年和2008年；威尼斯雙年展，2003年，2007年，2011年和2015年；伊斯坦布爾雙年展，2007年；「Brave New Worlds」，沃克藝術中心，明尼阿波利斯，2007–2008年；「中堅：新世紀中國藝術的八個關鍵形象」，尤倫斯當代藝術中心，北京，2009年；新美術館三年展，紐約，2009年；「1989年後的藝術與中國：世界劇場」，所羅門·R·古根海姆美術館，紐約，2017年。2010年，曹斐入圍了Hugo Boss獎；她分別於2006年和2016年獲得中國當代藝術獎(CCAA)的最佳青年藝術家獎和最佳藝術家獎。

Cao Fei

Since graduating from Guangzhou Academy of Fine Arts in 2001, Cao Fei has earned international acclaim for her groundbreaking multimedia works probing the interplay between virtual and real worlds, utopia and dystopia, and the body and technology. Born in 1978 in Guangzhou, Guangdong Province, Cao finds impetus in the precarious socioeconomic conditions of contemporary life. Her works are critical witnesses to the impact of hyper-economic growth, urban development, and rampant globalization on the individual in China.

Early works such as *Cosplayers* (2004) explored the alienation and longing to escape felt by youths who dress up as fantastical gaming characters. *Whose Utopia* (2006), which resulted from a six-month-long residency at a lighting factory in Foshan, outside Guangzhou, documents the factory workers as they metamorphose from their everyday roles into the incarnations of their dreams, such as a ballerina, a tai chi master, or a musician. With *RMB City: A Second Life City Planning by China Tracy (aka Cao Fei)* (2007), Cao moved her realm of observation into Second Life, a virtual platform where users can build an imagined "utopia" together through their avatars. Under the guise of China Tracy, Cao spent several years developing a virtual city where a floating giant panda, the Beijing Olympics "Bird's Nest" National Stadium, an upside-down CCTV building, and Shanghai's Oriental Pearl Tower are part of a topsy-turvy postmodernist landscape that both reflects the spectacle of today's rapid urban development and functions as a laboratory for pursuing a new world order.

The magical metropolis has been a key theme in Cao's works since she moved from Guangzhou to Beijing in 2006. *Haze and Fog* (2013) explores the spiritual malaise induced by China's pursuit of market capitalism and consumerism (here, the notion of a psychological state of "haze and fog" also evokes the smog in Beijing). The city's concrete esplanades and anonymous condo towers become the backdrop for a world of suspended reality, or what Cao describes as "zombie culture": "Zombie culture reflects a global situation — the numbness, brutality and loss of control. . . . In China, the magical comes to real life." In her most recent video work, *La Town* (2014), Cao turns to a surreal

段建宇

敘事性是段建宇輕盈、大尺幅的繪畫和私密雕塑背後的驅動力。1970年生於河南鄭州，1995年畢業於廣州美術學院油畫系，段建宇的創作往往以系列呈現，她將普通人、日常生活場景和超現實的元素編織在一起，創造出有關現代社會道德複雜性的寓言。例如，藝術家出版物《紐約巴黎駐馬店》(2008)始於一則男孩把生病的父親帶到大學一起生活的真實故事。在段建宇的講述中，兒子在撿到的硬紙板上給臥床不起父親畫畫，這對父子還通過怪異的日常活動如養雞和暢想環遊世界建立感情紐帶。段建宇用這個故事將一些紙板畫串連在一起：中國和歐洲的註釋地圖和威尼斯運河的風景線，事實上也都是她的「美麗的夢」系列(2008)的一部分。

經過折射的現實主義感知賦與段建宇的繪畫社會批判的維度。她常常在詭異的場景中插入反覆出現的母題，無論是她在2003年威尼斯雙年展帶去的九十九只雞的雕塑，或是《姐姐》(2004-12年)中描繪的在鄉間笨拙地站著的，或是拿著西瓜和裝魚水桶的空姐。這種批判在《殺，殺，殺馬特》(2014-16年)中得到了最有力的表達，這個標題來源於常遭到揶揄的亞文化現象「殺馬特」(smart的諧音)，其融合了哥特、朋克、視覺系和動漫的風格。盡管段建宇畫的是鄉村的場景，其中的人物(微笑的農民婦女，或是裸露或是穿著顏色俗氣的衣服)和她們的動作(在村間小屋前哺乳或是用籃子挎著鵝)將這些場景延展至中國現代化和農村身份認同間日益增長的緊張之中。

段建宇看似天真的視覺語言結合了西方現代主義的傳統和中國藝術史元素，從原始主義和抽象藝術到社會主義現實主義，以及二十世紀早期有意識地將西方繪畫風格融入實踐的中國畫家的作品。在《美與美術館No.2》(2011)中，段建宇嘲諷了全球化時代中歐洲藝術史教條的無所不在：怪異的幾何形狀的美術館在遠處中心的位置，遙望著赤裸的幾個女人體臥躺於蔥翠的畫面中央；在《回家No.3》(2010)中，藝術家又把裸女放置於在鄉村的稻田中勞作的村民之間，這種時代錯位和幽默的方法反映了藝術家對所謂真實性的質疑，以及為繼續這種真實性而建造起的「中心-外圍」關係，他們超越了簡單的挪用，並梳理了區域文化身份的焦慮。

除了大量在畫廊的個展之外，段建宇還在上海外灘美術館舉辦了雙個展：「醍醐：段建宇、胡曉媛」(2013)。她參與國際展覽和雙年展包括：威尼斯雙年展，2003年；廣州三年展，2005，2008年；「當代中國水墨的過去與現在」，大都會藝術博物館，紐約，2013-14年；「與繪畫有關」，OCAT西安館，2014年；亞太當代藝術三年展，澳大利亞布里斯班，2015-16年；「時代異托邦三部曲之III：從不扔東西的人」，時代美術館，廣州，2017年；「廣東快車：珠江三角洲的藝術」，M+展亭，香港，2017年。2010年段建宇被評為中國當代藝術獎(CCAA)最佳藝術家。

林一林

林一林1964年生於廣東廣州，致力於特定場域的多元行為表演。在全球化語境下，他從社會經濟的轉變、政治格局波動和文化錯位的經驗中重新想像自我、社區與周邊城鄉環境的關係。

1987年，林一林畢業於廣州美術學院雕塑專業。在20世紀90年代中國經濟高速增長的十年中，他以磚作為材料，創作了一系列關於「社會建設」主題的作品。在《1000塊的結果》(1994)中，他將自己的身體嵌入一堵磚牆中，牆縫中夾著鈔票，以此來討論「邊界」及其對移民和貨幣流通的影響。林一林最廣為人知的作品是《安全度過林和路》(1995)，他在廣州當時剛開發的一個新區中，把一堵臨時牆中的混凝土磚一塊一塊地從繁忙街道的一端搬到另一端，同時在這個九十分鐘的影像中被記錄下來的還有在全球化、新自由主義資本世界中作為商品的時間和勞動。林一林作為廣州的「大尾象工作組」(成立於1990年)的一員，其集體的工作過程，是他個人創作中回應和干預南方城市極速發展的關鍵。

自從2001年搬到紐約之後，林一林的工作範圍擴大到當地和國際社群——包括挪威大學生、中國家庭以及泰國農民。在他的作品中，牆作為社會交往和文化協商的場所，仍然是一個反覆出現的母題。用藝術家的話來說，「它把我作品中最核心和本質的內容運送到不同的現場和語境中」。在2007年的第12屆文獻展中，林一林在卡塞爾的諾德斯塔特公園憑空建起一道牆，搭建了本地居民和外國遊客各在一側的拔河比賽。這個名為《紀念碑式遊戲》質問了紀念碑的社會功能和公眾在確定紀念碑意義過程中的角色。2011年在舊金山卡迪斯特藝術基金會駐留期間，林一林組織了一系列關於舊金山中國移民的行為表演，探索了移民在新環境中如何重新協商身份。

林一林目前生活和工作於紐約和北京兩地，並任教於中央美術學院實驗藝術學院。他的個展包括：「大家庭：是兄弟，不是同志」，箭廠空間，北京，2009年；「誰的土地？誰的藝術？」，土地基金會，清邁以及當代唐人藝術空間，曼谷，2010-11年；「金色遊記」，美國，舊金山藝術學院，沃爾特·麥克拜恩畫廊，卡迪斯藝術基金會，舊金山，2012年；「假日」，Edicola Notte空間，羅馬，2013年；「林一林」，錄像局，北京，2014年。作為「大尾象」的成員林一林曾參與如下展覽，包括「大尾象」，伯爾尼藝術宮，1998年；「大尾象：一小時，沒空間，五回展」，時代美術館，廣州，2016年；林一林參與的國際雙年展、群展包括：光州雙年展，2002年；廣州三年展，2002年；威尼斯雙年展，2003年和2015年；第12屆文獻展，卡塞爾，德國，2007年；里昂雙年展，2009年；「行動的形象：五個當代影像」，亞洲協會，紐約，2010年；「行走之線」，以色列，海法藝術博物館，2011年；「1989後的藝術與中國：世界劇場」，所羅門·R·古根海姆美術館，紐約，2017年。

metropolis that exists outside a specific time or culture. Accompanied by the dialogue from the French postwar classic *Hiroshima Mon Amour* (1959), her camera slowly moves in and out of the daily lives of the residents of a postapocalyptic town—staged using miniature models the artist purchased online.

Cao's solo exhibitions include *COSplayers*, Para Site Art Space, Hong Kong, 2006; *Utopia*, Institute of Modern Art, Brisbane, Australia, 2009; *Haze and Fog*, Center for Contemporary Art, Tel Aviv, 2016; and *Cao Fei*, MoMA PS1, New York, 2016. Select group exhibitions and biennials include the Guangzhou Triennial, 2002, 2005, and 2008; Venice Biennale, 2003, 2007, 2011, and 2015; Istanbul Biennial, 2007; *Brave New Worlds*, Walker Art Center, Minneapolis, 2007–08; *Breaking Forecast: 8 Key Figures of China's New Generation Artists*, Ullens Center for Contemporary Art, Beijing, 2009; New Museum Triennial, New York, 2009; and *Art and China after 1989: Theater of the World*, Solomon R. Guggenheim Museum, New York, 2017. Cao Fei was the recipient of the Chinese Contemporary Art Award's (CCAA) Best Young Artist Award in 2006 and Best Artist Award in 2016. In 2010, she was a finalist for the Hugo Boss Prize.

Duan Jianyu

Narrative is the driving force behind Duan Jianyu's ethereal, large-scale paintings and intimate sculptures. Often working in series, Duan—who was born in 1970 in Zhengzhou, Henan Province, and graduated from the Department of Oil Painting at Guangzhou Academy of Fine Arts in 1995—weaves together images of ordinary people, everyday scenarios, and surreal elements into allegories of contemporary society's moral complexities. For instance, the real story of a boy who took his ailing father with him to live at university serves as the point of departure for the artist book *New York Paris Zhumadian* (2008). In Duan's interpretation, the pair bond over unusual daily activities such as rearing chickens, and imagine traveling together around the world, aided by the son's illustrations on found cardboard boxes. Duan interlaces the narrative with those very drawings: annotated maps of China and Europe and scenic vistas of Venetian canals, which in fact belong to her *Beautiful Dream* series (2008).

A refracted sense of realism gives Duan's paintings a dimension of social critique. She often inserts recurring motifs into peculiar settings, as with the ninety-nine sculptures of chickens she brought to the Venice Biennale in 2003, or the depictions of flight attendants who stand awkwardly in the countryside or carry watermelons and buckets of fish in the series *Sister* (2004–12). This reaches its most potent form in *Sharp Sharp Smart* (2014–16). The series' title references the oft-derided subcultural movement *shamate* (whose name is a phonetic play on the English "smart"), a blend of goth, punk, glam, and anime sensibilities that is popular among youth in rural China. Although Duan's paintings depict rustic settings, the figures (smiling peasant women who appear either naked or clothed in gaudy colors) and their actions (breast feeding in front of tribal huts or carrying geese in baskets) suspend these scenarios within the growing tension between China's modernization and its rural identity.

Duan's faux-naïve visual language incorporates references to both Western modernist tradition and Chinese art history, from primitivism and abstract art to Socialist Realism and the work of the early twentieth-century Chinese painters who consciously incorporated Western painting styles into their practices. In *Muse and Museum No. 2* (2011), Duan mocks the European art historical canon's ubiquity in the age of globalization by inserting reclining female nudes into a lush paradise overlooked by a geometrical contemporary museum building in the background; in *Go Home No. 3* (2010), she places one in a pastoral scene of villagers working in their rice paddies. Reflecting the artist's skepticism toward obsessions with locating authenticity, and the constructs of center and periphery that perpetuate them, this anachronistic and humorous approach surpasses simple appropriation to open up a third space for interpretation in painting after globalization, and tease out the cultural anxieties of regional identity.

Aside from numerous solo exhibitions at galleries, Duan has held a two-person exhibition at the Rockbund Art Museum, Shanghai, *A Potent Force: Duan Jianyu and Hu Xiaoyuan* (2013). She has participated in international exhibitions and biennials including the Venice Biennale, 2003; Guangzhou Triennial, 2005 and 2008; *Ink Art: Past as Present in Contemporary China*, Metropolitan Museum of Art, New York, 2013–14; *About Painting*, OCAT Xi'an, China, 2014; Asia Pacific Triennial of Contemporary Art, Brisbane, Australia, 2015–16; *Times Heterotopia Trilogy III: The Man Who Never Threw Anything Away*, Times Museum, Guangzhou, 2017; and *Canton Express: Art from the Pearl River Delta*, M+ Pavilion, Hong Kong, 2017. She received the Chinese Contemporary Art Award (CCAA) for Best Artist in 2010.

Lin Yilin

Born in 1964 in Guangzhou, Guangdong Province, Lin Yilin pursues a multifaceted practice rooted in site-specific performance. He draws from shifting socioeconomic conditions, the fluctuating political landscape, and experiences of cultural displacement to reimagine the relations between the self, community, and surrounding urban and rural environments in a globalized context.

Lin studied sculpture at the Guangzhou Academy of Fine Arts, graduating in 1987. Throughout the 1990s — a decade of rapid economic growth in China — he made a series of works using bricks under the rubric of "social construction." For *The Result of 1,000 Pieces* (1994), he embedded himself within a wall of bricks that had banknotes stuck between them, in a trenchant reflection on barriers and their effect on migratory and monetary circulation. Lin's most cited work is *Safely Maneuvering across Linhe Road* (1995), for which he moved a stack of concrete blocks one by one across a busy street in a newly developed zone in Guangzhou. Also documented in a video, this 90-minute action performed time and labor as commodities in a globalized, neoliberal capitalist world. Lin's involvement in the Guangzhou-based Big Tail Elephant Working Group (formed in 1990) was pivotal in shaping his responses to and interventions in the catalytic urban development of Southern China.

Since his move to New York in 2001, Lin has expanded his scope to working with both local and international communities, from college students in Norway to families in China and farmers in Thailand. The wall remains a recurring motif in his projects, acting as a site for social interaction and cultural negotiation. In the words of the artist, it "transports the most essential and intrinsic aspects of my work into a different field and context." For Documenta 12 in 2007, Lin built a freestanding wall with a small hole in it in the Nordstadtpark in Kassel, and staged a tug-of-war pitting local residents against visitors from abroad on opposing sides. Titled *The Game of Monumentality*, this work interrogates the social function of monuments and the public's role in determining their meaning. During his 2011 residency at Kadist Art Foundation in San Francisco, Lin organized a series of performances involving Chinese immigrants across the city, exploring how one renegotiates identity when navigating a new environment.

Lin now divides his time between New York and Beijing, where he teaches in the School of Experimental Art at the Central Academy of Fine Arts. Solo exhibitions include *Big Family: Brothers, Not Comrades*, Arrow Factory, Beijing, 2009; *Whose Land? Whose Art?* The Land Foundation, Chiang Mai, and Tang Contemporary Art, Bangkok, 2010–11; *Golden Journey*, San Francisco Art Institute Walter and McBean Galleries, San Francisco, 2012; *Holiday*, Edicola Notte, Rome, 2013; and *Archive 30: Lin Yilin*, Video Bureau, Beijing, 2014. Additionally, Lin has been featured in exhibitions of the Big Tail Elephant Group including *Big Tail Elephant*, Kunsthalle Bern, 1998, and *Operation PRD — Big Tail Elephants: One Hour, No Room, Five Shows*, Times Museum, Guangzhou, 2016. International group exhibitions and biennials include Gwangju Biennial, 2002; Guangzhou Triennial, 2002; Venice Biennale, 2003 and 2015; Documenta 12, Kassel, Germany, 2007; Lyon Biennial, 2009; *Go Figure: Five Contemporary Videos*, Asia Society, New York, 2010; *A Line Made by Walking*, Haifa Museum of Art, Israel, 2011; and *Art and China after 1989: Theater of the World*, Solomon R. Guggenheim Museum, New York, 2017.

Wong Ping

Repressed obsessions and unfulfilled desires; emasculation and submission before sexual and political dominance; lust and slippery morals. These are the themes that run through the strange and intimate stories told in Wong Ping's animation videos. Skirting the line between shock and humor, Wong relates his observations of contemporary society through invented anecdotes that allow glimpses into the deepest and often shameful traits of human nature. In *Stop Peeping* (2014), a young man's obsession with a female neighbor he observes through

黃炳

壓抑的迷戀和無法滿足的欲望，獲得性和政治主導權之前的去勢和順從，肉欲和遊移的道德準則，這些都是貫穿在黃炳的動畫中詭異又親密的故事主題。黃炳在驚詫和幽默之間劃出一條線，將他自己通過觀察當代社會創造出的軼事聯繫起來，以窺視人性中最深也往往是最可恥的部分。在《太陽留住我》(2014)中，一名年輕男子由於迷戀女鄰居，長期通過牆孔觀察她的生活，不由自主地去收集女鄰居的汗水來為自己制做冰棒。《狗仔式的愛》(2015)講述了一個男孩愛上了一個乳房長在背上女孩的故事。而一個極為虔誠的女人和一個無神論男人通過約會軟件促成了相遇，最終在塑料袋裏生了個孩子，則是《妳要熱烈地親親爹地》(2017)的場景。自始至終，黃炳的霓虹色調、低保真、復古流行的視覺語言抵消了這些敘事中令人不適的弦外之音。

有時，黃炳通過色彩斑斕的裝置將他的動畫世界擴展到三維空間。《欲望Jungle》(2015)講述了一個無法滿足自己妻子的陽痿男人的故事，妻子最終在家賣淫並被一個警察勒索。這件作品首次展出是在香港的非營利機構咩事藝術空間，黃炳正是受到這個空間所在之處深水埗的啟發，創造了一個真正的欲望叢林。這裏是九龍的工薪階層街區，當地也以性交易而著稱。他用招財貓填滿了展覽空間——在中國餐館經常見到日本裝飾物——但是擺動手臂則被替換成陰莖的樣子。這組裝置還包括一個巨大的陰莖雕塑，最上面是一顆面容悲傷的心，裸露的女性身體的性器官從內部亮起來，如同霓虹燈一般。這個充滿挑釁的場景設置反映了深水埗在士紳化過程中和香港城市景觀變遷中的緊張對峙，同時也使用男性氣質的圖像去揭露權力的底線和濫用。

黃炳1984年生於香港，於2005年在澳洲珀斯科廷大學取得文學學士學位。從香港的地下文化出發，黃炳有一條不同尋常的藝術創作道路，他的職業生涯始於廣播行業，2014年創辦了黃炳動畫廊。接受包括香港M+視覺文化博物館、NOWNESS和時尚品牌普拉達的委任創作。黃炳的個展包括「欲望JUNGLE」，咩事藝術空間，香港，2015年；「妳要熱烈地親親爹地」，馬凌畫廊，香港，2017年。部分群展包括「M+進行：流動的影像」，香港，2015年；「基本問題」，布魯森當代博物館，伊斯坦布爾，2015年；「稀有之物·中國」，中國當代藝術中心，曼徹斯特，2016年；和「留在暗處：阿裏斯托芬」，墨爾本藝術中心，2017年；新美術館三年展，紐約，2018。他的影片曾參與以下放映：倫敦國際動畫節，2013年；墨爾本國際動畫節，2013年；戛納國際創意節，2013年。黃炳獲得2013年亞洲電影及視覺媒體孵化器(ifva)金獎，以及香港2016年第三屆文化電影節頒發的香港最佳動畫及精神獎。

楊嘉輝

楊嘉輝的作曲、繪畫、裝置、廣播和行為表演涉及了諸如軍事沖突、身份、移民和政治邊界的過去和當下等話題。聲音及其文化政治是貫穿楊家輝敘事多重、典故豐富之實踐的核心。1979年生於香港，楊嘉輝在2013年獲得了普林斯頓大學的音樂博士(作曲)學位之後，涉足當代藝術領域。

暴力與聲音之間的關係是楊嘉輝作品中反複出現的研究線索。在2015年紐約Team畫廊的個展上，楊嘉輝在作品《夜曲》(2015)中穿著軍裝，坐在一系列音響設備和一個播放著不同戰場夜襲場景的小型監視器前。如同擬音師一樣，他重現了監視器上表現出來爆炸和槍擊圖像的聲音，並通過一個本地FM發射器進行廣播。楊嘉輝的繪畫則將上述關懷轉化成一種更為私密的表達形式，如在向後殖民主義思想家弗蘭茨·法農(Frantz Fanon)致敬的系列《致法農》(2016–)中，藝術家通過覆蓋圖像、混合媒體的方法肆意破壞了自己早期的作曲。

楊嘉輝的許多項目都是從大量的研究中發展而來。在《喪鐘為誰而鳴：沖突的音頻史之旅》(2015–)中，楊嘉輝獲得寶馬藝術之旅的支持，前往五大洲三十多個地點追蹤鐘的歷史和用途。通過建構一個包含錄音、草圖和物件的檔案，楊嘉輝揭示了鐘如何被卷入到領土、信仰和文化的沖突中。2016年的作品《Canon》，楊嘉輝穿著一身1979年皇家香港警察部隊制服，通過LRAD(遠距離聲學裝置)，一種用於驅散示威者的非致命聲音武器，來播放鳥類遇險時的呼叫。聲音專門朝向坐在遠處房間裏的觀眾，房間內同時填滿了與1979年越南難民危機有關的物品。2700名難民當時被香港拒絕入境後被迫滯留在貨船上四個月之久。

在2017年威尼斯雙年展香港館的個展中，楊嘉輝的作品借用了八十年代極其流行的巨星錄制「慈善單曲」的形式，批評這些單曲背後的潛台詞——其中包括「慈善」這種姿態與新自由主義政策和文化帝國主義的共謀——楊嘉輝通過挪用熱門歌單中的知名歌曲創作出繪畫、物件、錄像和場域特定的裝置。

楊嘉輝生活和工作於香港，並從事古典音樂作曲。他的個展包括「論音樂一般美麗的」，歌德學院，香港，2013年；「錄像藝術系列之46：楊嘉輝」，廣島市現代美術館，2015年；「黑暗讓我停留此處，我將譜出支離破碎的音樂」，杜塞爾多夫美術館，2016年；「楊嘉輝的賑災專輯」，香港館，威尼斯雙年展，2017年。部分群展包括「因腦維新族：新媒體藝術的華麗旅程」，台北當代藝術館，2013年；「巫師的房間」，溫特圖爾藝術館，瑞士，2013年；「疫年日誌：恐懼、鬼魂、叛軍、沙士、哥哥和香港的故事」，Para Site藝術空間，香港，2013年；「48小時時間」，4A當代亞洲藝術中心，悉尼，2015年；「逆行」，洛根中心畫廊，芝加哥大學，2016年；第14屆文獻展，希臘雅典和德國卡塞爾，2017年。楊嘉輝也是2007年彭博新秀藝術家獎得主，並於2015年獲得寶馬藝術之旅獎。

a peephole compels him to collect her sweat to make a Popsicle for his own consumption. *Doggy Love* (2015) tells the story of a boy who falls in love with a girl whose breasts are on her back, while a dating-app-facilitated encounter between a deeply religious woman and an atheist man, resulting in the delivery of a baby in a plastic bag, is the scenario for *Who's the Daddy* (2017). Throughout, Wong's neon-hued, lo-fi, retro-pop visual language offsets the uncomfortable undertones of these narratives.

In some cases, Wong creates colorful installations that extend the animation world of his videos into three dimensions. *Jungle of Desire* (2015) is a tale of an impotent man incapable of sexually fulfilling his wife; she ultimately turns to at-home prostitution and is extorted by a cop. When he exhibited the work at the nonprofit art space Things That Can Happen in Hong Kong in 2015, Wong was inspired by the gallery's surroundings in Sham Shui Po, a working-class neighborhood in Kowloon that is also known as the center of the local sex industry, to create an actual jungle of desire. He filled the space with *maneki neko* cat figurines — the Japanese good-luck charms often seen in Chinese restaurants — but reworked their swinging arms to resemble penises. The installation also incorporated a giant phallic sculpture topped by a sad-faced heart, and transparent sculptures of headless, naked female bodies with their sexual organs illuminated from within as neon lights. The provocative setup reflected tensions over gentrification in Sham Shui Po and the transformation of the urban landscape in Hong Kong, while also using images of masculinity to expose the underside of power and its abuse.

Wong was born in Hong Kong in 1984 and obtained his BA from Curtin University, Perth, Australia, in 2005. Emerging from the underground cultural scene in Hong Kong, he took an unconventional path to art making, starting his career in broadcasting before founding Wong Ping Animation Lab in 2014. Commissions include M+, Hong Kong; NOWNESS; and the fashion house Prada. Wong's solo exhibitions include *Jungle of Desire*, Things That Can Happen, Hong Kong, 2015. Select group exhibitions include *Mobile M+: Moving Images*, M+, Hong Kong, 2015; *Essential Matters*, Borusan Contemporary, Istanbul, 2015; *RareKind China*, Centre for Chinese Contemporary Art, Manchester, 2016; *XO State Dark:*

Aristophanes, Arts Centre Melbourne, 2017; and New Museum Triennial, New York, 2018. His films have been featured in screening events such as the London International Animation Festival, 2013; Melbourne International Animation Festival, 2013; and the Cannes Lions International Festival of Creativity, 2013. Wong Ping was the recipient of the Incubator for Film and Visual Media in Asia (ifva) Gold Award in 2013, and the Best Animation and Spirit of Hong Kong awards from the Third Culture Film Festival, Hong Kong, in 2017.

Samson Young

Samson Young's compositions, drawings, installations, radio broadcasts, and performances touch upon topics such as military conflict, identity, migration, and political frontiers past and present. Sound and its cultural politics are at the heart of a practice that interlays multiple narratives and references: born in Hong Kong in 1979, Young obtained a doctorate in music composition from Princeton University in 2013 while becoming involved in contemporary art.

The relationship between violence and sound is a recurrent line of investigation in Young's works. In *Nocturne* (2015), presented in New York in a solo exhibition at Team Gallery in 2015, Young dresses in military garb and sits before an array of sound-effects equipment and a small monitor showing found footage of night bombings in various war zones. Like a Foley artist, he recreates the sounds of the explosions and gunshots as they appear on the monitor, and then broadcasts them through a localized FM transmitter. Young's drawings transpose these concerns into a more intimate format, as in the series *To Fanon* (2016–), an homage to the postcolonial thinker Frantz Fanon, in which the artist vandalizes his own early scores by overlaying them with images and mixed media.

Young develops many of his projects via extensive research. For *For Whom the Bell Tolls: A Journey into the Sonic History of Conflicts* (2015–), supported by BMW Art Journey, he traveled to over thirty sites on five continents to trace the histories of bells and their usage. Amassing an archive of recordings, sketches, and objects, he reveals how the bells have been implicated in territorial, religious, and cultural conflicts. In *Canon* (2016), Young wears a 1979 Royal Hong Kong Police Force uniform and projects the distress calls of birds through an LRAD (Long Range Acoustic Device), a nonlethal sonic weapon used to disperse protesters. The sound is targeted at individual audience members, who sit in a distant room filled with paraphernalia related to the 1979 Vietnamese refugee crisis, when 2,700 refugees were forced to remain onboard a cargo vessel for four months after being refused entry to Hong Kong.

For his solo exhibition in the Hong Kong Pavilion at the 2017 Venice Biennale, Young took on the "charity singles" made by supergroups of recording artists that were especially popular in the 1980s. Critical of the subtexts behind these singles — among them, the complicity of such gestures of "charity" with neoliberal policies and cultural imperialism — Young created drawings, objects, videos, and site-specific installations by appropriating well-known songs from the roster of hits.

Young lives and works in Hong Kong and maintains an active practice in classical music composition. His solo exhibitions include *On the Musically Beautiful*, Goethe-Institute, Hong Kong, 2013; *Video Program: Samson Young*, Hiroshima City Museum of Contemporary Art, 2015; *A Dark Theme Keeps Me Here, I'll Make a Broken Music*, Kunsthalle Düsseldorf, 2016; and *Songs for Disaster Relief*, Hong Kong Pavilion, Venice Biennale, 2017. Select group exhibitions include *Innovationist: The Spectacular Journey of New Media Art*, Taipei Contemporary Art Museum, 2013; *The Wizard's Chamber*, Kunsthalle Winterthur, Switzerland, 2013; *A Journal of the Plague Year*, Para Site Art Space, Hong Kong, 2013; *48HR Incident*, 4A Centre for Contemporary Asian Art, Sydney, 2015; *Retrograde*, Logan Center Gallery, University of Chicago, 2016; and Documenta 14, Athens, Greece, and Kassel, Germany, 2017. Young was a recipient of the Bloomberg Emerging Artist Award in 2007, and the BMW Art Journey award in 2015.

作者簡介
About the Contributors

由安輝景整理
Compiled by Kyung An

黃裕邦

黃裕邦(生於1979年)在香港城市大學獲得碩士學位。他是《天裂》(卡亞出版社,2015年)的作者,2016年度「浪達文學獎」男同志組別香港首位得獎者,以及2016香港藝術發展獎「藝術新秀獎」(文學藝術)的獲得者。他的詩歌曾發表於*Gulf Coast*、*Copper Nickel*、*Third Coast*、*Missouri Review Online*、*Wasafiri*等英文刊物。中文版《天裂》將於2018年由水煮魚文化在香港和台灣出版。黃裕邦現居住在香港,擔任香港筆會副會長。

烏青

烏青(生於1978年)是一位生活在上海的詩人和作家。烏青以一種新的詩意敘述生活小事的方式,不講究韻律,被稱為「廢話體」或「烏青體」。2013年,江蘇文藝出版社出版了他的詩集《烏青詩選:天上的白雲真白啊》。烏青出版的中文小說包括短篇小說和詩集《有一天》(壞蛋出版計劃,2009年)和小說《逃跑家》(江蘇文藝出版社,2012)。《我就是丁西拌》的英文譯本於2011年在文學雜誌《天南》上發表。

許立志

許立志(1990-2014)的詩歌關注他作為農民工在專門生產電子產品以及諸如蘋果、黑莓、諾基亞和索尼等品牌配件的台灣富士康科技集團深圳工廠的經歷。許立志的詩歌曾發表在《打工詩人》、《打工文學》、《深圳特區報》等刊物上。他的作品也出現在《我的詩篇:當代工人詩典》(作家出版社,2015年),這本詩集的英文選集譯本由白松出版社於2017年出版。繼許立志24歲自殺之後,他的作品受到了媒體廣泛關注,最終由網絡眾籌出版了他詩集《新的一天》(作家出版社,2015)。

許煜

許煜任教於德國呂訥堡大學哲學研究所(IPK),並負責該校的研究項目「參與的技術生態學」。他是中國美術學院的客座教授,同時也是巴黎人文科學研究院西蒙東國際研究中心的研究員。他對科技和媒體哲學的研究發表在多份國際同行評審的期刊上,如*Metaphilosophy*、*Research Phenomenology*、*Techné*、*Angelaki*、*Cahiers Simondon*和*Deleuze Studies*等。許煜的專著包括《論數碼物的存在》(明尼蘇達大學出版社,2016年)和《論中國技術問題》(Urbanomic,2016年),並且編有《「非物質展」三十年後:藝術、科學與理論》(Meson出版社,2015)。

張羞

張羞(生於1979年)是詩人和獨立出版物「壞蛋繼續出版」(曾為「壞蛋出版計劃」)創始人。他以其荒謬、幽默的寫作風格著稱,他的詩歌出版包括:《瀑布》(壞蛋出版計劃,2010年)、《瀑布2》(聯邦走馬制作,2012年)、《瀑布3》(壞蛋繼續出版,2016年)和《瀑布4》(壞蛋繼續出版,2017年)。張也是小說家,他早期發表在網上的作品《大象》(2002年)因顛覆傳統敘事結構受到重視。其他小說包括聯邦走馬制作出版的《散裝麻雀》(2013年)和《百鳥無踏》(2016年)。張羞現在居住於北京。

Nicholas Wong

Nicholas Wong (b. 1979) received his MFA at City University of Hong Kong. He is the author of *Crevasse* (Kaya Press, 2015), winner of the 2016 Lambda Literary Award in Gay Poetry, and the recipient of the 2016 Young Artist Award in Literary Arts in Hong Kong. His poems have previously appeared in *Gulf Coast*, *Copper Nickel*, *Third Coast*, *Missouri Review Online*, and *Wasafiri*, among other publications. The Chinese edition of *Crevasse* will be published by Spicy Fish Cultural Production in Hong Kong and Taiwan in 2018. Wong currently lives in Hong Kong, where he is vice president of PEN Hong Kong.

Wu Qing

Wu Qing (b. 1978) is a poet and writer based in Shanghai. Wu first gained recognition on online platforms for his "nonsense style" poetry drawing on mundane events in everyday life. In 2013, Jiangsu Literature and Art Publishing House published the poetry collection *Wu Qing Poems: Ode to a White Cloud*. Wu's published fiction includes the collection of short stories and poems *One Day* (Bad Egg Plan, 2009) and a novel, *The Escapist* (Jiangsu Literature and Art Publishing, 2012), both in Chinese. The English translation of "My Name Is Ding Xiban" was published in the literary magazine *Chutzpah!* in 2011.

Xu Lizhi

The poetry of Xu Lizhi (1990–2014) drew on his experiences as a migrant worker employed at the Shenzhen factory of the Taiwanese conglomerate Foxconn Technology Group, which manufactures electronic products and components for brands including Apple, BlackBerry, Nokia, and Sony. Xu's poems have been included in journals including *Worker Poets*, *Worker Literature*, and *Shenzhen Special Zone Daily*. His work was also featured in the anthologies *My Poems: Contemporary Workers' Poetry* (The Writers Publishing House, 2014) in Chinese, and *Iron Moon: An Anthology of Chinese Migrant Worker Poetry*, published in English by White Pine Press in 2017. Following Xu's suicide at the age of twenty-four, his work received widespread media attention, leading to the poetry collection *A New Day* (The Writers Publishing House, 2015).

Yuk Hui

Yuk Hui teaches at the Institute of Philosophy and Theory of Art (IPK) at Leuphana University Lüneburg in Germany, where he is responsible for the project Technoecologies of Participation. He is a visiting professor at the China Academy of Art in Hangzhou and a member of the Centre international des études simondoniennes at Maison des Sciences de l'Homme Paris Nord (MSH Paris Nord). His research on the philosophy of technology and media has been published in international peer-reviewed journals such as *Metaphilosophy*, *Research in Phenomenology*, *Techné*, *Angelaki*, *Cahiers Simondon*, and *Deleuze Studies*. He is author of *On the Existence of Digital Objects* (University of Minnesota Press, 2016) and *The Question Concerning Technology in China: An Essay in Cosmotechnics* (Urbanomic, 2016), and a coeditor of *30 Years after Les Immatériaux: Art, Science and Theory* (Meson Press, 2015).

Zhang Xiu

Zhang Xiu (b. 1979) is a poet and founder of the independent publishing house Bad Egg Continuing Plan (formerly Bad Egg Plan). He is known for his nonsensical, humorous style of writing. His poems have been published in a series of collections: *The Falls* (Bad Egg Plan, 2010), *The Falls 2* (One Villain and 49 Horses, 2012), *The Falls 3* (Bad Egg Continuing Plan, 2016), and *The Falls 4* (Bad Egg Continuing Plan, 2017). Zhang is also a novelist. His early work *Elephant* (2002), published online, was highly regarded for its subversion of traditional narrative structure. Other novels include *Shoot the Sparrows* (2013) and *No Birds Can Touch* (2016), both published by One Villain and 49 Horses. Zhang currently resides in Beijing.

插圖目錄
List of Illustrations

參加展覽「單手拍掌」的作品由星號標記(*),作品完整圖注請查看本書所含展覽明信片。

除另行標註,所有作品為藝術家版權所有。

《詩和遠方》

19頁 鍾在本,《讓高產「衛星」永遠在天空運轉》,1958
海報,52×73 cm
私人收藏
圖片由社會歷史國際機構惠允

20頁 匿名創作者,《全民動員,保證鋼鐵翻一番!》,1958
海報,76.5×52.5 cm
私人收藏
圖片由社會歷史國際機構惠允

21頁 圖片由英國Methuen Drama, an imprint of Bloomsbury Publishing惠允

23頁 《有圖山海經》,1597–1620
文字:郭璞(276–324),插圖:蔣應鎬、吳臨父,刻版師:李文孝
18卷,4冊
圖片由美國國會圖書館惠允

24頁 圖片:Johannes Eisele/AFP/Getty Images

25頁 圖片:VCG via Getty Images

26頁 寧納·華納·法斯賓德,《世界旦夕之間》,1973年
16毫米,彩色有聲
圖片©寧納·華納·法斯賓德基金會惠允
攝影:Peter Gauhe

28頁 圖片:Daniel Maurer/Associated Press

* 29,33頁 曹斐,《Asia One》,2018(局部)
多頻彩色錄像,尺寸可變
所羅門·R·古根海姆美術館,紐約,何鴻毅家族基金藏品,2018.12

* 30頁 楊嘉輝,《Possible Music #1 (feat. NESS and Shane Aspegren)》,2018(數碼效果圖)
所羅門·R·古根海姆美術館,紐約,何鴻毅家族基金藏品,2018.17

31頁 圖片:AP Photo/Kin Cheung

32頁 亨利·盧克,《許立志肖像》,2014
紙上馬克筆,30.5×22.9 cm
圖片©亨利·盧克惠允

《單手拍掌?散論可能的現實》

38頁 林一林,《XX億零一個》,1998
磚頭、人民幣,尺寸可變,行為表演現場
行為表演現場:「大尾象」,伯恩美術館,1998年9月5日至10月18日

39頁 丹尼爾·布罕,《繪畫—雕塑》,1971
特定場域裝置
展覽現場:所羅門·R·古根海姆美術館,紐約,1971
攝影:Robert E. Mates 和Paul Katz
©DB-ADAGP,巴黎/Artists Rights Society (ARS),紐約,2018

40頁 段建宇,《殺,殺,殺馬特No.1》,2014
布面油畫,181×217 cm

41頁上圖 卡茲米爾·馬列維奇,《割草機》,1911–12
布面油畫,114.3×67.2 cm
俄羅斯夏諾夫哥羅德國家博物館
圖片由俄羅斯夏諾夫哥羅德國家博物館惠允

41頁下圖 保羅·高更,《我們從何處來?我們是誰?我們向何處去?》,1897–98
布面油畫,139.1×374.6 cm
波士頓美術館,湯普斯金藏品
©2018波士頓美術館

43頁上圖 黃炳,《慾望Jungle》,2015
彩色動畫錄像,有聲,6分50秒

44頁下圖 攝影:AP Photo/Kin Cheung

45頁 楊嘉輝,《Stanley》,2014
16張裝裱彩色印刷,作品每張84.1×59.4 cm,含外框每張:98×73.5 cm,霓虹燈:100×400 cm,沙,尺寸可變,聲音
展覽現場:「黑暗讓我停留此處,我將譜出支離破碎的音樂」,杜塞爾多夫美術館,2016年12月16日至2017年3月5日
攝影:Simon Vogel
圖片由藝術家和Gisela Capitain畫廊惠允

47頁 曹斐,《誰的烏托邦》,2006
彩色錄像,有聲,20分鐘
所羅門·R·古根海姆美術館,紐約,由國際總監理事會和執行理事會員基金購入2007.130

48頁上圖 曹斐,《人民城寨:第二人生城市計劃(由曹斐化身「中國·翠西」創造)》,2007
彩色錄像,有聲,6分鐘
所羅門·R·古根海姆美術館,紐約,由年輕藏家顧問基金以及上海灘基金購入2008.30

48頁下圖 攝影:STR/AFP/Getty Images

Works in the exhibition *One Hand Clapping* are marked by an asterisk (*). For complete captions, see postcard inserts.

All artworks © and courtesy the artist, unless otherwise noted.

"Poetry and Place Afar"

p. 19 Zhong Zaiben, *Let the "Sputnik" of high production circle around the sky forever*, 1958
Poster, 52 × 73 cm
Private collection
Photo: Courtesy International Institute of Social History

p. 20 Unknown artist, *Mobilize the whole population, to make sure that steel is doubled!*, 1958
Poster, 76.5 × 52.5 cm
Private collection
Photo: Courtesy International Institute of Social History

p. 21 Photo: Courtesy Methuen Drama, an imprint of Bloomsbury Publishing, UK.

p. 23 *Illustrated Classic of Mountains and Seas*, 1597–1620
Text by Guo Pu (276–324), with illustrations by Jiang Yinghao and Wu Linfu, and engraving by Li Wenxiao
Manuscript in eighteen volumes
Library of Congress
Photo: Courtesy Library of Congress

p. 24 Photo: Johannes Eisele/AFP/ Getty Images

p. 25 Photo: VCG via Getty Images

p. 26 Rainer Werner Fassbinder, dir., *World on a Wire*, 1973
16 mm film with sound, 205 min.
Photo: Peter Gauhe, © Rainer Werner Fassbinder Foundation

p. 28 Photo: Daniel Maurer/Associated Press

*pp. 29, 33 Cao Fei, *Asia One*, 2018 (detail)
Multichannel color video installation, with sound, dimensions variable overall
Solomon R. Guggenheim Museum, New York, The Robert H. N. Ho Family Foundation Collection 2018.12

*p. 30 Samson Young, *Possible Music #1 (feat. NESS and Shane Aspegren)*, 2018 (digital rendering)
Solomon R. Guggenheim Museum, New York, The Robert H. N. Ho Family Foundation Collection 2018.17

p. 31 Photo: AP Photo/Kin Cheung

p. 32 Henry Luke, *Portrait of Xu Lizhi*, 2014
Ink on paper, 30.5 × 22.9 cm
Photo: © and courtesy Henry Luke

"Clapping with One Hand? Fragmentary Notes on Possible Realities"

p. 38 Lin Yilin, *X Billion and First Person*, 1998
Bricks, Chinese yuan banknotes, dimensions variable; and performance
Performance view: *Big Tail Elephant*, Kunsthalle Bern, September 5–October 18, 1998

p. 39 Daniel Buren, *Peinture-Sculpture* (*Painting-Sculpture*), 1971
Work in situ
Installation view: Solomon R. Guggenheim Museum, New York, 1971
Photo: Robert E. Mates and Paul Katz
© DB-ADAGP, Paris / Artists Rights Society (ARS), New York 2018

p. 40 Duan Jianyu, *Sharp, Sharp, Smart No. 1*, 2014
Oil on canvas, 181 × 217 cm

p. 41, top: Kazimir Malevich, *The Mower*, 1911–12
Oil on canvas, 114.3 × 67.2 cm
Nizhny Novgorod State Art Museum, Russia
Photo: Courtesy Nizhny Novgorod State Art Museum

p. 41, bottom: Paul Gauguin, *Where Do We Come From? What Are We? Where Are We Going?*, 1897–98
Oil on canvas, 139.1 × 374.6 cm
Museum of Fine Arts, Boston, Tompkins Collection — Arthur Gordon Tompkins Fund
Photo: © 2018 Museum of Fine Art, Boston

p. 43 Wong Ping, *Jungle of Desire*, 2015
Animated color video, with sound, 6 min., 50 sec.

p. 44 Photo: AP Photo/Kin Cheung

p. 45 Samson Young, *Stanley*, 2014
Sixteen framed chromogenic prints, image: 84.1 × 59.4 cm; frame: 98 × 73.5 cm each; neon lights: 100 × 400 cm; sand, dimensions variable; and sound
Installation view: *A Dark Theme Keeps Me Here, I'll Make a Broken Music*, Kunsthalle Düsseldorf, December 16, 2016–March 5, 2017
Photo: Simon Vogel, courtesy the artist and Galerie Gisela Capitain

p. 47 Cao Fei, *Whose Utopia*, 2006
Color video with sound, 22 min.
Solomon R. Guggenheim Museum, New York, Purchased with funds contributed by the International Director's Council and Executive Committee Members 2007.130

p. 48, top: Cao Fei, *RMB City: A Second Life City Planning by China Tracy (aka Cao Fei)*, 2007
Color video with sound, 6 min.
Solomon R. Guggenheim Museum, New York, Purchased with funds contributed by the Young Collectors Council, with additional funds contributed by Shanghai Tang 2008.30

p. 48, bottom: Photo: STR/AFP/ Getty Images

段建宇

64–79頁《春江花月夜》研習小稿，2018

64–65頁《祕密的花園No.9》，2017
紙上壓克力，38 × 26.2cm

66、70頁《祕密的花園No.2》，2017
紙上鋼筆、壓克力、水彩、油畫棒和拼貼，
24.5 × 25cm

67、79頁《祕密的花園No.8》，2017
紙上圓珠筆和鉛筆，38 × 26.2cm

68、75頁《祕密的花園No.4》，2017
紙上鋼筆、墨、壓克力和拼貼，25 × 24cm

69、78頁《祕密的花園No.1》，2017
紙上水彩鋼筆、壓克力和拼貼，25 × 23cm

71、77頁《祕密的花園No.7》，2017
紙上壓克力、鉛筆和鋼筆，25 × 24cm

72–73頁《祕密的花園No.3》，2017
紙上鋼筆和拼貼，24.5 × 25cm

74頁《祕密的花園No.5》，2017
紙上鋼筆、彩色鋼筆、壓克力和拼貼，
24.5 × 25cm

76頁《祕密的花園No.6》，2017
紙上圓珠筆和拼貼，25 × 25cm

黃炳

88–105頁《親，需要服務嗎?》的旅行日記和概念手稿，2018

林一林

144–25頁《單子》的創作手稿和方案效果圖，2018

曹斐

134–49頁《Asia One》的錄像截屏，攝影記錄和創作過程中的參考素材，2018

* 134–42，144–49頁《Asia One》，
2018（局部）
多頻彩色錄像，尺寸可變
所羅門·R·古根海姆美術館，紐約，何鴻義家族基金藏品，2018.12

楊嘉輝

160–75頁《Possible Music #1（feat. NESS and Shane Aspegren）》方案效果圖，參考素材和與作品調研有關的繪畫手稿，2018

162–63頁《To Fanon（Resonance Studies I）》，2016（局部）
原始作曲手稿（紙上馬克筆）上的蠟筆、彩色鉛筆、絲網印刷和綜合媒介，
每張29.7 × 42 cm，5張

164頁，由上至下：

《Furniture music（avec une ironie contagieuse）》，2017
攝影燈箱，塗鴉記號，31 × 47 cm
圖片由藝術家和Gisela Capitain畫廊惠允

《Furniture music（continuez, sans perdre connaissance）》，2017
攝影燈箱，塗鴉記號，31 × 47 cm
圖片由藝術家和Gisela Capitain畫廊惠允

165頁，由上至下

《Stanley》，2014
16張裝裱彩色印刷，作品每張：84.1 × 59.4 cm，含外框每張：98 × 73.5 cm，
霓虹燈：100 × 400 cm，沙，尺寸可變，聲音
展覽現場：「黑暗讓我停留此處，我講譜出支離破碎的音樂」，杜塞爾多夫美術館，
2016年12月16日至2017年3月5日
攝影：Simon Vogel
圖片由藝術家和Gisela Capitain畫廊惠允

《Studies for Pastoral Music（M18 Claymore Antipersonnel Mine）》，2015
紙上馬克筆、塑形膠、鉛筆和水彩，
18.5 × 27.5 cm
圖片由藝術家惠允

《Studies for Pastoral Music（Kodiak Rifle）》，2015
紙上馬克筆、塑形膠、鉛筆和水彩，
18.5 × 27.5 cm
圖片由藝術家惠允

166頁《Nocturne》，2015
聲音表演（一個表演者使用手槍、錄音介面、大鼓、壓縮空氣、連線麥克風、烹飪紙、玉米片、電剃鬚刀、電子有聲玩具、FM發射器、玻璃瓶、電腦、混聲器、浪聲鼓、米、新科收音機、指向性麥克風、土、茶葉、雷鳴器、雷鳴管、特百惠盒子、風鈴），
尺寸可變
表演現場：「田園音樂」，Team畫廊，紐約，
2015年11月5日至12月20日
攝影：Joerg Lohse，圖片由紐約Team Gallery惠允

167頁《Canon》，2016
繪畫（紙上炭筆、馬克筆、蠟筆、鉛筆、印章和水彩）：28 × 38cm，聲音表演（一個表演者使用錄音介面、電腦、定向聲波發射器［LRAD］、話筒）和裝置（3D打印水盆、訂製長椅、原聲音樂、牆上印字、金屬圍欄），尺寸可變
表演現場：「黑暗讓我停留此處，我將譜出支離破碎的音樂」，杜塞爾多夫美術館，
2016年12月16日至2017年3月5日
攝影：Simon Vogel
圖片由藝術家和Gisela Capitain畫廊惠許

Duan Jianyu

pp. 64–79 Studies for *Spring River in the Flower Moon Night*, 2017–18

pp. 64–65 *Garden of Secrets No. 9*, 2017
Acrylic on paper, 38 × 26.2 cm

pp. 66, 70 *Garden of Secrets No. 2*, 2017
Pen, acrylic, watercolor, oil pastel, and collage on paper, 24.5 × 25 cm

pp. 67, 79 *Garden of Secrets No. 8*, 2017
Ballpoint pen and pencil on paper, 38 × 26.2 cm

pp. 68, 75 *Garden of Secrets No. 4*, 2017
Pen, ink, acrylic, and collage on paper, 25 × 24 cm

pp. 69, 78 *Garden of Secrets No. 1*, 2017
Color pen, acrylic, and collage on paper, 25 × 23 cm

pp. 71, 77 *Garden of Secrets No. 7*, 2017
Acrylic, pencil, and pen on paper, 25 × 24 cm

pp. 72–73 *Garden of Secrets No. 3*, 2017
Pen and collage on paper, 24.5 × 25 cm

p. 74 *Garden of Secrets No. 5*, 2017
Pen, color pen, acrylic, and collage on paper, 24.5 × 25 cm

p. 76 *Garden of Secrets No. 6*, 2017
Ballpoint pen and collage on paper, 25 × 25 cm

Wong Ping

pp. 88–105 Travel notes and concept drawings for *Dear, can I give you a hand?*, 2018

Lin Yilin

pp. 114–25 Preparatory drawings and digital renderings for *Monad*, 2018

Cao Fei

pp. 134–49 Film stills, visual documentation, and reference material related to the production of *Asia One*, 2018

*pp. 134–42, 144–49 *Asia One*, 2018 (detail)
Multichannel color video installation, with sound, dimensions variable overall
Solomon R. Guggenheim Museum, New York, The Robert H. N. Ho Family Foundation Collection 2018.12

Samson Young

pp. 160–75 Digital renderings, reference material, and drawings related to the research process for *Possible Music #1 (feat. NESS and Shane Aspegren)*, 2018

pp. 162–63, all: *To Fanon (Resonance Studies I)*, 2016 (detail)
Pastel, colored pencil, photocopy print, silkscreen print, and mixed media on original composition manuscripts (ink on paper), 29.7 × 42 cm each, set of five

p. 164, from top:

Furniture music (avec une ironie contagieuse), 2017
Photographic light box and graphical notation, 31 × 47 cm
Photo: Courtesy the artist and Galerie Gisela Capitain

Furniture music (continuez, sans perdre connaissance), 2017
Photographic light box and graphical notation, 31 × 47 cm
Photo: Courtesy the artist and Galerie Gisela Capitain

p. 165, from top:

Stanley, 2014 (detail)
Sixteen framed chromogenic prints, image: 84.1 × 59.4 cm; frame: 98 × 73.5 cm each; neon lights: 100 × 400 cm; sand, dimensions variable; and sound
Installation view: *A Dark Theme Keeps Me Here, I'll Make a Broken Music*, Kunsthalle Düsseldorf, December 16, 2016–March 5, 2017
Photo: Simon Vogel, courtesy the artist and Galerie Gisela Capitain

Studies for Pastoral Music (M18 Claymore Antipersonnel Mine), 2015
Ink, modeling paste, pencil, and watercolor on paper, 18.5 × 27.5 cm

Studies for Pastoral Music (Kodiak Rifle), 2015
Ink, modeling paste, pencil, and watercolor on paper, 18.5 × 27.5 cm

p. 166 *Nocturne*, 2015
Sound performance (for solo performer with airsoft pistol, audio interface, bass drum, compressed air, contact microphone, cooking paper, cornflakes, electric shavers, electrical sound toys, FM transmitter, glass bottle, laptop, mixer, ocean drum, rice, Shinco radio, shotgun microphone, soil, tea leaves, thunder sheet, thunder tube, Tupperware, wind chime), dimensions variable
Installation view: *Pastoral Music*, Team Gallery, New York, November 5–December 20, 2015
Photo: Joerg Lohse, courtesy Team Gallery, New York

p. 167 *Canon*, 2016
Charcoal, ink, pastel, pencil, stamp, and watercolor on paper, 28 × 38 cm; sound performance (for solo performer with audio interface, laptop, Long Range Acoustic Device [LRAD], microphone); and installation (3-D-printed water basin, custom-designed bench, soundtrack, stamped text on wall, wire fencing), dimensions variable
Installation view: *A Dark Theme Keeps Me Here, I'll Make a Broken Music*, Kunsthalle Düsseldorf, December 16, 2016–March 5, 2017
Photo: Simon Vogel, courtesy the artist and Galerie Gisela Capitain

《單手拍掌》出版於展覽之際

展覽由翁笑雨和侯瀚如策劃

所羅門·R·古根海姆美術館，紐約
2018年5月4日至10月21日

此展覽和出版物由何鴻毅家族基金贊助

ISBN 978-0-89207-540-9

第一版

古根海姆美術館出版物
紐約州紐約市第五大道1071號，
郵編10128
guggenheim.org

發行
ARTBOOK | D.A.P.
紐約市紐約州Broad大道75號630，
郵編10004
電話：212 627 1999
artbook.com

北美以外地區經銷發行
Thames & Hudson, Ltd.
英國倫敦High Holborn路
181A號，WC1V7QX
thamesandhudson.com

設計：Wkshps(吳承桓、陳穎)
製作：Jonathan Bowen、Shiori Kawasaki
編輯：Andrew Maerkle、吳建儒
中譯英：賈世怡(Breanna Chia)、
李佳桓、朱又佳，文學部分譯者：
費正華(Jennifer Feeley)、顧愛玲
(Eleanor Goodman)、柯夏智
(Lucas Klein)

英譯中：杜可柯(18–34頁)、莫修(106–72頁)、徐丹羽(176–84頁)、余小蕙(36–50頁)、張思銳(10、12–14、185–90頁)，封底部分譯者：陳璽安，文學部分譯者：徐晞文

比利時Die Keure印刷公司印刷

出版物預行編目資料可見於國會圖書館

Published on the occasion of
the exhibition *One Hand Clapping*

Organized by Xiaoyu Weng and
Hou Hanru

Solomon R. Guggenheim Museum,
New York
May 4–October 21, 2018

This exhibition and publication are made possible by The Robert H. N. Ho Family Foundation.

何鴻毅家族基金
THE ROBERT H. N. HO
FAMILY FOUNDATION

ISBN 978-0-89207-540-9

First printing

Published by
Guggenheim Museum Publications
1071 Fifth Avenue
New York, New York 10128
guggenheim.org

Available through
ARTBOOK | D.A.P.
75 Broad Street, Suite 630
New York, New York 10004
Tel: 212 627 1999
artbook.com

Distributed outside the United States and Canada by
Thames & Hudson, Ltd.
181A High Holborn
London WC1V 7QX, United Kingdom
thamesandhudson.com

Design: Wkshps (Chris Wu, Janet Chan)
Production: Jonathan Bowen and Shiori Kawasaki
Editorial: Andrew Maerkle and Jianru Wu

Translations from the Chinese by Breanna Chia, Alvin Li, and Yvette Zhu, with literary translations by Jennifer Feeley, Eleanor Goodman, and Lucas Klein

Translations from the English by Du Keke (pp. 18–34), Xu Danyu (pp. 176–84), Yu Hsiao-hwei (pp. 36–50), Sirui Zhang (pp. 10, 12–14, 185–90), Wayne Zhou (pp. 106–12), and Zian Chen (back cover), with literary translation by Aurora Tsui

Printed in Belgium by Die Keure

Note to the Reader:
Hanyu Pinyin romanization is used throughout the text; exceptions are made for spellings of Chinese proper names.

第72頁部分引用出自T.S.艾略特的《四個四重奏》，《情歌 · 荒原 · 四重奏》，湯永寬譯，上海譯文出版社，1994年。
The quotation on p. 72 is from T. S. Eliot, "Burnt Norton," in *The Poems of T. S. Eliot*, ed. Christopher Ricks and Jim McCue, vol. 1, *Collected and Uncollected Poems* (Baltimore: Johns Hopkins University, 2015).

第78頁部分引用出自蕭紅，《回憶魯迅先生》，《蕭紅全集·第二卷》，時代文藝出版社，2000年1月，第956頁。
The quotation on p. 78 is as cited in Xiao Hong, "A Remembrance of Lu Xun," trans. Howard Goldblatt, *Renditions*, no. 15 (Spring 1981).

第157頁的引用部分譯自羅蘭·巴特，《中國行日記》，Anne Herschberg Pierrot 編輯，Andrew Brown翻譯，第78頁，Polity出版社，英國劍橋，2012年。
The quotation on p. 157 is from Roland Barthes, *Travels in China*, ed. Anne Herschberg Pierrot, trans. Andrew Brown (Cambridge, UK: Polity, 2012).

Cataloguing-in-Publication Data is available from the Library of Congress.